Financial Markets, Institutions & Services

Financial Markets, Institutions & Services

Second Edition

Dr. N.K. Gupta
Senior Reader, Ramjas College
University of Delhi

&

Dr. Monika Chopra
Senior Lecturer in Finance, ICFAI Business School
Gurgaon

Ane Books Pvt. Ltd.

New Delhi ♦ Chennai

Financial Markets, Institutions & Services

N.K. Gupta and Monika Chopra

First Edition : 2008
Second Edition : 2010
Reprint : 2011, 2018,2019, **2020, 2023**

Published by

Ane Books Pvt. Ltd.

4821, Parwana Bhawan, 1st Floor, 24 Ansari Road, Darya Ganj,
New Delhi - 110 002, Tel.: +91(011) 23276843-44, Fax: +91(011) 23276863
e-mail: kapoor@anebooks.com, Website: www.anebooks.com

Branch Office:

- Avantika Niwas, 1st Floor, 19 Doraiswamy Road, T. Nagar,
  Chennai - 600 017, Tel.: +91(044) 28141554, 28141209
  e-mail: anebookschennai@gmail.com, rathinam@anebooks.com

ISBN : 978-93-8015-660-6

Printed at : Repro Knowledgecast Limited, Thane

Preface to the Second Edition

This edition brings in additional details on several areas like *Reforms in Indian Financial System, Book Building Method, Mutual Funds including SEBI guidelines for asset management companies. Further, a new chapter on* ***Internet Banking*** *has been added and the chapter on* ***Venture Capital*** *has been considerably improved.*

The text has been simplified and made student friendly. Numerous typos, omissions and other errors that slipped through the original proof-reading of the first edition have also been corrected. We are grateful to colleagues and students for critical appraisal of the first edition and response towards the book. However, the structure and context of the book remains unchanged.

We hope that this second edition will be more helpful to serve the course curriculum for various universities and institutes.

Dr. N.K.Gupta
Dr. Monika Chopra

Preface to the First Edition

The financial system in India has undergone revolutionary changes in recent times due to the development of new products and services, globalization and privatization of the economy and development of improved regulatory framework.

The present book has been written to give the students of finance a comprehensive knowledge about the development, operation and organization of Indian financial system. The book makes an attempt to cover each aspect of functioning of the financial system in simple and coherent manner. It presents the technical aspects of financial system in a way which is easy to grasp for any student.

The subject matter of the book has been divided into three parts –

Part I which gives detailed knowledge about financial markets. This section has two subsections namely – Money markets which discusses about various instruments of money market like call money, REPOS, T-Bills, Commercial Paper, Gilt-Edged securities, Certificate of Deposit etc. The other subsection is of Capital Markets which discusses the concept of Primary and Secondary markets covering various stock exchanges and their indices, share trading etc.

Part II deals with Financial Institutions and has been divided into 4 parts:

Regulatory and Promotional Institutions – RBI and SEBI.

Developmental Financial Institutions – IDBI, ICICI, IFCI, EXIM Bank, NABARD etc.

Specialized Financial Institutions – LIC, UTI, Banking companies, involving commercial banks and cooperative banks,

Non-Banking Finance Companies.

Part III deals with financial services sector. It covers financial services like venture capital, mutual funds, credit rating and merchant banking. It also discusses International finance instruments namely – ADRs and GDRs and other financial Services like Merchant Banking, Venture Capital, Debt Securitization, Insurance, Disinvestment etc.

The book draws influence from the views and ideas expressed by various distinguished authors in different books, journals, magazines and working papers.

The authors hope that the book will serve a useful purpose to students and teachers of the subject at graduation and postgraduation levels. It will also serve as a text due to its coverage of the syllabi of various universities. The book will function as a complete guide to provide valuable and resourceful information on all the topics related to financial markets and institutions in India.

In the preparation and editing of this book we have received help from various sources. At first we record a high sense of gratitude and indebtness to Dr. Rajinder Prasad, Principal, Ramjas College, University of Delhi and Shri K.S. Maheshwari, Executive Director, Delhi Productivity Council, for all the encouragement and support they extended to us.

We are thankful to our students and colleagues from various universities for their comments and suggestions which have been extremely useful.

Benevolence of Dr. Sanjiv Mittal, Professor, G.G.S.I.P. University, Delhi, who has been constant source of inspiration to us, cannot be forgotten any time. We wish to express our sincere thanks to our publisher Sh. Sunil Saxena, Chairperson, Sh. Jai Raj Kapoor, CEO, Ane Books India and Sh. P.R.Verma for their keen interest in the publication of the book.

Last but not the least, our family members, especially Mrs. Kusum Gupta and Mr. Vishal Chopra who bore the brunt of the crunches of time, deserve all thanks, appreciation and gratitude.

We are also thankful to our parents for their blessings which made it possible to bring the book in its present form.

We welcome all the suggestions and comments for further improvement of the book.

Dr. N.K. Gupta
Dr. Monika Chopra

Contents

Preface	*v*
Introduction to Financial System	**1-16**
• Introduction	1
• Components of Financial System	3
• Growth and Development of Financial System in India	7
• Reforms in the Indian Financial System	7
• *Questions*	15
PART - I : FINANCIAL MARKETS	
Section - I : Money Market	**17-70**
1. Introduction to Money Market	**19-26**
• Definition of Money Market	19
• Need for Money Market	19
• Players in Money Market	20
• Money Market Instruments	22
• Evolution of Money Market in India	24
• *Questions*	25
2. Call Money Market	**27-34**
• Introduction	27
• Features	27
• Functions of Call Money Market	29
• Mechanism of Operations in Call Money Market	29
• Location of Call Money Market	29
• Growth and Development of Call Money Market in India	30
• Guidelines for Call/Notice Money Market	30
• *Questions*	33
3. Commercial Paper	**35-42**
• Introduction	35
• Issuers of Commercial Paper	35
• Investors in Commercial Paper	36
• Procedure of Issuing Commercial Paper	37
• Cost involved for Issuing Commercial Paper	37

- Rating Requirements for Issue of Commercial Paper 39
- Steps Taken by RBI to Develop the Commercial Paper Market Further 40
- *Questions* 41

4. Certificates of Deposit **43-48**
- Introduction 43
- System of Issue 44
- Payment of Certificate of Deposit 46
- *Questions* 47

5. Gilt Edged Securities Market (Dated Securities) **49-54**
- Introduction 49
- Purpose of Issue 49
- Participants 50
- Process of Issue 50
- Secondary Market for Government Securities 51
- Settlement of Traders in Government Securities 51
- Constitution of Security General Ledger Account (SGL Account) 51
- *Questions* 53

6. Treasury Bills **55-64**
- Introduction 55
- Features 55
- Issuers of T-Bills 55
- Investors in T-Bills 56
- Types of T-Bills 56
- Process of Issuance 56
- Yield of T-Bills 57
- Trading 57
- Clearing and Settlement 58
- Risk Weightage 58
- Treasury Bills Market Abroad 59
- Secondary Market for T-Bills Abroad 60
- Yield Curve and Interest Rate Analysis 60
- Types of Yeild Curve 61
- Theories of Yeild Curve 62
- *Questions* 63

7. Repos (Repurchase Agreement) **65-70**
- Introduction 65
- Securities Treated in REPO 66
- Secondary Market in REPO 67
- Changes in the REPO Market 67
- *Questions* 70

Section - II : Capital Markets 71-148

8. Primary Markets **71-86**

- Introduction 71
- Public Issue 71
- Unlisted Companies 72
- Book Building Process 72
- Types of Investors 75
- Role of SEBI in Primary Market 77
- Intermediaries involved and their Role in Primary Market 78
- Issue of Prospectus 79
- *Questions* 84

9. Dematerialization 87-92

- Concept of Dematerialization 87
- Dematerialization 87
- Depository 87
- Depository Participant 88
- Operation of the Depository System 88
- Preference of Brokers to Deal in DEMAT Shares 89
- Process of Dematerialization 89
- Dividend on Dematted Shares 90
- Conversion of Dematted Shares Back into Physical Shares 90
- Multiple Accounts 91
- Security of Holdings 91
- *Questions* 91

10. Secondary Market 93-104

- Introduction 93
- History and Growth of Stock Markets in India 93
- Stock Market Indices 94
- Determinants of a Stock Index 94
- Methods of Index Construction 95
- Popular Indian Indexes 96
- Major U.S. Indexes 96
- Advantages of Stock Exchanges 98
- Types of Brokers in a Stock Exchange 98
- Trading Mechanism on a Stock Exchange 99
- Insider Trading 100
- Insider Defined 101
- *Questions* 103

***Appendix* 105-128**

11. Investor Education and Protection Fund (IEPF) 129-134

- Introduction 129
- IEPF Act (Section 205c) 129

- Credits to the Fund 130
- *Question* 133

12. Major Stock Exchanges of India **135-148**

- Bombay Stock Exchange 135
- Trading System 137
- Surveillance 137
- National Stock Exchange 138
- NSE & Its Subsidiaries 138
- S & P CNX NIFTY 140
- CNX NIFTY Junior 141
- CNX Mid Cap 142
- S & P CNX DEFTY 142
- CNX Midcap 200 142
- Over the Counter Exchange of India (OTCEI) 143
- Continuous Listing Requirements 145
- Participants in the OTC Market 146
- Risk Management in OTCEI 147
- *Questions* 148

PART II – FINANCIAL INSTITUTIONS

Section I – Regulatory and Promotional Institutions 149-172

13. Securities Exchange Board of India (SEBI) **151-156**

- Introduction 151
- Activities of SEBI 152
- SEBI and Primary Market 152
- SEBI and Secondary Market 153
- SEBI and Mutual Funds 153
- SEBI and Takeover Norms 154
- *Questions* 155

14. Reserve Bank of India **157-172**

- Introduction 157
- Offices 158
- Reform Measures 160
- RBI's Regulatory Environment 161
- Functions of RBI 162
- Norms Regarding Capital Adequacy, Asset Classification, Income Recognition and Provisioning Along with Action on the Recommendations 164
- *Questions* 172

Section II – Banking System in India 173-210

15. Commercial Banking System **173-194**

- Introduction 173
- History and Growth of Banking System in India 173

- Scheduled and Unscheduled Commercial Banks in India 174
- Banking Services in India 179
- Methods of Lending 183
- Consortium Lending 185
- Reasons for Consortium Lending 185
- Participants in Consortium Lending 185
- Benefits of Consortium Lending 186
- Documentation Required 187
- Credit Gaps 188
- Shift towards Universal Banking 189
- Universal Banking in India 190
- Approach to Universal Banking 190
- Global Face of Indian Banking 191
- *Questions* 192

16. Cooperative Banking in India 195-204

- Introduction 195
- Overview 196
- Categories 196
- RBI Policies 198
- Cooperative Banks RBI Perspective 199
- Cooperative Credit Structure: Committee Recommendations 200
- Future of Cooperative Banks 200
- *Questions* 204

17. Non-Banking Financial Companies 205-210

- Definition 205
- NBFCS Exempted from Registration 206
- Requirements for Registration with RBI 206
- Acceptance of Public Deposits by NBFCS 207
- Regulations on Acceptance of Deposits by NBFCS 207
- Acceptance of deposits from NRIs 208
- Prudential Regulations Applicable to NBFCS 209
- *Questions* 209

Section III – Developmental Financial Institution 211-226

18. Brief Profile of Various Developmental Financial Institutions in India 211-226

I. Industrial Credit and Investment Corporation of India Limited (ICICI) 211
- Functions/Services offered by ICICI 212

II. Industrial Finance Corporation of India (IFCI) 213
- Products and Services 213

III. Industrial Development Bank of India (IDBI) 215
- History and Growth 215

IV. National Bank for Agriculture and Rural Development (NABARD) 218

V. Small Industries Development Bank of India (SIDBI) 219
- Schemes 220

VI. EXIM Bank of India 222
- Export Services 223
- Development Banks: Future Ahead 224
- The Role of Development Banks & Impact of Liberalization 225
- *Questions* 226

Section IV – Specialised Financial Institutions **227-236**

19. Insurance Institutions **227-236**

I. Life Insurance Corporation of India (LIC) 227

II. Unit Trust of India (UTI) 230
- US. 64. Functioning and Downfall of the Scheme 231
- The Scheme's Functionsing 232
- Benefits to Investors 232
- Points of Downfall 233
- Gravest Misendeavour 234
- *Questions* 235

PART III – FINANCIAL SERVICES

20. Venture Capital **239-248**
- Definition 239
- History of Venture Capital 239
- Growth and Development of Venture Capital in India 240
- Types of Venture Funds in India 240
- Investment Process 242
- Exploring Investment Opportunities 244
- Analyzing the Investment Proposal 244
- Investment Valuation 245
- Structuring a Deal 245
- Monitoring and Follow-Up 246
- *Questions* 247

21. Credit Rating **249-254**
- Introduction 249
- Role of Credit Rating Agencies in the Evaluation of Issuers of Securities 249
- Importance of the Role of Credit Rating Agencies 251
- Limitations of Credit Rating - Rating Downgrades 253
- *Questions* 254

22. Merchant Banking **255-264**
- Introduction 255
- Origin of Merchant Banking in India 255
- Nature of Merchant Banking 256

- Merchant Banking Functions 256
- Pre-Issue Management 256
- Types of Issues 256
- Role of Merchant Banker in Pre-Issue Management 257
- Post Issue Management 259
- Difference between Merchant Bankers and Investment Bankers 261
- *Questions* 263

23. Mutual Funds 265-288

- Definition of a Mutual Fund 265
- Evolution and Growth of Mutual funds in India 266
- Organisation of a Mutual Fund 268
- Types of Mutual Funds 269
- By Investment Orientation 271
- Other Schemes 271
- Real Estate Mutual Funds (REMFS) 274
- Investment Plans of Mutual Funds 275
- Costs Involved in Mutual Fund Investment 280
- SEBI Guidelines On : Constitution and Management of Asset Management Company 281
- *Questions* 288

24. American and Global Depository Receipts 289-296

- ADR Defined 289
- Concept of ADRs 289
- Types of ADRs 290
- Level I ADR 290
- Level II ADR 290
- Level III ADR 291
- Other Kinds of ADRs 292
- The ADR Purchase and Issuance Process: Three Scenarios 293
- GDRs and EDRs 295
- *Questions* 296

25. Debt Securitization 297-308

- Definition of Securitization 297
- History of Securitization 297
- Securitizable Assets 298
- Reasons for Securitization 298
- Benefits of Securitization to Investors 300
- Parties in a Securitization Transaction 301
- Securitization Process 303
- Documentation 303
- Structuring Considerations 303
- Securitization in India 304
- Benefits of securitization in India 304

- Future strategies 305
- *Questions* 308

26. Disinvestment **309-325**

- Global Perspective 309
- Evolution of Public Sector in India 310
- Genesis and Rationale for Disinvestment in India 311
- Disinvestment Policy 313
- Major Issues in Disinvestment 314
- Employee issues 316
- Methods of Disinvestment 316
- *Questions* 325

27. Insurance **327-338**

- Principles of Insurance 327
- Insurance VS. Gambling 328
- History of Insurance 329
- Types of Insurance 329
- Types of Insurance Companies 331
- Insurance in India 331
- Life Insurance 333
- Key Features of Life Insurance Industry 333
- Benefits of Life Insurance 333
- Role of Life Insurance in the Growth of the Economy 334
- Major Market Players 334
- Products 336
- Non-Life Insurance/General Insurance 336
- *Questions* 338

28. Internet Banking : An Innovation in Banking Services **339-350**

- Traditional Banking 340
- Internet Banking 341
- Evolution of Internet Banking 342
- Need for Internet Banking 343
- Internet Banking India 344
- Drivers of Internet Banking 344
- Indian Banks on Web 344
- Internet Banking Services Available 345
- Steps in Netting the Transactions 346
- Conditions for Growth of Internet Banking 347
- Emerging Challenges 348

29. Leasing **351-354**

- Concept of Leasing 351
- *Questions* 354

Bibliography 355
Index 357

INTRODUCTION TO FINANCIAL SYSTEM

INTRODUCTION

A financial system is that part of economy, which includes all the financial institutions and markets involved in—

- moving savings from savers (households & firms) to borrowers; and
- transferring, sharing and insuring risks.

The significance of financial system can be understood only after studying the constituents of the economy who participate in the system in order to derive its benefits

A nation consists of 3 economic units basically –

- Government;
- Industry; and
- Household.

These units may perform various activities due to which they may be facing surplus or deficit budgetary situations.

- Industry sector may be able to generate funds from their activities and use them for various investment decisions like expansion, diversification, modernization, replacement etc.
- Government needs funds for financing public expenditure. It requires them mainly for developmental purposes and as the expenditure involved is quite high, it generally is in deficit budgetary situation.
- Individuals/household sector requires funds for meeting basic necessities as well as for expenditure on luxury items. They however may have been surplus funds in the form of savings.

So at any point of time some units may have excess funds while some may be in deficit and some may need extra funds to grow. Idle money does not yield any value while shortage may hinder growth and development. Surplus funds may be coming from household sector while shortage may be faced by government and industry. Thus, there should be some mechanism to ensure that savings move from household to government and corporate, which would ensure proper utilization of those and enhance their value.

Importance of Financial System

Financial system acts as such a channel, which allows funds to move from people, who lack productive investment opportunities (*i.e.* savers) to those who have such opportunities. By doing so the financial system contributes to higher production and efficiency in the economy. It also improves the well-being of consumers by allowing them to time their purchases better.

The above linkage provided by financial system between savers and investors can be shown as follows:

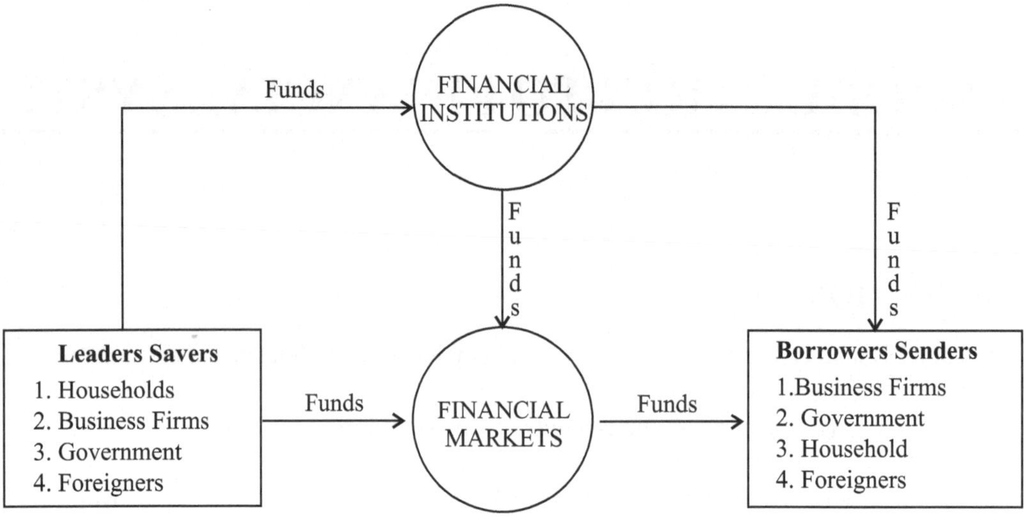

Fig. 1.1: Linkage of financial system between savers and investors

Taking the above into consideration we can say that financial system is very important in present day economy so as to allow judicious allocation of resources. It is similar to arterial circulation system in the human body wherein the flow of blood represents the flow of money and arterial arrangement symbolizes the financial system itself.The absence of financial system stops the flow of money leading to death of the economy in the same way as the absence of the arterial circulation system prohibits the flow of blood in the human body, forcing the death of the body.

Financial system helps in providing liquidity to the economy by promoting savings. Lack of financial system makes it difficult for people to save and acts as an obstacle for entrepreneurs to borrow funds. Due to this difficulty in borrowing experienced by the entrepreneurs, the economy experiences a low level of investment, resulting in slow or no economic growth, which further retards the growth of the financial system. This forms a vicious cycle as shown below:

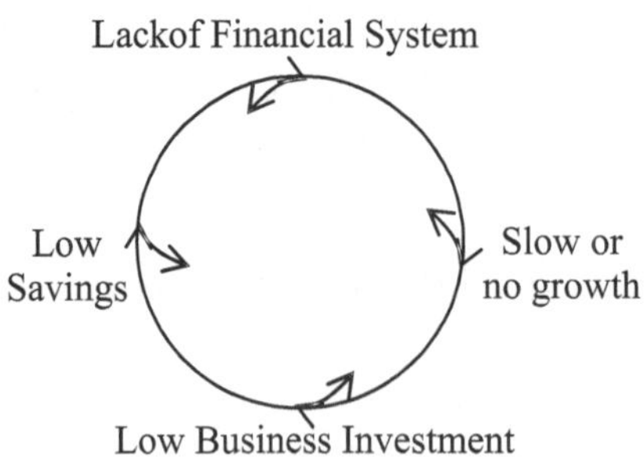

Fig. 1.2 : Vicious cycle on lack of financial system

The lack of Financial System may lead to other poverty traps also. Due to absence of Financial System, the cost of obtaining information about investment opportunities and funds availability by savers and borrowers respectively, is extremely high. This high information cost may, in addition, reduce the level of business investment and slower the economic growth.

The compounding effect of low savings, increased information cost, low investment and thus low or no economic growth may be shown below:

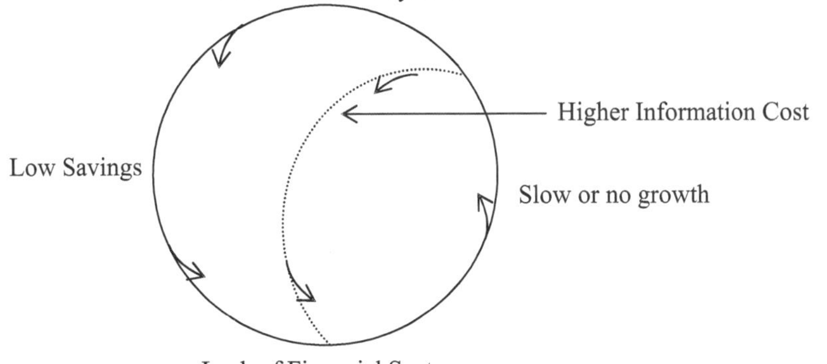

Fig. 1.3 : Low economic growth

COMPONENTS OF FINANCIAL SYSTEM

Financial system primarily comprises of –

- Financial Institutions and
- Financial Markets

Both of these further consist of the **ORGANIZED AND UNORGANIZED SECTOR**

Unorganized sector is made-up of money lenders, indigenous bankers, pawnbrokers, landlords, traders etc.

Organized Sector comprises of various constituents which may be separately classified for financial institutions and financial markets as follows:

Financial Institutions :

1. Regulatory and Promotional Institutions: The two major Regulatory and Promotional Institutions in India are :

1. Reserve Bank of India (RBI) and
2. Securities Exchange Board of India (SEBI)

Both RBI and SEBI administer, legislate, supervise, mentor, control and discipline the entire financial system. The reigns of financial institutions lie in the hands of RBI, while the financial markets are monitored by SEBI. Both of these have laid down several policies, procedures and guidelines, which are changed from time to time so as to set the financial system in the right direction in order to enable it to contribute towards healthy functioning of the economy.

2. Banking Institutions : Banking Institutions are the depositors and lenders of money and have been categorized on the basis of the functions being performed by them. The basic three categories are-

- **Commercial Banks :** Their function is to act as depositors of public savings and function with profit motive. They accept deposits and lend them to those in need for a charge called interest which is their profit.
- **Cooperative Banks :** Cooperative Banks are a part of Cooperative institutions which are based on principles of cooperation and mutual help. They accept deposits and lend short-term and long-term credit at reasonable rate of interest.
- **Developmental Banks :** They are set-up for the purpose of promoting certain sectors of the economy and cater to those only for *e.g.,* NABARD (National Bank for Agricultural and Rural Development), set-up for providing agricultural credit and development of the rural sector of the economy.
- **Non-Banking Finance Companies :** These are small privately owned financial intermediaries, which are engaged in accepting and disbursing funds. They are categorized into various types depending on the fund based activities performed by them. The most common of them are :

1. Investment Companies which provide loans for personal as well as commercial purpose and charge a higher rate of interest as compared to banks. Inspite of the interest rate charged being higher they are popular due to the hassle free procedure of providing loans on which no security is sought as compared to commercial banks which provide secured loans. They also provide higher interest on deposits accepted by them as compared to commercial banks.

2. Housing Companies : Housing companies provide loan for the purpose of house construction in lieu of a charge or interest for different time periods. This loan is a secured loan and involves hypothecation of the land or building against it. Housing companies in India include Housing and Urban Development Corporation (HUDCO), State Housing Finance Societies (SHFS), Housing Development and Finance Corporation (HDFC), other than these LIC, GIC, UTI also have entered into the area of housing finance. All these institutions are monitored and controlled by a committee set-up by RBI.

3. Lease Financing : A lease may be defined as a contractual arrangement in which lessor (one who owns the asset) provides the asset for the use to the lessee (who requires the asset) in return for a periodic payment (rentals) with or without further payment called premium. After the end of the lease period the equipment goes back to the lessor. So there is a separation of ownership and economic use of the asset. Major leasing companies in India are Infrastructure Leasing and Financial Services Ltd.(IL&FS), ICICI, Industrial Reconstruction Bank of India (IRBI), LIC, GIC, IFC, HDFC, some State Industrial Investment Corporations (SIICS).

4. Hire Purchase Companies : Hire purchase is a system under which term loan is provided for purchase of goods or services and this loan is then amortized in installments as laid down through a contract, under the contract the ownership of asset is transferred to the owner once the contract of loan is signed. Commercial Banks, IDBI, ICICI, SFCs, NSIC etc. are involved in such financing.

5. Specialized Financial Institutions : They include EXIM Bank providing loan for Export Import, NABARD-National Bank for Agricultural and Rural Development, Tourism & Finance Corporation of India. Technology Development and Information Company of India Ltd.

6. Investment Institutions like Unit Trust of India providing portfolio management services, Life Insurance Corporation providing cover for risk of loans of life, retirement etc. General Insurance Corporation providing cover for risks other than life.

7. State Level Institutions : They include State Financial Corporation (SFCs), which provide credit within the state and State Industrial Development Corporation (SIDCs) providing State Industrial Credit.

Financial Markets:

1. Capital Market : These are markets where securities of life greater than one year are traded. They can be further subdivided into.

(*a*) **Primary Market :** It is a market where securities are floated for the first time. It consists of:

- New Issue Market;
- Euro Issue Market; and
- Private Placements

(*b*) **Secondary Market :** It is a place where securities which have already been issued are traded. It is made-up of:

- Securities Exchanges;
- STCI (Securities Trading Corporation of India); and
- OTCEI (Over-the-Counter Exchange of India).

2. Money Market : These are the markets where securities having life of less than one year are traded. It is also divided into:

(*a*) **Primary Market :** It is made-up of new issues of instruments like T-Bills, Commercial Paper, Certificates of Deposit, Gift Edged Securities, Call Money, and Reports etc.

(*b*) **Secondary Market :** It includes Discount and Finance House of India.

(DFHI)

3. FOREX Market: It is a market where one currency is exchanged for another. It consists of:

1. **Wholesale Market:** It is made-up of primary price makers, *i.e.,* Banks who buy and sell one currency for another for a margin called Spread.
2. **Retail Market:** Retail Market is made-up of secondary price makers which are money changers catering tourists and travelers.
3. **Brokers:** Brokers act as intermediaries in both primary and secondary markets.
4. **Debt Market:** It includes securities issued by the Central and State Government and Bonds which may be issued by Financial Institutions, Public Sector Undertakings or Corporates (Debentures).

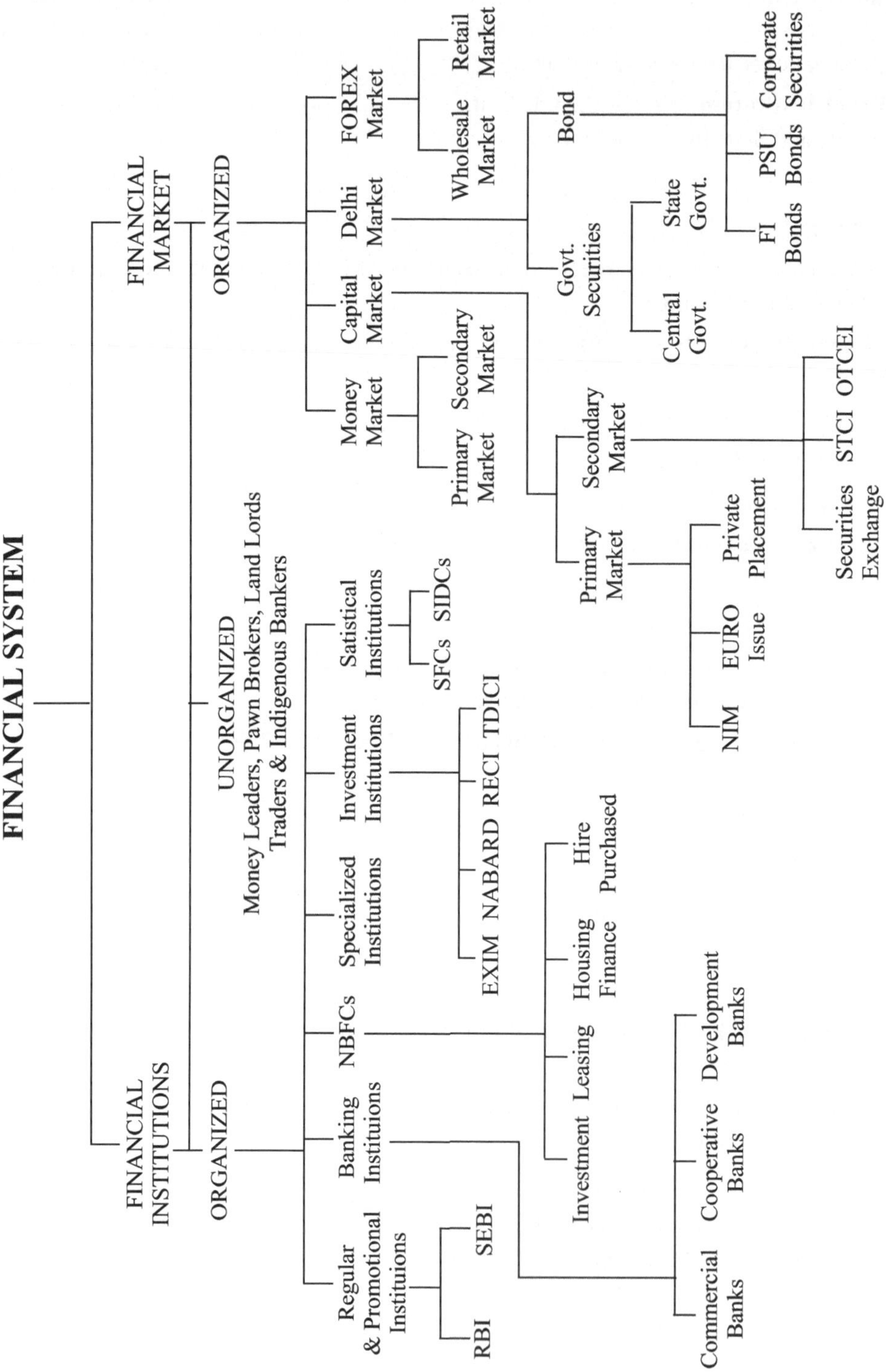

Composition of Financial System

GROWTH AND DEVELOPMENT OF FINANCIAL SYSTEM IN INDIA

The Indian Financial System has grown significantly over years. During the pre-reform period financial system essentially catered to the needs of planned development in a mixed economy framework where the government sector had a predominant role in economic activity. During this period India's macro economic policy moved from fiscal consolidation to fiscal activism as a part of planned development which led to developmental expenditures to finance long-gestation projects requiring long-term finance. In order to fulfill the government's requirement of funds interest rates on government securities were artificially lowered which was not in line with the market conditions. The government securities market as a result lost its appeal as lower rates of interest and early maturity reflected the needs of issuer (Government) for funds.

Moreover during these years the financial sector was characterized by segmented and underdeveloped financial markets and low number of financial instruments. There was a multiplicity and complexity of interest rates.

By the end of the eighties, the financial system was considerably stretched. Profitability of banking sector was also affected due to directed and concessional availability of bank credit with respect to certain sectors. There was a rising burden of NPAs due to lack of transparency, accountability and proper norms.

All these necessitated the introduction of reforms so as to increase the liquidity, profitability and viability of financial markets and institutions.

REFORMS IN THE INDIAN FINANCIAL SYSTEM

As the Indian economy grows and becomes more sophisticated, the financial system has to develop *pari pasu* in a manner that it supports and promotes such growth. With increasing global integration, the Indian banking and financial system as a whole has to be strengthened so as to be able to compete globally.

Pre reform, era

Reforms in the Indian financial system till have been measured, gradual, cautious, and steady as compared to other countries. Until the beginning of the1990s, the state of the financial sector in India could be described as a classic example of "financial repression" à la MacKinnon and Shaw. The sector was characterized, by administered interest rates, large pre-emption of resources by the authorities and extensive micro-regulations directing the major portion of the flow of funds to and from financial intermediaries.

Most of the financial intermediaries were public sector entities governed by opaque accounting norms and limited disclosure which had slowered their growth.

Insurance companies – both life and non-life – were all publicly owned and offered very little product choice.

In the securities market, new equity issues were governed by a large number of complex regulations and extensive restrictions. There was very little transparency and depth in the secondary market trading of such securities.

Interest rates on government securities, the predominant segment of fixed-income securities, were administered by the government. The market for such securities was confined mainly to financial intermediaries, *i.e.,* banks etc. who had to invest in government securities to fulfill high statutory reserve requirements. As a result there was low level of competition, efficiency and productivity in the financial sector, on the one hand, and severe credit constraints of the productive entities, on the other, especially for those in the private sector. The other major drawback of this regime was the inadequate attention that was placed on the financial health of the intermediaries.

However after 1991 India has had more than a decade of financial sector reforms during which there has been substantial transformation and liberalization of the whole financial system.

Indian financial sector over the last decade has been transformed into a reasonably sophisticated, diverse and resilient system. Reforms in the Indian financial system have marked the end of extensive well sequenced and coordinated policy measures aimed at making the Indian financial sector efficient, competitive and stable.

The main objectives, of the financial sector reform process in India initiated in the early 1990s have been to:

- Remove financial repression that existed earlier.
- Create an efficient, productive and profitable financial sector industry.
- Enable price discovery, particularly, by the market determination of interest rates that then helps in efficient allocation of resources.
- Provide operational and function autonomy to institutions.
- Prepare the financial system for increasing international competition.
- Open the external sector in a gradual way.
- Promote the maintenance of financial stability.

METHODS ADOPTED FOR REFORMS IN INDIAN FINANCIAL SYSTEM

The initiation of financial reforms in the country during the early 1990s was to a large extent conditioned by the analysis and recommendations of various committees/ working groups set up to address specific issues. The process has been marked by 'calibration' with measures being undertaken after extensive consultations with experts and market participants.

Reform measures were introduced across sectors as well as within each sector were planned in such a way so as to reinforce each other. Attempts were made to simultaneously strengthen for commercial decision-making and market forces in an increasingly competitive framework. At the same time, the process did not lose sight of the social responsibilities of the financial sector. However, for fulfilling such objectives, rather than using administrative force by government, attempts were made to provide operational flexibility and incentives so that the desired ends are attended through interaction of market forces.

Despite several changes in government there has not been any reversal of direction in the financial sector reform process over the last 15 years.

As pointed by Ex-Governor Reddy (Reddy, 2002 a), the approach towards financial sector reforms in India is based on *panchasutra* or five principles:

- Cautious and appropriate sequencing of reforms measures.
- Introduction of norms that are mutually reinforcing.
- Introduction of complementary reforms across sectors (most importantly, monetary, fiscal and external sector).
- Development of financial institutions.
- Development of financial markets.

Several advisory groups (*e.g.,* Standing Committee on International Financial Standards and Codes) were designed to benchmark India practices with international standards in several crucial areas of importance like monetary policy, banking supervision, data dissemination, corporate governance etc. and the recommendations contained therein have either been implemented or are in the process of implementation.

REFORMS IN BANKING SECTOR

After the nationalization of major banks in two waves, starting in 1969, the Indian banking system became predominantly government owned by the early 1990s. Banking sector reform essentially consisted of a two-pronged approach.

The first approach was introduction of international best practices in prudential regulation and supervision early in the reform cycle, to increase competition in the system gradually. In this approach special emphasis was placed on building up the risk management capabilities of the Indian banks.

The second approach involved recapitalisation of banks from government resources to bring them to appropriate capitalisation standards. This was done through diversification of ownership to private investors up to a limit of 49 per cent, thereby keeping majority ownership and control with the government.

With such widening of ownership most of these banks have been publicly listed; this helped to bring about greater market discipline in bank management and greater transparency through enhanced disclosure norms. This phased introduction of new private sector banks, and expansion in the number of foreign bank branches, provided for new competition. However, tight capital adequacy and prudential supervision norms were applied equally to all banks, regardless of ownership.

The following were the reforms in banking sector:

Prudential Measures

Introduction and phased implementation of international best practices and norms on risk-weighted capital adequacy requirement, accounting, income recognition, provisioning and exposure.

Measures were taken to strengthen risk management through recognition of different components of risk, assignment of risk-weights to various asset classes, norms on connected lending, risk concentration, application of marked-to-market principle for investment portfolio and limits on deployment of fund in sensitive activities.

Competition Enhancing Measures

Granting of operation autonomy to public sector banks by reduction of public ownership in public sector banks by allowing them to raise capital from equity market up to 49% of paid-up capital.

Transparent norms for entry of Indian private sector, foreign and joint-venture banks and insurance companies, granting of permission for foreign investment in the financial sector in the form of Foreign Direct Investment (FDI) as well as portfolio investment, permission to banks to diversify product portfolio and business activities.

Measures Enhancing Role of Market Forces

Sharp reduction in pre-emption through reserve requirement, market determined pricing for government securities, disbanding of administered interest rates with a few exception and enhanced transparency and disclosure norms to facilitate market discipline.

Introduction of pure inter-bank call money market, auction-based repo, reserve-repos for short-term liquidity management, facilitation of improved payments and settlement mechanism.

Institutional and Legal Measures

Setting up of Lok Adalats, debt recovery tribunals, asset reconstruction companies, settlement advisory committees, corporate debt restructuring mechanism, etc. for quicker recovery/restructuring of debt.

Promulgation of Securitization and Reconstruction of Financial Assets and Enforcement of Securities Interest (SARFAESI) Act and its subsequent amendment to ensure creditor rights.

Setting up of Credit Information Bureau for information sharing on defaulters as also other borrowers.

Setting up of Clearing Corporation of India Limited (CCIL) to act as central counter party for facilitating payments and settlement system relating to fixed income securities and money market instruments.

Supervisory Measures

Establishment of the Board for Financial Supervision as the apex supervisory authority for commercial. banks, financial institutions and non-banking financial companies.

Introduction of CAMELS supervisory rating system, move towards risk-based supervision, consolidated supervision of financial conglomerates, strengthening of off-site surveillance through control returns.

Recasting of the role of statutory auditors, increased internal control through strengthening of internal audit.

Strengthening corporate governance, enhanced due diligence on important shareholders, fit and proper tests for directors.

Technology Related Measures

Setting up of INFINET as the communication backbone for the financial sector, introduction of Negotiated Dealing System (NDS) for screen-based trading in government securities and Real Time Gross Settlement (RTGS) system.

REFORMS IN THE GOVERNMENT SECURITIES MARKET

Institutional Measures

Administered interest rates on government securities were replaced by an auction system for price discovery.

Automatic monetization of fiscal deficit through the issue of ad hoc Treasury Bills was phased out.

Primary Dealers (PD) were introduced as market makers in the government securities market.

Delivery versus Pay (DvP) settlement system was introduced for ensuring transparency in the trading of government securities.

Repurchase agreements (repo) was introduced as a tool of short term liquidity adjustment. Subsequently, the Liquidity Adjustment Facility (LAF) was introduced. LAF operates through repo and reverse auctions to set up a corridor for short-term interest rate. LAF has emerged as the tool for both liquidity management and also signaling device for interest rates in the overnight market.

Market Stabilisation Scheme (MSS) has been introduced, which has expanded the instruments available to the Reserve Bank for managing the surplus liquidity in the system.

Increase in Instruments in Government Securities Market

91-day Treasury bill was introduced for managing liquidity and benchmarking. Zero Coupon Bonds, Floating Rate Bonds, Capital

Indexed Bonds were issued and exchange traded interest rate futures were introduced. OTC interest rate derivatives like IRS/FRAs were introduced.

Enabling Measures

Foreign Institutional Investors (FIIs) were allowed to invest in government securities subject to certain limits.

Introduction of automated screen-based trading in government securities through Negotiated Dealing System (NDS).

Setting up of risk-free payments and settlement system in government securities through Clearing Corporation of India Limited (CCIL). Phased introduction of Real Time Gross Settlement System (RTGS).

Introduction of trading of government securities on stock exchanges for promoting retailing in such securities, permitting non-banks to participate in repo market.

DEBT MARKET REFORMS

A large number of reforms have been carried out in the government securities (G-Sec) debt market. In 1990s the system had to essentially move from administered interest rates and to a more market oriented system. Prescription of a "statutory liquidity ratio" (SLR), *i.e.* the ratio at which banks are required to invest in approved securities, though originally devised as a prudential measure, was used as the main instrument of this movement to market oriented system in the pre-reform period. The high

SLR requirement created a captive market for government securities, which were issued at low administered interest rates. After the initiation of reforms, this ratio has been reduced in phases to the statutory minimum level of 24%.

Over the past few years numerous steps have been taken to broaden and deepen the Government securities market and to raise the levels of transparency.

Automatic monetization of the Government's deficit has been phased out and the market borrowings of the Central Government are presently undertaken through a system of auctions at market related rates.

However still an appropriate institutional framework has to be created for such a market to be built and operated in sustained manner. Legislative provisions, technology development, market infrastructure such as settlement systems, trading systems, and the like have all be developed.

FOREX MARKET REFORMS

The Indian forex exchange market had been heavily controlled since the 1950s, along with increasing trade controls designed to foster import substitution. Consequently, both the current and capital accounts were closed and foreign exchange was made available by the RBI through a complex licensing system. The task facing Indian in the early 1990s was therefore to gradually move from total control to a functioning forex market. The move towards a market-based exchange rate regime in 1993 and the subsequent adoption of current account convertibility were the key measures in reforming the Indian foreign exchange market.

Following are the major reforms in forex markets:

Authorised Dealers of foreign exchange have been allowed to carry on a large range of activities.

Banks have been given large autonomy to undertake foreign exchange market. A large number of products including currency futures have been introduced and entry of newer players has been allowed in the market.

The Indian approach is opening the external sector and developing the foreign exchange market in a phased manner from current account convertibility to the ongoing process of capital account opening.

Exchange rate regime has evolved from a single currency fixed-exchange rate system to fixing the value of rupee against a basket of currencies and further to market-determined floating exchange rate regime.

Institutional Framework

Institutional framework for forex Replacement of the earlier Foreign Exchange Regulation Act (FERA), 1973 by the market friendly Foreign Exchange Management Act, 1999.

Delegation of considerable powers by RBI to Authorised Dealers to release foreign exchange for a variety of purposes.

Increase in Instruments in forex market

A number of instruments were introduced in the forex markets such as development of rupee-foreign currency swap market, Introduction of additional hedging instruments, such as, foreign currency-rupee options. Authorized dealers were permitted to use innovative products like cross-currency options, interest rate and currency swaps, cap/collars and forward rate agreements (FRSs) in the international forex market.

Among the liberalization several authorized dealers were permitted to initiate trading positions, borrow and invest in overseas market subject to certain specifications and ratification by respective Banks' Boards.

Banks are also permitted to fix interest rates on non-resident deposits, subject to certain specification, use derivative products for asset-liability management and fix overnight open position limits and gap limits in the foreign exchange market, subject to ratification by RBI.

Permission to various participants in the foreign exchange market, including exporters, Indian investing abroad, FIIs, to avail forward cover and enter into swap transactions without any limit subject to genuine underlying exposure.

FIIs and NRIs are permitted to trade in exchange traded derivative contracts subject to certain conditions.

Foreign exchange earners are permitted to maintain foreign currency accounts.

Residents are permitted to open such accounts within the general limit of US$25,000 per year.

REFORMS IN OTHER SEGMENTS OF FINANCIAL SECTOR

Measures aimed at establishing prudential regulation and supervision and also competition and efficiency enhancing measures have also been introduced for nonblank financial intermediaries as well. Towards this end, non-banking financial companies (NBFCs), especially those involved in public deposit taking activities, have been brought under the regulation of RBI. Development Finance Institutions (DFIs), specialized term-lending institutions, NBFCs, Urban Cooperative Banks and Primary Dealers have all been brought under the supervision of the Board for Financial Supervision (BFS). With the aim of regulatory convergence for entities involved in similar activities, prudential regulation and supervision norms were also introduced in phases for DFIs, NBFCs and cooperative banks.

The insurance business remained within the confined of public ownership until the late 1990s. Subsequent to the passage of the Insurance Regulation and Development Act in 1999, several changes were initiated, including allowing newer players/joint ventures to undertake insurance business on risk-sharing/commission basis.

CAPITAL MARKET REFORMS

With the objective of improving market efficiency, increasing transparency, integration of national markets and prevention of unfair practices regarding trading, a package of reforms comprising measures to liberalize, regulate and develop capital market was introduced.

An important step has been the establishment of the Securities and Exchange Board of India (SEBI) as the regulator for equity markets. Since 1992, reform measures in the equity market have focused mainly on regulatory effectiveness, enhancing competitive conditions, reducing information asymmetries, developing modern technological infrastructure, mitigating transaction costs and controlling of speculation in the securities market. Another important development under the reform process has been the opening up of mutual funds to the private sector in 1992, which ended the monopoly of Unit Trust of India (UTI), a public sector entity. These steps have been buttressed by measures to promote market integrity.

The Indian capital market was opened up for foreign institutional investors (FIIs) in 1992. The Indian corporate sector has been allowed to tap international capital markets through American Depository Receipts (ADRS), Global Depository Receipts (GDRS), Foreign Currency Convertible Bonds (FCCBs) and External Commercial Borrowing (ECBs). Similarly, Overseas Corporate Bodies (OCBs) and non-resident Indian (NRIs) have been allowed to invest in Indian companies. FIIs have been permitted in all types of securities including Government securities and they enjoy full capital convertibility. Mutual funds have been allowed to open offshore funds to invest in equities abroad.

REFORM IN MONETARY POLICY FRAMEWORK

The transition of economic policies in general and financial sector policies in particular, from a control oriented regime to a liberalized but regulated regime has also been reflected in changes in the nature of monetary management. While the basic objectives of monetary policy, namely price stability and ensuring adequate credit flow to support growth, have remained unchanged, the underlying operating environment for monetary policy has under gone a significant transformation. An increasing concern is the maintenance of financial stability. The basic emphasis of monetary policy since the initiation of reforms has been to reduce market segmentation in the financial sector through increase in the linkage between various segments of the financial market including money, government securities and forex market.

The Pursuit for Financial Stability

With growing liberalization, globalization and financial openness, financial stability issues have come up. It was believed earlier that monetary or macro-economic stability leads to financial stability. But this relationship although may be true in long run, in the short run a number of other factors hold true.

The basic factors affecting financial stability are increasing pace of financial innovations and growing acceptance of market processes as basic determinants of resource allocation.

Financial liberalization has come out in various sectors including banking and insurance. It has led to massive capital inflows and instability in exchange rates.

Financial markets need a greater supervision and liberalization as any destabilization can affect even those who are not a part of it.

Broadly, operating financial stability in India would mean.

(*a*) Ensuring uninterrupted settlement of financial transactions.

(*b*) Maintaining confidence among all participants and stockholders of the financial system.

(*c*) Remove excessive volatility that may adversely affect economic activity.

For improving financial stability Reserve Bank has taken three broad steps –

- Maintenance of overall economic balance.

- Improvement in function of institutions and markets, and
- Strengthening soundness among the institutions and market through regulation and supervision.

Reserve Bank has taken steps in this regard by improving the monetary policy to lower down inflation. It has also moved towards integration, widening and deepening of various segments of financial markets. It has also tried to lower the transaction costs and enhance liquidity in the markets. Ensuring orderly conditions in the financial markets is an important aspect of Reserve Bank's approach towards maintaining financial stability.

A robust financial system is characterized by smooth and secure payments system and RBI has taken initiative in matching the Indian payment system with the global standards. Electronic Clearing Initiatives like Electronic Fund Transfer, Electronic Clearing Services, Real Time Gross Settlement System, Centralized Fund Management System and the Structured Financial Messaging System have been introduced by RBI to quicken the settlement process.

A major initiative towards preventing crises has been the strengthening of regulation and supervision system.

Stability in financial system can be ensured only when markets and institutions function on basis of informed decisions. For ensuring this RBI has taken various steps by prescribing comprehensive disclosure requirements to ensure greater accountability and transparency.

Going by the above, it can be said that Financial Stability in India has moved to the center stage and has been an integral responsibility of RBI. In fact the efforts of RBI have made our financial system well functioning, stable and vibrant. The approach towards financial stability will be vigorously pursued so as to bench-mark ourselves with the international standards. This will in fact make our financial institutions emerge as global players and convert India or the international financial center of the new millennium.

QUESTIONS

Fill in the blanks:

1. A nation consists of __________ economic units.
2. Financial system primarily comprises of _________ and __________.
3. Banking institutions are the ___________ and ____________ of money.
4. Capital markets can be subdivided into _______ and _______.
5. A robust financial system is characterized by ________ and __________.

Define:

1. Lease financing.
2. Hire purchase

State whether true or false:

1. Financial system helps in imparting liquidity to the economy by promoting savings.
2. Primary market is a place where securities already issued are traded.
3. Money market involves trading of securities having life greater than a year.
4. A person who acts as an intermediary in both primary and secondary market is called a broker.
5. Derivatives include options and swaps.

Answer in detail:

Q.1. Classify the various components of financial system and bring out their features.

Q.2. "Financial Stability is difficult to achieve in context of growing globalization and liberalization", comment.

Q.3. "Indian Financial System remains weak in spite of the presence of suitable legislative measures", comment.

Q.4. Discuss how reforms have changed the face of Indian Financial System.

❑❑❑

PART–I
FINANCIAL MARKETS

Section - I : Money Market

Section - II : Capital Market

Section-I
Money Market

1 INTRODUCTION TO MONEY MARKET

DEFINITION OF MONEY MARKET

Money market is a place for large institutions and government to manage their short-term cash needs. It specializes in very short-term debt securities. Short-term rate refers to a period of less than one year. Money market investments are also called cash investments because of their short maturities. The securities of money market may be issued by government, large corporation, or financial institutions. These instruments are liquid and are considered extra-ordinarily safe. As they are extremely conservative, money market securities offer significantly lower rate than most other securities. To be eligible for classification as a money market instrument, a debt must be classified as.:

- Un-collateralized short-term (less than one year) debt of an issuer with high credit rating.
- Highly liquid and readily transferable.
- Bear an annualized "Discount Yield" and are quoted by it.

NEED FOR MONEY MARKET

Businesses need working capital for their day-to-day operations and major component of this working capital is cash. Neither the shortage or excess of cash is beneficial for a firm. Lack of adequate cash or liquidity can lead to disruption in daily activities of the business. Businesses generally face short-term mismatch of funds as cash outflows may not be timed with the cash inflows. Short-term cash deficit if not met, may not be able to meet the day-to-day cash obligations or carry out production and this will also add to the costs of the firm.

On the other hand excess funds in short-term may lay idle and not yield any interest. So firms should not maintain idle funds as they take away its profitability and also add costs of holding them. So to prevent maintenance of idle funds a firm should search for investment avenues. Short-term liquidity crises should be met with fund availability while surplus funds in short-term should be invested prudently.

During the pre-1950 era the requirement of short-term funds was met by lenders, pawnbrokers or indigenous banks. But later the need of the financial market grew to an extent became unmanageable for such unorganized sector. This led to the evolution of money market as a formal financial market, *i.e.,* an organized market to deal with short-term fund management.

So we can say that money market has come into existence because of the fundamental need of working capital management where balance between liquidity and profitability is paramount. The market provides a platform for cash surplus and deficient organizations to transact and reach an equilibrium regarding the rate of interest charged on these funds.

Borrowing and lending in money markets is in high volume and is less risky short-term. Due to short-term nature of transactions, cost of transactions is high, due to which volumes transacted are large. Most of the transactions have a maturity period overnight to one week. Difference between money market and capital market are following:

Difference between Money Market and Capital Market

Money Market	Capital Market
Finance is transacted for a period of less than one year.	Finance is transacted for a period greater than one year.
Money market securities trade in awfully high denominations.	Capital market securities in lower denominations.
It is a dealer market, *i.e.,* firms buy and sell securities in their own accounts, at their own risk.	A broker receives commission to act as an agent while investor takes the risk of holding the stock.
It lacks a central trading floor or exchange. Deals are transacted over phone or electronic system.	It has well-organised stock exchanges.
Securities traded have high face values may be in lakhs.	Securities traded have face value of denomination 10 or 100.
Instruments traded include commercial paper, certificate of deposit, T-Bills, G-Sees etc.	Instruments traded include shares, futures, options, debentures, bonds etc.

PLAYERS IN MONEY MARKET

The players in money market include:

1. Government : Government intervenes in money market to increase the stability of financial institutions and markets. It intervenes in the interest rates and money supply in the money market. This is done by two policies : Fiscal Policy and Monetary Policy.

Under the fiscal and monetary policies government intervenes in the forex market in order to adjust the exchange rate and affect the supply of money. When currency falls, government buys foreign currency and this leads to reduced money supply, similarly when currency rises, it sells foreign currency leading to increased money supply. For doing this the government may issue or buy securities to decrease or increase the money supply and thus protect the currency which is done in money market. The government also intervenes in money market to adjust its budget deficit. It borrows money by issuing short-term securities and adjusts its deficits.

2. Central Bank : Central Bank acts as an intermediary between government and money market. It issues securities on behalf of the government. It also regulates the money markets by issuing guidelines from time to time. Central Bank regulates money supply in the money market by issuing guidelines to banks regarding cash reserve ratio manipulating the interest ratio and involving in open market operations.

3. Banks : They act as borrowers and issuers in the money market they take debt when they fall short of statutory reserve requirements-due to change in rates or when they fall short of reserves to meet the withdrawal requirements of customers.

When Banks loan debt when they have surplus funds they may also require short-term funds. If they have some attractive loan proposal at their disposal but do not have funds they may at that time borrow funds from the money market.

4. Discount and Acceptance Houses : They act as Market Makers and participate in Bill Market. Discount houses perform the function of discounting/rediscounting the T-Bills or commercial bills. Acceptance houses accept the bills of exchange on behalf of their clients in lieu of commission, which increases the liquidity of the bill.

5. Financial institutions act as Borrowers and Lenders of short-tem funds.

6. Corporate houses act as Issuers of securities for meeting their working capital requirements.

7. Mutual Funds and Foreign Institutional Investment (FIIs) etc. act as investors in money market and FIIs contribute a small share in total participation as per the restrictions to investment laid down on them.

8. Various Dealers/Satellite Dealers also participate as intermediaries in the Money Market. The role of all the above players in the money market can be summarized as below:-

Player	Role
Government	Issuer/Borrower
Central Bank	Intermediary
Banks	Issuers/Borrowers
Discount Houses	Market Makers
Acceptance Houses	Market Makers
Financial Institution	Issuers/Borrowers
MFs	Investors/Lenders
FIIs	Investors
Corporate Houses	Issuers
Dealers	Intermediaries

MONEY MARKET INSTRUMENTS

Money market borrowing and lending involves various instruments. These include:

- Deposits and Loans
- REPO (Repurchase Options) and a number of securitized debt instruments
- Treasury Bills
- Bankers Acceptances
- Commercial Paper
- Certificates of Deposit
- Call and Notice Money Market
- Government Dated Securities (G-SRCS)
- Commercial Bills (Bill of Exchange)
- Money Market Mutual Funds

A detailed description of each instrument will be discussed in the subsequent chapters, given below is a brief profile of each:

Inter-Corporate Deposits (ICD) : An ICD is a loan extended by one corporate to another. It exists as a refuge for low rated corporates and allows corporates with surplus funds to lend to those in deficit. Moreover the better-rated corporates can borrow from banking system and lend in the market. So both borrowers and lenders are corporates. Rates of interest in this market are higher due to higher risk premium, which makes cost of the funds for corporates higher than a bank. The deposits are unsecure and therefore the risk underlying them is high. The ICD market is not well-organised very little information about transaction details.is available publicly.

REPO (Repurchase Opions): REPO is short for repurchase agreement. It is basically a contract entered into by two parties, which may include the RBI, a bank or NBFC. In this contract, a holder of government securities sells the securities to a lender and agrees to repurchase them at an agreed future date at an agreed price. They are usually short-term overnight or 30 days or more, which makes them less risky. REPO may be called a reuse REPO when a dealer buys government securities from an investor and then sells them back on a later date at a higher price and a term REPO when the maturity period is greater than 30 days.

Treasury Bills (T-Bills) : T-Bills are issued by the government to fill the deficit between revenue and expenditure in the budget. They may have a maturity period ranging from a fortnight to a year. They are risk free and highly marketable. Both institutional and private investors may bid on T-Bills. Institutional investors include banks, government, mutual funds etc. Private investors include brokers/dealers, who may buy the bill for resale in the secondary market.

Banker's Acceptance : Banks use banker's acceptance to finance import and export with firms in foreign countries. An importer's bank backs the importer by paying the foreign party on importer's behalf. The importer is then obliged to pay the bank within a period of 3-6 months. If the bank so desires, it can call the contract before it is repaid so as to replenish its cash, which makes BA highly liquid. If the importer defaults, bank becomes liable for payment on the importers behalf.

Commercial Paper : Commercial Paper is an unsecured short-term instrument saved by corporates with good credit record. Proceeds from Commercial Paper are used to buy inventories. Banks and brokerage houses buy it to resell to individuals in smaller lots. Commercial Papers are issued for a maturity period of 90 days and have denomination of Rs. 2.5 million. They can also be issued for a period of 180 days but more popular ones are those issued for 90 days. For issuing a Commercial Paper a company must get them rated by a recognized credit rating agency and only those companies can issue a Commercial Paper, having a credit rating of P_1. Secondary funds raised through Commercial Papers do not represent fresh borrowings for the corporate issuer, but merely substitute a part of banking limits available to it. Hence, a company issues Commercial Papers to save interest cost, *i.e.,* when market conditions are such that Commercial Paper issuance will be at rates lower than the rate at which company borrows money from the bank.

Certificate of Deposit (CD) : After treasury bills, the next lowest risk category investment option is the Certificate of Deposit (CD). It is a negotiable promissory note, secure and short-term (up to a year) in market. It is issued at discount to face values and this discount note (which is the interest) is negotiable between the issuer and the investor. Although RBI allows CDs to have maturity up to one year, mostly the maturity quoted is of 90 days. It does not have a well-developed secondary market.

CDs are issued by banks and financial institutions mainly to augment funds by attracting deposits from corporates having surplus funds or from high net-worth individuals, trusts, etc. Rates on CDs are determined by various factors. Foreign and private banks having lower deposit base use CDs to raise funds.

Call and Notice Money Market : It is a market for borrowing funds from a period of one day up to a year. In Notice Money Market, funds are not issued for a fiscal repayment period but borrower is issued a notice 2-3 days prior to repayment date and the borrower has to pay it on the specified date.

In case of Call Money Market, however, the borrower is specified a date prior to the deal.

Both of these serve as mechanisms of bridging the deficits in short-term.

Government Dated Securities : Government Dated Securities are issued by the Government of the India and form a part of borrowing program approved by the Parliament in the Finance Bill every year. They are issued in denominations as low as Rs. 100 in physical certificate form, with maturity ranging from 1 to 30 years. Despite long-term maturity, they form a part of the money market. This is because they are issued by the Government due to which they have very high liquidity and are characterized not only by their short-term nature but also by their liquidity. They are issued at a discount to face value and carry a coupon rate.

Commercial Bills : They are Bills of Exchange and denote negotiable financial instruments that provide funds immediately needed for a transaction. They are of various types depending on the date of maturity. They are issued for commercial transactions involving exchange of goods and services. They are discounted by banks, who further get them rediscounted with each other or RBI.

Money Market Mutual Funds : Money Market Mutual Funds pool money from retail investors and invest them in short-term securities. It enables investors to invest their surplus funds in money market instruments to get a higher return as compared to other avenues of investment. They are more liquid as compared to other investment alternatives and are safer also as they invest in highly rated securities like government bank, etc.

EVOLUTION OF MONEY MARKET IN INDIA

In 1985, a committee under the Chairmanship of Shri Surrmoy Chakravorty was set-up to make recommendations for the development of the money market. After this in 1987, RBI set-up a working group on Money Market under the Chairmanship of Shri N Vaghul, based on whose recommendations a number of measures were taken in the eighties for the widening of the money market. These initiatives were:

- DFHI, *i.e.,* Discount and Finance House of India was set-up to impart liquidity to money market instruments and develop a secondary market for them. DFHI was a joint venture of RBI & Public Sector Banks and Financial Institutions. Later RBI reduced its stake and it is now a minority shareholder.
- Commercial Paper, Certificates of Deposits and Inter-Bank Participation Certificates were introduced in 1988-89 to increase the range of money market instruments.
- In 1988-89 operations of DFHI in the Call and Notice Money Market were freed from interest rate ceiling and in May 1989 this interest rate ceiling was rediscounting of commercial bills and inter-bank participation certificates. Presently money market interest rates are determined by market forces.

Risks in Money Market

Money market is exposed to several risks as shown below.

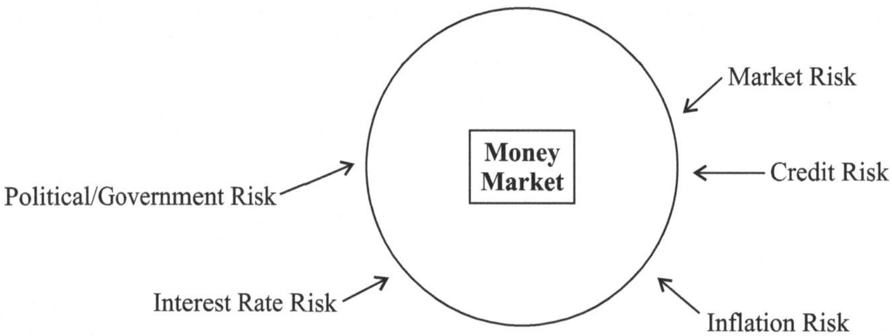

Market Risk : It occurs as prices and yields of all securities. It may rise and fall due to broad outside influences affecting the market. This rise and fall in prices of instruments may lead to capital loss/gain. This risk can be minimized by increasing the liquidity of the instrument.

Interest Rate Risk : It arises due to change in interest rate of securities. The investors putting funds in them will have to reinvest the funds at a lower rate of interest if interest rate falls or the value of security held by them may fall, if interest rate rises.

Inflation Risk : Inflation leads to rise in prices of securities and reduces their purchasing power. All the money market instruments are exposed to this risk but their exposure to this risk is lower than capital market instruments, which are of long-term nature.

Political Risk : Political Risk implies the risk inherent in change of government policies. This is because government policies have an impact on money supply, interest rates etc. and thus the money markets. Government policies may affect the role of players present in the money market, thus having a direct or indirect affect on the money market.

Credit Risk : It arises due to inability of borrowers to pay back because of their bankruptcy. It is more in case of money market securities issued by corporates than in case of those issued by the government.

After analyzing the money market development in India and its current progress it can be said that India has created a base for a variety of products in the money market. Although money market in India is not wide in terms of volume and liquidity actet the reforms in progress are considered to provide the necessary depth.

Money market may gradually get integrated with FOREX and debt market, and pave way for the Reserve Bank's increased dependence on indirect tools of monetary regulation.

QUESTIONS

Fill in the blanks:

1. Short-term refers to a period ____________.
2. ___________ acts as an intermediary between government and money market.
3. Full form of REPO is _______________.
4. Call money market helps to raise funds for ________ while notice money market helps to raise funds for _____________.
5. The risk arising out of borrower's inability to pay back is called _____________.

Define:

1. Money Market
2. Treasury Bills
3. Certificate of Deposit
4. Commercial Bills.

State whether true or false:

1. Borrowing and lending in money market involves high risk.
2. Financial institutions act as lenders of short-term funds in money market.
3. Money market lacks a centralized trading floor.
4. Commercial Paper is a secured usance promissory note issued by corporates.

Answer in detail:

Q.1. Bring out the differences between Capital Market and Money Market.

Q.2. What are various components of money market? Discuss the features of each.

Q.3. What are the deficiencies in Indian Money Market?

Q.4. What are the risks inherent in a money market?

❑❑❑

2

CALL MONEY MARKET

INTRODUCTION

Call/Notice Money is an amount borrowed or lent on demand for a very short period. If the period is more than one day, it is called "Notice Money" otherwise the amount is called "Call Money". The rate at which funds are borrowed in this market is called "Call Money Rate".

Whether the time period of the borrowing may be 1 day or 14 days or in between, the borrower is intimated about repayment, which enable him to arrange funds by the due date. In case money is lent for more than 14 days, it is called term money. Holidays/Sundays are excluded in the duration of borrowing. The transactions do not involve deposit of any collateral security due to their short-term nature.

FEATURES

- The Call Market enables the banks and institutions to even out their day-to-day deficits and surpluses of money.
- Commercial Banks, Cooperative Banks and Primary Dealers borrow and lend in the market for adjusting their cash reserve requirement.
- Specified All India Financial Institutions, Mutual Funds and certain specified entities are allowed to access Call/Notice Money Market only as lenders.
- It is also called inter-bank market as non-bank entities are not allowed to access it.
- Call rates are market determined.
- Due to short-term unsecured nature of market both the parties, *i.e.,* borrowers and lenders need to have current account with RBI.
- It provides an avenue for deploying funds on short-term basis to those who want continuous inflow of funds.
- The market is highly liquid as money lent can be called back any time.

Participants in the Call Money Market

Call Money Markets were basically inter-bank markets. But gradually the participation in these markets was extended to non-bank participants also.

The Chakravorty Committee (1985) first recommended the entry of non-bank institutions in the Call Money Market as it felt that allowing these participants will only lead to a re-distribution of existing resources from one participant to another and not dilute the strength of monetary regulation by RBI.

Vagrul Committee (1990) recommended to keep Call Money Market restricted to only the banking sector as it felt that participation of other non-bank entities would distort the call rates, which were market determined. It proposed that these non-bank entities should instead invest in other new money market instruments, which the committee recommended to bring into the market.

The Narsimhan Committee-II (1998) felt that non-bank entities being not subject to reserve requirements as Banks and should be completely phased out of Call Money Markets and must invest in other money market instruments.

In December, 2000, RBI constituted a Technical Group for phasing out non-banks from Call/Notice Money Market. The group put forward its recommendations in March, 2001 in which it proposed that non-bank entities should not be allowed to participate in the Call Money Market but this should not be immediate. They should be phased out gradually and made to enter other money market instruments so that there is no disturbance in the Call Money Market.

The guidelines regarding participation in the Call Money Market were changed from time to time (described later).

As per various policy guidelines Initially only DFHI and STCI were allowed to directly participate in the Call Money Market but in 1996 Primary Dealers other than those like SBI Gilts, Gilts Securities Trading Corporation etc. were also allowed to lend and borrow directly in the market. Presently 18 Primary Dealers are operating in the Call Money Market.

From 1991 onwards Corporate were also allowed to enter (lend) in the Call Money Markets. At first, they were allowed to lend through DFHI and then through any of the Primary Dealers. Earlier they were allowed to lend Rs. 20 crore, which was phased out to Rs. 3 crore in 1998. After June 2001 however, corporates were denied access to Call Money Market.

UTI and LIC have been permitted to lend in the call money markets since 1971. Other financial institutions have also been allowed to lend. All the registered mutual funds have been allowed to lend in the market since 1997. Thus, mutual funds, financial institutions, corporates operate on the lending side only whereas Banks and Primary Dealers can operate on both the sides i.e. lending and borrowing.

Bank participants can be further divided into two categories: (*a*) banks which are predominantly lenders, these include public sector banks. (*b*) banks which are predominantly borrowers, these include foreign and private sector banks.

State Bank of India is the largest lender in the market lending about 15% of the funds. While three public sector banks *viz.*, Canara Bank, Central Bank and Punjab National Bank along with five financial institutions *viz*,. ICICI, IDBI, LIC, SIDBI, UTI accounted for nearly 30% of lending in last few years.

Rates of Call Money

Call rates are market determined. The amount of call rate signifies the interest paid on call loans. It reflects whether there is surplus or deficit of funds in the market. If money supply is high, money will be easily available *i.e.*, high supply will lower the call rate, whereas if money supply is low which means shortage of money in the economy, *i.e.*, low supply will increase the call rate.

FUNCTIONS OF CALL MONEY MARKET

Call Money Market serves the following basic functions:

- Banks may face some short-term mismatch of funds as sometimes the withdrawals may exceed deposits. Due to this banks require immediate money to meet their demand liabilities which they can borrow from call money market.
- Banks borrow money from Call Money Market to maintain their Cash Reserve Requirements (CRR) and Statutory Liquidity Ratio (SLR).
- Money is also borrowed from Call Money Market for discounting commercial bills which forms a small portion of transaction in India due to underdeveloped bill market.
- Some banks also lend and borrow in Call Money Market in order to earn profit from the difference between borrowing and lending rates.

MECHANISM OF OPERATIONS IN CALL MONEY MARKET

Call Money market is a floorless market, *i.e.,* it lacks a central trading floor or exchange. Lenders and borrowers contact each other over phone and arrive at a deal specifying the amount of loan and interest rate. After the deal is struck between the two parties the lender issues a cheques in favour of the borrower. The cheque is a bank's pay order which is cleared by the special high value clearing cell in the RBI. The borrower then issues a borrowing receipt and after repayment the lender returns the same to the borrower.

The same can also be done through Discount and Finance house of India. Both borrowers and lenders can deal with DFHI and get or give funds in case they are in deficit or surplus respectively. The same procedure is followed for submission of cheques and issue of call deposit receipt as is done in case of borrowers and lenders dealing directly.

An extension on call loan can be made for a maximum period of 14 days.

LOCATION OF CALL MONEY MARKET

Call Money Market is located in main commercial center and industrial centers like Delhi, Mumbai, Kolkata, Chennai and Ahmedabad. Of these the most significant contribution is by Mumbai and Kolkata.

GROWTH AND DEVELOPMENT OF CALL MONEY MARKET IN INDIA

The call/notice money market was predominantly an inter-bank market till 1990, except for UTI and LIC which were allowed to play as lenders since 1971. Despite the recommendation of Vaghul Committee, RBI gradually liberalized its policy for entry of non-banking institutions into the call money market in order to increase liquidity of the market and widen the number of participants. The entities with surplus funds have been allowed to provide lendings to the market through primary dealers. This policy was followed to help corporates with surplus funds to supply these funds for short-terms and get some return. The minimum size of transactions has also been gradually reduced from Rs. 20 crore to Rs. 3 crore in order to increase participation and provide more flexibility.

Presently, banks and primary dealers function as both borrowers and lenders while a large number of financial institutions and mutual funds operate only as lenders. Different banks play different roles in the market. Private sector and foreign banks mainly act as borrowers while public sector banks are major lenders in the market. RBI plays a major role by enhancing the liquidity and volatility of the market from time to time.

The size of the Call Money Market in India is somewhere between Rs.60,000 to Rs.70,000 million, of which public sector banks account for 80% borrowings and foreign banks/private sector banks account for the balance 20%.

Call rates are most affected by short-term liquidity conditions. Supply side of call rates is affected by deposit mobilisation of banks, capital flow, CRR ratio etc. While demand side is affected by government borrowings, tax outflows, fluctuations in credit offtake etc.

The behaviour of call rates (average) from 1999-2000 to 2003-04 can be shown as follows:-

Year	Avg. Rate (%) p.a.
1999-2000	8.9
2000-2001	9.2
2001-2002	7.2
2002-2003	5.89
2003-2004	4.33

GUIDELINES FOR CALL/NOTICE MONEY MARKET

The following guidelines have been issued from time to time by RBI regarding participation in Call/ Notice Money Market.

2000-2001

- Access to call money market by non-bank participants such as financial institutions and mutual funds may be reduced in three stages by placing a cap in relation to their average daily lendings during April, 2000-March, 2001.

- In Stage-I, each such non-bank institutions should be allowed to lend only up to 70% of their average daily lendings in Call Money Market.
- In Stage-II, access should be further reduced to 40% of their daily lendings.
- In final stage, Clearing corporation should be set-up and access to Call Money Market should be permitted to 10% of their average daily lendings during 2000-01. This is considered essential so as to enable these particular classes of non-bank participants to be familiar with the operations of Clearing Corporation. After the ends of this stage, these entities would not be permitted to lend in the Call Money Market at all.

2001-2002

The following recommendations were made during 2001-02 with respect to Call Money Market.

- Permission to corporates to route their call transactions through primary dealers would be available up to June 30, 2001.
- Access to other non-bank institutions (including financial institutions, mutual funds and insurance companies) to operate in Call/Notice Money Market would be gradually reduced in three stages.
- In stage-I, w.e.f. May 5, 2001 non-banks would be allowed to lend up to 85 per cent of their average daily lendings in Call Money Market during 2000-01.
- In Stage-II, w.e.f. the date of operationalisation of Clearing Corporation, non-banks would be allowed to lend 70% of their average daily lendings in the Call Market during 2000-01.
- In stage-III, w.e.f. three months after stage-II access of non-banks to Call/Notice Money Market would be equivalent to 40 per cent of their average daily lendings in 2000-01.
- In stage-IV, w.e.f. three months after stage III access of non-banks to Call/Notice Money Market would be equal to 10% of their average daily lendings during 2000-01.
- From a date to be notified by RBI, after the onset of stage-IV, non-banks will not be permitted to lend in the Call/Notice Money Market.

2002-2003

- In the first stage with affect from the fortnight beginning October 5, 2002, lending schedules of commercial banks in the Call/Notice Money Market, on a fortnightly average basis should not exceed 50% of their owned funds (paid-up capital plus reserves as at the end of March of the previous financial year; however, banks are allowed to lend a maximum of 100% of their funds on any day, during a fortnight. Borrowings by scheduled commercial banks should not exceed (on a fortnightly average basis) 150% of their owned funds or 2% of aggregate deposits as at the end of March of previous financial year (whichever is higher), however, banks are allowed to borrow a maximum of 250% of their owned funds on any day, during a fortnight.
- In the second stage w.e.f. fortnight beginning December 14, 2002, lending schedules of commercial banks on a fortnightly average basis should not exceed 25% of their owned funds; however, banks are allowed to lend a maximum of 50% on any day during a fortnight.

Similarly, borrowings by schedule commercial banks should not exceed 100% of their owned funds or 2% of aggregate deposits, whichever is higher, however banks are allowed to borrow a maximum of 125% of their owned funds on any day, during a fortnight.

2003-2004

(*a*) Moving towards Pure Inter-Bank Call/Notice Money Market

In order to move further towards a pure inter-bank Call/Notice Money Market, RBI Governor proposed that w.e.f. fortnight beginning December 27, 2003, non-bank participants would be allowed to lend, on an average in a reporting fortnight, up to 60% of their average daily lending in Call/Notice Money Market during 2000-2001. The time table for further phasing out of non-bank participants would be announced in consultation with market participants.

(*b*) Rationalization of Standing Facilities

In order to move further towards phasing out sector specific standing facilities and rationalize the rates at which liquidity is injected into the system, RBI Governor proposed that the "normal" and "back stop" standing facilities will be available in the ratio of one-third to two-thirds (33:67) from the fortnight beginning December 27, 2003.

(*c*) Primary Dealers Access to Call/Notice Money Market

With a view to develop further the reputation of market and ensure balanced development of various segments of money market, RBI Governor proposed that w.e.f. February 7, 2005, Primary Dealers will be allowed to borrow, on average basis, in a reporting fortnight, up to 200% of their Net Owned Funds (NUF) as at end-March of preceding financial year.

(*d*) Reporting of Call/Notice Money Transaction on NDS Platform

Though there has been a significant increase in the reporting of NDS platform, RBI Governor observed that complete dissemination of trade information related to money, government securities and foreign exchange market will improve transparency and strengthen efficiency of the market. In this direction, all NDS members should report their deals as soon as deals are concluded.

2004-2005

- With effect from June 11, 2005, non-bank participants were allowed to lend up to 10% of their average daily lending in Call/Notice Money Market during 2000-2001.
- w.e.f. August 6, 2005, non-bank participants were completely phased out of Call/Notice Money Market.
- w.e.f. April 30, 2005, the benchmark for fixing prudential limits as exposure to Call/Notice Money Markets in case of scheduled commercial banks were linked to their capital funds (sum of Tier-I & Tier-II Capital).
- w.e.f. April 30, 2005 all members/participants are required to report their term money deals on Negotiated Dealing Screen (NDS) platform.
- A screen based negotiated quote-driven system for all dealings in Call/Notice Money Market transactions are proposed.

QUESTIONS

Fill in the blanks:

1. Money lent for more than 14 days is called ___________.
2. For participating in money market, borrowers and lenders need to have _______ account with RBI.
3. Extension for call loan in call Money Market can be got for a maximum period of ________ days.
4. _________ and ____________ function as both borrowers and lenders in call money market.

Define:

1. Call Money Rate.
2. Notice money.

State whether true or false:

1. Call rates are least affected by short-term liquidity conditions.
2. Non-bank participants were completely phased out of Call/Notice Money Market wth effect from August 6, 2005.

Answer in detail:

Q.1. What are the features of Call Money Market in India? Discuss its functioning.

Q.2. How has the Call Money Market in India changed over years due to various reforms implemented?

❑❑❑

3

COMMERCIAL PAPER

INTRODUCTION

Commercial Paper as it is popularly known, is in the nature of an unsecured usance promissory note, transferable by endorsement and delivery. It bears a fixed maturity.

Corporates need short-term funds in order to finance their working capital requirements. For this they raise funds through various means and one of them is **Commercial Paper**.

Features of Commercial Paper —

- It is an unsecured, short-term loan issued by a corporation.
- It helps in financing the accounts receivable and inventories of a corporation.
- It is usually issued at a discount, reflecting current market rates of interest.
- It is a very safe investment instrument because the financial situation of a company can be easily predicted over a few months.
- Typically only companies with high credit ratings and credit worthiness issue commercial paper.
- Mostly, large established corporates sell commercial paper.
- It does not carry any backing of assets so it is of a unsecured nature.

ISSUERS OF COMMERCIAL PAPER

Corporates, Primary Dealers, Satellite Dealers and All India Financial Institutions that have been permitted to raise short-term resources under the umbrella limit fixed by Reserve Bank.

A company can issue a Commercial Paper provided that:-

1. The company should have a maximum tangible net worth of Rs. 40 million as per the latest balance sheet.

Tangible Net Worth : As per RBI guidelines tangible net worth would be calculated as follows:

A – Paid-up Capital

Add:

B – General Reserve

C – Share Premium Account

D – Capital Debenture Redemption Reserve

E – Other free reserves not being created to meet any future liability or depreciation in assets or bad debts or reserves created by revaluation of assets. Other free reserves include Dividend Equalization Reserve, Development Rebate Reserve, Development Allowance Reserve, Investment Allowance Reserve and Capital Reserve created through profit on sale of assets realized in cash or otherwise.

F – Accumulated Losses.

G – Deferred Revenue Expenditure.

H – Other Intangible Assets

2. The company should have been sanctioned working as a "Standard Asset" by the Financing Banks/FIs.
3. The company should have minimum credit rating from an agency approved by RBI (which is PR2). The issuer shall ensure at the time of issuance of Commercial Paper that the rating obtained is current and have not fallen due for review.
4. An FI can issue Commercial Paper within the overall umbrella limit fixed by RBI, *i.e.,* issue of Commercial Paper together with other instruments like term deposits, term money borrowings, certificates of deposit and inter-corporate deposits should not exceed 100% of its net owned funds, as per the latest audited balance sheet.

The minimum amount, which can be issued, is Rs. 5 lakhs and multiples thereof. The aggregate amount of Commercial Paper from an issuer shall be within the limit as approved by its Board of Directors or the quantum for which rating is availed; whichever is lower. However Banks/FIs have the flexibility to fix working capital limits taking into account the borrower's financing pattern, including Commercial Paper. As per RBI circular dated October 10, 2000, Commercial Paper has been de-linked from the working capital limits and can be issued as a 'stand alone' product.

INVESTORS IN COMMERCIAL PAPER

Commercial Papers may be bought by individuals, banking companies, other corporate bodies registered or incorporated in India and unincorporated bodies, non-resident Indians (NRIs) and foreign institutional investors (FIIs). However, involvement by FIIs would be within the limits set for their investments by Securities and Exchange Board of India (SEBI). When NRIs subscribe to Commercial Paper issue, the conditions regarding non-repatriability and non-endorsability are indicated on the Commercial Paper.

Investors have the advantage of getting good returns on their short-term surplus funds by investing in Commercial Paper.

PROCEDURE OF ISSUING COMMERCIAL PAPER

Once a company decides to issue Commercial Paper for a specific amount a resolution is required to be passed by the Board of Directors approving the issue and authorizing the officials to execute the relevant documents, as per RBI norms. The Commercial Paper issued is required to be rated by an approved rating agency.

The company selects an Issuing and Paying Agent, which must be a scheduled bank. The company also arranges for dealers for placement of Commercial Papers. The issue has to be completed within two weeks of opening. Every Commercial Paper issue needs to be reported to RBI through an Issuing and Paying Agent. Commercial Paper is issued at a discount to the face value.

Denominations : Commercial Paper can be issued in denominations of Rs. 5 lakhs or multiples there of.

Commercial Paper can be issued for maturities between a minimum of 15 days and maximum of up to one year from the date of issue. If the maturity date is a holiday, the company would be liable to make payment on the immediate preceding working day.

On maturity of Commercial Paper, the holder of Commercial Paper will have to get it redeemed through the depository and receive payment from the Issuing and Paying Agent.

COST INVOLVED FOR ISSUING COMMERCIAL PAPER

The following costs are involved in the issue of Commercial Paper :

1. **Stamp Duty :** This varies across the tenure of the instrument and the investor profile. It will be applicable in the respective states. In general it is 0.025%.
2. **Rating Fees :** 0.1% (subject to minimum of 1,00,000).
3. **Issuing and Paying Agent Fee :** 0.1%

Responsibilities of Issuing and Paying Agent (IPA) during Issue of CP

IPA would ensure that issuer has the minimum credit rating as stipulated by RBI and amount mobilized through issuance of Commercial Paper is within the quantum indicated by Credit Rating Agency (CRA) for the specified noting. IPA has to verify all the documents submitted by the issuer, *i.e.,* copy of board resolution, signatures of authorized executants and issue a certificate that documents are in order. It should also certify that it has a valid agreement with the issuer. Certified copies of original documents verified by the IPA should be held in the custody of IPA.

Responsibilities of Credit Rating Agency (CRA)

Code of conduct prescribed by the SEBI to CRAs for undertaking rating of capital market instruments shall be applicable to them for rating Commercial Paper. Further the credit rating agency would henceforth have the discretion to determine the validity period rating depending upon its perception about the strength of the issuer.

Accordingly, CRA shall at the time of rating, clearly indicate the date when the rating is due for review. While the CRAs can decide the validity period of credit rating assigned to issuers *vis-à-vis* their track record at regular intervals and would be required to make its revision in the public ratings through its publications and website.

Mode of Issuance

Earlier Commercial Paper was issued in the form of a promissory note or in a dematerialized form through any of the depositories approved by and registered with SEBI. However, with effect from November 2001, banks, FIs, PDs & SDs were directed to make fresh investments and hold Commercial Papers only in dematerialized form.

Redemption of Commercial Paper

If the date of maturity of Commercial Paper is a holiday, payment of Commercial Paper shall be made on the preceding working day. If as a result of this the issuance of Commercial Paper falls below the minimum period of 15 days, the Commercial Paper will be deemed to be issued for a period of less than 15 days. As per the Negotiable Instrument Act, the maturity date of the Commercial Paper should not go beyond the date up to which the credit rating of the issuer is valid.

Advantages to Corporates on Issue of Commercial Paper

(1) Commercial Paper gives highly rated companies access to cheaper funds as compared to the working capital finance from banks or other sources.

(2) If minimizes documentation requirements. The maturity of Commercial Paper can be suitably adjusted according to the cash flow requirements of the issuers.

(3) Commercial Paper helps to enhance the finances of a company.

Advantage to Investors —

Investors have advantage of getting good returns on their short-term surplus funds with relatively low risk.

Documents Required by the Investors Include:

- Original Certificates Stamped.
- Copies of Board Resolution and signatures of Authorized Signatory of the Corporate.
- Rating Letter of an approved Credit Rating Agency.

Commercial Paper is an actively traded instrument on the National Stock Exchange. DFHI, STCI, PNB Gilts etc. play an important role in developing the secondary market for Commercial Paper by providing liquidity. They act as market makers and give two-way quotes for Commercial Paper everyday. Commercial Paper cannot be underwritten or co-accepted.

Banks/FIIs can provide credit enhancements for issue of a Commercial Paper.The quality of credit (indicated by credit rating), liquidity in the money market, call money rates, outlook and yield from alternative investment etc. Non-Bank entities are allowed to provide unconditional guarantee for Commercial Paper issue provided:

(*i*) Issuer fulfills the eligibility criteria prescribed for issuance of Commercial Paper;

(*ii*) The guarantor has a credit rating of at least one point higher than the issuer by an approved credit rating agency; and

(*iii*) The offer document for Commercial Paper properly discloses; the net worth of the guarantor company, the names of the companies to which guarantor has issued similar guarantees, extent of guarantee offered by the guarantor company and the conditions under which guarantee will be involved.

The Banks are allowed to invest in Commercial Papers guaranteed by non-bank entities, provided their exposure remains within the regulatory ceiling as prescribed by RBI.

RATING REQUIREMENTS FOR ISSUE OF COMMERCIAL PAPER

The Company should satisfy the minimum eligibility requirements for issue of Commercial Paper as notified by RBI from time to time. The issuing companies have to satisfy the relevant provisions of the Income Tax Act, 1961, Companies Act, 1956 and Negotiable Instruments Act, 1881. The minimum credit rating shall be P-2 for CRISIL or such equivalent for other rating agencies. The participants shall ensure that the rating so obtained is current and not fallen due for review at the time of issuance. Credit Rating increases the acceptability of Commercial Paper and makes it less risky.

Recent Trends in the Commercial Paper Market : The amount of Commercial Paper outstanding since 1993 till 2004 December has been listed as under –

As on March 31	Total Outstanding Amount (Rs. Cr.)	Range of Discount %
1993	577	15.76 – 16.00
1994	3264	11.01 – 12.00
1995	604	14.00 – 15.00
1996	76	20.15
1997	646	11.25 – 12.25
1998	1500	14.22 – 15.50
1999	4770	10.05 – 12.00
2000	5663	10.00 – 12.00
2001	5846	08.75 – 11.25
2002	7224	07.41 – 10.25
2003	5749	06.00 – 07.75
2004	9131	04.70 – 06.50
Dec. 2004	12107	05.10 – 07.10

(*Source:* RBI Handbook of Statistics (2003-2004)

The Commercial Paper issued has seen a risk over the last 10 years. This has been due to relaxation of Commercial Paper, eligibility criteria, conditions of issue etc. Moreover they have become an attractive investment alternative for Mutual Funds.

Among the issuers, the issue of Commercial Paper by manufacturing companies has seen a decline from 8.6% in 2000-01 to 34% in 2004-05. This has been due to better management of cash, increased production efficiency and availability of bank finance without additional costs like Stamp Duty, IPA Fees, Demat Costs etc., which are associated with the issue of Commercial Paper.

On the other hand, Financial Institutions share has risen dramatically from 1% in 2001-02 to 18% in 2003-04.

The share of Leasing and Finance Companies has risen from 13% in 2000-01 to 38% in 2003-04.

In other trends the domination of 93% of market share by issuers with tangible net worth of 50 crore during 2002-03 and 2003-04 has declined to 83% during 2004-05.

The companies with medium size have however risen their share from 7% to 13% in the market.

STEPS TAKEN BY RBI TO DEVELOP THE COMMERCIAL PAPER MARKET FURTHER

The following recommendations have recently been given by RBI to develop the Commercial Paper Market further.

- Reduction in minimum maturity period from 16 days to 7 days. This has been implemented w.e.f. October 26, 2004.
- Reporting of issuance of Commercial Paper on the Negotiated Dealing System (NDS) platform at the end of the day for which various softwares have been developed.
- Constitution of a group comprising of market participants to standardize, wherever possible, various aspects of processing, settlement and documentation of Commercial Paper with a view to achieving settlement on T + 1 basis. This group was set-up under the Chairmanship of the Chief General Manager, State Bank of India.

Other recommendations, which were given but are still under consideration are:-

- **Rating** : It was proposed to bring down the minimum credit rating to P-3 of CRISIL or its equivalent to increase the issuers and investors. But the rating still remains P-2 as the minimum for issuing a Commercial Paper.
- **Asset Backed Commercial Paper :** The report of RBI recommended introduction of ABCP for further developing the Commercial Paper Market.

  ABCP is a pass through security with accounts receivable and other current assets as backing assets that is being passed through. ABCP issuers scrutinize a portfolio of cash generating asset funded by liabilities including Commercial Paper. This will help smaller firms even with higher risks to access the Commercial Paper market. This proposal is under examination of RBI.
- **Reference Rate :** Presently the issuer of Commercial Paper decides on Commercial Paper Note on account of demand and supply prevailing in the market. The status paper recommended to make the Commercial Paper deals in line with Call Money/Notice Money deals

  This would help in benchmarking and further enhance the liquidity of the market.

So, the growth and development of Commercial Paper Market in India is immensely important as it not only provides an investment avenue for short-term but also provides funds to meet working capital needs of the issuers.

QUESTIONS

Fill in the blanks:

1. Commercial paper can be issued to finance working capital requirement as well as a ______ product.
2. A company should have a maximum tangible net worth of _________ to issue commercial paper.
3. Commercial paper can be issued in denominations of _________ or multiples thereof.
4. The maturity period of commercial paper should be between a minimum of ________ and maximum of _______ from the date of issue.
5. The minimum credit rating required for issue of commercial paper is ________.

Define:

1. Asset backed commercial paper.
2. Issuing and paying agent.
3. Rating a commercial paper.

State whether true or false:

1. Commercial paper does not bear a fixed maturity.
2. Commercial paper is rated in order to establish the standing of issuing corporate.
3. Commercial paper can be backed by an underwriter.
4. Banks can participate in commercial paper market.

Answer in detail:

Q.1. What are the features, procedures for issue of commercial paper in India?

Q.2. Discuss the development of Commercial Paper Market in India.

Q.3. What is the role played by Issuing and Paying Agent in the issue of Commercial Paper?

❑❑❑

4

CERTIFICATES OF DEPOSIT

INTRODUCTION

Certificates of Deposits (CDs) are negotiable money market instruments issued in dematerialized form or as Usance Promissory Note, for funds deposited at a bank or other financial institutions for a specified period of time. Allowed in 1989 CDs were one of RBIs measures to deregulate the cost of funds for banks and FIs.

Features of CDs

- CDs are short-term rupee denominated deposits made with Indian Banks and India Development Finance Institutions (DFIs)
- CDs may or may not be rated; most CD issuers prefer to get these rated to target a large number of investors.
- Banks can issue CDs with initial maturity between 15 days to 1 year, whereas DFIs can issue CDs with an initial maturity of 1-3 years.
- CDs have a initial lock-in period of 15 days.
- They are issued at discount to face value.
- They may be bearer document or registered.
- CDs are highly liquid and marketable.
- All scheduled banks (except RBIs and Cooperative Banks) are eligible to issue CDs.
- They are freely transferable by endorsement and delivery. At present CDs are issued in physical form.

Aggregate amount of CD Allowed for Issue

- Banks have the freedom to issue CDs depending on their requirement, *i.e.,* no limit is fixed for them.

- An FI may issue CDs within the overall umbrella limit fixed by RBI, *i.e.,* issue of CD together with other instruments like term money, term deposits, commercial papers and inter-corporate deposits should not exceed 100% of its net-owned funds, as per the latest audited balance sheet.

SYSTEM OF ISSUE

Banks and FIs issue CDs on tap, *i.e.* they are available to the investors all the time. There is no fixed time when they are available.

Investors and Markets

Major investors in CDs are public and private sector companies and provident funds, high net worth individuals invest in CDs issued by banks. NRIs are allowed to invest in CDs on a non-transferable and non-repatriable basis. FIIs are not permitted to invest in CDs.

Trading in CDs

CDs are not listed as trading, is over the counter only. Market participants quote dealing levels on a yield basis specified to two decimal places. Transaction sizes vary and trades between Rs.10 lakhs and Rs. 50 crores have taken place. Two-way quotes are not offered on CDs. Brokers charge a commission of 0.05% - 0.25% for intermediated secondary market deals. Deals between direct parties do not affect any transaction costs. CDs issued by DFIs do not attract any stamp duty but primary issuances of CDs by banks attract a stamp duty at rate, which depend on the period for which the CD has been issued. CDs do not bear any withholding taxes.

Clearing and Settlement of CDs

CDs are subject to clearance by endorsement and delivery. Deals are settled on trade date or on the following business day.

Minimum Size and Denomination

Minimum Size of a CD should be Rs. 1 Lakh, *i.e.,* minimum deposit, which can be accepted from a single subscriber should not be less than Rs. 1 Lakh and in multiples of Rs. 1 Lakh thereafter.

Subscribers

CDs can be subscribed by individuals, corporations, companies, trusts, funds, associations etc. NRIs may also subscribe to CDs but only on non-repatriate basis and this has to be clearly stated on the certificate. They are also non-transferable in case of NRIs.

Maturity

The maturity period of CDs issued by banks should not be less than 15 days and not more than one year.

FIs can issue CDs for a period of not less than one year and not more than three years from the date of issue.

Discount Rate/Coupon Rate

CDs are issued at discount to face value. FIs (Developmental) also issue coupon-bearing CDs. Banks are allowed to issue floating rate CDs, where the rate on CDs is periodically set in accordance with the prevailing rates of interest in the market on other money market instruments. They may even offer different rates to different customers.

Transferability

Except for NRIs, CDs are freely transferable by endorsement and delivery. There is no lock-in period for CDs. CDs in DEMAT form can be transferred just like other DEMAT securities.

Buy-Back/Loans on CDs

There is no buy-back of CDs, nor can any loan be granted against them.

Discount Rate on CDs/Yield

$$\text{Discount Rate} = \frac{\text{F.V.}}{\text{I} + (\text{Int.} \times \text{N}/100 \times 365)}$$

F.V. = Face value

Int. = Interest rate per annum

N = No. of years of issue

Reserve Requirements

Banks have to maintain the appropriate reserve requirement, *i.e.* CRR (Cash Reserve Ratio) and SLR (Statutory Liquidity Ratio) for the issue of CDs.

Format of CDs

CDs are issued in dematerialized form. The investors can however opt for physical form of certificate also. In case of repayment of CD by Banks/FIs, no grace period is allowed. The payment is made on a preceding day if the date of maturity happens to be a holiday.

Issuing Procedure

There is no issuing procedure for CDs. They are available on tap, *i.e.,* any investor willing to invest in CDs can go to any banker. The bank may accept the deposit or in case it is not willing to do the same, it may quote rates, which are not very high than term deposits of similar maturity so as to discourage the investor from investing in CDs.

Stamp Duty

In case the subscriber/investor is in eligible class of investor (*i.e.,* commercial and cooperative banks and specified FIs like IFCI, IDBI, SFCS) then the stamp duty applicable to :

Up to 3 months	Re. 0.50 per 1000
3 – 6 months	Rs. 1.00 per 1000
6 – 9 months	Rs. 1.50 per 1000
9 – 12 months	Rs. 2.00 per 1000
12 – 24 months	Rs. 4.00 per 1000
24 – 36 months	Rs. 6.00 per 1000

Where the subscriber/investor is not an eligible class of investor then the stamp duty applicable is :

Up to 3 months	Rs. 1.25 per 1000
3 – 6 months	Rs. 2.50 per 1000
6 – 9 months	Rs. 3.75 per 1000
9 – 12 months	Rs. 5.00 per 1000
12 – 24 months	Rs. 10.00 per 1000
Above 24 months up to 36 months	Rs. 15.00 per 1000

PAYMENT OF CERTIFICATE OF DEPOSIT

On maturity, the CD may be redeemed by the issuing Bank.

- In case of investors who hold CDs in physical form, the last holder (as CDs are transferable) may present the CD for payment.
- In case of investors holding CDs in DEMAT form, the holder approaches the respective Depository Participant (DP) and gives delivery instructions to transfer the DEMAT security represented by the specific ISIN to the 'CD Redemption Account' maintained by the issuer. The same may be communicated to the issuer along with intimation of the place at which payment may be made. After the credit of CDs in the 'CD Redemption Account' the issuer arranges payment to holder by Banker's Cheque/High Value Cheque.

Accountancy

Banks/FIs account the issue price under the head 'CD Issued' and show it under deposits. According to the guidelines issued to them they should maintain a register of CDs issued with complete particulars.

Secondary Market

Inspite of free transferability of CDs and a well-established primary market, the secondary market is less developed. This is because of high yields on CDs due to which investors prefer to hold them till maturity in the primary market.

CDs are freely transferable by endorsement and delivery. So precautions are taken to guard against tempering with the document. They should be signed by two or more authorized signatories.

In case of loss of physical CD certificates, duplicate certificates can be issued if the following are compiled with:-

(*a*) A notice is required to be given in at least one local newspaper.

(*b*) Lapse of a reasonable period from the date of notice in the newspaper (This is around 15 days).

(*c*) Execution of an Indemnity Bond by investor to the satisfaction of issuer of CD.

No stamp duty is to be paid in case of issue of duplicate CD.

In case of mutilated CDs, duplicate can be issued by the branch/office which issued the original CD and retained. The original CD itself will be to ensure a suitable move on it so that it does not come in the market for trading.

Growth in CD Market

Government and RBI have taken a number of measures to enhance and develop the CD market.

Earlier, there was a limit on issue of CDs as average of aggregate deposits of banks. This was 1% of aggregate deposits. This limit was raised and in 1993 it was removed completely.

Minimum size of issue was reduced from Rs. 1 crore and multiples of Rs. 25 lakhs to Rs. 5 lakhs and multiples of 1 lakh thereof. Lock-in period was reduced from 45 days to 15 days. Restriction on transferability was removed. DFHI was promoted for development of secondary market in CDs.

There has been slow growth in the CD market (both primary and secondary) due to various reasons like high yield on primary instruments; lack of investor awareness, option of other sources of funds by banks as compared to CDs due to higher interest cost. Inspite of this there is a potential for the CD market. This is because of the high cash flows with financial institutions, corporates etc.

The extra funds can be deployed in the CD market, which offer assured high yield. What is needed presently is the awareness of investors, promotion of discount houses as an active participant in CD market and increased support of RBI so as to make CD market an attractive investment opportunity for investors.

QUESTIONS

Fill in the blanks:

1. CDs are traded in __________ exchange.
2. The initial lock-in period for certificate of deposit is ___________ .
3. CDs are issued in _________ form.
4. __________ forms the secondary market for CDs.

Define:

1. Discount rate on CDs
2. Promissory note

State whether true or false:

1. Certificates of deposits are issued at premium to face value.
2. CDs are available on tap.
3. Issue of duplicate CDs is not subject to any stamp duty.
4. CDs are freely transferable by endorsement and delivery.
5. Loan can be granted against certificates of deposits.

Answer in detail:

Q.1. What are the features of (Certificate of Deposits) CDs and what have been the reforms in the development of CD market in India?

Q.2. What are the reasons for an underdeveloped CD market in India?

❑❑❑

5 GILT EDGED SECURITIES MARKET (DATED SECURITIES)

INTRODUCTION

The government securities are commonly referred to as gilt edged securities, these comprise of dated securities issued by both central and state government including financial institutions owned by the government.

They are thus the debt obligations of the government 'Gilt' refers to 'gold'. As the securities are floated by the government and repayment of principal and interest are the obligations of the government itself so these securities are completely risk free, *i.e.*, there is no risk of default at all on these. Due to this they are called 'gilt edged securities'.

PURPOSE OF ISSUE

Government securities are issued in order to enable the open market operations by RBI as well as to overcome the fiscal deficit of the government.

Form

They are not generally in the form of securities but in the form of entries in RBIs Subsidiary General Ledger (SGL) account.

Period of Issue

These securities are issued with various maturities ranging from 2 to 31 years. Dated securities presently have a maturity period of upto 20 years. Such securities whose maturity period is above 10 years are called long dated securities while those having tenure between 5-10 and less than 5 years are called medium and short-term securities respectively. The securities are issued in denomination of Rs.10,000/- and multiples thereof.

PARTICIPANTS

Participants in the market include issuers and investors.

Issuers

- Central government issues dated securities to fund budgetary deficits and meet other short-term funding requirements through RBI.
- RBI participates through open market operations as well as through Liquidity Adjustment Facility.
- Primary Dealers, who are market intermediaries appointed by RBI underwrite and make market in government securities by providing two way quotes and have access to call and REPO market for funds.
- State governments, municipal and local bodies issue securities in debt markets to fund their developmental projects as well as to finance their budgetary deficits.
- Public sector undertakings and their finance corporations issue securities to meet the long-term and working capital need.
- DPs issue securities for funding their financing requirements and working capital needs.

Investors

- Banks are the largest investors in the debt market, particularly in the gilt edged securities market to meet their SLR requirements.
- Insurance companies invest in these in order to meet their investment norms.
- Mutual funds have emerged as important players in the market due to the growing number of debt funds that have been able to attract a large number of investors.
- DFIs invest in dated securities but they are permitted this only up to a limit.
- Provident and pension funds are large investors in this market but due to government regulations they are not permitted to sell their holdings until they have some funding requirement which cannot be met through regular accruals as contributions.
- Charitable institutions, trusts and societies are also large investors in the market.
- Since January 2002, retail investors have also been permitted to submit non-competitive bids at primary auction through any bank or primary dealers. They can submit bids amounting to Rs.10,000 or multiples thereof subject to a maximum limit of Rs.1 crore.

PROCESS OF ISSUE

Primary Market in Government Securities.

Government Securities are issued through an auction process, RBI through a press notification announces the auction and invites bids for the same. There are two types of treasury auctions:

- Discriminatory Price Auction also called French auction.
- Uniform Price Auction or Dutch auction.
  - In case of Discriminatory Price Auctions, the bidder who quotes the maximum price is the successful bidder. All the successful bidders pay the actual price which they quoted for.
  - However in Uniform Price Auction, all successful bidders pay a uniform price which is the cut-off price (yield).

For example, Assume that in an auction RBI decides the cut-off price for a 11.50% 2013 paper as Rs.120.2582 then bids up to the next highest price of Rs.120.2582 will be declared successful, while bidders at the cut-off price will receive allotments on pro-rata basis.

If all the successful bidders have to pay the cut-off price of 120.2582 then the auction is called a Dutch auction, or a Uniform Price Auction. If the successful bidders have to pay the prices they have actually bid and the auction fills up the notified amounts in various prices at which each of the successful bidders bid, then the auction is called French auction or Discriminatory Price Auction.

The prices and yield of government securities is decided by Fixed Income Money Market and Derivates Association of India (FIMMDA) on the basis of a yield curve calculated by FIMMDA for the purpose of valuation.

SECONDARY MARKET FOR GOVERNMENT SECURITIES

Government Securities are listed on the NSE's Wholesale Debt Market (WDM) after their issue. The settlement of these securities occurs through Security General Ledger (SGL) Account with RBI. SGL holder after the trade, have to report the same within 24 hours. The settlement period is T+1, but in case of settlement through a broker of a permitted stock exchange the settlement period is T+2.

SETTLEMENT OF TRADERS IN GOVERNMENT SECURITIES

All traders in Government Securities are reported to RBI-SGL Account for settlement. These securities are held in dematerialized form in the SGL Account. The settlement of transactions through SGL Account is overseen by Public Debt Office (PDO). Transfer of funds is done by crediting/debiting the current account of seller/buyer maintained with RBI. Securities are transferred through credits/debits in the SGL Account.

CONSTITUTION OF SECURITY GENERAL LEDGER ACCOUNT (SGL ACCOUNT)

SGL Account is a facility provided by RBI to large banks and PDs so as to enable electronic book entry of investment in government securities and treasury bills. It helps these banks and PDs to settle their trades in securities held in SGL Account through a Delivery *versus* Payment (DVP) mechanism which helps in the simultaneous movement of funds and securities. Those entities who do not have an SGL Account are permitted by RBI to open constitutional SGL accounts. Constituent SGL Accounts provide the following facilities :

- Dematerialisation
- Rematerialisation
- Buy/sell transactions with
    - Any other NSCCL constituent account holder
    - Any SGL Account holder with RBI
    - Any constituent SGL Account holder with RBI
    - RBI under its open market operations.
- Payment of interest on securities
- Redemption or conversion of securities.

Government of India issued a revised general notification on May 6, 2002 specifying the general terms and conditions applicable to all issues of government securities. The revised notification incorporates the following additional features:-

(*a*) The auctions for issue of securities (on either yield basis or price basis) would be held either on 'Uniform Price' method or on 'Multiple Price' method or any other method as may be decided. Under 'Uniform Price' method, competitive bids offered with rates up to and including the maximum rate of yield or the prices up to and including the minimum offer price, as determined by RBI, would be accepted at the maximum rate of yield or minimum after so determined. Bids quoted higher than the maximum rate of yield or lower than the minimum price as determined by RBI would be rejected. Under 'Multiple Price' method, the competitive bids offered at the maximum rate of yield of the minimum offer price as determined by RBI would be accepted. Other bids tendered at lower than the maximum rate of yield or higher than the minimum offer price determined by RBI would be accepted at the rate of yield or price as quoted in the respective bid.

(*b*) Individuals and institutions can participate in the auctions on 'non-competitive' basis, indirectly through a scheduled bank or a primary dealer offering such services or any other agency permitted by RBI for this purpose. Allocation of securities to non-competitive bidders would be at the discretion of RBI and at a price not higher than the weighted average price arrived at on the basis of the competitive bids accepted at the auction or any other price announced in the specific notification. The nominal amount of securities allocated on such basis would be restricted to a maximum percentage of the aggregate nominal amount of the issue, within or outside the nominal amount, as specified by GOI/RBI.

(*c*) Government securities can also be issued by credit to investor's bond ledger account maintained with RBI or any institution authorized by RBI.

(*d*) Offer for purchase of government securities can be submitted in electronic form. Payment for the government securities can be made by successful participants through Electronic Fund Transfer (EFT) in a secured environment.

(*e*) Government may issue securities with embedded derivatives. Such securities may be repaid, at the option of Government of India or at the option of the holder of the security, before the specified redemption date, where a "call option/put option" is specified in the specific notification relating to the issue of a government security. Where neither a call option nor a put option is specified or exercised, the government security would be repaid on the date of redemption specified in the specific notification.

(*f*) RBI would have discretion to retain the excess subscription to the extent specified in the specific notification when securities are issued through pre-announced coupon rates.

(*g*) RBI can participate in auction as a 'non-competitor' and will be allocated securities at cut-off price/yield.

QUESTIONS

Fill in the blanks:

1. The debt obligation of government gilt refers to __________.
2. Government Securites are issued in denominations of ________ and multiples thereof.
3. Primary dealers who act as intermediaries in Government Securites market are appointed by _______.
4. Gilt edged means ________.
5. Gilt-edged securities are issued in__________ form.

Define:

1. Uniform Price Auction
2. Discriminatory Price Auction
3. SGL Account

State whether true or false:

1. Gilt edged securities are the least risky of all the money market instruments.
2. Retail investors cannot participate in gilt edged market.
3. Government issues gilt edged securities to meet its fiscal deficit.

Answer in detail:

Q.1. What are the various procedures for issue of gilt edged securities?

Q.2. Discuss the features and constituents of SGL Account.

Q.3. Describe the various issuers and investors participating in Government Securities market and their purpose of participation.

❑❑❑

6

TREASURY BILLS

INTRODUCTION

Treasury Bills are short-term debt instruments issued by Central Government to raise funds to overcome short-term liquidity problems.

Being issued by the Central Government T-Bills are considered to be highly liquid, have zero default risk, have assured return and are widely available. They are issued in form of Promissory Notes or finance bills. A considerable part of government borrowings occurs through T-Bills of various maturities.

FEATURES

The main features of Treasury Bills are:

I. Government issued zero risk instruments.

II. Bills have maturity of 91 or 364 days.

III. Available in primary and secondary market.

IV. Issued at discount to face value, *i.e.,* investors will buy T-Bills at a discount to face value of Rs.100, and on maturity the face value of Rs.100 is received by the investor.

V. No tax deduction at source.

VI. Convenience of CSGL Account as in case of Central Government Securities such as automatic credit of redemption money.

VII. Highly liquid.

VIII. Attractive returns.

ISSUERS OF T-BILLS

Reserve Bank of India acts as an issuer of T-Bills on behalf of Government of India.

INVESTORS IN T-BILLS

Banks are the major investors in T-Bills and they invest in these so as to maintain their Statutory Liquidity Ratio (SLR) as prescribed by RBI. Other than banks Financial Institutions, Mutual Funds, Non-Banking Finance Companies, Provident Funds, State Governments, Insurance Companies etc. also act as investors in the T-Bills market.

TYPES OF T-BILLS

Until 1986 the only kind of T-Bills which was available was the 91-day bill which was issued on tap at the fixed rate of 4.5%. In 1987, 182-day T-Bills were introduced and the auction process for T-Bills was started. In April, 1992, 364-day. Bill was also introduced. In 1992, RBI suspended the issue of 182-day T-Bills and resumed it from 1999. In 2001, (May) RBI did away with 14-day and 182-day T-Bills, RBI now sells all T-Bills through an auction process according to an auction calendar. *Adhoc* treasury bills have also been eliminated. Currently only 2 types of T-Bills are issued: *i.e.,* 91-day and 364-day Bills.

PROCESS OF ISSUANCE

T-Bills are *issued in the form of discounted promissory note or by credit to the Subsidiary General Ledger (SGL) Account maintained with the Reserve Bank.* The RBI also functions as a depository and maintains SGL Accounts of the various banks and others wherein transaction holding is represented by a book entry. Physicals are also available on request. The minimum denomination of T-Bills is Rs. 25,000. Trading and bidding usually takes place in multiples of Rs. 5 crore.

T-Bills are *sold through an auction process*, in which banks and primary dealers are major bidders. Non-competitive bidders, who may not quote the rate of yield at which they desire to pay T-Bills can participate in these auctions. These non-competitive bidders include provident funds and others allotted bids at the weighted average yield arrived at on the basis of the yields quoted by competitive bidders in the auction. Allocations of T-Bill to these non-competitive bidders are outside the amount notified for sale.

The Reserve Bank issues a calendar of auctions along with the exact dates, amount to be auctioned and payment dates by issuing a calendar of T-Bills auction. *The Calendar of auctions given by RBI –*

Type of Bill	Periodicity	Notified Amount (Rs.Crores)	Date of Auction	Day of Payment
91-Days	Weekly	500	Every Wednesday	Following Friday
364-Days	Fortnightly	1000	Every alternate Wednesday	Following Friday

Since May, 1999, development of Primary Dealers (PDs) in T-Bill auctions has been done away with; any development being on RBI alone, while PDs manage T-Bills as an interest rate policy tool. *Auction method followed earlier was a Uniform Price Auction, which has now been changed to Multiple Price Auction System.*

- Uniform Price Auction Method is one where all the successful bidders pay a uniform price, *i.e.,* the cut-off price is decided in the auction.
- In case of Multiple Price Auction, however, successful bidders would get the security at the rates they have bid. Under this system successful bidders may have to pay a premium, which is the difference between the price quoted by the bidder and the cut-off price fixed in the auction. This is called 'winners' curse. Thus, as against Multiple Price Auction Method, Uniform Price Auction Method would eliminate the payment of premium by the bidders.

YIELD OF T-BILLS

T-Bills do not carry any coupon rate. They are issued at a discount and redeemed at par. They are preferred by risk averse investors and banks although the interest rate (Difference between Issue and Redemption Price) is lower than other money market instruments.

The yield of a T-Bill is the rate at which the issue price has to be compounded for the number of days to maturity to equal the maturity value.

For example, If a T-Bill of Face Value 100 is issued for Rs. 87.50 for a period of 70 days, then yield will be calculated as –

$$\frac{\text{days} \times \text{Yield}}{365} = \frac{\text{Face Value} \times \text{Price}}{\text{Price}}$$

i.e.

$$\frac{85 \times \text{Yield}}{365} = \frac{12.5 \times 87.50}{87.50}$$

$$85 \times \text{Yield} = \frac{12.5 \times 87.50}{87.50 \times 85} = \frac{4562.5}{7437.5}$$

$$\text{Yield} = 61.34\%$$

TRADING

Trading in T-Bills is usually done Over The Counter (OTC) or National Stock Exchange (NSE). Market participants usually quote on a yield basis specified up to 2 decimal places. For trade on the NSE, equivalent prices specified up to 4 decimal places are quoted. Daily trading volumes average about Rs. 150 crore with a usual transaction size of Rs. 5 to 20 crore. The Bid offer spread is 5 – 10 basis points depending on market liquidity. Brokerage withholding taxes are applied.

CLEARING AND SETTLEMENT

Clearing and Settlement for T-Bills is through Delivering vs Payment (DVP) System, that requires the parties to submit an SGL note to the Public Debt Office dealing in the transaction. The RBI will then make entries in the SGL account and current account of the parties concerned. Inter Bank T-Bills usually settle on the same business day, whereas trades with the non-bank counter parties settle either on the same day or one business day after trade date.

RISK WEIGHTAGE

The Risk Weight for T-Bill is 2.5% for the purpose of capital adequacy requirements.

Apart from auctioned T-Bills, the other types of T-Bill issued are –

Adhoc Treasury Bills : Adhoc T-Bills are issued by RBI on behalf of government in order to enable the government to tide over the temporary fiscal deficits. They provide cash to the government whenever it needs. They are issued by RBI, who holds them in its Issue Department and issues currency notes against them. The bills are renewed at maturity.

These bills are used to replenish the balance of government with RBI, which should be is 50 crore on Fridays and Rs. 4 crore on other days. Adhoc T-Bills have a maturity period of 91-days and a discount rate of 4.6%. The maximum outstanding amount in T-Bills should be Rs. 5000 crore at the end of a year and within the year it cannot exceed Rs.9000 crores for a period more than 10 consecutive days. In case this limit is exceeded RBI automatically reduces it by either selling the adhoc T-Bills or by issuing fresh Government of India securities. T-Bill can be closed before maturity. They have to be repaid by the Government whenever it has sufficient balance and its budget deficit is filled up. But as the budget deficit of the Government was never filled up, adhoc T-Bills once became a permanent source of financing the fiscal deficit of the Government. So in 1994-95 it was decided to phase-out the system of adhoc T-Bills to bridge the fiscal gap, which was leading to serious imbalance in the economy. It was decided that RBI will not finance the fiscal deficit through T-Bills but will grant advances called ways and means advances up to a limit to the government in order to overcome the short-term finance requirements and these should be repaid within a period of 3 months. An excess drawal beyond the limit was allowed for a maximum period of ten consecutive days. So adhoc T-Bills have been removed from the present system.

On-tap Treasury Bills : On-tap Treasury Bills are issued by RBI to investors on any business day. There is no limit to the amount of investment in them. They have a maturity period of 91 days and are redeemable at face value on maturity. They carry a discount rate of around 4.6%. They can be rediscounted after a period of 14 days with the RBI. They are considered to be highly liquid from point of view of investment as they can be discounted with RBI at any point of time and any amount. They also have been discounted w.e.f. 1st April, 1997 along with adhoc T-Bills.

History and Growth of T-Bills in India

- There was an active T-Bills market in the Bank's history before 1960's when 91-day Treasury Bills were auctioned weekly and the bills were widely held in the market. During the period there were two important developments.

- First, in mid 1950's the system of adhoc 91 day Treasury Bills was introduced to replenish on automatic basis, the Central Government's cash balance with the RBI and bring it to its minimum required level. This opened up on era of uncontrolled monetization of Central Government's deficit.
- The adhoc bills were replaced by on-tap T-Bills in mid 1960's. During this period there was no congenial environment for development of T-Bills. But the interest in development of this market came up with the introduction of 182 day T-Bills on auction basis in November, 1986 and constitution of DFHI as a money market institution.
- 182 day Bill was replaced by 364 day bills on fortnightly auction since April, 1992 as a part of reform measures.
- In January, 1993, 91-day bill were introduced on auction. In April, 1997 14-day intermediate T-Bill and auction bills were introduced.
- In the current situation T-Bill issues consist of 91-day bill auctions and 364 day bill auctions on a fortnightly basis along with 14 day intermediate bills available for state governments and foreign central banks.
- A number of significant initiatives have been taken up by RBI in this area. The auction procedures have been streamlined to have notified amounts of all auctions and to accept non-competitive bids outside the notified amounts. A uniform price auction for 91-day bills has been introduced. Another important development has been in the area of open market sale window of the Bank.
- The Reserve Bank has been continuously revising the development of money market T-Bills.
- The demand for T-Bills is mostly related to call rates. Supply of T-Bills is adjusted turning into account the demand condition and short-term needs of Central Government.

Secondary Market Activity in T-Bills: T-Bills are mostly held to maturity by buyers and secondary market activity is quite spare. The average turnover in secondary market, transactions in T-Bills has been as follows:

TREASURY BILLS MARKET ABROAD

Primary Market

- Treasury Bills are issued by the US Treasury to cover government budget deficit and to refinance maturing debt.
- Standard original maturities of these Bills are 13 weeks, 26 weeks or 52 weeks.
- They are issued in denominations of $1000 but typical round lot is $5 million.
- They are virtually default risk free.
- Auction of 13-week and 26-week T-Bills offered is announced weekly.
- Bids are submitted by government securities dealers financial and non-financial corporations and individuals.
- Individual competitive bidders are limited to 35% of total issue size and can submit more than one bid, allocations being made beginning with the highest bidder.

Non-competitive bidders indicate quantity desired and agree to pay a weighted average of the rate on winning competitive bids. They get preferential allocation.

SECONDARY MARKET FOR T-BILLS ABROAD

It is the largest of any US money market security. Approximately 30 financial institutions "make" a market in T-Bills by buying and selling securities for their own accounts and by trading for their customers, including depository institutions, insurance companies pensions funds etc.

In secondary market Federal Reserve Bank acts as an intermediary to transfer T-Bills from one account to another Bank, average firms and bond houses are the major participants. These market makers invest in T-Bills to get liquidity and risk free investment. The customers participating in the market are insurance companies, non-financial institutions, government etc. T-Bills are issued at discount to the face value and redeemed at face value.

YIELD CURVE AND INTEREST RATE ANALYSIS

Yield curve is the relation between the interest rate (or cost of borrowing) and the time to maturity of the debt for a given borrower in a given currency. For example, the interest rates paid on Treasury Bills for various maturities are commonly plotted on a graph which is called "the yield curve."

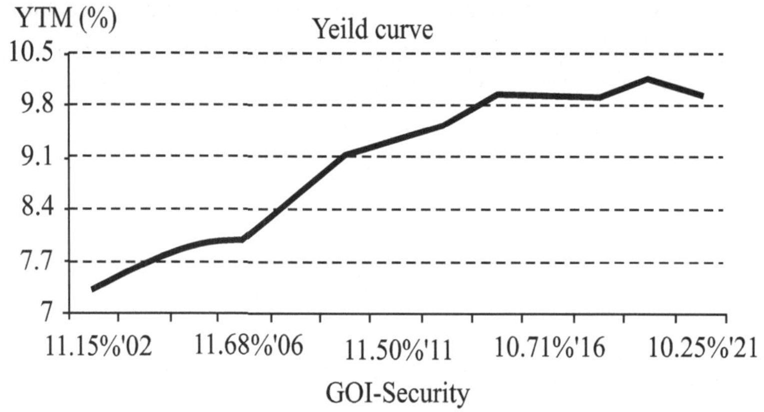

Fortnightly closing YTM for benchmark securities (16th July, 2001 to 31st July, 2001)
Source: Debt to Date,SHCIL,Issue no.14

The shape of the yield curve gives an idea of future interest rate change and economic activity. Yield curves are used by fixed income analysts, who analyze bonds and related securities, to understand conditions in financial markets and to seek trading opportunities. Economists use the curves to understand economic conditions.

Yield curves move on a daily basis, reflecting the market's reaction to news. Also they tend to move in parallel, *i.e.,* the yield curve shifts up and down as interest rate levels rise and fall.

TYPES OF YIELD CURVE

Normal yield curve

Normal yield curve means that yields rise as maturity lengthens (*i.e.,* the slope of the yield curve is positive). This positive slope reflects investor expectations for the economy to grow in the future. Moreover this growth is associated with a greater expectation that inflation will rise in the future rather than fall. This expectation of higher inflation leads to expectations that the central bank will tighten monetary policy by raising short term interest rates in the future to slow economic growth and dampen inflationary pressure. It also creates a need for a risk premium associated with the uncertainty about the future rate of inflation and the risk this poses to the future value of cash flows. Investors price these risks into the yield curve by demanding higher yields for maturities further into the future.This makes yeild curve go up as maturity increases.

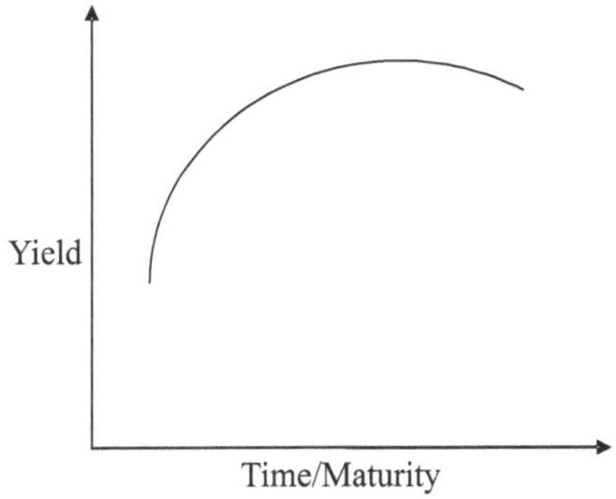

Fig. 6.1 : Normal yield curve

Flat or humped yield curve

A flat yield curve is observed when all maturities have similar yields, whereas a humped curve results when short-term and long-term yields are equal and medium-term yields are higher than those of the short-term and long-term. A flat curve sends signals of uncertainty in the economy. This mixed signal can revert back to a normal curve or could later result into an inverted curve.

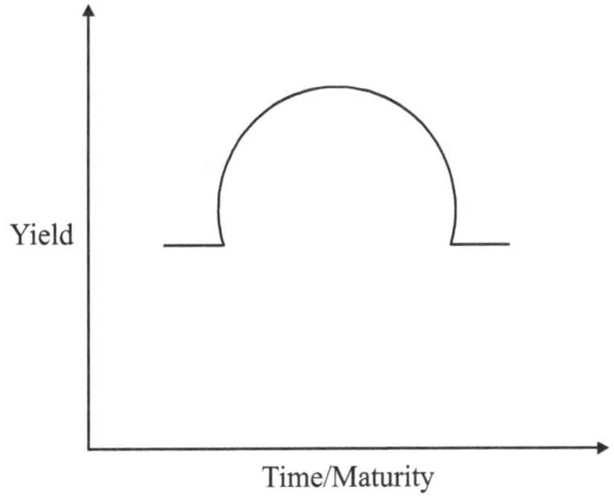

Fig. 6.2 : Flat or humped yield curve

Inverted yield curve

An inverted yield curve occurs when long-term yields fall below short-term yields. Under this abnormal and contradictory situation, long-term investors will settle for lower yields as they think the economy will slow or even decline in the future. An inverted curve may indicate a worsening economic situation in the future. In addition to signaling an economic decline, inverted yield curves also implies that the market believes inflation will remain low.

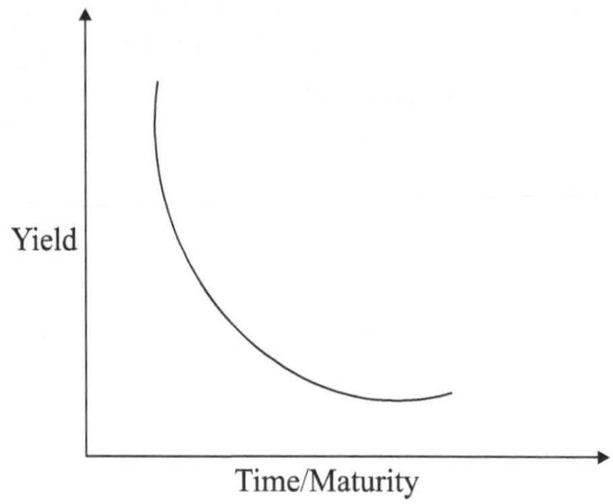

Fig. 6.3 : Inverted yield curve

THEORIES OF YEILD CURVE

There are four main economic theories which explain how yields vary with maturity.

Market expectations (pure expectations) hypothesis

This hypothesis assumes that the various maturities are perfect substitutes and suggests that the shape of the yield curve depends on market participants' expectations of future interest rates. This also assumes that arbitrage opportunities will be minimal. For example, if investors have an expectation of what 1-year interest rates will be next year, the 2-year interest rate can be calculated as the compounding of this year's interest rate by next year's interest rate. This stands as under:

$$(1+i_t)^n = (1+i_1)^1 \; (1+i_2)^2 \cdots\cdots\cdots (1+i_t)^n$$

where i stands for interest rate

t stands for time period ranging from 1 to n.

This theory, fails to explain the persistence in the shape of the yield curve.

Liquidity preference theory

The Liquidity Preference Theory, states that long-term interest rates not only reflect investors' assumptions about future interest rates but also include a premium for holding long-term bonds, called the term premium or the liquidity premium. This premium compensates investors for the added risk of having their money tied up for a longer period, including the greater price uncertainty. Because of the term premium, long-term bond yields tend to be higher than short-term yields, and the yield curve slopes upward.

Market segmentation theory

This theory is also called the **segmented market hypothesis**. In this theory, financial instruments of different terms are not substitutable. The supply and demand in the markets for short-term and long-term instruments is determined independently. Prospective investors would have to decide in advance whether they need short-term or long-term instruments. As nvestors prefer their portfolio to be liquid, they will prefer short-term instruments to long-term instruments. Therefore, the market for short-term instruments will receive a higher demand. Higher demand for the instrument implies higher prices and lower yield. This explains the fact that short-term yields are usually lower than long-term yields. This theory explains the normal yield curve shape. However, because the supply and demand of the two markets are independent, this theory fails to explain the observed fact that yields tend to move together (*i.e.,* upward and downward shifts in the curve).

Preferred habitat theory

The Preferred Habitat Theory states that in addition to interest rate expectations, investors have different investment horizons and require a meaningful premium to buy bonds with maturities outside their preferred maturity, which is also called habitat. Further the theory believes that short-term investors are more prevalent in the fixed-income market and therefore, longer-term rates mostly tend to be higher than short-term rates, but short-term rates can be higher than long-term rates occasionally. This theory is a middle way between between the Market Segmentation Theory and the Market Expectations Theory. Moreover, it seems to explain both the persistence of the normal yield curve shape and the tendency of the yield curve to shift up and down while retaining its shape.

QUESTIONS

Fill in the blanks:

1. T-Bills are issued in ________ or ________ form.
2. T- Bills have a maturity of _________ days.
3. ________ are the major investors in T-Bills.
4. ________ issue T-Bills on behalf of the government.
5. Standard maturity of US T-bills is _______ , ________ , or _________ days.
6. _____________ is the relation between the interest rate (or cost of borrowing) and the time to maturity of the debt for a given borrower in a given currency.

State whether true or false:

1. T-bills carry coupon rate.
2. Adhoc T-bills are issued till today.
3. T-bills are not subject to TDS.
4. Both uniform and multiple price auction systems constitute the market for treasury bills.
5. Yield curves move on a daily basis in parallel i.e., the yield curve shifts up and down as interest rate levels rise and fall.

Answer in detail:

Q.1. Discuss yield of T-Bills and how it is calculated.

Q.2. What are the various types of T-Bills and their features?

Q.3. In spite of the presence of Government Securies what is the need for the government to issue T-bills?

Q.4. What is the mechanism of trading, clearing and settlement of T-bills?

Q.5. What are the various theories of yield curve? How do they explain its movement?

❑❑❑

7 REPOS (REPURCHASE AGREEMENT)

INTRODUCTION

REPO (Repurchase Agreement) is a contract between two parties to buy/sell securities with the agreement that the transaction reverses after a predetermined period of time at pre-determined prices.

A REPO is a combination of an outright purchase and (later) an outright sale. The purchase and sale prices are determined by the REPO rate. A REPO in other words is a collateralized borrowing. The transaction is called a REPO when viewed from the prospective of seller of the securities and reverse REPO when described from the point of view of supplier of funds. Thus, whether a given agreement is termed a REPO or a reverse REPO depends on which party initiated the transaction.

The lender or buyer in a REPO transaction is entitled to receive compensation for use of funds provided to the counter-party. The seller of security borrows money for a period of time (REPO period) at a particular rate of interest mutually agreed with the buyer of the security, who has lent the funds to the seller. The rate of interest agreed upon is called REPO rate. The REPO rate is negotiated by the counter-parties independent of the coupon rate or rates of the underlying securities and is influenced by the overall money market conditions.

Features

- Collateralized short-term lending and borrowing agreement.
- Also called ready forward transaction, as it is a means of funding by selling a security held on spot basis and repurchasing the same on forward basis.
- REPO rate is the annualized interest rate for the funds transferred by the lender to the borrower.
- REPO transaction is comprised of two transactions – sale of security and repurchase of the same.

In the first part, *i.e.,* sale, the sale price is usually based on the prevailing market price while in the second part, *i.e.,* purchase of the security again by the seller the price is based on prevailing interest as well as tax elements.

Although REPO are collateralized transactions yet they are subject to counter-party risk and issuer risk associated with the collateral counter-party risk (non-payment of interest) can be overcome by sale of securities kept as collateral while against this the issuer risk (non-return of lent securities) the seller/ lender will keep cash and other securities as protection against non-return of the lent securities.

Participants

RBI, all scheduled commercial banks, primary dealers, satellite dealers, financial institutions and mutual funds are allowed to participate in the REPO market. A Subsidiary General Ledger (SGL) account as well as current account with RBI is a pre-requisite to be a party to REPO transaction in government securities.

Time

REPO may be done for a period of 3 months but mostly they are reversed within a fortnight or less. Maximum period permitted is not restricted, which minimum is of one day.

Volumes

The average volume transacted in REPO is Rs. 1000 crore per fortnight.

Use of REPO for Participants

- Help in collateralized borrowing for meeting liquidity requirements.
- The money received in the first part (*i.e.* sale) may be used for meeting short-term liquidity requirements.

SECURITIES TREATED IN REPO

All government securities and all listed debt securities in dematerialized form can be reposed.

Operational Aspects of a REPO

- The Borrower initially decides the size of REPO depending on the amount of money, he requires. Borrowers may be banks who wish to buy securities for short-term in order to meet their Statutory Liquidity Ratio set by RBI.
- Tenders are submitted to RBI in denominations of Rs. 1 crore and the multiples thereof.
- RBI announces the securities eligible for REPO. All Government of India Securities, T-Bills, PSU Bonds, which are in DEMAT form are eligible for REPOS.
- The interest rate on borrowing is mutually agreed between the borrower and the lender of securities and depends on the prevailing market rates of other money market instruments.
- RBI performs the Government Securities Settlement System for those having SGL account in public department office through *Delivery* vs. *Payment*. In this system trades are settled on a "trade by trade" basis simultaneously by ensuring that there are sufficient funds in the buyer's account and sufficient securities in the sellers account.

Advantages of REPO

REPO provide a variety of advantages to the financial markets, which may be as follows:

- REPO market helps in increasing turnover in the money market, thereby improving liquidity and depth of the market.
- REPO provides a source of inexpensive finance and offer investment opportunities of borrowed money at market rates.
- REPOS are used by Central Bank as a Monetary Policy measure for injecting/ withdrawing liquidity in the market.
- They help the borrower to raise funds at better rates.

SECONDARY MARKET IN REPO

Secondary market transactions in REPOS are settled through RBI SGL accounts. Minimum time period in which REPOS can be done away is within 1 day while the maximum period varies and the most common occurring period is 14 days.

The average weekly volume of REPO transactions in Secondary Market has grown from Rs. 763 crores in 1998-1999 to Rs. 1591 crore in 1999-2000, Rs. 2423 crore in 2000-2001 and Rs. 6960 crore in 2001-2002. REPOS in Central Government Securities dominate the market.

CHANGES IN THE REPO MARKET

REPOS have been used by RBI for controlling liquidity in the market. It is a tool for regulating the money supply. So, RBI controls the REPO market and issues instructions in this regard, some changes brought about by RBI in the REPO market have been –

- With effect from September 30, 1995, the minimum period of REPO transaction was decided to be of three days so as to differentiate the REPO Market from Call Money Market.
- With effect from October 31, 1998, it was decided to withdraw.
- Since June 2000, RBI conducts REPO operations on a daily basis on all working days, through uniform price auctions, in which PDs and Banks are permitted to participate.
- Earlier REPOS were held only in government securities and subsequently State Government Securities were included in the set of eligible securities. It has been further decided to extend REPOS into PSU Bonds and private corporate debt securities, provided they are held in dematerialized form in a depository and transactions are done in recognized stock exchanges.
- With effect from April, 2001, it has been decided to phase out non-banks from call markets and use the REPO markets for the short-term operations of non-bank players.
- The REPO markets are now available for banks and primary dealers. Along with this mutual funds, financial institutions, corporates, provident funds, etc. have also been recommended to become participants in the REPO market.
- It has also been decided to adopt international usage for the term "REPO" and "Reverse REPO" under Liquidity Adjustment Facility Operations. Accordingly, current "REPO" operation where Reserve Bank of India absorbs liquidity is termed as "Reverse REPO" and the current "Reverse REPO" operation, where RBI injects liquidity is termed "REPO".

Example

Bank-A tends to borrow an amount of 150 crores from Bank-B under a REPO transaction. The period of REPO is 12 days and interest rate is 9%. The underlying security is 13.05% Government of India Securities. The time period of coupon payments of the security is –

Last Coupon Date	—	22nd April, 2004
Date of Leg of REPO	—	10th May, 2004
REPO Rate	—	9%
No. of Days for which REPO occurs	—	12
Value of Security	—	Rs. 116.40
Interest occurred	—	0.6384
Gross Price	—	116.40 + 0.6384 = 117.03
Second Leg Date	—	22nd May 2004
Gross Price	—	117.03 (1 + 9% x 12/365)=117.3029
Date of Reversal of Transaction	—	22nd May
Interest accrued (from the date of last payment to the date of reversal of the transaction) *i.e.* 30 days	—	1.2485
Price Security	—	117.3029 – 1.2485 = 116.05

Guidelines for Uniform Accounting for REPO/Reverse REPO Transactions

1. In order to ensure uniform accounting treatment in respect of REPO transactions and to impart an element of transparency, it has been decided to lay down uniform accounting principles for REPO/ reverse REPO transactions undertaken by all housing finance companies (HFCs).
2. The uniform accounting principles will be applicable from the financial year 2003-04. On implementation, market participants may undertake REPOS from any category of investments.
3. The legal character of REPO under the current law, *viz.* as outright purchase and outright sale transactions will be kept intact by ensuring that the securities sold under REPO (the entity selling referred to as "seller") are excluded from the Investment Account of the seller of securities and the securities bought under reverse REPO (the entity buying referred to as "buyer") are included in the Investment Account of the buyer of securities.
4. At present REPO transactions are permitted in Central Government Securities including Treasury Bills and dated State Government Securities. The first leg of the REPO should be contracted at prevailing market rates. Further, the accrued interest received/paid in a REPO/reverse REPO transaction and the clean price (*i.e.,* total cash consideration less accrued interest) should be accounted for separately and distinctly.

5. The other accounting principles to be followed while accounting for REPOs/reverse REPOs will be as under –

(*i*) *Coupon* : In case the interest payment date of the security offered under REPO falls within the REPO period, the coupons received by the buyer of the security should be passed on to the seller on the date of receipt as the cash consideration payable by the seller in the second leg does not include any intervening cash flows. While the buyer will book the coupon during the period of the REPO, the seller will not accrue the coupon during the period of the REPO. In the case of discounted instruments like Treasury Bills, since there is no coupon, the seller will continue to accrue the discount at the original discount rate during the period of the REPO. The buyer will not therefore accrue the discount during the period of the REPO.

(*ii*) REPO Interest Income/Expenditure

After the second leg of the REPO/reverse REPO transaction is over,

(*a*) The difference in the clean price of the security between the first leg and the second leg should be reckoned as REPO Interest Income/Expenditure in the books of the buyer/seller respectively;

(*b*) The difference between accrued interest paid between the two legs of the transaction should be shown as REPO Interest Income/Expenditure account, as the case may be; and

(*c*) The balance outstanding the REPO Interest Income/Expenditure account should be transferred to the Profit and Loss Account as income or expenditure.

As regards REPO/reverse REPO transactions outstanding on the balance sheet date, only the accrued income/expenditure till the balance sheet date should be taken to the Profit and Loss Account. Any REPO income/expenditure for the subsequent period in respect of the outstanding transactions should be reckoned for the next accounting period.

(*iii*) *Mark to Market* : The buyer will mark to market the securities acquired under reverse REPO transactions as per the investment classification of the security. The valuation for securities acquired under reverse REPO transactions may be in accordance with the valuation norms followed by them in respect to securities of similar nature.

In respect of the REPO transactions outstanding as on the balance sheet date

(*a*) The buyer will mark to market securities on the balance sheet date and will account for the same as laid down in the extent valuation norms prescribed in the Housing Finance Companies (NHB) Direction, 2001.

(*b*) The seller will provide for the price difference in the Profit and Loss account and show this difference under "Other Assets" in the balance sheet if the sale price of the security offered under REPO is lower than the book value.

(*c*) The seller will ignore the price difference for the purpose of Profit and Loss account but show the difference under "Other Liabilities" in the balance sheet if the sale price of the security offered under REPO is higher than the book value; and (*d*) Similarly the accrued interest paid/received in the REPO/reverse REPO transactions outstanding on balance sheet dates should be shown as "Other Assets" or "Other Liabilities" in the balance sheet.

(*iv*) *Book value on repurchase* : The seller shall debit the REPO account with the original book value (as existing in the books on the date of the first leg) on buying back the securities second leg.

(*v*) *Disclosure* : The following disclosures should be made by banks in the "Notes on Accounts" to the Balance Sheet.

(Rs. in Lakhs)

	Minimum Outstanding during the year	**Maximum Outstanding during the year**	**Daily Average Outstanding**	**As on March 31 Outstanding during the year**
Securities sold under REPOS				
Securities purchased under reverse REPO				

QUESTIONS

Fill in the blanks:

1. REPO transaction is comprised of two transactions *i.e.* ______and_______.
2. REPOS have been used by RBI for controlling _______ in the market.
3. Accrued interest paid/received in the REPO/Reverse REPO transaction outstanding on Balance Sheet dates should be shown as ____________or __________ in B/S.
4. Secondary market transactions in REPOS are settled through _____________.

State whether true or false:

1. Repurchase agreements between two parties do not have predetermined period of time at predetermined price.
2. Maximum period permitted is not restricted in REPO.
3. T-Bills cannot be included as an underlying security for REPO.
4. REPO rate is negotiable between buyer and seller.

Answer in detail:

Q.1. Discuss the need for REPO markets.

Q.2. What guidelines have been adopted for uniform accountancy of REPOs?

❑❑❑

Section-II

Capital Markets

8 PRIMARY MARKETS

INTRODUCTION

Primary Market is a place where securities are introduced as an offer to the public. This offer may be for the first time *i.e.,* New Issue or an issue by an existing listed company.

Every company needs funds for its business. Fund requirements can be for short-term or long-term. Short-term requirement of funds can be met through banks, lenders, institutions etc. Whereas to meet long-term requirements, capital is raised through private placements of shares, rights issue or public issue. These constitute the primary market.

PUBLIC ISSUE

Public Issue means raising funds from the public. The company may require funds to invest in some profitable projects. For this purpose the company may raise funds from the public by the issue of its shares which may later on be listed on any of the stock exchanges.

In order to bring out a Public Issue a company is required to comply with the following laws:

- Provisions of Companies Act, 1956.
- Securities Contracts (Regulations) Act, 1956.
- SEBI rules and regulations.
- Compliance of listing agreement with the concerned stock exchanges after the listing of securities.
- RBI regulations in case of foreign/NRI equity participation.

Keeping in view investor protection, greater transparency and development of capital market SEBI from time to time, has amended the entry norms for companies to bring out a public issue.

The norms for entry are divided into the following:

- Unlisted Companies.
- Listed Companies.

UNLISTED COMPANIES

Unlisted companies are those public limited companies which are presently not listed at any of the recognized stock exchanges in India. Their shares are therefore not traded at any of the stock exchanges. In case of unlisted companies there are two options to bring out a public issue:

Option-I

- The company should have a track record of distributable profits for at least 3 out of 5 preceding years and;
- The pre-issue net worth should be at least Rs. 1 crore in 3 out of 5 years with the minimum net worth in the immediately preceding 2 years.

The issue size including offer to public, firm allotment, promoters contribution through offer document should not exceed 5 times its pre-issue net worth as per the last available audited accounts.

Option-II

Earlier it was considered that if a company cannot satisfy the first option then it can come out with a public issue provided the project is appraised by any bank or public financial institution with at least 10% of project cost financed by such appraiser.

But w.e.f. August 4,2000, SEBI has amended its guideline stating that if the company is unable to satisfy the first option or if the issue size is more than 5 times of its pre-issue net worth then the second option to come out with the issue is through book building process only. The issue can come out through book building process provided 60% of the issue size is allotted to Qualified Institutional Buyers (QIB's). In case it is not so, the money so received shall be refunded.

BOOK BUILDING PROCESS

Corporates may raise capital in the primary market by way of an initial public offer, rights issue or private placement. An Initial Public Offer (IPO) is the selling of securities to the public in the primary market. This Initial Public Offering can be made through the fixed price method, book building method or a combination of both.

Book-building is a process of price discovery used in public offers. The issuer sets a base price and a band within which the investor is allowed to bid for shares.

Book Building is essentially a process used by companies raising capital through Public Offerings- both Initial Public Offers (IPOs) or Follow-on Public Offers (FPOs) to aid price and demand discovery. It is a mechanism where, during the period for which the book for the offer is open, the bids are collected from investors at various prices, which are within the price band specified by the issuer. The process is directed towards both the institutional as well as the retail investors. The issue price is determined after the bid closure based on the demand generated in the process.

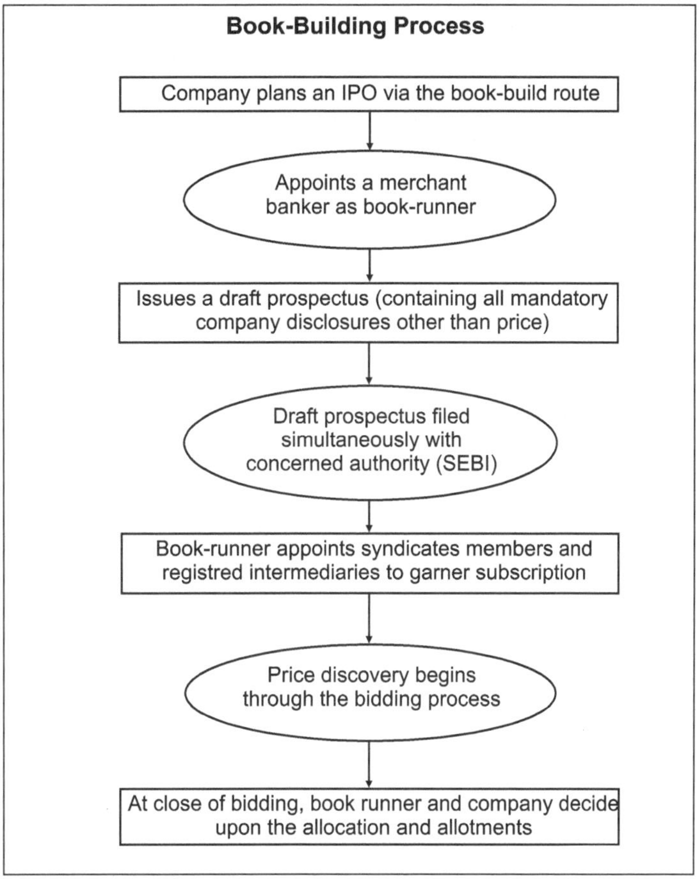

The Process

- The Issuer who is planning an offer nominates lead merchant banker(s) as 'book runners'.
- The Issuer specifies the number of securities to be issued and the price band for the bids.
- The Issuer also appoints syndicate members with whom orders are to be placed by the investors.
- The syndicate members input the orders into an 'electronic book'. This process is called 'bidding' and is similar to open auction.
- The book normally remains open for a period of 5 days.
- Bids have to be entered within the specified price band.
- Bids can be revised by the bidders before the book closes.
- On the close of the book building period, the book runners evaluate the bids on the basis of the demand at various price levels.
- The book runners and the Issuer decide the final price at which the securities shall be issued.

- Generally, the number of shares is fixed, the issue size gets frozen based on the final price per share.
- Allocation of securities is made to the successful bidders. The rest get refund orders.

Every public offer through the book-building process has a book running lead manager (BRLM), a merchant banker, who manages the issue.

Further, an order book, in which the investors can state the quantity of the stock they are willing to buy, at a price within the band, is built. Thus, the term 'book-building.'

An issue through the book-building route remains open for a period of 3 to 7 days and can be extended by another three days if the issuer decides to revise the floor price and the band. The public issue made by an infrastructure company, satisfying the requirements in Clause 2.4.1 (iii) of Chapter II may be kept open for a maximum period of 21 working days.

Open bookbuilding

In book-built issues, it is mandatory to have an online display of the demand and bids during the bidding period. This is known as open book system. (Under closed book building, the book is not made public and the bidders have to take a call on the price at which they intend to make a bid without having any information on the bids submitted by other bidders). As per SEBI, only electronic facility is allowed to be used in case of book building.

Price band

The offer document may have a floor price for the securities or a price band within which the investors can bid. The spread between the floor and the cap of the price band can not be more than 20%. In other words, it means that the cap should not be more than 120% of the floor price. The company decides the price band in consultation with the investment bankers, and typically after undertaking a pre-marketing exercise with some leading QIBs. The price band can have a revision. SEBI requires that any revision in the price band has to be widely disseminated by informing the stock exchanges, by issuing press release and also indicating the change on the relevant website and the terminals of the syndicate members. When the price band is revised, the bidding period has to be extended for a further period of three days, subject to the total bidding period not exceeding thirteen days.

Floor price

Floor price is the minimum price at which bids can be made.

Cut-off price

Once the issue period is over and the book has been built, the BRLM along with the issuer arrives at a cut-off price. The cut-off price is the price discovered by the market. It is the price at which the shares are issued to the investors.

Investors bidding at a price below the cut-off price are ignored. So those investors who apply at a price higher than the cut-off price have a higher chance of getting the stock. So the question that arises is:

Determination of cut-off price

The cut-off price is arrived at by the method of Dutch auction. In a Dutch auction the price of an item is lowered, until it gets its first bid and then the item is sold at that price.

Let's say a company wants to issue one million shares. The floor price for one share of face value, Rs 10 and the band is between Rs 19 and Rs 25.

At Rs 25, on the basis of the bids received, the investors are ready to buy 200,000 shares. So the cut-off price cannot be set at Rs 25 as only 200,000 shares will be sold. So as a next step, the price is lowered to Rs 24. At Rs 24, investors are ready to buy 400,000 shares. So if the cut-off price is set at Rs 24, 600,000 shares will be sold. This still leaves 400,000 shares to be sold.

The price is now lowered to Rs 23. At Rs23, investors are ready to buy 400,000 shares. Now if the cut-off price is set at Rs 23, all one million shares will be sold.

Investors who had applied for shares at Rs 25 and Rs 24 will also be issued shares at Rs 23. The extra money paid by these investors while applying will be returned to them.

The movement of bids and percentage subscription can be shown as below:

Bid Quantity	Bid Price	Cumulative Quantity	Subscription
200000	25	200000	20%
400000	24	600000	60%
200000	23	1000000	100.0%
50000	22	1050000	105%
25000	19	1075000	107.5%

From the above table it can be seen that the highest price at which the issuer is able to issue the desired number of shares is the price at which the book cuts off, *i.e.,* Rs. 23 in the above example. Which means that the number of shares offered to the public will be subscribed to by them at or above such price The issuer, in consultation with the book running lead managers, will finalise the issue price at or below such cut off price, *i.e.,* at or below Rs. 23. All bids at or above this issue price and cut-off bids are valid bids and are considered for allocation in the respective categories.

TYPES OF INVESTORS

There are three kinds of investors in a book-building issue. The retail individual investor (RII), the non-institutional investor (NII) and the Qualified Institutional Buyers (QIBs).

RII is an investor who applies for stocks for a value of not more than Rs 100,000. Any bid exceeding this amount is considered in the NII category. NIIs are commonly referred to as high networth individuals. On the other hand QIBs are institutional investors who possess the expertise and the financial muscle to invest in the securities market.

Mutual funds, financial institutions, scheduled commercial banks, insurance companies, provident funds, state industrial development corporations, etc. fall under the definition of being a QIB.

Each of these categories is allocated a certain percentage of the total issue. The total allotment to the RII category has to be at least 35% of the total issue. RIIs also have an option of applying at the cut-off price. This option is not available to other classes of investors. NIIs are to be given at least 15% of the total issue.

And the QIBs are to be issued not more than 50% of the total issue. Allotment to RIIs and NIIs is made through a proportionate allotment system. The allotment to the QIBs is at the discretion of the BRLM. The following graph shows changes in norms for issue of shares to various class of investors.

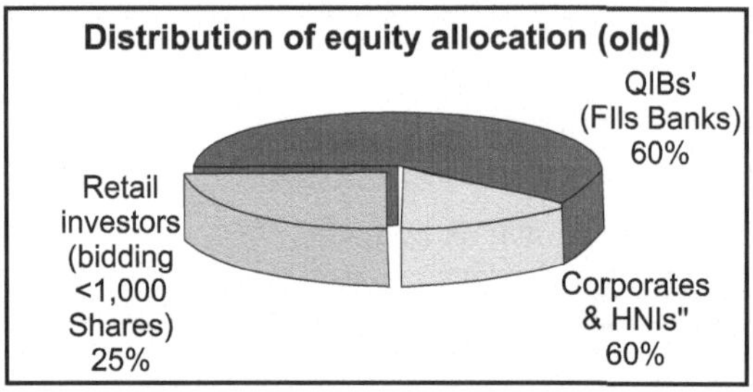

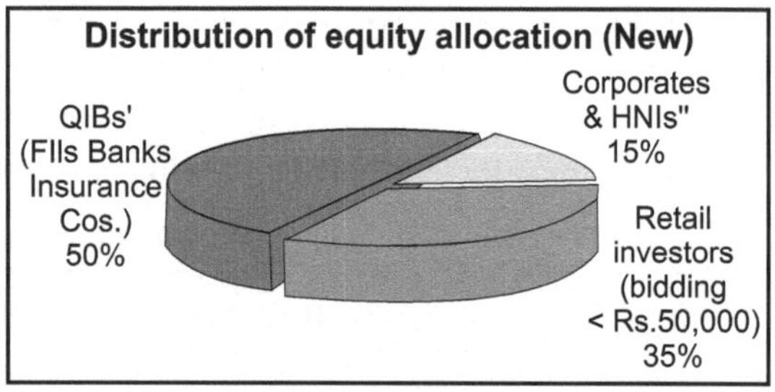

Determination of allotment

Let's suppose, A Ltd., makes an offer for 200,000 shares. The issue is oversubscribed, *i.e.,* there is demand for more shares than the issuer plans to issue. Further, a minimum allotment of 100 shares is to be made for every investor.

The cut-off price has been decided and now the allotments are to be made. In the RII category, 1,500 applicants have applied for 100 shares each, *i.e.,* there is a demand for 150,000 shares.

A Ltd. plans to issue 35% of the total issue to this category, *i.e.,* 70,000 shares. In the NII category, 200 applicants have applied for 500 shares each, *i.e.,* 100,000 shares. A Ltd. plans to issue 15% of the total issue to this category, *i.e.,* 30,000 shares.

The cut-off price has already been decided, so adjusting the quantity remains the only way of reaching the equilibrium. Applying the proportionate allotment system each investor in the RII category will get 46.67 shares [(70,000/ 150,000) x 100)]. But the minimum allotment has to be 100 shares.

So through a lottery, 700 investors are chosen and allotted 100 shares each, making a total of 70,000 shares. In the NII category every investor will get 150 shares [(30,000/100,000) x 500)]. And that is how equilibrium is reached.

Green shoe option

In case the issue has been oversubscribed, as was the case with A Ltd, the company has to exercise a green shoe option to stabilize the post-listing price. When a particular issue is oversubscribed the appetite of investors for the stock has not been satisfied and once it gets listed they tend to pick up the stock from the secondary market.

Since the demand is greater than supply the prices tend to rise way beyond what the fundamentals of the stock would justify. So in order to stabilise the post-issue price of the stock, the issuer has to issue more shares in case of oversubscription.

These shares are taken from the pre-issue shareholders or promoters and are issued to the investors who have come in through the public offer on a prorata basis. The green shoe option can be a maximum of 15% of the public offer.

Book-building has become the preferred route of raising capital, as can be seen from the table below. Though there are fixed price issues, by amount, the book-building IPOs dominate.

Year	BOOKBUILDING			FIXED PRICE			TOTAL	
	No.of IPOs	Amount (Rs.crore)	%	No.of IPOs	Amount (Rs.crore)	%	No.of IPOs	Amount (Rs.crore)
2004-05	9	2641.04	82.8	10	550.07	17.2	19	3191.10
2005-06	15	14507.04	98.9	8	155.28	1.1	23	14662.32
2006-07	53	10225.43	94.7	23	572.45	5.3	76	10797.88
2008-09	65	23469.07	99.0	11	237.10	1.0	76	23706.16

In order to safeguard investor interests includes making the board of the company more responsible towards what they state in the book building document. Also, the CFO of the company has to authenticate the financial statements stated with this document. Bottom-line, the chief executive officer or the chief financial officer of a company will certify the disclosures in the offer document. Thus, the recent amendments announced by SEBI, aim at strengthening investor confidence and make book building a successful process for Indian investors.

ROLE OF SEBI IN PRIMARY MARKET

- Upto 1992, the capital primary market was controlled by the Controller of Capital Issue (CCI) formed under the Capital Issues Control Act. During that period, the pricing of capital issues was controlled by CCI. The premium on issue of equity shares issued through the primary markets was done in accordance with the Capital Issues Control Act.
- The CCI guidelines were abolished with the introduction of Securities and Exchange Board of

India (SEBI) formed under the SEBI Act, 1992 with the prime objective of protecting the interests of investors in securities, promoting the development of, and regulating the securities market and for matters connected therewith or incidental thereto.

- The SEBI Act came into force on 30th January, 1992 and with its establishment, all public issues are government by the rules and regulations issued by SEBI.
- SEBI was formed to promote fair dealing in issue of securities and to ensure that the capital markets function efficiently, transparently and economically in the better interest of both the issuers and the investors.
- The promoters should be able to raise funds at a relatively low cost. At the same time, investors must be protected from unethical practices and their rights must be safeguarded so that there is a steady flow of savings into the market. There must be proper regulation and code of conduct and fair practice by intermediaries to make them competitive and professional.
- Since, its formation, SEBI has been instrumental in bringing greater transparency in capital issues. Under the umbrella of SEBI, companies issuing shares are free to fix the premium provided adequate disclosure is made in the offer documents. SEBI has become a vigilant watchdog with the focus towards greater investor protection.

INTERMEDIARIES INVOLVED AND THEIR ROLE IN PRIMARY MARKET

Many intermediaries are involved in connection with the public issue. Following are the intermediaries who have to be registered with SEBI and must have valid certificate from SEBI to act as intermediaries:

- Merchant Bankers
- Registrar and Share Transfer Agents
- Bankers to the issue
- Underwriters
- Stock Brokers and Sub-Brokers
- Depositories

Merchant Bankers play the most vital role amongst all intermediaries. They assist the company right from preparing prospectus to the listing of securities at the stock exchanges. Merchant bankers have to satisfy themselves about the correctness and propriety of all the information provided in the prospectus. It is mandatory for them to carry due diligence for all the information provided in the prospectus and they must issue a certificate to this effect to SEBI. A Company may appoint more than one merchant banker provided *inter se* allocation of responsibilities between the merchant bankers is properly structured.

Underwriters are those intermediaries who underwrite the securities offered to the public. In case there is under subscription (in short, the company does not receive good response from public and amount received from is less than the issue size), underwriters subscribe to the unsubscribed amount so that the issue is successful.

Registrar and Share Transfer Agents process all applications received from the public and prepare the basis of allotment. The dispatch of share certificates/refund orders are handled by them.

Bankers to the Issue are banks which accept applications from the public on behalf of the company. These applications are then forwarded to Registrar and Share Transfer Agents for further processing.

Stock Brokers and Sub-Brokers are those intermediaries who through their contacts/sources invite the public for subscribing shares for which they get commission.

Depositories are the intermediaries who hold securities in dematerialized form on behalf of the shareholders.

ISSUE OF PROSPECTUS

Prospectus is the most important document for the company to come out with a public issue. As per Section 2 (36) of the Companies Act, "Prospectus" means any document described or issued as a prospectus and includes any notice, circular, advertisement or other document inviting deposits from the public or inviting offers from the public for the subscription or purchase of any shares in, or debentures of, a body corporate.

Prospectus is a document by way of which the investor gets all the information pertaining to the company in which they are going to invest. It gives the detailed information about the Company, Promoter / Directors, Group Companies, Capital Structure, Terms of the present issues, details of proposed project, particulars of the issue etc. There are certain mandatory disclosures which have to be made in the prospectus. SEBI has issued guidelines, SEBI (Disclosure for Investor and Protection), Guidelines, 2000 which gives details about the contents of prospectus.

Regulations regarding Issue of Prospectus

- A company cannot come out with public issue unless draft prospectus is filed with SEBI.
- A company cannot file prospectus directly with SEBI. It has to be filed through a merchant banker. After the preparation of prospectus, the merchant banker along with the due diligence certificates and other compliance sends the same to SEBI.
- SEBI on receiving the same scrutinizes it and may suggest changes within 21 days of receipt of prospectus. (Earlier, the situation was that the company was required to obtain Acknowledgement Card from SEBI).
- If the issue size is up to Rs.20 crore then the merchant bankers are required to file prospectus with the regional office of SEBI falling under the jurisdiction in which registered office of the company is situated.
- If the issue size is more than Rs. 20 crore, merchant bankers are required to file prospectus at SEBI, Mumbai office.
- Prospectus is also required to be filed with the concerned stock exchanges along with the application for listing its securities. Presently, companies approaching the stock exchange for public issue should obtain in-principal approval from such stock exchanges.

After making changes, if any made by SEBI / Stock Exchanges, the final Prospectus duly signed by all the Directors (or by Authorised representatives through its Power of Attorney) must be filed with the Registrar of Companies (ROC) along with the copy of all material documents.

The Registrar of Companies may suggest changes which should also be reported to SEBI / Stock Exchanges. The date on which ROC Card is obtained is the date of the prospectus.

Provisions Regarding Promoter's Contribution and Lock-in Requirement

Some specific provisions have been inserted with regard to the contribution of the promoters in the capital of the company.

In case of public issues by **listed companies**, the promoter's contribution should be either 20% of the proposed issue or 20%, then the excess of 20% shall attract the provisions of the guidelines on preferential allotment, if the issue price is lower than the price as determined on the basis of said preferential allotment guidelines.

Promoters Contribution to be Brought in Before the Issue

Promoters are required to bring the full amount of the promoter's contribution at least one day prior to the opening of the public issue and should be kept in an escrow account with a scheduled bank.

Exemption from Requirement of Minimum Promoters' Contribution

If the company is a listed company for at least 3 years and has a track record of dividend payment for at least 3 immediately preceding years, the requirement of promoter's contribution will not be applicable.

Lock-in Requirements

- The eligible promoter's contribution is locked-in for 3 years.
- The entire pre-issue share capital, other than that locked-in as promoter's contribution, shall be locked-in for a period of one year.
- All the securities issued on firm allotment basis shall be locked in for a period of one year.
- The date of the lock-in shall be reckoned from the date of commencement of commercial production or the date of allotment in the public issue, whichever is later.

Other Lock-in Requirement

- The shares held by promoter's and are locked-in may be pledged with banks or financial institutions for loans, provided the pledge of shares is one of the terms of the sanction of loan.
- The locked-in shares held by promoters can be transferred between the promoters provided they are disclosed as promoters in the prospectus and there would be no change in the period of lock-in.
- The Share Certificates issued for lock-in shares should inscribe the word 'Non-Transferable up to——- 'or 'Lock-in up to——'

Rules Regarding Reservations and Firm Allotment

- In case of unlisted company, Public Issue should be at least 25% of the post issue capital.
- In case of a listed company, Public Issue should be at least 25% of the issue size.

- The above is relaxed in case of a public issue of unlisted companies in information technology sector where at least 10% of the securities may be offered to public subject to (*i*) 20 lakh securities are offered to public and (*ii*) issue size is minimum Rs. 50 crore.
- The company can **reserve** shares in the issue on competitive basis wherein allotment of shares is made in proportion to the shares applied for by the concerned reserved categories which are as follows—
  - Permanent Employees including working directors and in case of new company the permanent employees of the promoting company.
  - Shareholders of the promoting companies in case of new company and shareholders of group companies in case of existing company.
  - Indian Mutual Funds
  - FII's including NRI's and OCB.
  - Indian and multilateral development institutions.
  - Scheduled banks.

  Company is allowed to make **firm allotment** to the following:
  - Indian and Multilateral Development Financial Institutions
  - Indian Mutual Funds
  - FII
  - Permanent / regular employees of the company
  - Scheduled Banks
  - Merchant Bankers (subject to 5% of the issue size)
- The aggregate **of reservations and firm allotment** for employees cannot exceed 10% of the issue size.
- For shareholders, it cannot exceed 10% of the issue size.

Pre-Issue Obligation (*i.e.,* before the opening of issue)

- Board Resolution for approving the draft prospectus and related resolutions.
- Shareholder's Resolution pursuant to Section 81 (1A) of the Companies Act, 1956.
- Filing of Form 23 with ROC for passing special resolution for issuing shares as above.
- Appointment of intermediaries and entering into MOU with them.
- Due diligence by a merchant banker.
- Submission of all required papers/documents with merchant bankers.
- Preparation of draft prospectus in consultation with the merchant banker and submitting the same with SEBI alongwith the fees and other requirements and submitting the same with stock exchanges as per guidelines.
- Receipt of queries from SEBI/stock exchanges, if any and make changes in prospectus, if required.

- Reply to SEBI / stock exchanges in connection with changes in prospectus.
- Obtaining in-principle approval from stock exchanges.
- File final prospectus with SEBI / stock exchanges / ROC
- Statutory Advertisements
- Submission of 1% Security Deposit with the Regional Stock Exchange.
- Depositing Promoter's Contribution in the issue in a separate bank account.

Post-Issue Obligation (*i.e.,* after the closure of issue)

- Collection of Application forms and processing the same at the Registrar and Share Transfer Agent in consultation with the Merchant Banker.
- Separate account to be opened for the applications received from public.
- Submitting 3-day post issue monitoring report with SEBI by merchant banker.
- Basis of allotment in consultation with the regional stock exchange.
- Post-Issue Advertisement
- Dispatch of share certificate / refund orders.
- File Form No.2 for Return of Allotment with ROC
- Entering into a listing agreement
- Obtaining permission from Stock Exchanges for listing and trading of securities
- Commencement of trading of securities
- 78-day Post-Issue monitoring report to be submitted by Merchant Banker with SEBI.
- Redressal of Investors Grievances
- Application to SEBI/Stock Exchange for refund of security deposit.

Some important issues pertaining to public issues

- Companies can freely price its securities
- Company cannot come out with public issue unless all its existing partly paid-up shares, if any, are made fully paid-up.
- Before filing the final prospectus, the company can keep a price band of maximum 20%. It means that if the company is not sure of the issue price, it may keep a floor price with price band of 20%.
- Companies are now free to determine the denomination of shares.
- Net offer to public should be at least 25% of the issue size.
- Public-Issue should be opened for at least 3 working days and not more than 10 working days.
- The minimum amount to be received from each investor should be Rs.2,000/-.
- Promoter may at its discretion arrange for buy back facility or safety net facility in the prospectus

subject to a maximum 1000 shares per allottee. The validity of such scheme, if any shall be for at least 6 months from the date of dispatch of share certificates.

- Company can come out with an issue within 365 days from the date of the observation letter received from SEBI or where such letter is not received, issue can come out within 365 days from the 22nd day of the date of filing of the prospectus with SEBI.
- Company is required to appoint Compliance Officer to directly liaise with SEBI/Stock Exchanges to comply with various laws and investor's complaint related matters.
- Trading of securities of all new public issues will be in dematerialized form only.
- The refund orders demat credit, allotment and submission of listing documents to stock exchanges should be completed within 2 working days of finalization of the basis of allotment.

Other Methods of Raising Money in Primary Market

- **Bought-Out-Deals** : It is the sale of securities under a negotiated agreement between an issuer and investing institutions as an alternative to a Public Issue. The reason for the buyer doing this is to offload the securities later in the market at a profit. Bought-Out-Deals are commonly done in the issue of the Over. The Counter Exchange of India (OTCEI). It provides an advantage of saving time and cost to the issuing company. It also serves as a gestation stage for the unlisted companies or projects before they tap the primary market. It is another avenue of investing funds for institutions and mutual funds. But there can be some disadvantages to the issuer such as interference by the institutional investor or restrictive covenants in the initial subscription agreement. While on the other hand institutional investor or the sponsor in these Bought-Out-Deals bears the risk of capital loss due to fall in price of the securities.
- **Private Placement** : It is the sale, by a company, of its securities to one or a few financial institution through a process of direct negotiations, or to a limited number of individual investors. The financial institutions can later sell the securities to the public.

  This method of issuing securities helps in lowering the cost of raising capital as it does not involve any underwriting agreement. Moreover, advertisement, postage, brokerage charges etc. are also not present. There is no listing requirement as not only public limited but also closely held private companies can also raise capital through this method. It also provides an advantage of adjusting the issue according to the requirement of buyer and there is no lower limit to the size of the issue. It also takes lesser time to raise money through a private placement then through public issue. But this method is generally preferred to bring issues of small size as compared to a public issue.
- **Rights Issue :** The issue of Equity Shares to the existing shareholders in proportion of their existing holding is called Rights Issue. It is thus an issue of shares on pro rata basis to the existing holders. The shares in the rights issue are offered mostly at a lower rate than the market price.

The value of a right is found by the following formula –

$$\frac{MP_C - SP}{N+1}$$

Where:

MPC $\rightarrow$ Market Price of Share-cum-Right.

SP $\rightarrow$ Subscription price at which shares are offered to shareholders.

N $\rightarrow$ No. of rights needed to obtain one new share.

Rights issue is useful for the company as it avoids dilution of control because of the shares being offered first to existing shareholders only.

Moreover it is less costly due to lower floatation costs. The rights issue also has more chances of being successful because of being offered at a price lower than the market price. But it may lead to loss of wealth of the shareholders who do not exercise their rights.

QUESTIONS

Fill in the blanks:

1. Public Issue means __________.
2. Book Building is a process used in ___________ for efficient price discovery.
3. The final prospectus during a public issue must be filed with __________ after being duly signed by all the directors.
4. In a public issue, the aggregate of reservation and firm allotment to the employees cannot exceed __________ % of the issue size.
5. Public Issue should be kept open for atleast ___________ days.
6. Issue of shares to the existing shareholders in proportion to their existing holding is called _____________.
7. The document which gives all information pertaining to the company to an investor is called _____________.

State whether true or false:

1. Primary market is a place where securities are offered first time.
2. In book building mechanism offer price of an IPO is determined before the bid closing date.
3. The company can reserve shares in IPO for its permanent employees.
4. Shares should compulsorily be in DEMAT form for trading.

Answer in detail:

Q.1. Describe the process of Book Building and how is it better as compared to other traditional methods of raising an IPO?

Q.2. What details should be disclosed by a company while issuing a prospectus during a public issue?

Q.3. Who are the intermediaries involved in primary market and discuss their respective roles?

❑❑❑

9 DEMATERIALIZATION

CONCEPT OF DEMATERIALIZATION

Keeping in mind the risks involved on account of fake / forged certificates, bad delivery and delays in transfer SEBI has made recent changes by which all the public issues shall be in **dematerialized** form only. It means that no physical share certificate will be given to the shareholders. The shares shall be electronically transferred to the shareholders account opened its Depository Participant.

Trading in the shares of any Company is compulsory in dematerialized form for all investors.

DEMATERIALIZATION

Dematerialization ("Demat" in short form) signifies conversion of a share certificate from its physical form to electronic form for the same number of holdings which is credited to the demat account which the investor opens with a Depository Participant (DP).

Dematerialization is a process by which the physical share certificates of an investor are taken back by the Company and an equivalent number of securities are credited in electronic form at the request of the investor. An investor will have to first open an account with a Depository Participant and then request for the dematerialization of his share certificates through the Depository Participant so that the dematerialized holdings can be credited into that account. This is very similar to opening a bank account.

Dematerialization of shares is optional and investors can still hold shares in physical form. However, he/she will have to demat the shares if he / she wishes to sell the same through the Stock Exchanges. Similarly, if an investor purchases shares, he / she will get delivery of the shares in demat form.

DEPOSITORY

A Depository (NSDL & CDSL) is an organization like a Central Bank where the securities of a shareholder are held in the electronic form at the request of the shareholder through the medium of a Depository Participant.

If an investor wants to utilize the services offered by a Depository, the investor has to open an account with the depository through a Depository Participant.

So a depository is just another form of a custodial service, the difference being that the securities are held in an electronic form

Moreover, the Depository can legally transfer beneficial ownership which a custodian cannot. The main objective of a Depository is to minimize paper work involved with the ownership, trading and transfer of securities.

DEPOSITORY PARTICIPANT

Similar to the brokers who trade on behalf of investors in and outside the Stock Exchange, a Depository Participant (DP) is the representative (agent) of the investor in the depository system providing the link between the Company and investor through the Depository. Depository Participants maintain the securities account balances of the investors and intimate them the status of their holding from time to time. According to SEBI guidelines, Financial Institutions like banks, custodians, stock brokers etc. can become depository participants. A DP is one with whom an investor needs to open an account to deal in electronic form. While the Depository can be compared to a Bank, DP is like a branch of the bank with which an investor can have an account. Total Depository Participants in India are 76.

OPERATION OF THE DEPOSITORY SYSTEM

The Depository System functions very much like the banking system. A bank holds funds in accounts whereas a Depository holds securities in accounts for its clients. A Bank transfers funds between accounts whereas a Depository transfers securities between accounts. In both systems, the transfer of funds or securities happens without the actual handling of funds or securities. Both the Banks and the Depository are accountable for the safe keeping of funds and securities respectively.

Benefits of a DEMAT Account :

(*a*) Trading in the shares of the Company is now under the compulsory demat segment. With SEBI making demat mandatory on most of the traded scripts, electronic transaction will be the only way everyone will trade.

(*b*) No stamp duty for transfer of securities in the electronic form. In case of transfer of physical shares, stamp duty of 0.5 per cent is payable on the market value of shares being transferred.

(*c*) All risks associated with physical certificates such as delays, loss in transit, theft, mutilation, bad deliveries, etc. are eliminated. Shares can be kept in the "Frozen Mode" by the Depository Participant under specific instructions by the investor.

(*d*) The concept of an "odd lot" in respect of dematerialized shares stands abolished, *i.e.,* in the demat mode, market lot becomes one share.

(*e*) Dematerialized securities are most preferred by banks and other financiers for providing credit facility against securities. Generally, demat securities attract lower margin and lower rates of interest compared to physical securities.

(*f*) Even in the electronic mode of trading, the payment mechanism (usually through a broker) between the buyer and seller continues to be as before. Also the usual brokerage charges would have to be incurred. However, after the settlement, pay in and pay out are on the same day for script-less trading which means the investor gets his securities as well as cash immediately.

(*g*) Shares bought or sold are transferred in investor's name on the very next day of pay-out. In case of physical shares, transfer of ownership takes 30 days or sometimes even more.

(*h*) No courier / postal charges for sending share certificates / transfer deeds.

(*i*) Facility for freezing / locking of investor accounts, which enables him to make his account non-operational, for instance if he is abroad.

(*j*) Facility to pledge and hypothecate securities available with the investor.

(*k*) As the Depository System becomes popular, brokers will be increasingly reluctant to deal with physical shares.

(*l*) Investors prefer to buy shares which are already in dematerialized form, because when they buy shares already in the depository mode, they become the owner of those shares in the depository within a day of the settlement being completed. As a result they do not have to apply to the Company for registering the shares in their name. Thus, there will be no possibility of loss or theft when the share certificates are posted to the Company. The investor will have no fear that any fake or stolen shares may have been delivered to him.

PREFERENCE OF BROKERS TO DEAL IN DEMAT SHARES

Apart from the risk arising out of having to deal with the paper work and keeping account of the share certificates, the brokers are exposed to the risk of bad deliveries in the present system. It may take up to one year for the broker to discover that such a risk exists. As against this in the depository mode the broker will be free from the worries of bad deliveries. The broker's only risk will be that the investor does not own the shares which the investor has sold. But this will be known within the settlement period (10-15 days). The broker will thus prefer to sell securities that are in the depository mode.

PROCESS OF DEMATERIALIZATION

The process of opening an account with a Depository Participant is similar to the opening of a bank account.

1. First, the investor has to open an account with a Depository Participant (DP) of his choice by filling up an Account Opening Form and signing a "Participant-Client Agreement". The investor will be then given a unique client ID number, which must be quoted in all correspondence with the DP.
2. Thereafter, the investor will have to fill up and submit a Dematerialization Request Form (DRF) provided by the DP duly signed by all the holders and surrender the physical shares intended to be dematted to the DP.

3. The DP upon receipt of the shares and the DRF, will issue to him an acknowledgement and will send an electronic request to the Company/ Registrars and Transfer Agents of the Company through the Depository for confirmation of demat.
4. The DP will simultaneously surrender the DRF and the shares to the Company / Registrars and Transfer Agents of the Company with covering letter requesting the Company to confirm demat.
5. The Registrars and Transfer Agents of the Company, after necessary verification of the documents received from the DP, will cancel the physical shares and confirm demat to the Depository.
6. This confirmation will be passed on by the Depository to the DP which holds the account of the investor. After receiving this confirmation from the Depository, the DP will credit investor's account with the number of shares dematerialized. The DP will hold the shares in the dematerialized form thereafter on investor's behalf. And he will become the beneficial owner of these dematerialized shares.
7. When the investor submits the shares for dematerialization, his DP will deface the share certificates with the stamp "SURRENDERED FOR DEMATERIALISATION". This ensures that his shares are not lost in transit or misused till credit is received by the investor in his demat account.

Charges to be paid for opening an account and to demat one's physical share

Each DP can levy charges by way of account opening fees, transaction fees, custody fees and so on and these charges differ from Depository Participant to Depository Participant.

DIVIDEND ON DEMATTED SHARES

The Depositories will give the list of demat account holders and the number of shares held by them in electronic form on the Record date to the Registrars and Transfer Agents of the Company (known as BENPOS). On the basis of BENPOS, the Company will issue dividend warrants in favour of the demat account holders.

The rights of the shareholders holding shares in demat form are at par with the holders in physical form. Hence the investor will be eligible to get the Annual Report and will have the right to attend the AGM as a shareholder.

CONVERSION OF DEMATTED SHARES BACK INTO PHYSICAL SHARES

If the investors wish to get their securities in the physical form all they have to do is

1. Submit a re-materialization Request Form (RRF) through their DP in the same manner as Dematerialization.
2. The Depository Participant will forward their request to the Depository after verifying that they have the necessary securities in balance.

3. The Depository in turn will intimate the Registrar and Transfer Agents of the Company who will print and dispatch to them the share certificates for the number of shares so rematerialized and the investors' account will be debited by the Depository and credited with the Company.
4. The Registrar and Transfer Agents will print new certificates with a new range of certificate numbers and provide them to the investor.

MULTIPLE ACCOUNTS

Earlier there were absolutely no restrictions on the number of DPs an investor can open accounts with. Opening an account with a DP is very similar to opening a bank account. Just as a person can have savings or current accounts with more than one bank, in the same way he can open accounts with more than one Depository Participant. But w.e.f. 2006 due to frauds in allotment of shares in IPOs, SEBI has issued new guidelines where an investor cannot have more than one Demat account and can open it with one Depository Participant only.

SECURITY OF HOLDINGS

When an investor opens an account with a DP, an agreement is signed by him with the Depository Participant, in which the DP indemnifies him for any misuse of his holdings. The Depository will also ensure that the interests of the investors are protected, so that the grievances, if any, against the DP will be resolved by the Depository.

Moreover every transaction in investor's account will be authorised by him. He can authorize any transaction either by affixing clients' signatures or by using any smart card similar to the use of an ATM or a credit card.

There is a facility by which the investor can lock his account so that the Depository Participant will not be able to carry out any transaction in his absence without the investors' authorisation.

QUESTIONS

Fill in the blanks:

1. For getting the shares dematerialized an investor has to open an account with a _________.
2. In case of bad deliveries shares can be kept in _____________ mode by a DP as per the instruction of the investor.
3. While opening a DMAT account an investor has to sign a ____________agreement.
4. Conversion of DMAT shares back into physical form is called _____________.

State whether true or false:

1. Brokers prefer to deal in physical shares than DMAT shares.
2. DMAT shares are not subject to stamp duty while transferring them.
3. Once DMAT, shares cannot be converted back to physical form.
4. An investor can have multiple DMAT accounts with as many DPs as he wants.
5. Transactions in DMAT account can be done by a DP only as per the instructions of the Investor.

Answer in detail:

Q.1. What is the advantage of dematerialization of shares over holding them in physical form?

Q.2. Discuss the process of dematerialization and re-materialization of shares.

Q.3. How safe is holding securities in e-form? What is the method of preventing any default on behalf of investors in case of dematerialization?

❑❑❑

10

SECONDARY MARKET

INTRODUCTION

Secondary market is a place where already issued securities (Shares and Bonds) of the Companies listed on recognized exchanges in the market are traded. Secondary markets, therefore, are another name of the stock markets which comprises of four players : Stock Exchanges, Companies, Investors and Brokers.

Indian Stock Markets have a history which dates back to nearly 200 years.

HISTORY AND GROWTH OF STOCK MARKETS IN INDIA

- It was at the close of the eighteenth century when East India Company was a dominant institution that business in loan securities of the company used to be transacted.
- By 1830's business on corporate stocks and shares in Bank and Cotton Presses took place in Bombay.
- In 1850, there was a rapid development of commercial enterprises and the number of brokers increased to 60 in 1860.
- In 1874, after the American Civil War, the brokers who thrived out of the Civil War in 1874, found a place in a street (now called Dalal Street) where they would conveniently assemble and transact business.
- In 1897, they formally established in Bombay, the "Native Share and Stock Brokers Association" and in 1895, the Stock Exchange acquired a premises in the same street and was inaugurated in 1899 named as Bombay Stock Exchange or BSE.
- After this in 1908, Calcutta Stock Exchange was formed. The Madras Stock Exchange came into existence in 1920.
- After the Second World War, Stock Exchanges were floated in all parts of the country namely, Uttar Pradesh Stock Exchange Limited (1940), Nagpur Stock Exchange Limited (1940) and Hyderabad Stock Exchange Limited (1944).

- In June, 1947, Delhi Stock Exchange was formed by the amalgamation of Delhi Stock and Share Brokers' Association and Delhi Stock and Share Limited.
- After Independence, Securities Contracts (Regulation) Act, 1956 was introduced. During early sixties there were eight recognized stock exchanges in India. During eighties many stock exchanges were established: Cochin Stock Exchange (1980) Pune Stock Exchange (1982), Ludhiana Stock Exchange (1983), Gauhati Stock Exchange (1984), Kanara Stock Exchange (1985), Magadh Stock Exchange (1986), Jaipur Stock Exchange (1989), Bubhneshwar Stock Exchange (1989), Saurashtra Kutch Stock Exchange (1989), Vadodara Stock Exchange (1990).

Thus, at present there are 23 recognized stock exchanges in India including the National Stock Exchanges, Bombay Stock Exchange and Over-The-Counter – Exchange of India.

STOCK MARKET INDICES

Stock Index is a representative of the price and value of various companies listed on the Stock Exchange. It is a single figure, which sums up the overall performance of the market on a daily basis.

A Stock Index is the pulse rate of an economy and reflects the expectations of investors. It measures the general movement of the market.

Various types of Stock Indexes are :

1. **Broad Market Index :** It consists of all the large, liquid stocks of the country and becomes the benchmark for the capital market in the whole country *e.g.* S&P CNX 500, Sensex.
2. **Specialized Index :** These are industry or sector specific indexes, which act as a benchmark for that particular industry, *e.g.* CNX Mid Cap, which is composed of companies with market capitalization between 500-1500 crore, NASDA, which comprises of IT shares, CNX IT sector index, CNX Bank Index, CNX FMCG Indexes.

DETERMINANTS OF A STOCK INDEX

1. **Liquidity :** The Index should have stocks with high liquidity. This is measured by the 'impact cost' criterion. Impact cost is measured as :

$$\frac{\text{Purchase Price of Stock} - \text{Market Price}}{\text{Market Price}} \times 100$$

   Purchase price of the stock involves transaction costs. Higher the difference between purchase price and market price of the stock, higher will be the impact cost.
2. **Diversification :** Index should be will diversified *i.e.* reflect the economy by having a balanced representation of all sectors.
3. **Optimum Size :** The Index should not be too small as it will not represent the market properly, on the other hand it should not be too big otherwise it may include ill-liquid stocks in it.
4. **Market Capitalization :** The Index should include the stocks of companies that have significant market capitalization with respect to the index such that any change in the price of the stock is reflected in the Index.

5. **Averaging :** Index movement occurs due to news about the company and about the economy. The Index must be averaged so as to reduce the impact of company news and is affected only due to changes in economy.

METHODS OF INDEX CONSTRUCTION

1. **Price Weighted Method :** It is the ratio of sum of prices of certain shares in a certain year (or month or week or day) with reference to base year. For example. if Index comprises of 5 stocks

	Price in Base Year	Price in Current Year
X	40	60
Y	55	78
Z	72	100
M	30	55
N	65	80
Total	262	373

Then Price Index is given as:

$$\frac{373 \times 100}{262} = 142.36$$

It is based on the assumption that investors buy one share of each stock included in the Index.

2. **Equal Weighted Index :** It is the ratio of the sum of relative prices of shares in the current year with reference to the base year. For example considering the above case.

Relative Price in current year =

X	60 x 100 / 40	=	150.00
Y	78 x 100 / 55	=	141.81
Z	100 x 100 / 72	=	138.88
M	55 x 100 / 30	=	183.33
N	80 x 100 / 65	=	123.07
	Total	=	737.09
	EWI = 737.09 x 100 / 500	=	147.41

It is assumed that investors assign equal weights to all the stocks included in the Index.

3. **Value Weighted Index/Market Capitalization Weighted Index :** It is the ratio of aggregate market capitalization in current year to the aggregate market capitalization in the base year. This can be shown as:

Price in Base Year (Rs.)	Price in Current Year (Rs.)	No. of Ordinary Share Outstanding (Rs. mm)	Market Capital in Current Year (Rs. mn)	Market Capital in Base Year (Rs. mn)
(1)	(2)	(3)	(2 x 3)	(1 x 3)
40	60	15	900	600
55	78	10	780	550
72	100	25	2500	1800
30	55	12	660	360
65	80	20	1600	1300
			6440	**4610**

Value Weighted = 6440 / 4610 = 139.69

POPULAR INDIAN INDEXES

1. **NSE's S & P CNX Nifty :** It is a value weighted index comprised of 50 stocks with base period as the closing price of November 3, 1995 and base value of Index as 1000.
2. **BSE Sensex-Bombay Stock Exchange Sensitive Index :** It comprises 30 shares and is a value weighted index with base period as 1978-79 w.e.f. Sept 1, 2003 the free float, government and promoter holdings as well as locked-in-shares are excluded for calculating market capitalization of the companies and this is called Free Float Cap. Weighing.
3. **The Economic Times Index of Ordinary Share Prices :** It is an Equal Weighted Index comprising of 72 shares with a base year of 1984-85.
4. **The Financial Express Equity Index :** It comprises of 100 actively traded shares with base year as 1979. It is a value weighted index.

MAJOR U.S. INDEXES

1. **Dow Jones Indexes**

   (*a*) Dow Jones Industrial Average Index comprising of 30 stocks, current Divisor value is 0.12560864.

   (*b*) Dow Jones Transportation Index with 20 stocks. Its current divisor value is 0.23720855.

   (*c*) Dow Jones Utility Index with 15 stocks. Its current divisor value is 1.5940823.

   All of these are price weighted indices.
2. **NYSE Composite Index :** It comprises of 2,100 stocks and calculated as Price Weighted Index with a base value of 5000.
3. **NASDAQ (National Association of Stock Dealers Automated Quotations) :** It is a market value weighted index. It is a floorless exchange. NASDAQ Indexes are calculated as:

$$\text{NASDAQ Index Level} = \frac{\text{Current Market Value}}{\text{Adjusted Based Period Market Value}} \times \text{Base Value}$$

$$\text{Where Adjusted Base Period Market Value} = \frac{\text{CMVAA}}{\text{CMVBP}} = \text{PBPMV}$$

CMVAA = Current Market Value after Adjustments

CMVBA = Current Market Value before Adjustment

PBPMV = Provision Base Period Market Value

Major NASDAQ Indices are —

- NASDAQ : 100 Index which includes 100 largest domestic and non-financial companies with a base value equal to A 125.
- NASDAQ : 100 Equal Weighted Index, Base value equal to 1000 and same securities as NASDAQ 100 but weight of 1% of the Index.
- NASDAQ Financial 100 Index containing 100 domestic and international financial companies having a base value equal to 250.
- NASDAQ Biotechnology Index, comprising pharmaceutical and biotech firms and having base value equal to 200.
- NASDAQ Composite Index consisting of all domestic and international based common type stocks of 3000 companies and a base value of 100.
- NASDAQ National Market Composite Index value which is a subset of NASDAQ Composite Index and has a base, of 100.

Others:

- NASDAQ Computer Index
- NASDAQ Health Care Index
- NASDAQ Industrial Index
- NASDAQ National Market Industrial Index
- NASDAQ Insurance Index
- NASDAQ Other Finance Index
- NASDAQ Telecommunication Index
- NASDAQ Transportation Index

4. **Standard's and Poor's**

Major S and Ps Indices are

- S&P 500 Index
- S&P 100 Index
- S&P 400 Mid Cap Index
- S&P 600 Small Cap Index
- S&P 1500 Super Composite Index

These are calculated by Free Float Methodology and Equal Weighted Methodology.

Other Popular Indices and their countries :

- FTSE – London
- KOSPI – Korea
- NIKKEI – Japan
- HENG SENG – Hong Kong
- Street Times – Singapore

ADVANTAGES OF STOCK EXCHANGES

1. Increased Liquidity of Securities : They provide increased liquidity to securities by facilitating their buying and selling and hence increase the marketability of securities.
2. They increase savings and investment in the economy.
3. They help in ensuring flow of money from spenders to borrowers.
4. They reflect the performance of industry and economy.
5. They are a means of getting foreign investment in the country and hence a source of foreign funds.
6. They provide a significant alternative investment avenue for portfolio creation and diversification.
7. They lead to flow of money into profitable channels.

TYPES OF BROKERS IN A STOCK EXCHANGE

The following are the kinds of brokers operating in a stock exchange :

1. **Jobbers or Tarawanwiwallas :** These brokers are also called Market Makers in London Stock Exchange and Specialists in New York Stock Exchange while in India they are popular as Jobbers. Jobbers give two way quotes or prices at which they are ready to buy a security as well as selling quote or price at which they are ready to sell the same security. Both the quotes are given by the Jobber to sell or buy in his own name. So a Jobber buys or sells securities in his own name and earns a profit margin in turn. He specializes in a few securities and does not get any commission as he operates on his own behalf. A Jobber may strike a deal with a broker operating on behalf of a client or another Jobber. In BSE every company with a market capitalization greater than 3 crores must appoint a Jobber to increase market liquidity of its stocks.
2. **Commission Brokers :** They are simply brokers who operate on behalf of their clients *i.e.* buy and sell securities not on their behalf (as a Jobber) but on behalf of their clients. A broker on getting order from the client executes it on behalf of the client and settles the deal. He charges a commission for this purpose and this may range from 0.75% to 1%.
3. **Sub-Brokers :** As broker cannot be present everywhere so on behalf of these sub-brokers deal with the clients. So these sub-brokers bring the clients in contact of the broker. But they cannot buy or sell securities on clients' behalf. They are registered with stock exchange. They charge commission for bringing the client in contact of the broker and this commission is paid

out of the commission received by the broker from the client. However, the maximum commission received by a sub-broker can be 40% of the total commission paid by the client.

4. **Authorized Clerks :** They are appointed by a broker to act on his behalf in his absence. So they have the power of attorney and can sign documents or buy and sell shares on broker's behalf and in his absence. Brokers are liable for any action of the authorized clerks and have to pay entrance as well as annual subscription fee for them. He can also remove them at any time after prior information to the exchange.

TRADING MECHANISM ON A STOCK EXCHANGE

The following are the steps of buying and selling securities on a stock exchange –

1. **Choice of a Broker :** An individual buys or sells securities directly so he/she has to appoint a broker for this purpose. The broker may be chosen on the basis of accessibility, references, repute etc.
2. **Placement of Order :** Once a broker has been appointed next step is to place an order with him for buying/selling securities.

The various types of orders are :

1. **Market Order :** It is an order to buy a certain number of securities at the best prevailing market price within a certain time period. For *e.g.* "Buy 100 CIPLA at best".
2. **Limit Order :** It is an order for purchase or sale of securities at a fixed price *i.e.* the client places a price limit which should not be crossed *e.g.* "Buy 100 CIPLA @ Rs.150".
3. **Discretionary Order :** Here the client leaves the decision to buy/sell at the discretion of the broker *i.e.,* whatever time and price he thinks the best.
4. **Immediate or Cancel Order** *i.e.,* to buy/sell securities immediately quoted prices or cancel the order *e.g.* Buy 100 CIPLA @ 150 immediately.
5. **Stop Loss Order :** It is an order to buy as soon as the price of securities rises to a particular level and sell as soon as it falls to a particular level to avoid any loss.

As soon as the order is place, it is recorded in an 'Order Book'.

3. **Execution of Order :** After the order is entered matching bids are required. The buying and selling bids should match the order to be executed. The buyer and seller may negotiate with each other and come to a mutually agreed price acceptable to both. As soon as order is executed a confirmation memo is prepared and given to the client.
4. **Preparation of Contract Note :** After issue of confirmation memo, a contract note is signed between the broker and the client stating the transaction fees (commission of broker), number of shares bought or sold, price at which they are brought or sold etc.
5. **Settlement of Transaction :** Earlier there was a system of account settlement in which settlement cycle was 'T+7' or weekly settlement cycle which was Monday to Friday in BSE & Wednesday to Tuesday in NSE. But now both the exchanges have entered into compulsory rolling settlement which is 'T+2' cycle of settlement.

The Cycle is –

T – Day of trade

T+1 – Confirmation of order, preparation of contract note

T+2 – Pay-in / Pay-out

T+3 – Auction for shortages

T+4 – ********

T+5 – Pay-in/Pay-out of auctioned securities

6. **Transfer of Ownership :** Once the trading is complete the buyer holds the possession of securities given by the seller along with a transfer deed which specifies the number of shares to be transferred in the buyer's name. The buyer then lodges these shares with the Registrar and Transfer Agent of the company and then requisite action is taken to transfer the shares in the name of the buyer.

Internet Trading : Since June 2000, internet trading has gained popularity over physical trading. For the purpose of internet trading a brokerage firm provides a platform *e.g.* ICICI securities, KOTAK MAHINDRA.

A unique 'User ID' and password is given to the client and the client has to open a cash account and DEMAT account with the firm. Quotes can be put by the client using the ID and password and then as soon as the order is confirmed and finalized, cash or securities are debited or credited from the respective accounts.

Carry Forward/Badla : Badla or carry forward is a deal between the Bull and the Bear in which the bull asks the Bear to carry forward the settlement of securities to the next cycle. Bull may buy securities in anticipation of price rise but the price may not actually rise towards the end of settlement cycle. So he may enter into an agreement with the seller to delay the settlement till the next cycle. For this he pays an interest on the amount due to the seller or badla financer.

In case the transaction is initiated from seller's side, it is called 'ulta badla' or 'backwardation'.

Badla was allowed till 1993 but in Jan 1994 it was banned by SEBI. Later in 1994 (March), SEBI received a proposal to modify Badla but it rejected the same. In February 1995 a three member committee was appointed by SEBI to review Badla and its report was submitted in 1997. According to the report carry forward or Badla is allowed only till 90 days. After the 75th day it was necessary to take delivery of shares. Total value of transaction per broker in the settlement badla cannot exceed Rs.20 crore. Although the stocks in which badla is allowed was to be decided by exchange, however, SEBI has laid restrictions that this trading should be done only in liquid stocks.

Risk Management : The various margins are required to be deposited with the broker to ensure liquidity and safety of trades in the market. It helps in reducing speculative transactions and liquidity.

INSIDER TRADING

Insider trading may be defined as the trading of a company's shares or other securities (*e.g.,* bonds or stock options) by corporate insiders such as officers, key employees, directors, or holders of more than ten per cent of the firm's shares.

Insider trading is believed to lead some persons to make extra gains in stock market through use of some information like information on expected dividends, expected decline or rise in profits, any information on merger, acquisition, potential threats etc or any other price-sensitive information.

Hence, insider trading is considered illegal.Illegal insider- trading in India includes an insider giving advice or tip to any outsider about such price-sensitive information.

INSIDER DEFINED

An insider is a person who is or was connected to the company and who is reasonably expected to have access to unpublished price-sensitive information in respect to the securities of that company.

"Price-sensitive information" has been defined as periodical financial results of companies, dividend declaration, issue or buy-back of securities, any major expansion plans or execution of new projects, amalgamation, mergers or takeovers, disposal of whole or substantial part of undertaking and significant changes in policies, plans or operations of the company.

Despite the existence of the detailed regulation, the stock prices of a company invariably tend to move up or down at least a couple of weeks ahead of any price-sensitive announcement.

Should Insider Trading be Stopped?

The prevention of insider trading is gaining wide significance in securities regulation. In United States, regulators appear to devote significant resources in fighting against insider trading. This has led the regulators in India to believe that the prohibition of insider trading is an important function. In most countries other than the US, government actions against insider trading are much more limited.

The ideal securities market is one which efficiently allocates capital in the economy. Market efficiency is the situation where the market price of each security accurately reflects the risk and return in its future *i.e.,* all information is freely available to everybody. The primary function of regulation and policy is to promote market efficiency, hence to find out whether insider trading should be stopped, we must evaluate the impact of insider trading upon market efficiency.

It is well established that when company insiders trade on the secondary market, they speed up the flow of information and forecasts into prices. Company insiders are in a unique position to make forecasts about the future risk and return of the shares and bonds of their company, hence they might often correctly perceive market prices to be "too low" or "too high".

Insider trading is different from market manipulation. Manipulation is about making market prices move *away* from their fair values; manipulators *reduce* market efficiency. Insider trading brings prices *closer* to their fair values; insiders *enhance* market efficiency.

Insider trading *appears* unfair, especially to speculators outside a company who face difficult competition from inside traders. Individual speculators and fund managers are able to get inferior returns when markets are more efficient owing to the actions of inside traders. Insider trading hurts individual and institutional speculators.

For example, If we consider two countries with different policy regimes. In country A, insider trading is instantly detected and severally punished, hence it is essentially absent. In country B, insider trading is free. How would price formation on the two islands differ?

In country B, insiders would play a major role in price discovery. Individual and institutional speculators would find it very difficult to compete, and they would settle into passive strategies like owning index funds. In country A, in the absence of insider trading, market inefficiencies would flourish, which would attract significant resources into research and speculation by both individuals and institutions.

From this analysis, it can be said that through insider trading the monopoly of outside speculators in exploiting market inefficiencies gets finished. It appears that both countries can achieve the desired outcome, *i.e.,* a state of market efficiency. Country A uses greater human resources on research and speculation as compared with country B, where these resources become available for other purposes. Hence the insider trading approach is probably a preferable way for an economy to obtain efficient markets at the minimum cost.

From this viewpoint, the State could enhance market efficiency by imposing a *reporting* requirement. Since trades by insiders are unusually informative, it would help market efficiency if these were required to be rapidly disclosed. The price, quantity and identity of the insider should be revealed shortly after a trade is consummated.

Given the higher degree of automation of the Indian markets, it is not difficult to imagine a situation where trades by insiders are disclosed to the market within five minutes of the trade being matched by the computer. Such a reporting requirement would harness the informational potential of insider trading, and enhance market efficiency by speeding up the full impact of the trade upon market prices.

Looking at the *Cost-benefit analysis of inside trading* even if restrictions on insider trading were considered desirable, their sound implementation is extremely expensive. A wide variety of individuals can be classed as insiders by virtue of possessing information material to securities prices — top management, upstream and downstream producers, regulatory and enforcement authorities, professional advisors, etc. Further, the number of persons through whom insiders could route their trades is very large — family, friends, business associates who are "paid" in information, etc. Enforcement of restrictions upon insider trading runs the risk of either being ineffective. Even if there are high quality restrictions, they would not appear fair in an environment where insider trading is otherwise uncontrolled. Even in the US, where significant resources have been expended on preventing insider trading, there is subjective evidence that a great deal of successful speculation continues based on insider trading.

Hence, if we view securities regulation in terms of maximising the impact upon market efficiency given a scarce supply of regulation and supervision, then insider trading would be a low priority.

The insider trading guidelines given by SEBI in 1992 are enclosed herewith in *APPENDIX.*

QUESTIONS

Fill in the Blanks:

1. Four players in secondary market are _________,_______,________and__________.
2. Stock index is a representative of __________and__________ of various companies listed on the stock exchanges.
3. The facility to carry forward a transaction from one settlement period to another is known as ______________.
4. A person appointed by a stock broker to assist him in a business of securities is called _____.
5. _______ give two way quotes in the secondary market.
6. The order to buy certain no. of securities at the best prevailing market price within a certain time period is called ___________.
7. Liquidity of stocks in an Index is measured by __________ criterion.
8. _______ is a person who is or was connected to the company and who is reasonably expected to have access to unpublished price-sensitive information in respect to the securities of that company.

State whether true or false:

1. Stock Index measures the general movement of the market.
2. Carry forward transactions are facilitated by Badlawalas.
3. There are 24 recognised stock exchanges in India.
4. Economic Times Index is a Value Weighted Index.
5. Currently settlement cycle of stocks is T+2 cycle.
6. Insider trading is an evil in stock markets.

Answer in detail:

Q.1. What are the determinants of Stock Index and how are the various Indexes constructed?

Q.2. Discuss the trading mechanism on a stock exchange.

Q.3. What is carry forward and how is it done? What are the present regulations laid down by SEBI for carry forward of transactions?

Q.4. Should Insider trading be stopped? Why or why not?

❑❑❑

APPENDIX

SECURITIES AND EXCHANGE BOARD OF INDIA ([1][PROHIBITION OF] INSIDER TRADING) REGULATIONS, 1992

In exercise of the powers conferred by Section 30 of the Securities and Exchange Board of India Act, 1992 (15 of 1992), the Board, with the previous approval of the Central Government, hereby makes the following regulations, namely:—

CHAPTER 1

PRELIMINARY

Short title and commencement

1. (1) These regulations may be called the Securities and Exchange Board of India ([2][Prohibition of] Insider Trading) Regulations, 1992.

(2) These regulations shall come into force on the date of their publication in the Official[3] Gazette.

Definitions

2. In these regulations, unless the context otherwise requires:—

(*a*) "Act" means the Securities and Exchange Board of India Act, 1992 (15 of 1992);

(*b*) "body corporate" means a body corporate as defined in section 2 of the Companies Act, 1956 (1 of 1956);

(*c*) "connected person" means any person who—

(*i*) is a director, as defined in clause (13) of section 2 of the Companies Act, 1956 (1 of 1956), of a company, or is deemed to be a director of that company by virtue of sub-clause (10) of Section 307 of that Act; or

(*ii*) occupies the position as an officer or an employee of the company or holds a position

---

1 *Inserted by the SEBI (Insider Trading) (Amendment) Regulations,* 2002,*w.e.f.* 20.02.2002.

2 *Ibid.*

3 19.11.1992.

involving a professional or business relationship between himself and the company [4][whether temporary or permanent] and who may reasonably be expected to have an access to unpublished price sensitive information in relation to that company. [5][*Explanation* :— For the purpose of clause (*c*), the words "connected person" shall [6][mean] any person who is a connected person six months prior to an act of insider trading;]

(*d*) "dealing in securities" means an act of [7][subscribing,] buying, selling or agreeing to [8][subscribe,] buy, sell or deal in any securities by any person either as principal or agent

(*e*) "insider" means any person who, is or was connected with the company or is deemed to have been connected with the company, and who is reasonably expected to have access [9][***] to unpublished price sensitive information in respect of securities of [10][*a*] company, or who has received or has had access to such unpublished price sensitive information;

(*f*) "investigating authority" means any officer of the Board or any other person, not being a firm, body corporate or an association of persons, having experience in dealing with the problems relating to the securities market and who is authorised by the Board under Chapter III;

(*g*) "officer of a company" means any person as defined in clause (30) of Section 2 of the Companies Act, 1956 (1 of 1956) including an auditor of the company;

(*h*) "person is deemed to be a connected person", if such person—

(*i*) is a company under the same management or group, or any subsidiary company thereof within the meaning of sub-section (1B) of Section 370, or sub-section (11) of Section 372, of the Companies Act, 1956 (1 of 1956), or sub-clause (*g*) of Section 2 of the Monopolies and Restrictive Trade Practices Act, 1969 (54 of 1969), as the case may be;

[11][(*ii*) is an intermediary as specified in Section 12 of the Act, Investment company, Trustee Company, Asset Management Company or an employee or director thereof or an official of a stock exchange or of clearing house or corporation;]

(*iii*) is a merchant banker, share transfer agent, registrar to an issue, debenture trustee, broker, portfolio manager, Investment Advisor, sub-broker, Investment Company or an employee thereof, or, is a member of the Board of Trustees of a mutual fund or a member of the Board of Directors of the Asset Management Company of a mutual fund or is an employee thereof who has a fiduciary relationship with the company;

---

4 Ibid.

5 *Ibid.*

6 Substituted for "include" by the SEBI (Prohibition of Insider Trading) (Second Amendment) Regulations, 2002, w.e.f. 29.11.2002.

7 Inserted by the SEBI (Insider Trading) (Amendment) Regulations, 2002,w.e.f. 20.02.2002.

8 *Ibid.*

9 Words, "by virtue of such connection", omitted, *ibid.*

10 Substitued for "the", *ibid.*

11 Substituted, *ibid.* Prior to its substitution,sub-clause (ii) read as under:

" (ii) is an official or a member of a stock exchange or of a clearing house of that stock exchange, or a dealer in securities within the meaning of clause (c) of Section 2, and Section 17 of the Securities Contracts (Regulation) Act, 1956 (42 of 1956) respectively or any employee of such member or dealer of a stock-exchange;"

(*iv*) is a Member of the Board of Directors, or an employee, of a public financial institution as defined in Section 4A of the Companies Act, 1956;

(*v*) is an official or an employee of a Self-regulatory Organisation recognised or authorised by the Board of a regulatory body;

(*vi*) is a relative of any of the aforementioned persons;

(*vii*) is a banker of the company;

[12][(*viii*) relatives of the connected person; or

[13][(*ix*) is a concern, firm, trust, Hindu undivided family, company or association of persons wherein any of the connected persons mentioned in sub-clause (*i*) of clause (*c*), of this regulation or any of the persons mentioned in sub-clause (*vi*), (*vii*) or (*viii*) of this clause have more than 10 per cent of the holding or interest;]]

[14][(*ha*) "price sensitive information" means any information which relates directly or indirectly to a company and which if published is likely to materially affect the price of securities of company.

Explanation : The following shall be deemed to be price sensitive information :—

(*i*) periodical financial results of the company;

(*ii*) intended declaration of dividends (both interim and final);

(*iii*) issue of securities or buy-back of securities;

(*iv*) any major expansion plans or execution of new projects;

(*v*) amalgamation, mergers or takeovers;

(*vi*) disposal of the whole or substantial part of the undertaking; and

(*vii*) significant changes in policies, plans or operations of the company;]

(*i*) "relative" means a person, as defined in Section 6 of the Companies Act, 1956 (1 of 1956);

(*j*) "stock exchange" means a stock exchange which is recognised by the Central Government [15][or Securities and Exchange Board of India] under Section 4 of Securities Contracts (Regulation) Act, 1956 (42 of 1956);

---

12 Inserted by the SEBI (Insider Trading) (Amendment) Regulations, 2002, w.e.f. 20.02.2002.

13 Substituted, by the SEBI (Prohibition of Insider Trading)(Second Amendment)Regulations,2002, w.e.f. 29-11-2002. Earlier it was inserted by the SEBI (Insider Trading) (Amendment) Regulations,2002, w.e.f. 20-02-2002. Prior to its substitution, sub-clause(ix)read as under:

"a concern, firm, trust, Hindu undivided family, company, association of persons wherein the relatives of persons mentioned in sub-clauses (vi),(vii) and (viii) has more than 10 percent of holding interest;"

14 Inserted by the SEBI (Insider Trading) (Amendment) Regulations, 2002, w.e.f. 20.02.2002.

15 Inserted, *ibid.*

[16][(*k*) "unpublished" means information which is not published by the company or its agents and is not specific in nature.

Explanation.— Speculative reports in print or electronic media shall not be considered as published information.]

---

16 Substituted, *ibid*, Prior to its substitution, clause (k) read as under:

'(k) "unpublished price sensitive information" means any information which relates to the following matters or is of concern, directly or indirectly, to a company, and is not generally known or published by such company for general information, but which if published or known, is likely to materially affect the price of securities of that company in the market –

(*i*) financial results (both half-yearly and annual) of the company:

(*ii*) intended declaration of dividends (both interim and final);

(*iii*) issue of shares by way of public rights, bonus, etc.;

(*iv*) any major expansion plans or execution of new projects;

(*v*) amalgamation, mergers and take-overs;

(*vi*) disposal of the whole or substantially the whole of the undertaking;

(*vii*) such other information as may affect the earnings of the company.

(*viii*) any changes in policies, plans or operations of the company.

CHAPTER II

PROHIBITION ON DEALING, COMMUNICATING OR COUNSELLING

Prohibition on dealing, communicating or counselling on matters relating to insider trading.

3. No insider shall—

(*i*) either on his own behalf or on behalf of any other person, deal in securities of a company listed on any stock exchange [17][when in possession of] any unpublished price sensitive information; or

[18] [(*ii*) communicate counsel or procure directly or indirectly any unpublished price sensitive information to any person who while in possession of such unpublished price sensitive information shall not deal in securities :

Provided that nothing contained above shall be applicable to any communication required in the ordinary course of business [19][or profession or employment] or under any law.]

[20][***]

[21][**3A.** No company shall deal in the securities of another company or associate of that other company while in possession of any unpublished price sensitive information.]

[22][**Regulation 3A not to apply in certain cases.**

3B. (1) In a proceeding against a company in respect of Regulation 3A, it shall be a defence to prove that it entered into a transaction in the securities of a listed company when the unpublished price sensitive information was in the possession of an officer or employee of the company, if:

(*a*) the decision to enter into the transaction or agreement was taken on its behalf by a person or persons other than that officer or employee; and

---

17 Substituted for "on the basis of", *ibid.*

18 Substituted by the SEBI (Insider Trading) (Amendment) Regulations, 2002, w.e.f.20.2.2002. Prior to substitution, clause (ii) read as under:

"(ii) communicate any unpublished price sensitive information to any person, with or without his request for such information, except as required in the ordinary course of business or under any law; or"

19 Inserted by the SEBI (Prohibition of Insider Trading) (Second Amendment) Regulations, 2002, w.e.f. 29.11.2002.

20 Omitted by the SEBI (Insider Trading) (Amendment) Regulations, 2002, w.e.f. 20.02.2002. Prior to its omission clause (iii) read as under:

"(iii) counsel or procure any other person to deal in securities of any company on the basis of unpublished price sensitive information."

21 Inserted, *ibid.*

22 Inserted by SEBI (Prohibition of Insider Trading) (Second Amendment) Regulations, 2002, w.e.f. 29.11.2002.

(*b*) such company has put in place such systems and procedures which demarcate the activities of the company in such a way that the person who enters into transaction in securities on behalf of the company cannot have access to information which is in possession of other officer or employee of the company; and

(*c*) it had in operation at that time, arrangements that could reasonably be expected to ensure that the information was not communicated to the person or persons who made the decision and that no advice with respect to the transactions or agreement was given to that person or any of those persons by that officer or employee; and

(*d*) the information was not so communicated and no such advice was so given.

(2) In a proceeding against a company in respect of Regulation 3A which is in possession of unpublished price sensitive information, it shall be defence to prove that acquisition of shares of a listed company was as per the Securities and Exchange Board of India (Substantial Acquisition of Shares and Takeovers) Regulations, 1997.]

Violation of provisions relating to insider trading.

4. Any insider who deals in securities [23][***] in contravention of the provisions of Regulation 3 [24][or 3A] shall be guilty of insider trading.

[23] Words "or communicate any information or counsels any person dealing in securities" omitted by the SEBI (Insider Trading) (Amendment) Regulations, 2002, w.e.f. 20.2.2002.

[24] Inserted, *ibid.*

CHAPTER III

INVESTIGATION

[25][**Power to make inquiries and inspection.**

4. (1) If the Board suspects that any person has violated any provision of these regulations, it may make inquiries with such persons or any other person as mentioned in clause (*i*) of sub-section (2) of Section 11 as deemed fit, to form a *prima facie* opinion as to whether there is any violation of these regulations.

(2) The Board may appoint one or more officers to inspect the books and records of insider(s) or any other persons as mentioned in clause (*i*) of sub-section (2) of Section 11 for the purpose of sub-regulation (1).]

Board's right to investigate.

5. (1) Where the Board, [26][is of *prima facie*] opinion that it is necessary to investigate and inspect the books of account, either records and documents of an insider [27][or any other person mentioned in clause (*i*) of sub-section (1) of Section 11 of the Act] for any of the purposes specified in sub-regulation (2), it may appoint an investigating authority for the said purpose.

(2) The purpose referred to in sub-regulation (1) may be as follows :

(*a*) to investigate into the complaints received from investors, intermediaries or any other person on any matter having a bearing on the allegations of insider trading; and

(*b*) to investigate *suo motu* upon its own knowledge or information in its possession to protect the interest of investors in securities against breach of these regulations.

Procedure for investigation.

6. (1) Before undertaking any investigation under Regulation 5, the Board shall give a reasonable notice to insider for that purpose.

(2) Notwithstanding anything contained in sub-regulation (1), where the Board is satisfied that in the interest of investors or in public interest no such notice should be given, it may by an order in writing direct that the investigation be taken up without such notice.

(3) On being empowered by the Board, the investigating authority shall undertake the investigation and inspection of books of account and the insider against whom an investigation is being carried out [28][an insider or any other person mentioned in clause (*i*) of sub-section (1) of Section 11 of the Act] shall be bound to discharge his obligations as provided in regulation 7.

---

[25] Inserted by the SEBI (Insider Trading) (Amendment) Regulations, 2002, w.e.f. 20.02.2002.

[26] Substituted for "on the basis of written information in its possession is of the ", *ibid.*

[27] Inserted, *ibid.*

[28] Inserted by the SEBI (Insider Trading) (Amendment) Regulations, 2002, w.e.f. 20.02.2002.

Obligations of insider on investigation by the Board.

7. (1) It shall be the duty of every insider, who is being investigated [29][or any other person mentioned in clause (*i*) of sub-section (1) of Section 11 of the Act], to produce to the investigating authority such books, accounts and other documents in his custody or control and furnish the authority with the statements and information relating to the transactions in securities market within such time as the said authority may require.

(2) The insider [30][or any other person mentioned in clause (*i*) of sub-section (2) of Section 11 of the Act] shall allow the investigating authority to have reasonable access to the premises occupied by such insider and also extend reasonable facility for examining any books, records, documents and computer data in the possession of the stock-broker or any other person and also provide copies of documents or other materials which, in the opinion of the investigating authority are relevant.

(3) The investigating authority, in the course of investigation, shall be entitled to examine or record statements of any member, director, partner, proprietor and employee of the insider [31][or any other person mentioned in clause (*i*) of sub-section (2) of Section 11 of the Act].

(4) It shall be the duty of every director, proprietor, partner, officer and employee of the insider to give to the investigating authority all assistance in connection with the investigation, which the insider [32][or any other person mentioned in clause (*i*) of sub-section (2) of Section 11 of the Act] may be reasonably expected to give.

Submission of Report to the Board.

8. The investigating authority shall, within [33][reasonable time] of the conclusion of the investigation, submit an investigation report to the Board.

Communications of findings, etc.

9. [34][(1) The Board shall, after consideration of the investigation report communicate the findings to the person suspected to be involved in insider trading or violation of these regulations.

(2) The person to whom such findings has been communicated shall reply to the same within 21 days.

(3) On receipt of such a reply or explanation, if any, from such person, the Board may take such measures as it deems fit to protect the interests of the investors and in the interests

---

29 Inserted, *ibid.*

30 Inserted, *ibid.*

31 Inserted by the SEBI (Insider Trading) (Amendment) Regulations, 2002, w.e.f. 20.02.2002.

32 *Ibid.*

33 Substituted for "one month" by the SEBI (Insider Trading) (Amendment) Regulations, 2002, w.e.f. 20.02.2002.

34 Substituted, *ibid.* Prior to their substitution, sub-regulations (1) and (2) read as under:

"(1) The Board shall after consideration of the investigation report communicate the findings to the insider and he shall be given an opportunity of being heard before any action is taken by the Board on the findings of the investigating authority.

(2) On receipt of the explanation, if any, from the insider, the Board may call upon the insider to take such measures as the Board may deem fit to protect the interest of investors and in the interest of the securities market and for due compliance with the provisions of the Act, rules made thereunder and these regulations."

of the securities market and for the due compliance of the [35][provisions] of the Act, the regulations made thereunder including the issue of directions under Regulation 11.]

Appointment of Auditor.

10. Notwithstanding anything contained in [36][Regulation 4A and] Regulation 5, the Board may appoint a qualified auditor to investigate into the books of account or the affairs of the insider [37][or any other person mentioned in clause (*i*) of sub-section (1) of Section 11 of the Act]:

Provided that, the auditor so appointed shall have the same powers of the inspecting authority as stated in Regulation 5 and the insider shall have the obligations specified in Regulation 7.

[38][Directions by the Board.

11. The Board may without prejudice to its right to initiate criminal prosecution under Section 24 or any action under Chapter VIA of the Act, to protect the interests of investor and in the interests of the securities market and for due compliance with the provisions of the Act, regulation made thereunder issue any or all of the following order, namely :

(*a*) directing the insider or such person as mentioned in clause (*i*) of sub-section (2) of Section 11 of the Act not to deal in securities in any particular manner;

(*b*) prohibiting the insider or such person as mentioned in clause (*i*) of sub-section (2) of Section 11 of the Act from disposing of any of the securities acquired in violation of these regulations;

(*c*) restraining the insider to communicate or counsel any person to deal in securities;

(*d*) declaring the transaction(s) in securities as null and void;

(*e*) directing the person who acquired the securities in violation of these regulations to deliver the securities back to the seller :

Provided that in case the buyer is not in a position to deliver such securities, the market price prevailing at the time of issuing of such directions or at the time of transactions whichever is higher, shall be paid to the seller;

(*f*) directing the person who has dealt in securities in violation of these regulations to transfer an amount or proceeds equivalent to the cost price or market price of securities, whichever is higher to the investor protection fund of a recognised stock exchange.]

---

35 Substituted for "province" by the SEBI (Prohibition of Insider Trading) (Second Amendment) Regulations, 2002, w.e.f. 29.11.2002.

36 Inserted by the SEBI (Insider Trading) (Amendment) Regulations, 2002, w.e.f. 20.02.2002.

37 *ibid.*

38 Substituted by the SEBI (Insider Trading) (Amendment) Regulations, 2002, w.e.f. 20.02.2002. Prior to its substitution, regulation 11 read as under:

"11.On receipt of the explanation, if any, from the insider under sub-regulation (2) of Regulation 9, the Board may without prejudice to its right to initiate criminal prosecution under Section 24 of the Act, give such directions to protect the interest of investors and in the interest of the securities market and for due compliance with the provisions of the Act, rules made thereunder and these regulations, as it deems fit for all or any of the following purposes, namely :

(*a*) directing the insider not to deal in securities in any particular manner;

(*b*) prohibiting the insider from disposing of any of the securities acquired in violation of these regulations;

(*c*) restraining the insider to communicate or counsel any person to deal in securities."

[39]CHAPTER IV

POLICY ON DISCLOSURES AND INTERNAL PROCEDURE FOR PREVENTION OF INSIDER TRADING

Code of internal procedures and conduct for listed companies and other entities

12. (1) All listed companies and organisations associated with securities markets including :

(*a*) the intermediaries as mentioned in Section 12 of the Act, asset management company and trustees of mutual funds;

(*b*) the self-regulatory organisations recognised or authorised by the Board;

(*c*) the recognised stock exchanges and clearing house or corporations;

(*d*) the public financial institutions as defined in Section 4A of the Companies Act, 1956; and

(*e*) the professional firms such as auditors, accountancy firms, law firms, analysts, consultants, etc., assisting or advising listed companies, shall frame a code of internal procedures and conduct as near thereto the Model Code specified in Schedule I of these Regulations.

(2) The entities mentioned in sub-regulation (1), shall abide by the code of Corporate Disclosure Practices as specified in Schedule II of these Regulations.

(3) All entities mentioned in sub-regulation (1), shall adopt appropriate mechanisms and procedures to enforce the codes specified under sub-regulations (1) and (2).

(4) Action taken by the entities mentioned in sub-regulation (1) against any person for violation of the code under sub-regulation (3) shall not preclude the Board from initiating proceedings for violation of these Regulations.

Disclosure of interest or holding by directors and officers and substantial shareholders in a listed companies - Initial Disclosure.

13. (1) Any person who holds more than 5% shares or voting rights in any listed company shall disclose to the company [40][in Form A], the number of shares or voting rights held by such person, on becoming such holder, within 4 working days of —

[39] Inserted by the SEBI (Insider Trading) (Amendment) Regulations, 2002, w.e.f. 20.02.2002.

[40] Inserted by the SEBI (Insider Trading) (Amendment) Regulations, 2003, w.e.f. 11.7.2003.

(*a*) the receipt of intimation of allotment of shares; or

(*b*) the acquisition of shares or voting rights, as the case may be.

(2) Any person who is a director or officer of a listed company, shall disclose to the company [41][in Form B], the number of shares or voting rights held by such person, within 4 working days of becoming a director or officer of the company.

Continual disclosure

(3) Any person who holds more than 5% shares for voting rights in any listed company shall disclose to the company [42][in Form C] the number of shares or voting rights held and change in shareholding or voting rights, even if such change results in shareholding falling below 5%, if there has been change in such holdings from the last disclosure made under sub-regulation (1) or under this sub-regulation; and such change exceeds 2% of total shareholding or voting rights in the company.

(4) Any person who is a director or officer of a listed company, shall disclose to the company [43][in Form D], the total number of shares or voting rights held and change in shareholding or voting rights, if there has been a change in such holdings from the last disclosure made under sub-regulation (2) or under this sub-regulation, and the change exceeds Rs. 5 lakh in value or [44][25,000] shares or [45][1%] of total shareholding or voting rights, whichever is lower.

(5) The disclosure mentioned in sub-regulations (3) and (4) shall be made within 4 working days of :

(*a*) the receipts of intimation of allotment of shares, or

(*b*) the acquisition or sale of shares or voting rights, as the case may be.

Disclosure by company to stock exchanges

(6) Every listed company, within five days of receipt, shall disclose to all stock exchanges on which the company is listed, the information received under sub-regulations (1), (2), (3) and (4) [46][in the respective formats specified in Schedule III.]

---

40 Inserted by the SEBI (Insider Trading) (Amendment) Regulations, 2003, w.e.f. 11.7.2003.

41 *Ibid.*

42 *Ibid.*

43 *Ibid.*

44 *Ibid.*

45 Substituted for "2%", *ibid.*

46 Inserted by the SEBI (Insider Trading) (Amendment) Regulations, 2003, w.e.f. 11.7.2003.

Violation of provision relating to disclosure.

14. (1) A person who violates provisions of Regulation 12 shall be liable for action under Section 11 or 11B and/or Section 24 of the Act.

(2) A person who violates provisions of Regulation 13 shall be liable for action as specified in Regulation 11 or Sections 11, 11B or action under Chapter VIA or Section 24 of the Act.]

[47][Appeal to the Central Government

[48][**15.**] Any person aggrieved by an order of the Board under these regulations may prefer an appeal to the Securities Appellate Tribunal.]

---

47 Substituted by the SEBI (Insider Trading) (Amendment) Regulations, 2002, w.e.f. 20.02.2002. Prior to its substitution, it was substituted by the SEBI (Appeal to the Securities Appellate Tribunal) (Amendment) Regulations, 2000, w.e.f. 28.3.2000, read as under:

12. "Appeal to the Central Government- Any person aggrieved by an order of the Board made on and after the commencement of the Securities Laws (Second Amendment) Act, 1999,(*i.e.,* after 16th December, 1999), under these regulations may prefer an appeal to a Securities Appellate Tribunal having jurisdiction in the matter."

48 Regulation 12 renumbered as Regulation 15, *ibid.*

[49][*SCHEDULE I*
[*Under Regulation 12(1)*]
PART–A

MODEL CODE OF CONDUCT FOR PREVENTION OF INSIDER TRADING FOR LISTED COMPANIES

1.0 Compliance Officer

1.1 The listed company has appointed a Compliance Officer senior level employee who shall report to the Managing Director/Chief Executive Officer.

1.2 The compliance officer shall be responsible for setting forth policies, procedures, monitoring adherence to the rules for the preservation of "Price Sensitive Information", pre-clearing; of designated employees' and their dependents' trades (directly or through respective department heads as decided by the company), monitoring of trades and the implementation of the code of conduct under the overall supervision of the Board of the listed company.

Explanation: For the purpose of this Schedule, the term 'designated employee' shall include —

(*i*) officers comprising the top three tiers of the company management [50][***];

(*ii*) the employees designated by the company to whom these trading restrictions shall be applicable, keeping in mind the objectives of this code of conduct.

1.3 The compliance officer shall maintain a record of the designated employees and any changes made in the list of designated employees.

1.4 The compliance officer shall assist all the employees in addressing any clarifications regarding the Securities and Exchange Board of India (Prohibition of Insider Trading) Regulations, 1992 and the company's code of conduct.

2.0 Preservation of "Price Sensitive Information"

2.1 Employees/directors shall maintain the confidentiality of all Price Sensitive Information. Employees/Directors shall [51][not] pass on such information to any person directly or indirectly by way of making a recommendation for the purchase or sale of securities.

---

[49] Inserted, *ibid.*

[50] Words "and all employees in the finance department" omitted by the SEBI (Prohibition of Insider Trading) (Second Amendment) Regulations, 2002, w.e.f. 29.11.2002.

[51] Substituted for "no" by the SEBI (Prohibition of Insider Trading) (Second Amendment) Regulations, 2002, w.e.f. 29.11.2002.

2.2 Need to know

2.2.1 Price Sensitive Information is to be handled on a "need to know" basis, *i.e.*, Price Sensitive Information should be disclosed only to those within the company who need the information to discharge their duty.

2.3 Limited access to confidential information

2.3.1 Files containing confidential information shall be kept secure. Computer files must have adequate security of login and password etc.

3.0 Prevention of misuse of "Price Sensitive Information"

3.1 All directors/officers and designated employees of the company shall be subject to trading restrictions as enumerated below.

3.2 Trading window

3.2.1 The company shall specify a trading period, to be called "trading window", for trading in the company's securities. The trading window shall be closed during the time the information referred to in para 3.2.3 is unpublished.

3.2.2 When the trading window is closed, the employees/directors shall not trade in the company's securities in such period.

3.2.3 The trading window shall be, *inter alia*, closed at the time —

(*a*) Declaration of financial results (quarterly, half-yearly and annually).

(*b*) Declaration of dividends (interim and final).

(*c*) Issue of securities by way of public/rights/bonus etc.

(*d*) Any major expansion plans or execution of new projects.

(*e*) Amalgamation, mergers, takeovers and buy-back.

(*f*) Disposal of whole or substantially whole of the undertaking.

(*g*) Any changes in policies, plans or operations of the company.

[52][**3.2.3A** The time for commencement of closing of trading window shall be decided by the company.]

3.2.4 The trading window shall be opened 24 hours after the information referred to in para 3.2.3 is made public.

3.2-5 All directors/officers/designated employees of the company shall conduct all their dealings in the securities of the Company only in a valid trading window and shall not deal in any transaction involving the purchase or sale of the company's securities during the periods when trading window is closed, as referred to in para 3.2.3 or during any other period as may be specified by the Company from time to time.

---

[52] Inserted, *ibid.*

3.2.6 In case of ESOPs, exercise of option may be allowed in the period when the trading window is closed. However, sale of shares allotted on exercise of ESOPs shall 1[not] be allowed when trading window is closed.

3.3 Pre-clearance of trades

3.3.1 All directors/officers/designated employees of the company who intend to deal in the securities of the company (above a minimum threshold limit to be decided by the company) should pre-clear the transaction as per the pre-dealing procedure as described hereunder.

3.3.2 An application may be made in such form as the company may notify in this regard, to the Compliance Officer indicating the estimated number of securities that the designated employee/officer/director intends to deal in, the details as to the depository with which he has a security account, the details as to the securities in such depository mode and such other details as may be required by any rule made by the company in this behalf.

3.3.3 An undertaking shall be executed in favour of the company by such designated employee/director/officer incorporating, *inter alia*, the following clauses, as may be applicable :

(*a*) That the employee/director/officer does not have any access or has not received "Price Sensitive Information" upto the time of signing the undertaking.

(*b*) That in case the employee/director/officer has access to or receives "Price Sensitive Information" after the signing of the undertaking but before the execution of the transaction he/she shall inform the Compliance Officer of the change in his position and that he/she would completely refrain from dealing in the securities of the company till the time such information becomes public.

(*c*) That he/she has not contravened the code of conduct for prevention of insider trading as notified by the company from time to time.

(*d*) That he/she has made a full and true disclosure in the matter.

4.0 Other restrictions

4.1 All directors/officers/designated employees shall execute their order in respect of securities of the company within one week after the approval of pre-clearance is given. If the order is not executed within one week after the approval is given, the employee/director must pre-clear the transaction again.

4.2 All directors/officers/designated employees shall hold their investments in securities for a minimum period of 30 days in order to be considered as being held for investment purposes. The holding period shall also apply to subscription in the primary market (IPOs). In the case of IPOs, the holding period would commence when the securities are actually allotted.

4.3 In case the sale of securities is necessitated by personal emergency, the holding period may be waived by the compliance officer after recording in writing his/her reasons in this regard.

5.0 Reporting Requirements for transactions in securities

5.1 All directors/officers/designated employees of the listed company shall be required to forward following details of their securities transactions including the statement of dependent family members (as defined by the company) to the Compliance Officer:

(*a*) all holdings in securities of that company by directors/officers/designated employees at the time of joining the company;

(*b*) periodic statement of any transactions in securities (the periodicity of reporting may be defined by the company. The company may also be free to decide whether reporting is required for trades where pre-clearance is also required); and

(*c*) annual statement of all holdings in securities.

5.2 The Compliance Officer shall maintain records of all the declarations in the appropriate form given by the directors/officers/designated employees for a minimum period of three years.

5.3 The Compliance Officer shall place before the Managing Director/Chief Executive Officer or a committee specified by the company, on a monthly basis all the details of the dealing in the securities by employees/director/officer of the company and the accompanying documents that such persons had executed under the pre-dealing procedure as envisaged in this code.

6.0 Penalty for contravention of code of conduct

6.1 Any employee/officer/director who trades in securities or communicates any information for trading in securities in contravention of the code of conduct may be penalised and appropriate action may be taken by the company.

6.2 Employees/officers/directors of the company who violate the code of conduct shall also be subject to disciplinary action by the company, which may include wage freeze, suspension, [53][ineligible] for future participation in employee stock option [54][plans], etc.

6.3 The action by the company shall not preclude SEBI from taking any action in case of violation of SEBI (Prohibition of Insider Trading) Regulations, 1992.

7.0 Information to SEBI in case of violation of SEBI (Prohibition of Insider Trading) Regulations, 1992

7.1 In case it is observed by the company/Compliance Officer that there has been a violation of SEBI (Prohibition of Insider Trading) Regulations, 1992. SEBI shall be informed by the company.

---

[53] Substituted for "intelligibility" by the SEBI (Prohibition of Insider Trading) (Second Amendment) Regulations, 2002, w.e.f. 29.11.2002.

[54] Substituted for "plants", *ibid.*

PART–B

MODEL CODE OF CONDUCT FOR PREVENTION OF INSIDER TRADING FOR OTHER ENTITIES

1.0 Compliance Officer

1.1 The organisation/firm has a Compliance Officer (senior level employee) reporting to the Managing Partner/Chief Executive Officer.

1.2 The Compliance Officer shall be responsible for setting forth policies and procedures and monitoring adherence to the rules for the preservation of "Price Sensitive Information", pre-clearing of all designated employees and their dependents trades (directly or through respective department heads as decided by the organisation/firm), monitoring of trades and the implementation of the code of conduct under the overall supervision of the partners/proprietors.

1.3 The Compliance Officer shall also assist all the employees/directors/partners in addressing any clarifications regarding SEBI (Prohibition of Insider Trading) Regulations, 1992 and the organisation/firm's code of conduct.

1.4 The Compliance Officer shall maintain a record of the designated employees and any changes made in the list of designated employees.

2.0 Preservation of "Price Sensitive Information"

2.1 Employees/directors/partners shall maintain the confidentiality of all Price Sensitive Information. Employees/directors/partners must not pass on such information directly or indirectly by way of making a recommendation for the purchase [55][or] sale of securities.

2.2 **Need to know**

2.2.1 Price Sensitive Information is to be handled on a "need to know" basis, *i.e.*, Price Sensitive Information should be disclosed only to those within the organisation/firm who need the information to discharge their duty and whose possession of such information will not give rise to a conflict of interest or appearance of misuse of the information.

2.3 **Limited access to confidential information**

2.3.1 Files containing confidential information shall be kept secure. Computer files must have adequate security of login and password etc.

---

[55] Substituted for "of" by the SEBI (Prohibition of Insider Trading) (Second Amendment) Regulations, 2002, w.e.f. 29.11.2002.

2.4 Chinese Wall

2.4.1 To prevent the misuse of confidential information the organisation/firm shall adopt a "Chinese Wall" policy which separates those areas of the organisation/firm which routinely have access to confidential information, considered "inside areas" from those areas which deal with sale/marketing/investment advise or other departments providing support services, considered "public areas".

2.4.2 The employees in the inside area shall not communicate any Price Sensitive Information to any one in public area.

2.4.3 The employees in inside area may be physically segregated from employees in public area.

2.4.4 Demarcation of the various departments as inside area may be implemented by the organisation/firm.

2.4.5 In exceptional circumstances employees from the public areas may be brought "over the wall" and given confidential information on the basis of "need to know" criteria, under intimation to the compliance officer.

3.0 Prevention of misuse of Price Sensitive Information

3.1 Employees/directors/partners shall not use Price Sensitive Information to buy or sell securities of any sort, whether for their own account, their relative's account, organisation/firm's account or a client's account. The following trading restrictions shall apply for trading in securities.

3.2 Pre-clearance of trades

3.2.1 All directors/officers/designated employees of the organisation/firm who intend to deal in the securities of the client company (above a minimum threshold limit to be determined by the organisation/firm) shall pre-clear the transactions as per the predealing procedure as described hereunder.

3.2.2 An application may be made in such form as the organisation/firm may specify in [56][this] regard, to the Compliance Officer indicating the name and estimated number of securities that the designated employees/director/partner intends to deal in, the details as to the depository with which he has a security account the details as to the securities in such depository mode and such other details as may be required by any rule made by the organisation/firm in this behalf.

3.2.3 An undertaking shall be executed in favour of the organisation/firm by such designated employee/partners/directors incorporating, *inter alia*, the following clauses, as may be applicable:

(*i*) That the designated employee/director/partner does not have any access or has not received any "Price Sensitive Information" upto the time of signing the undertaking.

(*ii*) That in case the designated employee/director/partner has access to or receives "Price Sensitive Information" after the signing of the undertaking but before the execution of the transaction he/she shall inform the Compliance Officer of the change in his position and that he/she would completely refrain from dealing in the securities of the client company till the time such information becomes public.

---

[56] Substituted for "the" by the SEBI (Prohibition of Insider Trading) (Second Amendment) Regulations, 2002, w.e.f. 29.11.2002.

(*iii*) That he/she has not contravened the code of conduct for prevention of insider trading as specified by the organisation/firm from time to time.

(*iv*) That he/she has made a full and true disclosure in the matter.

4.0 Restricted/Grey list

4.1 In order to monitor Chinese wall procedures and trading in client securities based on inside information, the organisation/firm shall restrict trading in certain securities and designate such list as restricted/grey list.

4.2 Security of a listed company shall be put on the restricted/grey list if the organisation/firm is handling any assignment for the listed company or is preparing appraisal report or is handling credit rating assignment and is privy to Price Sensitive Information.

4.3 Any security which is being purchased or sold or is being considered for purchase or sale by the organisation/firm on behalf of its clients/schemes of mutual funds, etc. shall be put on the restricted/grey list.

4.4 As the restricted list itself is highly confidential information it shall not be communicated directly, or indirectly to anyone outside the organisation/firm. The Restricted List shall be maintained by Compliance Officer.

4.5 When any securities are on the Restricted List-trading in these securities by designated employees/ directors/partners may [57][be] blocked or may be disallowed at the time of pre-clearance.

5.0 Other restrictions

5.1 All directors/designated employees/partners shall execute their order within one week after the approval of pre-clearance is given. If the order is not executed within one week after approval is given the employee/director/partners must [58][pre] clear the transaction again.

5.2 All directors/officers/designated employees/partners shall hold their investments for a minimum period of 30 days in order to be considered as being held for investment purposes.

5.3 The holding period shall also apply to purchases in the primary market (IPOs). In the case of IPOs, the holding period would commence when the securities are actually allotted.

5.4 In case the sale of securities is necessitated by personal emergency, the holding period may be waived by the Compliance Officer after recording in writing his/her reasons in this regard.

5.5 Analysts, if any, employed with the organisation/firm while preparing research reports of a client company(s) shall disclose their shareholdings/interest in such company(s) to the Compliance Officer.

5.6 Analysts who prepare research report of a listed company shall not trade in securities of that company for thirty days from preparation of such report.

---

[57] Inserted by the SEBI (Prohibition of Insider Trading) (Second Amendment) Regulations, 2002, w.e.f. 29.11.2002.

[58] Substituted for "are", *ibid.*

6.0 Reporting Requirements for transactions in securities

6.1 All directors/designated employees/partners of the organisation/firm shall be required to forward following details of their securities transactions including the statement of dependent family members (as defined by the organisation/firm) to the Compliance Officer:—

(*a*) all holdings in securities by directors/officers/designated employees/partners at the time of joining the organisation;

(*b*) periodic statement of any transactions in securities (the periodicity of reporting may be defined by the firm or organisation. The organisation/firm may also be free to decide whether reporting is required for trades where pre-clearance is also required;

(*c*) annual statement of all holdings in securities.

6.2 The Compliance Officer shall maintain records of all the declarations given by the directors/ designated employees/partners in the appropriate form for a minimum period of three years.

6.3 The Compliance Officer shall place before the Chief Executive Officer/Partner or a committee notified by the organisation/firm, on a monthly basis all the details of the dealing in the securities by designated employees/directors/partners of the organisation/firm and the accompanying documents that such persons had executed under the pre-dealing procedure as envisaged in this code.

7.0 Penalty for contravention of code of conduct

7.1 Any employee/partner/director who trades in securities or communicates any information or counsels any person trading in securities, in contravention of the code of conduct may be penalised and appropriate action may be taken by the organisation/firm.

7.2 Employees/partners/directors of the organisation/firm who violate the code of conduct may also be subject to disciplinary action by the company, which may include wage freeze, suspension, etc.

7.3 The action by the organisation/firm shall not preclude SEBI from taking any action in case of violation of SEBI (Prohibition of Insider Trading) Regulations, 1992.

8.0 Information to SEBI in case of violation of SEBI (Prohibition of Insider Trading) Regulations

8.1 In case it is observed by the organisation/firm/compliance officer that there has been a violation of these Regulations, SEBI shall be informed by the organisation/firm.

9.0 Listed intermediaries to comply with both Parts A and B of Schedule I

9.1 The intermediaries such as credit rating agencies, Asset Management Companies, or broking companies etc. whose securities are listed in recognised stock exchange shall comply with both Part A and Part B of this Schedule in respect of its own securities and client's securities.

SCHEDULE II
[See *under Regulation 12(2)*]

CODE OF CORPORATE DISCLOSURE PRACTICES FOR PREVENTION OF INSIDER TRADING

1.0 Corporate Disclosure Policy

1.1 To ensure timely and adequate disclosure of price sensitive information, the following norms shall be followed by listed companies:—

2.0 Prompt disclosure of price sensitive information

2.1 Price sensitive information shall be given by listed companies to stock exchanges and disseminated on a continuous and immediate basis.

2.2 Listed companies may also consider ways of supplementing information released to stock exchanges by improving Investor access to their public announcements.

3.0 Overseeing and co-ordinating disclosure

3.1 Listed companies shall designate a senior official (such as compliance officer) to oversee corporate disclosure.

3.2 This official shall be responsible for ensuring that the company complies with continuous disclosure requirements. Overseeing and co-ordinating disclosure of price sensitive information to stock exchanges, analysts, shareholders and media and educating staff on disclosure policies and procedure.

3.3 Information disclosure/dissemination may normally be approved in advance by the official designated for the purpose.

3.4 If information is accidentally disclosed without prior approval, the person responsible may inform the designated officer immediately, even if the information is not considered price sensitive.

4.0 Responding to market rumours

4.1 Listed companies shall have clearly laid down procedures for responding to any queries or requests for verification of market rumours by exchanges.

4.2 The official designated for corporate disclosure shall be responsible for deciding whether a public announcement is necessary for verifying or denying rumours and then making the disclosure.

5.0 Timely Reporting of shareholdings/ownership and changes in ownership

5.1 Disclosure of shareholdings/ownership by major shareholders and disclosure of changes in ownership as provided under any Regulations made under the Act and the listing agreement shall be made in a timely and adequate manner.

Disclosure/dissemination of Price Sensitive Information with special reference to Analysts, Institutional Investors

6.0 Listed companies should follow the guidelines given hereunder while dealing with analysts and institutional investors:—

(*i*) *Only Public information to be provided* : Listed companies shall provide only public information to the analyst/research persons/large investors like institutions. Alternatively, the information given to the analyst should be simultaneously made public at the earliest.

(*ii*) *Recording of discussion* : In order to avoid misquoting or misrepresentation, it is desirable that at least two company representative be present at meetings with Analysts, brokers or Institutional Investors and discussion should preferably be recorded.

(*iii*) *Handling of unanticipated questions* : A listed company should be careful when dealing with analysts' questions that raise issues outside the intended scope of discussion. Unanticipated questions may be taken on notice and a considered response given later. If the answer includes price sensitive information, a public announcement should be made before responding.

(*iv*) *Simultaneous release of Information* : When a company organises meetings with analysts, the company shall make a press release or post relevant information on its website after every such meet. The company may also consider live webcasting of analyst meets.

7.0 Medium of disclosure/dissemination

(*i*) Disclosure/dissemination of information may be done through various media so as to achieve maximum reach and quick dissemination.

(*ii*) Corporates shall ensure that disclosure to stock exchanges is made promptly.

(*iii*) Corporates may also facilitate disclosure through the use of their dedicated Internet website.

(*iv*) Company websites may provide a means of giving investors a direct access to analyst briefing material, significant background information and questions and answers.

(*v*) The information filed by corporates with exchanges under continuous disclosure requirement may be made available on the company website.

8.0 Dissemination by stock exchanges

(*i*) The disclosures made to stock exchanges may be disseminated by the exchanges to investors in a quick and efficient manner through the stock exchange network as well as through stock exchange websites.

(*ii*) Information furnished by the companies under continuous disclosure requirements, should be published on the website of the exchange instantly.

(*iii*) Stock exchanges should make immediate arrangement for display of the information furnished by the companies instantly on the stock exchange website.

[59][*SCHEDULE III*

FORMS

FORM A

Securities and Exchange Board of India (Prohibition of Insider Trading) Regulations, 1992 [Regulations 13(1) and (6)]

Regulation 13(1) : Details of acquisition of 5% or more shares in a listed company

Name & address of share-holder with tele-phone number	*Sharehol-ding prior to acquisi-tion*	*No. and percentage of shares/ voting rights acquired*	*Date of receipt of allotment/ advice. Date of acquisition (specify)*	*Date of intimation to Company*	*Mode of acquisi-tion (market purchase/ public/ rights/ preferen-tial offer etc.)*	*Share-holding subse-quent to acquisi-tion*	*Trading member through whom the trade was executed with SEBI Registra-tion No. of the TM*	*Exch-ange on which the trade was executed*	*Buy quan-tity*	*Buy value*

FORM B

Securities and Exchange Board of India (Prohibition of Insider Trading) Regulations, 1992 [Regulations 13(2) and (6)]

Regulation 13(2): Details of shares held by Director or Officer of a Listed company

Name & address of Director/ Officer	*Date of assuming office of Director/ Officer*	*No. & % of shares/ voting rights held at the time of becoming Director/ Officer*	*Date of intimation to company*	*Mode of acquisition (market purchase/ public/rights/ preferential offer etc.)*	*Trading member through whom the trade was executed with SEBI Registration No. of the TM*	*Exchange on which the trade was executed*	*Buy quantity*	*Buy value*

59 Inserted by the SEBI (Insider Trading) (Amendment) Regulations, 2003, w.e.f. 11.7.2003.

FORM C

Securities and Exchange Board of India (Prohibition of Insider Trading) Regulations, 1992

[Regulations 13(3) and (6)]

Regulation 13(3): Details of change in shareholding in respect of persons holding more than 5% shares in a listed company

Name & Address of share holders	*Share holding prior to acquisition/sale*	*No. & % of shares/ voting rights acquired/ sold*	*Receipt of allotment advice/ acquisition of shares/ sale of shares specify*	*Date of intimation to company*	*Mode of acquisition on (market purchase/ public/ rights/ preferential offier etc.)*	*No. & % of shares/ voting rights post-acquisition/ sale*	*Trading member through whom the trade was executed with SEBI Registration No. of the TM*	*Exchange on which the trade was executed*	*Buy quantity*	*Buy value*	*Sell quantity*	*Sell value*

FORM D

Securities and Exchange Board of India (Prohibition of Insider Trading) Regulations, 1992

[Regulations 13(4) and (6)]

Regulation 13(4): Details of change in shareholding of Director or Officer of a Listed Company

Name & Address of Director Officer	*No. of % of shares/ voting rights held by the Director/ Officer*	*Date of receipt of allotment advice/ acquisition/sale of shares/ voting rights*	*Date of intimation to company*	*Mode of acquisition (market purchase/ public/ rights/ preferential offer etc.)*	*No. & % of shares/ post acquisition/ voting rights sale*	*Trading member through whom the trade was executed with SEBI Registration No. of the TM*	*Exchange on which the trade was executed*	*Buy quantity*	*Buy value*	*Sell quantity*	*Sell value*

11 INVESTOR EDUCATION AND PROTECTION FUND (IEPF)

1. INTRODUCTION :

Investor Education and Protection Fund (IEPF) has been established under Section 205C of the Companies Act, 1956 by way Companies (Amendment) Act, 1999 for promotion of investors' awareness and protection of the interests of investors. The following is the act as given by Ministry of Law Justice and Company Affairs on 1st October, 2001:

2. IEPF ACT (SECTION 205C) :

As per the Act

1. The Central Government shall establish a fund to be called the Investor Education and Protection Fund (hereafter in this section referred to as the "Fund")
2. There shall be credited to the Fund the following amounts, namely:-
   - (*a*) amounts in the unpaid dividend accounts of companies;
   - (*b*) the application moneys received by companies for allotment of any securities and due for refund;
   - (*c*) matured deposits with companies;
   - (*d*) matured debentures with companies;
   - (*e*) the interest accrued on the amounts referred to in clauses (*a*) to (*d*);
   - (*f*) grants and donations given to the Fund by the Central Government, State Governments, companies or any other institutions for the purposes of the Fund;
   - (*g*) the interest or other income received out of the investments made from the Fund;

Provided that no such amounts referred to in clauses (*a*) to (*d*) shall form part of the Fund unless such amounts have remained unclaimed and unpaid for a period of seven years from the date they became due for payment.

3. The Fund shall be utilized for promotion of investors' awareness and protection of the interests of investors in accordance with such rules as may be prescribed.
4. The Central Government shall, by notification in the Official Gazette, specify an authority or committee, with such members as the Central Government may appoint, to administer the Fund, and maintain separate accounts and other relevant records in relation to the Fund in such form as may be prescribed in consultation with the Comptroller and Auditor-General of India.
5. It shall be competent for the authority or Committee appointed under sub-section (4) to spend moneys out of the Fund for carrying out the objects for which the Fund has been established.

3. CREDITS TO THE FUND:

(*i*) Any amount required to be credited by the companies to the Fund, as provided in the Act shall be remitted into the concerned specified branches of Punjab National Bank, within a period of thirty days of such amounts becoming due to be credited to the Fund

(*a*) The amount shall be tendered by the companies on behalf of the Central Government in such branches of Punjab National Bank along with Challan (in triplicate) and the Bank will return two copies duly stamped to the Company as token of having received the amount.

(*b*) Every Company shall file with the concerned Registrar of Companies one copy of the Challan referred to in (a) evidencing deposit of the amount to the Fund.The Company shall fill in the full description and the nature of the amount tendered and its Head of Account.

(*i*) Every Company shall, when effecting a credit to the account of the Fund, will separately furnish to the concerned Registrar of Companies a statement in Form duly certified by a Chartered Accountant or a Company Secretary or a Cost Accountant practicing in India or by the statutory auditors of the company.Provided that each Company shall keep a record relating to folio number, Certificate Number etc. in respect of persons to whom the amount of unpaid or unclaimed dividend, application money, matured deposit or debentures, interest accrued or payable, for a period of three years and the Committee or Sub-Committee shall have powers to inspect such records of that period.

(*ii*) On receipt of this statement, the concerned Registrar of Companies shall enter the details of such receipt in a register and reconcile the amount so remitted and collected, with the concerned Pay and Accounts Officer, on monthly basis.

(*iii*) Each Registrar of Companies shall furnish an abstract of such receipt received during the month to Department of Company Affairs within seven days from the close of the month.

(*iv*) Department of Company Affairs shall maintain a consolidated abstract of receipts and shall reconcile them on a quarterly basis with Principal Pay and Accounts Office of the Department of Company Affairs.

4. Expenses of the Committee:

(*a*) The official member of the committee or sub-committee shall be entitled to Travelling Allowance according to the rules regulating their official position.

(*b*) For Journeys performed by a non-official member of the Committee or Sub-Committee or special invitee in connection with the work of the committee or a sub-committee shall be entitled for TA/DA as per supplementary Rules of Central Government.

(*c*) Committee shall have powers to recommend appointment/remuneration to any experts in such areas as may be considered necessary.

(*d*) Committee shall have powers to recommend appointment of Auditors and for scrutinizing the accounts of the voluntarily agencies registered with it.

5. Audit of Accounts: The accounts of the Fund shall be audited by internal audit party of the Department of Company Affairs every year and will also be subject to audit by the office of Comptroller and Auditor General of India.

6. Constitution and Functions of the Committee:

(*a*) The Committee shall consist of ten members, excluding the Chairperson who is Secretary, to the Department of Company Affairs. The members shall be nominated by Reserve Bank of India, the Securities and Exchange Board of India and or from any other Ministry or Department of Central Government dealing with investor protection activities and experts from the field of investors' education and protection.The non-official Members shall hold office for a period of two years.The Official members shall hold office for a period of two years or until they occupy their position which ever is earlier.The constitution of the Committee shall be notified in the Official Gazette.

(*b*) Functions of the Committee: The Committee shall recommend the following activities relating to investors' education, awareness and protection:

(*a*) Education Programmes through Media;

(*b*) Organizing Seminars and Symposia;

(*c*) Proposals for registration of Voluntary Associations or Institution or other Organizations engaged in Investor Education and Protection activities;

(*d*) Proposals for projects for Investors' Education and Protection including research activities and proposals for financing such projects;

(*e*) Coordinating with institutions engaged in Investor Education, awareness and protection activities; The Committee may also be entrusted with such other functions for carrying out the objects for which the Fund has been established.

(*f*) (*i*) The Committee may appoint one or more sub-Committees whenever it considers necessary to facilitate efficient and speedy discharge of its functions. (*ii*) Sub-Committee shall be constituted from amongst the members. (*iii*) The Chairperson of the Committee may nominate any one of the members of the Sub-Committee as its convener and where no such nomination has been made, the members of the Sub-Committee elect a convenor amongst themselves. (*iv*) The Committee may have Sub-Committee to examine the end use of grants and assistance and recommend release of funds.

7. **Power to call upon a Company:**

   (*i*) The Committee shall have *suo moto* powers to call upon any company to pay the amount due to the Fund.

   (*ii*) Committee shall call upon any company to give estimates of the amounts to be credited to the Fund in Form 2.

8. **Report by the Committee:** The Committee shall furnish its activity report for every six month's period to the Central Government.

9. **Meetings:**

   (*i*) One third of the total members subject to five members in the case of meeting of committee and three members in case of sub-committee meeting shall constitute a quorum.

   (*ii*) The Chairperson of the Committee and the convenor of a Sub-Committee, respectively, shall preside over the meetings of the Committee or the Sub-Committee as the case may be. In the event of the Chairperson or, as the case may be, the convenor being unable to attend the meeting for any reason, the members present may elect one amongst themselves to preside over the meeting.

   (*iii*) **The Chairperson of the Committee or the convenor of a sub-Committee may, call meeting of the Committee or a Sub-Committee:** Provided that the Chairperson or the Convenor, as the case may be, shall also call a meeting if a requisition for that purpose is presented to him by at least five members in the case of the Committee and three members in the case of a Sub-Committee.

   (*iv*) At least fourteen clear days' notice indicating the time and place of the meeting shall be sent to the members of the Committee or the Sub-Committee as the case may be: Provided that in case of urgency, a special meeting of the Committee or Sub-Committee may be called at any time by the Chairperson or the convenor, who shall inform the members at least three clear days in advance of the subject-matter for consideration at the meeting and the reasons for which he considers the meeting urgent; Provided further that no other business shall be transacted at such a meeting.

   (*v*) The Chairman or the convenor, as the case may be, may invite any person to attend any meeting of the Committee or Sub-Committee as a special invitee but such person shall not be entitled to vote.

10. **Agenda:**

   (*i*) At least seven clear days before any meeting of the Committee or a Sub-Committee, a list of business proposed to be transacted at the meeting shall be sent to the members of the Committee or of a Sub-Committee, as the case may be.

   (*ii*) No business, not included in the list of business, shall be transacted at a meeting without the permission of the Chairperson presiding over the meeting.

11. Voting:

(*i*) Every question brought before any meeting of the Committee or Sub-Committee, as the case may be, shall be decided by a majority vote of members present and voting at the meeting.No member shall vote by proxy.

(*ii*) In the event of equality of votes, at a meeting, the Chairperson or the convenor, as the case may be or in his absence, the person presiding, shall have a second or casting vote.

12. Minutes: The minutes of the meeting of the Committee or Sub-Committee shall be caused to be recorded and circulated among the members.

13. Conditions for Utilization of Funds by the Committee:

(*i*) The Committee may register from time to time various Associations or institutions or organizations, engaged in activities relating to investor awareness, education and protection and proposing for Investors programmes; organizing seminar, symposia and undertake projects for Investor Protecting including research activities.

(*ii*) Application for registration by such organisations referred to in sub-rule (*i*) be made in Form-3.

(*iii*) Application for release of funds for the activities listed in Rule 7(1) from the organizations or Institutes registered with the Department of Company Affairs shall be made in Form 4.

(*iv*) A copy of the summary or recommendations of the seminar or programme conducted and copy of Accounts for such activity by such organisation *e.g.,* registered associations or chambers of commerce or institutes shall be provided to the Committee within ten days of the conclusion of the seminar or programme.

(*v*) The organization or Associations registered shall be considered for grant of funds as a grant-in-aid either as one time measure or in stages or by way of reimbursement depending upon the nature of the activity proposed.

(*vi*) The Committee shall be entitled to examine the end use of grants and assistance before recommending release of funds.

(*vii*) The Committee shall cause to draw at the end of each Financial Year, a statement of Total Receipts from various sources indicated in Section 205C of the Companies Act, 1956 and the grants disbursed or the expenditure incurred in connection with the activities organized by the Committee or Sub-Committee and other expenditure incurred for holding the meetings.

(*viii*) The Committee shall maintain the necessary records showing amount disbursed, date of disbursal, the name of Organization or Voluntary agency, the activities of the agency for which such disbursal was made.

QUESTION

1. Explain the use of Investor Protection and Education fund for Indian investors.

❑❑❑

12 MAJOR STOCK EXCHANGES OF INDIA

BOMBAY STOCK EXCHANGE

Bombay Stock Exchange (BSE) was established in 1875. It was started as "The Native Share and Stock Brokers Association" and over the years it has become the premier stock exchange of the country. It is the first stock exchange to have obtained permanent recognition in 1956 from the Government of India under the Securities Contracts (Regulation) Act, 1956.

Organization

The exchange comprises of a governing board having 20 directors which regulates the exchange affairs and decides its policies. Among these 20 members there are 9 elected directors in the board of which one third retire every year by rotation, there are 3 nominees of SEBI, 6 public representatives, an Executive Director, Chief Operating Officer, and Chief Executive Officer.

The Executive Director as the Chief Executive Officer is responsible for the day-to-day administration of the Exchange he is assisted by the Chief Operating Officer and other Heads of Departments.

The average daily turnover of the exchange during the financial year 2003-04 and 2004-05 (April-March) was – Rs.1978.81 crore and Rs.2050.26 crore respectively.

Listing on BSE

A company which wishes to have its securities listed on the exchange has to comply with the listing requirements prescribed by the exchange. These are –

I. Minimum listing requirements for new companies –

A. Minimum Capital –

New companies can be listed on the exchange if their issued and subscribed capital after the public issue is Rs.10 crore and the company should have a post-issue net worth of Rs.20 crore.

In case of new companies in technology sector—

- Total income from main activity should not be less than 75% of the total income during the two immediately preceding years.
- Minimum post-issue paid-up equity capital should be Rs.5 crore.
- Minimum market capitalization should be Rs.50 crore.
- Post-issued net worth should be Rs.20 crore.

B. Minimum Public Offer –

- Minimum 20 lakh securities must be offered to the public and the minimum size of offer to public is Rs. 50 crore.

II. Minimum Listing Requirements for companies listed on other stock exchanges.

- Company should have minimum issued and paid-up capital of Rs.3 crore and a profit making track record for the last 3 years.
- Minimum net worth of company should be Rs.20 crore.
- Market capitalization should be at least two times of the paid-up capital.
- The company should have a dividend paying track record for the last 3 consecutive years and minimum dividend should be at least 10%.
- At least 25% of the capital issued must be with Non-Promoter Shareholders.
- The company should have at least two years listing record with any Regional Stock Exchange and sign an agreement with CDSL and NSDL for DEMAT trading.

III. In case of companies de-listed by BSE and seeking re-listing a fresh public offer must be made as per prevailing guidelines of SEBI and BSE.

IV. The companies who desire to list their securities offered through public issue are required to obtain prior permission to use the name of the exchange in their prospectus which is obtained from a duly formed "Listing Committee" who evaluates the promoters, company, project and several other factors before taking any decision in this regard.

V. Submission of Letter of Application : As per Section 73 of the Companies Act, 1956, a company seeking listing of its securities on the Exchange is required to submit a letter of application to all the stock exchanges where it propose to have its securities listed before filling the prospectus with the Registrar of Companies.

VI. Allotment of Securities : As per Listing Agreement a company is required to complete allotment of securities offered to the public within 30 days of the date of closure of the subscription list and approach the regional stock exchange *i.e.* stock exchange nearest to its registered office for approval of the basis of allotment. In case of book building issue, allotment shall be made not later than 15 days failing which 15% interest will have to be paid to the investor.

VII. Trading Permission : The issuer company should complete the formalities of trading at all stock exchanges where securities are to be listed within 7 working days of finalizing the basis of allotment for obtaining trading permission.

VIII. Requirement of 1% Security : The company has to deposit a refundable amount of 1% of the amount of issue with the regional stock exchange before the opening of issue as a security against any default by the company.

TRADING SYSTEM

Earlier BSE had an open outlay system of trading but now it has shifted to a fully computerized mode of trading known as BOLT (BSE On Line Trading) system w.e.f. March 14, 1995. In this system member-brokers enter orders for purchase or sale of securities, from Trader Work Stations (TWS) installed in their offices, instead of assembling in the trading ring. So the entire trading is anonymous *i.e.,* buyers and sellers do not know the names of each other. Trading is done from Monday to Friday between 9:55 a.m. and 3:30 p.m. and the scrips traded have been classified into A, B1, B2 and Z groups which represent certain qualitative and quantitative parameters which include number of trades, value traded etc. for the guidance and benefit of investors. 'F' group represents the fixed income securities. The exchange has also commenced trading in Government Securities for retail investors under "G" group w.e.f. January 16, 2003.

SURVEILLANCE

The Surveillance Department monitors the members on daily basis and scrutinizes the prices and volumes of the scrips on a daily basis. It monitors the movement of scrips, detects market manipulations like price rigging etc., monitors abnormal prices and volumes not consistent with the normal trading pattern along with the inspection of member-brokers' position to reduce the possibility of default.

As per SEBI guidelines, the following steps are being taken to reduce defaults:

- **Circuit Filters :** The exchange applies a daily circuit filter of 20% on all the scrips whose price moves beyond the limit on any particular day.
- In case of large variations in volumes of scrips, they are scrutinized and appropriate action is taken.
- The exchange also imposes special margins on scrips where it is suspected that there is an attempt to ramp up the prices by creating artificial volumes. The exchange also transfers the scrips for trading and settlement on a trade-to-trade basis resulting into giving / taking delivery of shares on a gross level.
- The exchange has developed an On Line Real Time (OLRT) Surveillance System w.e.f. July 15, 1999 which generates on-line alerts whenever there is any abnormal variation in price, volume, position taken by members.
- Besides this there exists a database with the exchange regarding the lost, stolen or misplaced securities.
- The Risk Management Department of the exchange has developed a client caution database to provide information to member brokers regarding the false/forged certificates issued by clients or sub-brokers. The member brokers have the database available with them and can use it for further verification.
- The exchange has an inspection department to check the records of the member brokers regarding compliance of the risk management procedures.

NATIONAL STOCK EXCHANGE

National Stock Exchange of India (NSE) was set-up in November 1992 under the recommendation of a high powered study group on establishment of new stock exchanges – The Pherwani Committee which recommended the setting up of NSE for removing the defects of the Indian Stock Market and provides equal access to investors across to country. NSE was promoted by leading financial institutions on behalf of the government of India and functioned as a tax paying company just like other existing stock exchanges.

It was recognized as a stock exchange in April 1993 under the Securities Contracts (Regulation) Act 1956. In June 1994 a Wholesale Debt Market (WDM) segment was started and in November 1994 the Capital Market (Equities) segment commenced its operation. The operations of the Derivatives segment commenced from June 2000.

Reasons for Setting-up of NSE

- To increase transparency, speed and efficiency of the Indian Stock Market.
- To introduce an exchange with well developed infrastructure and modern fully automated screen based trading system.
- Inability of various stock exchanges to coordinate and function under a legal and regulatory framework.

Objectives of NSE

- To play the role of a catalyst in Indian securities market in terms of trading volume and market practices.
- To introduce state-of-art technology for providing transparent trading, clearing and settlement mechanism.
- To introduce some innovations in products and services like – demutualization of the governance of stock exchange, screen based trading, reduction of settlement cycle, dematerialization and electronic transfer of securities, lending and borrowing of securities, professionalization of trading members, fine turned risk management systems, emergence of clearing corporations to assume counterparty risk market of debt and derivative instruments and intensive use of technology.

NSE & ITS SUBSIDIARIES

NSE has the following subsidiaries:

- **National Securities Clearing Corporation Ltd. (NSCCL):**

  NSCCL was established in August 1995 as a wholly owned subsidiary of NSE. The objective of NSCCL was to bring & sustain confidence in clearing & settlement of securities, to promote & maintain, short consistent settlement cycles; to provide counter-party risk guarantee and to operate a tight risk containment system. In April 1996 NSCCL started clearing operations. Presently it carried out the clearing & settlement of trades executed in the equities & derivatives segments & operates Subsidiary General Ledger (SGL) for settlement of trades in government securities. It assumes the counter-party risk of each member and guarantees financial settlement. It also undertakes settlement of transactions on other stock exchanges like OTCEI. The clearing & settlement mechanism of NSCCL is in line with international markets.

- **NSE IT Lld.**

  NSEIT a 100% subsidiary of National Stock Exchange of India Limited is the information technology arm of the largest stock exchange of the country. NSEIT has state-of-the art infrastructure and skills.

  It runs the trading and clearing infrastructure of NSE. NSEIT has the major focus on providing top-of-the line products, services and solutions in the area of trading, broker front-end and back office, clearing & settlement, web-based trading, risk management, treasury management, asset-liability management, banking, insurance etc. It has also been providing consultancy and implementation services in the areas of data warehousing, business continuity plans, status mainframe, facility management, site maintenance, real market analysis & financial news over NSE-Net etc. NSEIT has the plans to release products for broker back-office operations & enhance neat XS/neat IXS to support straight through processing on the net.

- **India Index Services and Products Ltd. (IISL)**

  IISL is a joint venture between NSE and CRISIL Limited. It was set-up in May 1998, to provide a variety of indices and index related services and products for the Indian capital markets. It has consulting and licensing agreement with Standard and Poor's (S&P) for co-branding equity indices. IISL provides a broad range of services, products and professional index services. It maintains over 80 equity indices comprising of broad-based benchmark indices, sectoral indices and customized indices. Based on IISL indices, a number of investment and risk management product have been developed within India and abroad. They include index based derivatives traded on NSE and Singapore Exchange (SIMEX) and a number of index funds.

- **National Securities Depository Limited (NSDL)**

  NSE along with Industrial Development Bank of India (IDBI) and Unit Trust of India (UTI) set-up the National Securities Depository Limited (NSDL), the first depository in India so as to solve the problems related to trading in physical securities.

  NSDL commenced its operations in November 1996 and since then it has established national infrastructure of international standard to handle trading & settlement in dematerialized form. This has helped to eliminate the risks associated with false, bad or stolen paper.

- **Dot Ex International Limited**

  Dot Ex was set-up as a joint venture between L-flex Solutions Ltd. & NSEIT. Ltd. Dot Ex was formed to provide a world-class internet trading platform which allows members of NSE to offer online trading facilities to their customers. With the help of this members of NSE can service a larger clientele by using automated risk management features and thus it increases volume of trading. It also enables the investors to get comprehensive and updated information necessary to trade along with single click convenience to fulfill their obligations. It provide a Dot Ex Plaza where multiple market participants such as members of NSE, depository participants and banks can offer web based services to their customers.

- **Technological Development of NSE**

  NSE has moved to electronic trading system which helps in providing wider reach and ease in trading. NSE's IT set-up uses satellite communication technology to connect around 400 cities around the country. The trading hardware of NSE can presently handle around 1 million trades per day. NSE's Internet Based Information System (NIBIS) helps in providing trading information over the internet. The exchange applications are being handled by the use of latest software platforms like RDBMS, ORACLE 7, ORACLE FORMS 4-5 etc. It manages its data center operations, system and database administration, development of in-house systems and design and implementation of telecommunication solutions. NSE has more than 4000 VSATs. It has also developed a corporate network connecting all the offices at Mumbai, Delhi, Calcutta and Chennai which enables speedy inter-office communications and data and voice connectivity between offices. NSE has gone online on the internet where live stock quotes can be seen on the website.

- **Indices**

  An index provides information about price movements of products in the financial, commodities and other markets. Price movements of stocks, bonds, T-Bills etc. are measured through financial indexes. Stock Market indexes are created by selecting a group of stocks that are representative of whole market or a specified sector or segment of the market. It reflects the overall behaviour of the equity markets.

- **National Stock Exchange Indices**

  With the objective of providing a variety of indices and Index related services, NSE has set-up India Index Service & Products Limited (IISL). IISL is a joint venture between National Stock Exchange of India Limited (NSE) and Credit Rating Information Services of India Limited (CRISIL). It has a consulting and licensing agreement with Standard and Poor's (S&P), the world's leading provider of investible equity indices, for co-branding IISL's equity indices.

  Major Indices of NSE are:

  - S & P CNX NIFTY
  - CNX NIFTY Junior
  - 58 P CNX 500
  - CNX Mid cap
  - S & P CNX Defty
  - CNX Mid cap 200

S & P CNX NIFTY

S & P CNX NIFTY is comprised of 50 stocks and represents 23 sectors of the economy.

NIFTY is computed using weighted average market capitalization method. (Ratio of weighted average market capitalization of all stocks to the weighted average market capitalization in the base period). The base period is November 3, 1995 and its value is 1000.

Criteria for Stock Selection in S & P CNX NIFTY

- Liquidity – Liquidity of a stock is also called impact cost. Impact cost is the ratio of difference between actual Buy/Sell price to the Ideal Price calculated as (Best Buy + Best Sell) /2 *i.e.* It is the percentage mark-up suffered during buying/selling the desired quantity of security as compared to its ideal price.

  For being included in the S & P CNX NIFTY the liquidity in terms of impact cost of 0.75% or less.
- The companies should have an average market capitalization of Rs.500 crores or more during the last six months.
- The companies should have at least 12% stock not held by promoters and associated entities (*i.e.* floating stock).

  S & P CNX NIFTY Stocks represent 60% of the total market capitalization.

CNX NIFTY JUNIOR

CNX NIFTY Junior comprises of 100 most liquid stocks in India. It is computed using weighted average market capitalization method. Stocks in CNX NIFTY Junior are stocks with highest liquidity excluded from S & P CNX NIFTY. The base date for CNX NIFTY Junior is Nov. 3, 1996 and base value is 1000.

Criteria for Selecting Stocks in CNX NIFTY Junior

- Liquidity (Impact cost)- The stocks with impact cost of 1.5% or less are included in the CNX NIFTY Junior Index.
- Market Capitalization of Stocks for inclusion in this index should be Rs.200 crores or more.
- At least 12% of the stocks should not be held by promoters and associated entities.

CNX NIFTY JUNIOR represents 10% of the total market capitalization.

S & P CNX 500

It is an Index which compares portfolios returns with market returns. The S & P CNX 500 companies are disaggregated into 72 industry indices. The weightage of stocks in the Index is in accordance with the weightage of stocks in the market. For example - A company having 10% weightage in universe of stocks traded on NSE; then pharma stocks in the Index (S&P CNX 500) will also have around 10% representation in the Index. The Index is calculated using weighted average method. 1994 is the base year for the Index and base value is 1000.

Criteria for selection of Stocks for inclusion S&P CNX 500 –

- Market Capitalization
- It should have industry representation *i.e.* Industry weightage in the Index must be representative of industry weightage in the market.
- The companies should have high turnover and high trading frequency along with a minimum listing period of 6 months.
- Companies should have positive net worth record of minimum 3 years.

CNX MID CAP

It represents the stocks of mid cap sector. It is computed on the basis of weighted average market capitalization with base period as Jan 1, 2003 and base value of 1000.

Criteria for Selection of Stocks for CNX Midcap —

- Market Capitalization- First a list of all stocks in descending order of capitalization is formed out of which those having more than 5% market capitalization are excluded. The weightage and then cumulative weightage of remaining stocks is determined. From this companies which form up to 75% (*i.e.* 75% and less) of the cumulative percentage of 75% and above form the CNX Midcap Index.
- Listing record of minimum 6 months.
- Positive net worth track record of 3 years.

S & P CNX DEFTY

It is S & P CNX NIFTY measured in Dollars. It enables foreign institutional investors and off-shore funds to measure their performance. Its calculation is done as –

$$\text{S\&P CNX Defty} = \frac{\text{S\&P CNX NIFTY at time } t \times \text{Exchange rate as on base date}}{\text{Exchange rate at time } t}$$

Base date is 3rd Nov. 1995

Base value is 1000

Exchange rate as on base date = 34.65 & Adjustment factor as on base date = 1.

CNX MIDCAP 200

It includes medium capitalization companies and represents 72% of market capitalization of Mid cap sector. Base date for Index is year 1994 & value is 1000.

Criteria for selection of stocks for CNX Midcap 200

- Market Capitalization – Midcap of the company's stock for being included in the index should be between 750-7500 crores.
- The weightage of industries in CNX Midcap 200. Index represents weightage of industries in Midcap segment of the market.
- Listing record should be a minimum of 6 months.
- Company should have had a track record of positive net worth for at least 3 years.

Other Indices of NSE are —

- CNX IT Sector Index
- CNX Bank Index

- CNX FMCG Index
- CNX PSE Index
- CNX MNC Index
- CNX Service Sector Index
- S&P CNX Industry Indices
- Customized Indices

OVER THE COUNTER EXCHANGE OF INDIA (OTCEI)

OTCEI was incorporated in 1990 under Section 25 of The Companies Act 1956 and is recognized as a stock exchange under Section 4 of the Securities Contract Regulation Act, 1956.

Need for OTCEI

There were many companies which were innovative and high growth and had been undergoing technological revolution. These companies needed a platform to raise timely, cost effective & long-term capital so as to carry out their operations and enhance growth. They were unable to fulfill the listing requirement and the minimum capital limit for getting listed on large exchanges. So OTCEI was set-up for providing transparent and efficient mode of trading for smaller companies.

Objectives of OTCEI

- To aid enterprising promoters in raising finance for new projects in a cost effective manner and to provide investors with transparent & efficient mode of trading.
- Introduction of new concepts to Indian market along the lines of NASDAQ, USA.
- Provide market for small companies who could not afford the listing fees of large exchanges.

Promoters of OTCEI

Promoters of OTCEI are LIC, GIC, UTI, ICICI, IDBI, IFCI, SBI, Capital Markets and Canbank Financial Services.

Securities Traded

OTCEI has 3 types of securities which are traded listed *i.e.* those which are listed on OTCEI and not traded elsewhere permitted *i.e.* securities of other recognized exchanges which are allowed to trade on OTCEI and initiated as start-up companies.

Listing Requirements

For getting listed on OTCEI:

- A company should have a minimum paid-up capital of Rs.30 lakhs and the minimum offer to the public should be 25% of the issue capital or Rs.20 lakhs worth of shares in face value whichever is higher. All the issues should be as per SEBI guidelines on Disclosure & Investor Protection.

- Every company that intends to get listed must be sponsored by a merchant banker of the exchange. The sponsor of the issue must arrange for Market Makers to give Buy & Sell quotes in the securities for an initial period of 18 months.

In addition companies which fulfill the following conditions are eligible to apply:-

- 3 year dividend paying record in the last 5 years.
- Sponsored by a Member / Sponsor of OTCEI.
- Have at least 2 market makers for continuous liquidity to their shares.

In case of companies not fulfilling 3 year dividend record / financial institution appraisal or funding criteria may go for Bought-Out-Deals.

Along with the above mentioned norms all Public Limited Companies have to fulfill the following criteria to get themselves listed on OTC.

1. Company Valuation	
Net Tangible Assets (or)	Rs. 1 crore (or)
Market Capitalization (or)	Rs. 5 crore (or)
Net Income (in latest fiscal year or 2 of last 3 fiscal years)	Rs. 0.25 crores
2. Shareholding	
Minimum Total Float (shares)	11,00,000
Minimum Public Float (shares)	5,00,000
Market value of Public Float	Rs.2.50 crores
Minimum offer to the public (as % of total paid-up capital)	25%
Minimum no. of shareholders	1000
3. Market Making	
No. of Market Makers	Minimum 2
Duration of Market Making	18 months
Obligation	Mandatory
Market making inventory (at the time of public issue)	Graded
4. Company Fact File	
Operating History (or)	1 year (or)
Minimum Market Capitalization	Rs.5 crore
Corporate Governance	Yes
Compliance Standards	No defaults
Additional Requirements for Finance Companies	
Registration with RBI As NBFC	Compulsory
Investment Grade Rating	In case of FDs or debenture issues
Continuous Profitability	Past 3 years
Market Making Inventory	
Principal & Additional Market Maker	10% minimum together
Debt Equity Ratio	As per RBI guidelines

CONTINUOUS LISTING REQUIREMENTS

The trading in equity shares of the company commences 3 days after the company is listed. Post listing, the company is required to provide a bank guarantee of 1% of the issue amount in favour of OTCEI for complying with continuous requirements. Apart from this the following are the continuous listing requirements:

1. Company Valuation	
Net Tangible Assets	0.75 crores or
Or Market Capitalization	3.75 crores or
Or Net Income (in latest fiscal year or last 3 fiscal years)	0.15 crores
2. Shareholding	
Minimum Total Float (shares)	8,25,000
Minimum Public Float (shares)	3,75,000
Market value of Public Float	Rs.1.90 crores
Minimum offer to the public (as % of total paid-up capital)	25%
Minimum no. of shareholders	1000
3. Company Fact File	
Operating History (or)	N/A (or)
Minimum Market Capitalization	Rs.3.75 crore
Corporate Governance	Yes
Compliance Standards	No Defaults

Procedure for Listing

- The company first appoints a sponsor. A sponsor does not participate in secondary market activities and only sponsors the issue.
- Sponsor appoints a market maker, who is actually involved in trading and underwriting activities for the issue.
- After this registration application (with relevant documents) is submitted to get approval which is valid for 6 months.
- A draft prospectus is then submitted with OTCEI for approval.
- After this Notice of Issue is submitted.
- The basis of allotment of securities is finalized.
- Listing application is filed.

The initial listing fee is Rs.7500.

The annual listing fee is:

Paid-up Capital	Amount of Annual Fees.
Up to 3 crores	Rs. 7500.00
3-10 crores	Rs.15000.00
10-20 crores	Rs. 25000.00
20-50 crores	Rs. 40000.00
50-100 crores	Rs.85000.00
Above Rs.100 crores	Rs.1000/- for every Rs. 10 crores or part thereof of the capital

PARTICIPANTS IN THE OTC MARKET

1. **Members, Dealers & Sponsors** – Members, Dealers & Sponsors contribute to the exchanges' activities by trading and enabling listing of companies on the Exchange. Members & Dealers may carry out the activities of trading, underwriting, market making & participation in bought-out deals. Sponsors perform the function of sponsoring the issue. They cannot participate in secondary market activities. The sponsor however has to carry out compulsory market making for a minimum period of 18 months from the date when public trading starts. He must also appoint an additional market maker to hold 5% of public offer. Sponsors/Members/Dealers may be banks, financial institutions or NBFC approved by SEBI.
2. **Investors** – Investors involve all those who participate in OTCEI for buying / selling scrips.
3. **Companies** – Their shares are listed and traded in OTCEI.

Apart from the participants, Registrar to the issue for maintaining accounts of members, Banker to clear payments and Regulatory authorities including government and SEBI are involved.

Trading of OTCEI

- An investor who wishes to buy/sell scrips at OTCEI first gets registered with the exchange and obtain an INVEST OTC CARD.
- The investor approaches the brokers (Members/Dealers) and views the screen displaying the best current quotes/prices offered.
- After viewing the quotes the investor can put a buy/sell order to match either the best quote or the best rate.
- Alternatively, the investor may put an order at a rate different from those currently available and the order may be executed against a corresponding order received within the same settlement period.
- After orders get matched and deal is confirmed if it is a buying order then the customer may make payment by cheques and get a temporary counter receipt from the seller which may be returned and final counter receipt may be collected when cheques get cleared. On the other hand if it is a selling order then the investor will have to give a counter receipt and transfer deed in lieu of sales confirmation slip which may be returned after the cheques is cleared and collected.

RISK MANAGEMENT IN OTCEI

Risk management in OTCEI is done by imposing margins on the members & dealers. These margins include:

- **Daily Margin:** It comprises of mark to market margins and value at risk margin.
  (*a*) **Mark to Market Margin** — It is computed on the basis of mark to market loss of a member. Mark to market loss is potential loss, increase the cumulative net outstanding position of the member in all securities at the end of day is closed out. It is computed by marking each transaction in a scrip to closing price of the scrip at the end of trading.
  (*b*) **Value at Risk Margin -** It is computed for all securities in the rolling settlement. All securities are classified into three groups for purpose of value at risk (VAR) margins.

Advantages of OTCEI:

- It is the first screen based nationwide stock exchange in India to introduce market making.
- It is the only exchange to allow listing of companies with paid-up capital below Rs.3 crore.
- It is the only exchange which allows companies with a trade record of less than 3 years to cap the market.
- The exchange has introduced a weekly settlement cycle which helps in early settlement of trades.
- It acts as a benchmark to value securities.
- It is an easier launch pad for an IPO.
- It helps to make the informal market of trading a broader & more liquid market.

OTCEI is an active market and has been receiving a positive response from investors in Indian markets. OTCEI proposes to introduce a vibrant and a well regulated market structure for trading in unlisted securities thereby giving an exit option for venture capital/private equity, offshore funds & other institutions and corporates. This provides improved investment opportunities in start-up enterprises, especially in the growth sectors with its new initiatives & developments. OTCEI has been setting benchmarks and proving to be of benefit to the corporates & individual investors of India.

QUESTIONS

Fill in the blanks:

1. BSE comprises of governing board having ____________ directors.
2. Shares traded in BSE have been classified into ______,______,______and_______ groups which represent certain quantitative and qualitative parameters.
3. BSE applies __________ of 20% on all scrips whose price moves beyond the limit on any particular day.
4. The mode of trading on BSE is called ____________.
5. NSE follows ____________ driven system.
6. NSEIT setup uses ________ technology to connect around 400 cities in India.
7. CNX Midcap represents stocks of ______________.
8. __________ committee recommended the setting up of NSE.
9. NSE has _________ subsidiaries.
10. _________ type of securities are traded on OTCEI.
11. Members of OTCEI are __________ only.
12. ______,_______and_______ contribute to trading and enable listing of companies on OTCEI.
13. Risk management in OTCEI is done by imposing _______ comprising of_______and______.

State whether true or false:

1. BSE is a national exchange.
2. Minimum net worth of a company should be 20 crores for getting listed on BSE.
3. F-Group on BSE represents securities of defaulter companies.
4. There is no trading floor on NSE.
5. Stocks in NSE indices are selected on the basis of market capitalization only.
6. NSE does not deal with trading of debt securities.
7. Registration is not necessary for an investor who wishes to buy/sell scrips at OTCEI.
8. A company intending to get listed on OTCEI must be sponsored by a merchant banker.
9. OTCEI is a national exchange.
10. OTCEI is an easier launch pad for an IPO.

Answer in detail:

Q.1. Discuss the surveillance mechanism adopted by BSE.

Q.2. Differentiate between BSE, NSE & OTCEI.

❑❑❑

PART–II
FINANCIAL INSTITUTIONS

Section - I : Regulatory and Promotional Institutions

Section - II : Banking System in India

Section - III : Developmental Financial Institutions

Section - IV : Specialised Financial Institutions

13 SECURITIES EXCHANGE BOARD OF INDIA (SEBI)

INTRODUCTION

Securities Exchange Board of India (SEBI) was established on April 12, 1988 with the dual objective of protecting the rights of small investors and regulating and developing stock markets in India. The Board was subsequently upgraded as a fully autonomous body (a statutory Board) in the year 1992 by passing a SEBI Act on 30th January, 1992.

In place of government control, a statutory and autonomous regulatory board with defined responsibilities to cover both development and regulation of the market and independent powers has been set-up.

The basic objectives of the Board were identified as—

- To protect the interest of investors in securities.
- To promote the development of Securities Market.
- To regulate the securities market.
- To promote fair dealing by the issuers of securities and ensure a market place where they can raise funds at relatively low cost.
- To provide a degree of protection to investors and safeguard their rights and interests so that there is steady flow of savings into the market.
- To regulate and develop a code of conduct and fair practices by intermediaries like brokers, and merchant bankers with a view to make them competitive and professional.

Since inception SEBI has been working towards targeting of securities and trying to fulfill its objectives with commendable zeal and dexterity.

Administration of SEBI

- The Securities and Exchange Board of India Act, 1992 came into force on January 30, 1992. Under this Act a Board named Securities and Exchange Board of India (SEBI) was constituted under the SEBI Act to administer its provisions.

- It consists of one chairman and five members: One each from the department of Finance and Law of the Central Government, one from the Reserve Bank of India and two other persons and having its head office in Bombay and regional offices in Delhi, Calcutta and Madras. The Central Government reserves the right to terminate the services of the Chairman or any member of the Board. The Board decides questions in the meeting by majority vote with the Chairman having a second or casting vote.

- Section 11 of the SEBI Act provides that to protect the interest of investors in securities and to promote the development and regulate the securities market by such measures, is the duty of the Board. It has given power to the Board to—
    - Regulate the businesses in Stock Exchanges
    - Register and regulate the working of stock brokers, sub-brokers, share transfer agents, bankers to an issue, trustees of trust deeds, registrar to an issue, merchant bankers, underwriters, portfolio managers, investment advisors etc.,
    - To register and regulate the working of collective investment schemes including mutual funds
    - To prohibit fraudulent and unfair trade practices and insider trading, to regulate takeover, to conduct enquiries and audits of stock exchanges etc.
- All the stock brokers, sub-brokers, share transfer agents, bankers to an issue, merchant bankers, underwriters, portfolios managers, investment advisors and other such intermediary who may be associated with the Securities Markets are to register with the Board under the provisions of the Act under Section 12 of the SEBI Act. The Board has the power to cancel or suspend such registration.
- The Board is bound by the direction vested by the Central Government from time to time on questions of policy and the Central Government reserves the right to supersede the Board. The Board is also obliged to submit a report to the Central Government giving true and full account of its activities, policies and programmes.

ACTIVITIES OF SEBI

SEBI has introduced from time to time the comprehensive regulatory measures, prescribed registration norms, eligibility criteria, code of obligations and code of conduct for different intermediaries like, bankers to issue, merchant bankers, brokers and sub-brokers, registrars, portfolio managers, credit rating agencies, underwriters and others. It has framed bye-laws, risk identification and risk management systems for clearing houses of stock exchanges, surveillance system etc., which has made dealing in securities both safe and transparent to the end investors.

SEBI AND PRIMARY MARKET

Public Issue

Any company or a listed company making a public issue or a rights issue of value of more than

Rs.50 Lakhs is required to file a draft offer document with SEBI for its observations. The company can proceed forward only after getting observations from SEBI. The company has to open its issue within three months from the date of SEBIs observation letter. SEBI has also laid down several entry norms for companies who are to make a public issue.

SEBI AND SECONDARY MARKET

Section 3 of SEBI Act protects the interests of investors in securities and also promotes the development of, and regulates, the security market and related matters.

The following are the financial products/instruments which are controlled by SEBI:-

- Equity Shares
- Rights Issue / Rights Shares
- Bonus Shares
- Preferred Stock / Preference Shares
- Cumulative Preference Shares
- Cumulative Convertible Preference Shares
- Participating Preference Shares
- Bond
- Zero Coupon Bond
- Convertible Bond
- Debentures
- Commercial Paper
- Coupons
- Treasury Bills

SEBI AND MUTUAL FUNDS

SEBI formulates policies to regulate the mutual funds for protecting the interest of investors. Mutual funds either promoted by public or by private sector entities including ones promoted by foreign entities are governed by these Regulations.

SEBI approved Asset Management Company (AMC) manages the funds by making investments in various types of securities, custodian, registered with SEBI, holds the securities of various schemes of the fund in its custody. The general power of superintendence and direction over AMC is vested with the trustees.

According to SEBI guidelines, two tricks of the directors of trustee company or board of trustees must be independent. They should not be associated with the sponsors 50% of the directors of AMC must be independent. All mutual funds are required to be registered before they launch a scheme.

SEBI AND TAKEOVER NORMS

SEBI has also laid down norms for take over. These are:-

- Imposing curb on off- market deals.
  - (*a*) Upto a threshold level of 5 per cent, off market deals are allowed.
  - (*b*) Between 5 per cent and 15 per cent all deals should be made only through stock market.
- SEBI has laid down the reduction of time limit for completion of the open offer from 4 months at present to 3 months.
- SEBI has put restrictions on the sale of shares by the acquirer during the open offer period.
- SEBI has made it mandatory for the board of directors to give independent comment to the shareholders of the target company regarding its future plans.
- Merchant Banker must stop dealing in the shares of the target company, following his appointment as manager to the offer and disclose its shareholding in the offer document.

SEBI and Foreign Institutional Investors

SEBI has laid down provisions regarding Foreign Institutional Investment. Under these provisions, an application for registration has to be made in Form A, the format of which is provided in the SEBI (FII) Regulations, 1995 and submitted with the prescribed documents in duplicate addressed to SEBI as well as to Reserve Bank of India (RBI).

SEBI and Derivatives Trading

Derivatives trading takes place under the Act 1992, and the framework including suggestive bye law and its clearing corporation / house has been laid down by Dr. L.C. Gupta Committee, constituted by SEBI.

Role of SEBI in Collective Investment Schemes

Registered with SEBI under the SEBI (Collective Investment Schemes) Regulations, 1999 and incorporated under the provisions of the Companies Act, 1956 whose object is to organize, operate and manage a collective Investment Scheme forms a collective Investment Management Company.

SEBI's Entry Norms for Banks

SEBI requires public sector banks to have two years' profitability record before pricing their public issues above par, while private banks can float public issues at par after one year of operation. But they cannot price it at premium until they have a profit and dividend track record of three years.

SEBI and Secondary Market

SEBI has taken the following initiatives in the Secondary Market:-

1. Reconstitution of Government Boards of Stock Exchanges to have:-
   - (*a*) 50:50 broker and non-broker representation in the board.

(b) Arbitration, Disciplinary and Default committees of exchanges to have 60% representation from non-broker members.

(c) Change of tenure of Vice President and President such that they are not able to hold office for long periods of time without break.

2. To ensure impartial and fair governance by public representatives and government nominees on governing Boards of the stock exchanges.
3. Filing of criminal cases against unrecognized stock exchanges.
4. Compulsory audit of broker books and filing of audit reports with SEBI.
5. Amendment of SCRA Section 19 (2*b*) to reduce the minimum percentage of securities to be issued to public from 60% to 25%.
6. Reporting of off-market deals by a special committee.
7. Set-up of 3 tier margin system to curtail build up of speculative volumes on brokers to ensure curtailment of speculative volumes and price rigging.
8. Guidelines for introduction of market making in less liquid scrip in a phased manner for the first time.
9. Continuous monitoring of stock exchanges by inspection.

QUESTIONS

Fill in the blanks:

1. SEBI has powers to grant approval to __________ of stock exchanges.
2. Any company making a public issue of value of more than Rs. ________ is required to file a draft offer document with SEBI.
3. ______committee was constituted by SEBI for deciding about derivatives trading.
4. Public Sector Banks should have profitability record of ________ years before pricing their public issues above par.

State whether true or false:

1. The objective of SEBI is to promote development of securities market.
2. Stock brokers do not come under SEBI regulations.
3. T-Bills issued are not controlled by SEBI.
4. AMC of a mutual fund should be approved by SEBI.

Answer in detail:

Q.1. What are the various objectives for which SEBI has been setup? What areas does it regulate and in what ways?

❑❑❑

14

RESERVE BANK OF INDIA

INTRODUCTION

The Reserve Bank of India (RBI) is the central bank of the country. It was established in April, 1935 with a share capital of Rs. 5 crore on the basis of the recommendations of the Hilton Young Commission. The share capital was divided into fully paid, shares of Rs. 100 each which was entirely owned by private shareholders in the beginning. The Government held shares of nominal value of Rs. 2,20,000.

Reserve Bank of India was nationalized in the year 1949. The general superintendence and direction of the Bank is entrusted to Central Board of Directors of 20 members, the governor and four deputy governors, one government official from the ministry of finance, ten nominated directors by the Government to give representation to important elements in the economic life of the country, and four nominated directors by the central government to represent the four local Boards with the headquarters at Mumbai, Kolkata, Chennai and New Delhi. Local Boards consist of five members each appointed by the central government for a term of four years to represent territorial and economic interests and the interests of cooperative and indigenous banks.

The Reserve Bank of India Act, 1934 was commenced on April 1, 1935. The Act, 1934 (II of a1934) provides the statutory basis of the functioning of the Bank.

Objectives of RBI:

The bank was constituted for the need of following:

- To regulate the issue of banknotes,
- To maintain reserves with a view to securing monetary stability, and
- To operate the credit and currency system of the country to its advantage.

Administrative Set-up

(*i*) **Central Board :** RBI is governed by the Central Board which is appointed/nominated by the Government of India for a period of four years. The Central Board consists of the governor and four deputy governors, as official directors. Additionally there are 14 non-official directors. 10 of them are nominated by government from various fields and one government official. The remaining four directors are selected one each from four Local Boards.

(*ii*) **Local Boards :** There are four Local Boards one each for the four regions of the country in Mumbai, Kolkata, Chennai and New Delhi. Membership of the Local Boards consists of five members each. They are appointed by the central government for a term of four years.

While Central Board looks after general superintendence direction of the bank's affairs, the function of the Local Boards is to advise the Central Board on local matters and to represent territorial and economic interests of local cooperative and indigenous banks, to perform such other functions as delegated by Central Board from time to time.

OFFICES

RBI has 22 regional offices, most of them in state capitals. It has six training establishments, of which three, College of Agricultural Banking, Bankers Training College and Reserve Bank of India Staff College as part of RBI. Others are autonomous institutions, such are National Institute for Bank Management, Indira Gandhi Institute for Development Research (IGIDR), Institute for Development and Research in Banking Technology (IDRBT)

Subsidiary Institutions

(*i*) **Fully Owned:** National Housing Bank (NHB), National Bank for Agriculture and Rural Development(NABARD), Deposit Insurance and Credit Guarantee Corporation of India (DICGC), Bharatiya Reserve Bank Note Mudran Private Limited (BRBNMPL)

(*ii*) **Majority Stake:** State Bank of India

(*iii*) **Minority Stake:** Infrastructure Development Finance Company (IDFC), Securities Trading Corporation of India(STCI), Discount and Finance House of India(DFHI).

In keeping with its approach to avoid the potential conflict of interest created by the ownership of regulated financial institutions, the Reserve Bank divested its entire holdings in the Securities Trading Corporation of India Ltd. and the Discount and Finance House of India. Similar disinvestment is proposed for its holding in the State Bank of India, the National Housing Bank and the National Bank for Agriculture and Rural Development. In pursuance of the objective of withdrawing from development financing functions, the Reserve Bank transferred assets on account of loans and advances to Development Financial Institutions out of National Industrial Credit (Long-term Operations) Fund to the Government, replacing them with long-term Government of India securities through private placement.

RBI Regulation of Banks – Pre-Reform Status

- The regulatory framework for the banking industry under the Banking Regulation Act was circumscribed by the special provisions of the Bank Nationalization Act, both of which had elements of corporate governance incorporated with regard to composition of Board of Directors in terms of representation of directors, etc.

- While technically there was competition between banks and non-banks and among banks, substantively, competition was conditioned by policy as well as regulatory environment, common ownership by the Government and agreement between the Government of India as an owner and the workers represented by the Unions.
- Subsequent efforts during the reform period were made in terms of hesitancy in permitting industrial houses as well as foreign owned banks.
- As regards the policy environment, the whole of financial intermediation was on account of public sector, with PSBs being the most important source of mobilization of financial savings. Resources for DFIs were also made available either by banks or mostly created money and governmental support.
- The major thrust was on expansion of bank's branches, provision of banking services and mobilization of deposits. The interest rate regime was administered with interest rates fixed both on deposits and lending.
- There was large pre-emption of banks' resources under the cash reserve ratio or in the form of statutory liquidity ratio. The delivery of credit was also by and large directed through an allocative mechanism or as an adjunct to the licensing regime. The private sector banks tended to be confined to the local areas and were unable to expand in such an environment.
- Banks, mainly public sector banks became the most dominant vehicle of the financial intermediation in the country. To a large extent, entry was restricted and exit was impossible and there was little or no scope for functions of risk assessment and pricing of risks. The Government thus combined in itself the role of owner, regulator and sovereign.
- The legal as well as policy framework emphasized coordination in the interest of national development as per Plan priorities, with the result the issue of corporate governance became subsumed in the overall development framework.
- Each bank, even after nationalization, maintained its distinct identity, governance structure as incorporated in the concerned legislations provided for a formal structure of relationship between the RBI, Government, Board of Directors and management.
- The role of the RBI as a regulator became essentially one of being an extended arm of the Government so far as highest priority was accorded to ensuring coordinated actions in regard to activities particularly of PSBs.
- SBI, which was owned by the RBI was in substance no different from the other banks owned by Government in terms of Board composition, appointment procedures of the executives and non-executive members of the Board of Directors.
- Both Government and RBI were represented on the Board of Directors of the PSBs.
- Cross holdings and inter-relationships were more a rule than an exception in the financial sector, since the basic objective was coordination for ensuring planned development, with the result, the concepts of conflicts of interest among players, checks and balances etc.,were subordinated to the social goals of the joint family headed by the Government.

REFORM MEASURES

The major challenge of the reform has been to introduce elements of market incentive as a dominant factor gradually replacing the administratively coordinated planned actions for development.

Such a paradigm shift has several dimensions, the *corporate governance* being one of the important elements. The evolution of corporate governance in banks, particularly, in PSBs, thus reflects changes in monetary policy, regulatory environment, and structural transformations and to some extent, on the character of the self-regulatory organizations functioning in the financial sector.

During the reform period, the policy environment enhanced competition and provided greater opportunity for exercise of what may be called genuine corporate element in each bank to replace the elements of coordinated actions of all entities as a "joint family" to fulfill predetermined Plan priorities. The measures taken so far can be summarized as follows :

- **First,** greater competition has been in the banking system by permitting entry of private sector banks (9 licences since 1993), and liberal licensing of more branches by foreign banks and the entry of new foreign banks. With the development of a multi-institutional structure in the financial sector, emphasis is on efficiency through competition irrespective of ownership. Since non-bank intermediation has increased, banks have had to improve efficiency to ensure survival.
- **Second,** the reforms accorded greater flexibility to the banking system to manage both the pricing and quantity of resources. There has been a reduction in statutory preemptions to less than a third of commercial banks resources. The mandatory component of market financing of Government borrowing has decreased. While directed credit continues, it is now on near commercial terms. Valuation of banks' investments is also attuned to international best practices so as to appropriately capture market risks.
- **Third,** the RBI has moved away from micro-regulation to macro-management. RBI has replaced detailed individual guidelines with general guidelines and now leaves it to individual banks' boards to set their guidelines on credit decisions. A Regulation Review Authority was established in RBI, whereby any bank could challenge the need for any regulation or guideline and the department had to justify the need and usefulness for such guideline relative to costs of regulation and compliance.
- **Fourth,** to strengthen the banking system to cope up with the changing environment, prudential standards have been imposed in a progressive manner. Thus, while banks have greater freedom to take credit decisions, prudential norms setting out capital adequacy norms, asset classification, income recognition and provisioning rules, exposure norms, and asset liability management systems have helped to identify and contain risks, thereby contributing to greater financial stability.
- **Fifth,** an appropriate legal, institutional, technological and regulatory framework has been put in place for the development of financial markets. There is now increased volume and transparency in the primary and secondary market operations. Development of the Government Securities, money and FOREX markets has improved the transmission mechanism of monetary policy, facilitated the development of a yield curve and enabled greater integration of markets. The interest rate channel of monetary policy transmission is acquiring greater importance as compared with the credit channel.

RBI'S REGULATORY ENVIRONMENT

Prudential regulation and supervision have formed a critical component of the financial sector reform programme since its inception, and India has endeavoured to international prudential norms and practices. These norms have been progressively tightened over the years, particularly against the backdrop of the Asian crisis. Bank exposures to sensitive sectors such as equity and real estate have been curtailed. The Banking Regulation Act, 1949 prevents connected lending (*i.e.,* lending by banks to directors or companies in which Directors are interested).

- Periodical inspection of banks has been the main instrument of supervision, though recently there has been a move toward supplementary 'on-site inspections' with 'off-site surveillance'.
- The system of 'Annual Financial Inspection' was introduced in 1992, in place of the earlier system of Annual Financial Review/Financial Inspections. The inspection objectives and procedures, have been redefined to evaluate the bank's safety and soundness; to appraise the quality of the Board and management; to ensure compliance with banking laws and regulation; to provide an appraisal of soundness of the bank's assets; to analyze the financial factors which determine bank's solvency and to identify areas where corrective action is needed to strengthen the institution and improve its performance. Inspections based upon the new guidelines have started since 1997.
- A high powered Board for Financial Supervision (BFS), comprising the Governor of RBI as Chairman, one of the Deputy Governors as Vice-Chairman and four Directors of the Central Board of RBI as members was constituted in 1994, with the mandate to exercise the powers of supervision and inspection in relation to the banking companies, financial institutions and non-banking companies.
- A supervisory strategy comprising on-site inspection, off-site monitoring and control systems internal to the banks, based on the CAMELS (capital adequacy, asset quality, management, earnings, liquidity and systems and controls) methodology for banks have been instituted. The RBI has instituted a mechanism for critical analysis of the balance sheet by the banks themselves and the presentation of such analysis before their boards to provide an internal assessment of the health of the bank. The analysis, which is also made available to the RBI, forms a supplement to the system of off-site monitoring of banks.
- Keeping in line with the merging regulatory and supervisory standards at international level, the RBI has initiated certain macro level monitoring techniques to assess the true health of the supervised institutions.
- The format of balance sheets of commercial banks have now been prescribed by the RBI with disclosure standards on vital performance and growth indicators, provisions, net NPAs, staff productivity, etc. appended as 'Notes of Accounts'.
- To bring about greater transparency in banks' published accounts, the RBI has also directed the banks to disclosure date on movement of non-performing assets (NPAs) and provisions as well as lending to sensitive sectors. These proposed additional disclosure norms would bring the disclosure standards almost on par with the international best practice.

FUNCTIONS OF RBI

Bankers' Bank and Lender of the Last Resort

- The Reserve Bank of India acts as the banker's bank. According to the provisions of the Banking Companies Act of 1949 every scheduled bank was required to maintain with the Reserve Bank a cash balance equivalent to 5 per cent of its demand liabilities and 2 per cent of its time liabilities in India.
- By an amendment of 1962, the distinction between demand and time liabilities was abolished and banks have been asked to keep cash reserves equal to 3 per cent of their aggregate deposit liabilities. The minimum cash requirements can be changed by the Reserve Bank of India.
- The scheduled banks can borrow from the Reserve Bank of India on the basis of eligible securities or get financial accommodation in times of need or stringency by rediscounting bills of exchange.
- Since commercial banks can always expect the Reserve bank of India to come to their help in times of banking crisis the Reserve Bank becomes not only the banker's bank but also the lender of the last resort.

Controller of Credit

- The Reserve Bank of India is the controller of credit, *i.e.,* it has the power to influence the volume of credit created by banks in India.
- It can do so through changing the bank rate or through open market operations. According to the Banking Regulation Act of 1949, the Reserve Bank of India can ask any particular bank or the whole banking system not to lend to particular groups or persons on the basis of certain types of securities.
- Since 1956, selective controls of credit are increasingly being used by the Reserve Bank.
- The Reserve Bank of India is armed with many more powers to control the Indian money market. Every bank has to get a license from the Reserve Bank of India to do banking business within India, the license can be cancelled by the Reserve Bank if certain stipulated conditions are not fulfilled.
- Every bank will have to get the permission of the Reserve Bank before it can open a new branch.
- Each scheduled bank must send a weekly return to the Reserve Bank, showing in detail, its assets and liabilities. This power of the Bank to call for information is also intended to give it effective control of the credit system.
- The Reserve Bank has also the power to inspect the accounts of any commercial bank.
- As supreme banking authority in the country, the Reserve Bank of India, therefore, has the following powers:

  (*a*) It holds the cash reserves of all the schedule banks.

  (*b*) It controls the credit operations of banks through quantitative and qualitative controls.

(*c*) It controls the banking system through the system of licensing, inspection and calling for information.

(*d*) It acts as the lender of the last resort by providing rediscount facilities to scheduled banks.

Custodian of Foreign Reserves

- The Reserve Bank of India has the responsibility to maintain the official rate of exchange.
- According to Reserve Bank of India Act of 1934, the bank was required to buy and sell at fixed rates any amount of Sterling in lots if not less than Rs. 10,000.
- After India became a member of the International Monetary Fund in 1946, the Reserve Bank has the responsibility of maintaining fixed exchange rates with all other member countries of the IMF.
- Besides maintaining the rate of exchange of the rupee, the Reserve Bank has to act as the custodian of India's reserve of international currencies.
- The vast Sterling balances were acquired and managed by Banks. Further, the RBI has the responsibility of administering the exchange controls of the country.

Supervisory Functions

- In addition to its traditional central banking functions, the Reserve bank has certain non-monetary functions of the nature of supervision of banks and promotion of sound banking in India.
- The Reserve Bank Act, 1934, and the Banking Regulation Act, 1949 have given the RBI wide powers of supervision and control over commercial and cooperative banks, relating to licensing and establishments, branch expansion, liquidity of their assets, management and methods of working, amalgamation, reconstruction and liquidation.
- The RBI is authorized to carry out periodical inspections of the banks and to call for returns and necessary information from them.
- The nationalization of 14 major Indian scheduled banks in July, 1969 has imposed new responsibilities on the RBI for directing the growth of banking and credit policies towards more rapid development of the economy and realization of certain desired social objectives.
- The supervisory functions of the RBI have helped a great deal in improving the standard of banking in India to develop on sound lines and to improve the methods of their operation.

Promotional functions

- With economic growth assuming a new urgency since Independence, the range of the Reserve Bank's functions has steadily widened.
- The Bank now performs a variety of developmental and promotional functions, which, at one time, were regarded as outside the normal scope of central banking.
- The Reserve Bank was asked to promote banking habit, extend banking facilities to rural and semi-urban areas, and establish and promote new specialized financing agencies. Accordingly, the Reserve Bank has helped in the setting-up of the IFCI and the SFC; it set-up the Deposit

Insurance Corporation in 1962, the Unit Trust of India in 1964, the Industrial Development Bank of India also in 1964, the Agricultural Refinance Corporation of India in 1963 and the Industrial Reconstruction Corporation of India in 1972.

- These institutions were set-up directly or indirectly by the Reserve Bank to promote saving habit and to mobilize savings, and to provide industrial finance as well as agricultural finance.
- As far back as 1935, the Reserve Bank of India set-up the Agricultural Credit Department to provide agricultural credit. But only since 1951 the Bank's role in this field has become extremely important.
- The Bank has developed the co-operative credit movement to encourage saving, to eliminate moneylenders from the villages and to route its short-term credit to agriculture.
- The RBI has set-up the Agricultural Refinance and Development Corporation to provide long-term finance to farmers.

NORMS REGARDING CAPITAL ADEQUACY, ASSET CLASSIFICATION, INCOME RECOGNITION AND PROVISIONING ALONG WITH ACTION ON THE RECOMMENDATIONS

(Extract taken from RBI report: Committee on Banking Sector Reforms Narasimham Committee-II October 31, 2001)

RBI appointed a Committee on Financial System under the Chairmanship of Mr. M. Narasimham in 1991. The Committee submitted its report in April, 1998. The recommendations in the report were studied and implemented and a new report was submitted in October, 1998 stating the action taken on the recommendations. The following is the extract related to Norms regarding Capital Adequacy, Asset Classification, Income Recognition and Provisioning along with action taken on the recommendations.

Recommendation	Action Taken
Capital Adequacy	
1. The Committee suggests that pending the emergence of markets in India where market risks can be covered, it would be desirable that capital adequacy requirements take into account market risks in addition to the credit risk Chapter-III Para 3.10)	Banks are now required to assign capital for market risk. A risk weight of 2.5% for market risk has been introduced on investments in Government and other approved securities with effect from the year ending 31st March, 2000. For investments in securities outside SLR, a risk weight of 2.5% for market risk has been introduced with effect from the year ending 31st March, 2001. (Circulars DBOD No.BP.BC.103/21.01.002/98 dated 31.10.98 and 121/21.04.124/99-2000 dated 3.11.99)

2. In the next three years, the entire portfolio of Government securities should be marked to market and this schedule of adjustment should be announced at the earliest. It would be appropriate that there should be a 5% weight for market risk for Government and approved securities. (Chapter-III para 3.11)	The percentage of banks' portfolio of Government and approved securities, which is required to be marked to market, has progressively been increased. For the year ending 31st March, 2000, banks were required to mark to market 75% of their investments. In order to align the Indian accounting standards with the international best practices and taking into consideration the evolving international developments, the norms for classification and valuation of investments have been modified with effect from September 30, 2000. The entire investment portfolio of banks is required to be classified under three categories, *viz.,* Held to Maturity, Available for Sale and Held for Trading. While the securities "Held for Trading' and 'Available for Sale' should be marked to market periodically, the securities 'Held to Maturity', which should not exceed 25% of total investments are carried at acquisition cost unless it is more than the face value, in which case, the premium should be amortized over a period of time. (Circular DBOD No. BP.BC.32/31.04.048/2000-2001 dt. 16.10.2000).
3. The risk weight for a Government guaranteed advance should be the same as for other advances. To ensure that banks do not suddenly face difficulties in meeting the capital adequacy requirement, the new prescription on risk weight for Government guaranteed advances should be made prospective from the time the new prescription is put in place. (Chapter III para 3.12)	In cases of Governmentguaranteed adavances, where the guarantee has been invoked and the concerned State Governmenthas remained in default as on March 31,2000, a risk weight of 20% on such advances, has been introduced. State Govts.who continue to be in default in respect of such invoked guarantees even after March 31,2001, a risk weight of 100% is being assigned. (Circular DBOD.No.BP.BC.103/21.01.002/98 dated 31.10.98)
4. There is an additional capital requirement of 5% of the foreign exchange open position limit. Such risks should be integrated into calculation of risk weighted assets. The Committee recommends that the foreign exchange open position limits should carry a 100% risk weight. (Chapter III para 3.13)	Risk weight of 100% has been introduced for foreign exchange open position limits with effect from March 31, 1999. (Circular DBOD. No.BP.BC.103/21.01.002/98 dt.31.10.98)

5. The Committee believes that it would be appropriate to go beyond the earlier norms and set new and higher norms and set new and higher norms for capital adequacy. The Committee accordingly recommends that the minimum capital to risk assets ratio be increased to 10% from its present level of 8%. It would be appropriate to phase the increase as was done on the previous occasion. Accordingly, the Committee recommends that an intermediate minimum target of 9% be achieved by the year 2000 and the ratio of 10% by 2002. The RBI should also have the authority to raise this further in respect of individual banks if in its judgment the situation with respect to their risk profile warrants such an increase. The issue of individual banks' shortfalls in the CRAR needs to be addressed in much the same way that the discipline of reserve requirements is now applied, *viz.,* of uniformity across weak and strong banks (Chapter III, Para 3.15 3.16)	The minimum capital to risk asset ratio (CRAR) for banks has been enhanced to 9% with effect from the year ending March 31, 2000. (Circular DBOD.No.BP.BC.103/21.01.002/98 dated 31.10.98).
6. In respect of PSBs, the additional capital requirement will have to come from either the Government or the market. With the many demands on the budget and the continuing imperative need for fiscal consolidation, subscription to bank capital funds cannot be regarded as a priority claim on budgetary resources. Those banks which are in a position to access the capital market at home or abroad should, therefore, be encouraged to do so. (Chapter III, para 3.17)	Banks are permitted to access the capital market. Till today, 12 banks have already accessed capital market.
Asset Classification and NPAs: 7. The Committee recommends that an asset be classified as doubtful if it is in the substandard category for 18 months in the first instance and eventually for 12 months and loss if it has	Banks have been advised that an asset will be classified as 'doubtful' if it has remained in the substandard category for 18 months instead of 24 months as at present, by March 31, 2001. Banks have been permitted to achieve these norms for additional provisioning in phases, as under: As on 31.3.2001

been so identified but not written off. These norms, which should be regarded as the minimum, may be brought into force in a phased manner. (Chapter III, para 3.18)	Provisioning of not less than 50% on the assets which have become doubtful on account of the new norm. As on 31.3.2002 Balance of the provisions not made during the previous year, in addition to the provisions needed as on 31.3.2002. (Circular DBOD.No.BP.BC.103/21.01.002/98 dt.31.10.98)
Introduction of the norm of 90 days for income recognition in a phased manner.	In the Monetary and Credit Policy announced in April, 2001, the banks have been advised to chalk out an appropriate transition path for smoothly moving over to 90 days norm. As a facilitating measure, banks should move over to charging of interest at monthly rests by April 1,2002. Banks should commence making additional provisions for such loans, starting from the year ending March 31, 2002, which would strengthen their balance sheets and ensure smooth transition to the 90 days norm by March 31, 2004.
8. The Committee has noted that NPA figures do not include advances covered by Government guarantees which have turned sticky and which in the absence of such guarantees would have been classified as NPAs. The Committee is of the view that for the purposes of evaluating the quality of asset portfolio such advances should be treated as NPAs. If, however, for reason of the sovereign guarantee argument such advances are excluded from computation, the Committee would recommend that Government guaranteed advances which otherwise would have been classified as NPAs should be separately shown as an aspect of fuller disclosure and greater transparency of operations. (Chapter III, para 3.21)	Prudential norms in respect of advances guaranteed by State Governments where guarantee has been invoked and has remained in default for more than two quarters has been introduced in respect of advances sanctioned against State Government guarantee with effect from April 1, 2000. Banks have been advised to make provisions for advances guaranteed by State Governments which stood invoked as on March 31, 2000, in phases, during the financial years ending March 31, 2000 to March 31, 2003 with a minimum of 25% each years. (Circular DBOD.No.BP.BC.103/21.01.002/98 dt.31.10.98)
9. Banks and financial institutions should avoid the practice of "evergreening" by making fresh advances to their troubled constituents only	The RBI has reiterated that banks and financial institutions should adhere to the prudential norms on asset classification, provisioning, etc. and avoid

with a view to settling interest dues and avoiding classification of the loans in question as NPAs. The Committee notes that the regulatory and supervisory authorities are paying particular attention to such breaches in the adherence to the spirit of the NPA definitions and are taking appropriate corrective action. At the same time, it is necessary to resist the suggestions made from time to time for a relaxation of the definition of NPAs and the norms in this regard (Chapter III, para 3.22)	the practice of "evergreening". (Cir.DBOD.No.BP.BC.103/21.01.002/98 dt.31.10.98)
10. The Committee believes that the objective should be to reduce the average level of net NPAs for all banks to below 5% by the year 2000 and to 3% by 2002. For those banks with an international presence the minimum objective should be to reduce gross NPAs to 5% and 3% by the year 2000 and 2002, respectively, and net NPA to 3% and 0% by these dates. These targets cannot be achieved in the absence of measures to tackle the problem of backlog of NPAs on a one time basis and the implementation of strict prudential norms and management efficiency to prevent the recurrence of this problem. (Chapter III, para 3.26)	This is the long-term objective which RBI wants to pursue. Towards this direction, a number of measures have been taken to arrest the growth of NPAs: banks have been advised to tone up their credit risk management systems; put in place a loan review mechanism to ensure that advances, particularly large advances are monitored on an on-going basis so that signals of weaknesses are detected and corrective action taken early; enhance credit appraisal skills of their staff, etc. In order to ensure recovery of the stock of NPAs, guidelines for one-time settlement have been issued in July, 2000.
11. The Committee is of the firm view that in any effort at financial restructuring in the form of hiving off the NPA portfolio from the books of the banks or measures to mitigate the impact of a high level of NPAs must go hand in hand with operational restructuring. Cleaning up the balance sheets of banks would thus make sence only if simultaneously steps were taken to prevent or limit the re-emergence of new NPAs which could only come about through a strict application of prudential norms and managerial improvement. (Chapter III, para 3.27)	Banks have been advised to take effective steps for reduction of NPAs and also put in place risk management systems and practices to prevent re-emergence of fresh NP As. (Cir.DBOD.No.BP.BC.103/21.01.002/98 dated 31.10.1998)

12. For banks with a high NPA portfolio, the Committee suggests consideration of two alternative approaches to the problem as an alternative to the ARF proposal made by the earlier CFS. In the first approach, all loan assets in the doubtful and loss categories – which in any case represent bulk of the hard core NPAs in most banks should be identified and their realizable value determined. These assets could be transferred to an Asset Reconstruction Company (ARC) which would issue to the banks NPA Swap Bonds representing the realizable value of the assets transferred, provided the stamp duties are not excessive. The ARC could be set-up by one bank or a set of banks or even in the private sector. In case the banks themselves decide to set-up an ARC, it would need to be ensured that the staff required by the ARC is made available to it by the banks concerned either on transfer or on deputation basis, so that staff with institutional memory on NPAs is available to ARC and there is also some rationalization of staff in the banks whose assets are sought to be transferred to the ARC. Funding of such an ARC could be facilitated by treating it on par with venture capital for purpose of tax incentives. Some other banks may be willing to fund such assets in effect by securitizing them. This approach would be worthwhile and workable if stamp duty rates are minimal and tax incentives are provided to the banks. (Chapter III, para 3.28)	The proposal to set-up an Asset Reconsturction Company (ARC) on a pilot basis to take over the NPAs of the three weak public sector banks, has been announced in the Union Budget for 1999-2000. The modalities for setting up the ARC are being examined.
13. An alternative approach could be to enable the banks in difficulty to issue bonds which could form part of Tier II capital. This will help the banks to bolster capital adequacy which has been eroded because of the provisioning requirements for NPAs. As the banks in difficulty may find it difficult to attract subscribers to bonds. Government will need to guarantee these instruments which would	Banks are permitted to issue bonds for augmenting their Tier II capital. Guarantee of the Government for these bonds is not considered necessary.

then make them eligible for SLR investments by banks and approve instruments by LIC, GIC and Provident Funds (Chapter III, para 3.29)	
Income Recognition and Provisions Norms	
14. With regard to income recognition, in India, income stops accruing when interest or instalment of principal is not paid within 180 days. The Committee believes that we should move towards international practices in this regard and recommends the introduction of the norm of 90 days in a phased manner by the year 2002. (Chapter III, para 3.35)	The recommendation of the Committee that we should move towards international practices in regard to income recognition is accepted in principle. However, tightening of the prudential norms should be made keeping in view the existing legal framework, production and payment cycles, business practices, the predominant share of agriculture in the country's economy, etc. The production and repayment cycles in the industry in the country generally involve a period of not less than from 4 to 6 months. A large number of SSIs also have difficulties in timely realization of their bills drawn on the suppliers. These have to be taken into account while contemplating any change in the norm. Implementation of the recommendation would have serious implications on the asset portfolio of banks and even good quality borrowers and find it difficult to comply with the norms recommended. There have been representations from banks and financial institutions seeking relaxation in the above instructions by increasing the period to 3-4 quarters. Keeping in view the current industrial scenario, implementation of the recommendation would have serious implications even to healthy borrowers. Furthermore, interest on advances is calculated by banks at quarterly rests. Keeping in view the large number and volume of accounts, if we have to implement the recommendation, a few preconditions should be met : (*a*) Banks should introduce calculation of interest at monthly rests; (*b*) There should be 100% computerization of banks' operations. Unless 100%

	computerization is made, it may not be feasible to implement the recommendation ; (*c*) It is also necessary to tone up the legal machinery for speedy disposal of the collateral taken as security for the advance. However, considering the need to bring our norms in line with the best international practices, the recommendations made by the Committee would be our long-term objective. As the level of gross NPAs of banks come down because of better management practices, the recommendation to introduce the norm of 90 days will be examined.
15. At present, there is no requirement in India for a general provision on standard assets. In the committee's view a general provision, say, of 1% would be appropriate and RBI should consider its introduction in a phased manner. (Chapter II, para 3.36)	To start with, a general provision on standard assets of a minimum of 0.25% from the year ended March 31, 2000 introduced. (Cir.DBOD.No.BP.BC.103/21.01.002/98 dt.31.10.98)
16. The Committee believes that in the case of future loans, the income recognition and asset classification and provisioning norms should apply even to Government guaranteed advances in the same manner as for any other advance. For existing Government guaranteed advances, RBI, Government and banks may work out a mechanism for a phased rectification of the irregularities in these accounts. (Chapter III, para 3.37)	

QUESTIONS

Fill in the blanks:

1. RBI is governed by a central board appointed by _______ for a period of __________.
2. RBI holds cash reserves of ___________.
3. CAMELS stands for __________.
4. RBI is the lender of last resort for ___________.

State whether true or false:

1. RBI regulates the issue of bank notes.
2. RBI acts as banker's bank.
3. RBI provides finance to farmers.
4. RBI applies only qualitative credit control on banks.

Answer in detail:

Q.1. What is the role of RBI in the Indian Banking System taking into account the recent trends of globalization and liberalization?

❑❑❑

Section-II
Banking System in India

15 COMMERCIAL BANKING SYSTEM

INTRODUCTION

A sound and efficient banking system is a prerequisite of a healthy economy. The banking system should be developed in a way to be able to meet the challenges posed by changing technology and various other factors external or internal to the economy.

HISTORY AND GROWTH OF BANKING SYSTEM IN INDIA

The Indian banking system traces sack its history to 1786 when the first Bank in India was established. From that year till today the journey of growth of the Indian Banking System can be divided into three phases:—

Phase I:

- This was the first phase of Indian Banking during which the first Bank called The General Bank of India was set-up in the year 1786. Next to it, the Bank of Hindustan and Bengal Bank came. During this period three banks, Bank of Bengal (1809), Bank of Bombay (1840) & Bank of Madras (1843), were set-up by the East India Company as independent units and were called Presidency Banks. These three were later merged in 1920 as Imperial Bank of India which had European shareholders.
- Later in 1865 Allahabad Bank was established followed by Punjab National Bank in 1894. Between 1906 and 1913, Bank of India, Central Bank of India, Bank of Baroda, Canara Bank, Indian Bank, and Bank of Mysore were set-up.
- In 1935, Reserve Bank of India came into being, which was later formed the Central Banking Authority under the Banking Regulation Act 1949.
- This period of Bank development witnessed slow growth and several bank failures. This was primarily due to lesser investor confidence, slow deposit mobilization, greater reliance of public on alternative investment facilities like those provided by the Postal Department.

Phase II:

- This phase was the post-independence phase. In 1955, Government nationalized Imperial Bank of India and formed it as State Bank of India for handling Central and State government's banking transactions and functioning as the principal agent of RBI.
- In 1959, seven subsidiaries of SBI were also nationalized. In 1961, insurance cover was extended to deposits and in 1969, 14 major commercial banks were nationalized under the Prime Ministership of Mrs. Indira Gandhi.
- Credit Guarantee Corporation of India was set-up in 1971 to guarantee insurance of deposit and mobilize credit to banks in need.
- Regional Rural Banks were introduced in 1975 and in 1980 seven banks with deposits over 200 crores were nationalized, bringing 80% of the banking sector under government's umbrella.
- During this phase banking sector grew tremendously showing an 800% growth in deposits and 11000% growth in advances. This was due to rise in public faith because of government's holding on banks and increased awareness among people towards banking.

Phase III:

- This phase started since 1991 during which liberalization of banking practices was introduced as per the report of a banking committee set-up under the chairmanship of Mr. M. Narasimham.
- From the start of this Phase till date tremendous changes have occurred in the Banking System with retail banking shifting to universal banking and orthodox methods being replaced by new ones so-as-to establish customer satisfaction as the highest priority.

SCHEDULED AND UNSCHEDULED COMMERCIAL BANKS IN INDIA

The commercial banking structure in India consists of:

- Scheduled commercial banks: These include those banks which have been included in the second schedule of Reserve Bank of India 1934 and satisfy the criteria laid down *vide* Section 46 (6) (a) of the Act. It is also defined as : "The State Bank of India under the State Bank of India Act, 1955, a subsidiary bank as defined in State Bank of India (Subsidiary Banks) Act, 1959, a corresponding new bank constituted under Section 3 of the Banking Companies (Acquisition and Transfer of Undertaking) Act, 1980, or any other bank being a bank included in the Second Schedule to Reserve Bank of India Act, 1934, but does not include a cooperative bank".
- "Non-scheduled bank in India" means a banking company as defined in Clause-C of Section 5 of the Banking Regulation Act, 1949, which is not a scheduled bank".

Public Sector Scheduled Banks in India are as under:

- State Bank of India
- State Bank of Bikaner and Jaipur
- State Bank of Hyderabad

- State Bank of Indore
- State Bank of Patiala
- State Bank of Saurashtra
- State Bank of Travancore
- Andhra Bank
- Allahabad Bank
- Bank of Baroda
- Bank of India
- Bank of Maharashtra
- Canara Bank
- Dena Bank
- Indian Overseas Bank
- Indian Bank
- Oriental Bank of Commerce
- Punjab National Bank
- Punjab and Sindh Bank
- Syndicate Bank
- Union Bank of India
- United Bank of India
- UCO Bank
- Vijaya Bank

The Following are the Scheduled Banks in India (Private Sector):

- Vysya Bank Ltd
- UTI Bank Ltd
- Industrial Bank Ltd
- ICICI Banking Corporation Bank Ltd
- Global Trust Bank Ltd
- HDFC Bank Ltd
- Centurion Bank of Punjab Ltd
- IDBI Bank Ltd

The Following are the Scheduled Foreign Banks in India:

- American Express Bank Ltd
- ANZ Gridlays Bank Plc
- Bank of America NT & SA
- Bank of Tokyo Ltd

- Banquc Nationale de Paris
- Barclays Bank Plc
- Citi Bank NC
- Deutsche Bank AG
- Hongkong and Shanghai Banking Corporation
- Standard Chartered Bank
- The Chase Manhattan Bank Ltd
- Dresdner Bank AG

Classification of Banks in India

Banks have been classified into the following main categories:

1. **Public Sector Banks in India:** Public sector banks are under government umbrella. The list of Public Sector Banks includes—
   - Allahabad Bank
   - Andhra Bank
   - Bank of Baroda
   - Bank of India
   - Bank of Maharashtra
   - Canara Bank
   - Central Bank of India
   - Corporation Bank
   - Dena Bank
   - Indian Bank
   - Indian Overseas Bank
   - Oriental Bank of Commerce
   - Punjab and Sindh Bank
   - Punjab National Bank
   - Syndicate Bank
   - UCO Bank
   - Union Bank of India
   - United Bank of India
   - Vijaya Bank
   - State Bank and its subsidiaries
2. **Private Sector Banks:** These are run by private promoters and are the following:-
   - Bank of Rajasthan
   - Catholic Syrian Bank

- Centurion Bank of Punjab
- City Union Bank
- Dhanlakshmi Bank
- Development Credit Bank
- Federal Bank
- HDFC Bank
- ISBI Bank
- Indus Industrial Bank
- ING Vysya Bank
- Jammu and Kashmir Bank
- Karnataka Bank
- Karur Vysya Bank
- Laxmi Vilas Bank
- South Indian Bank
- United Western Bank
- UTI Bank

3. **Foreign Banks:** Due to government policy of liberalization number of foreign banks have set-up their branches in India and these include:-

- ABN Amro Bank
- Abu Dhabi Commercial Bank
- Bank of Ceylon
- BNP Paribas Bank
- Citi Bank
- China Trust Commercial Bank
- Deutsche Bank
- HSBC
- JP Morgan Chase Bank
- Standard Chartered Bank
- Scotia Bank
- Taib Bank

Upcoming Foreign Banks in India:

- Royal Bank of Scotland
- Switzerland's UBS
- US based GE Capital
- Credit Suisse Group
- Industrial and Commercial Bank of China

4. **Cooperative Banks in India:** Cooperative banks are registered under the Co-operative Societies Act and are governed by the Banking Regulations Act 1949 and Banking Laws (Cooperative Societies) Act, 1955. They are an important constituent of Indian Financial System.

Cooperative banks in India finance rural areas under:

- Farming
- Cattle
- Milk
- Hatchery
- Personal finance

Cooperative banks in India finance urban areas under:

- Self-employment
- Industries
- Small scale units
- Home finance consumer finance
- Personal finance

Cooperative banks have been successful in India mainly due to local reach, personal interaction with customers and their ability to catch the nerve of the local clientele.

5. **Regional Rural Banks in India:** Earlier rural banks mainly focused on agro sector but now they have penetrated in every corner of the country and have extended a helping hand in the growth process of the country.

   SBI has 30 RRBs spread in 13 states from Kashmir to Karnataka and Himachal Pradesh to North East. The total number of branches of these RRBs is 2349 and till date there are 14,475 rural banks in the country of which 2126 are located in remote rural areas.

Some of the major rural banks are:

(*a*) **Haryana State Cooperative Apex Bank Limited (HARCO Bank)** plays a vital role in rural banking in economy of Haryana state and has been providing aids for financing farmers, rural artisans, agricultural labourers, entrepreneurs etc. in the state and giving service to depositors.

(*b*) **National Bank for Agriculture and Rural Development (NABARD)** is a development bank in the sector of Regional Rural Banks in India. It provides and regulates credit and gives services for the promotion and development of rural sectors mainly agriculture, small scale, cottage and village industries. It also helps in promoting integrated rural development and prosperity.

(*c*) **United Bank of India (UBI)** also plays a vital role in regional rural banks. It has expanded its branch network to participate actively in development of rural and semi-urban areas.

(*d*) **Syndicate Bank :** It has rooted itself in rural area and has a clear vision of future India due to its understanding of grass root realities. It has kept itself abreast of the progressive banking in India during the entire years.

BANKING SERVICES IN INDIA

Banks provide the following services to their customers –

1. **Bank Account :** The most common and basic service provided by banks is deposit account. These are of the following types –
   (*a*) **Bank Savings Account :** It can be opened by individuals, organizations or agencies (as advised by RBI from time to time).
   (*b*) **Bank Current Account :** It can be opened by individuals, partnership firms, private and public limited companies, HUFs, societies, trusts etc.
   (*c*) **Bank Account On-line :** Due to technological development, banks have facilitated their customers to open Bank Account online where they are registered through a PC with an internet connection. This helps in saving operating cost of a bank and time of customers.
2. **Plastic Money :** Another facility being provided by banks in Plastic Money. It involves –
   (*a*) Credit Cards and
   (*b*) Debit Cards
   (*a*) **Credit Cards :** Credit Card are a facility provided by banks to buy now and pay later. The borrower is assigned a credit limit under which he can make purchases and pay later for them. A grace period is given to the borrower which is the number of days between the statement date and due date of payment. This period is generally of 2-3 weeks and after this interest is charged on the amount due. There is no grace period on previous month's balance carried forward and purchases made thereafter. The following are the types of credit cards issued by banks :
   - *Standard Card* : It is the most basic card offered by issuers, Standard Card issued by VISA is also classic card.
   - *Gold Card/Executive Card* : It requires higher credit than standard card. It also provides extra perks or incentives to cardholders.
   - *Platinum Card* : A Credit Card with higher limit and additional perks than a gold card.
   - *Titanium Card* : A card with an even higher limit than a platinum card.

Banks offering credit cards in India are:

- State Bank of India Credit Card (SBI Credit Card)
- Bank of Baroda Credit Card or (BOB Credit Card)
- ICICI Credit Card
- HDFC Credit Card
- IDBI Credit Card
- ABN AMRO Credit Card
- Standard Chartered Credit Card
- HSBC Credit Card
- Citibank Credit Card

Varieties of Credit Cards in India are:

- ANZ – Gold
- ANZ – Silver
- Bank of India – India Card
- BOI – Taj Premium
- BOI – Gold
- BOB – Exclusive
- BOB – Premium
- Canara Bank – Can Card
- Citibank – Gold
- Citibank – Silver
- Citibank WWF Card
- Citibank Visa Card for women
- Citibank Cry Card
- Citibank Silver International Credit Card
- Citibank Gold International Credit Card
- Citibank Electronic Credit Card
- Citibank Maruti International Credit Card
- Citibank Times Card
- Citibank India Oil International Card
- Citibank Citi Diners Club Card
- HSBC Gold
- HSBC – Classic
- ICICI Sterling Silver Credit Card
- ICICI Solid Gold Credit Card
- ICICI True Blue Credit Card
- SBI Card
- Standard – Gold
- Standard – Executive
- Standard Classic
- Thomas Cook Standard Chartered Global Credit Card

Apart from extended credit facility credit cards offer the following facilities also.

- Hotel Discounts
- Travel Fare Discounts
- Free Global Calling Card

- Loss Baggage Insurance
- Accident Insurance
- Waiver of Payment in case of Accidental Deals.
- Household Conscience

(*b*) **Debit Card :** Debit Cards are a way to pay now without the burden of carrying excess cash. On payment through a debit card, money is deducted from the Bank Account. So it is a way by which the card holder uses his own money and not the issuer's money. In India, Debit Card is issued by almost all banks to their account holders.

3. **Loans :** Banks in India have become easily accessible for getting loans for use by individuals. The following types of loans are being provided by banks:
   - Personal Loan given to individuals for personal needs and range between Rs.25,000 – Rs.10,00,000.
   - Car Loans sanctioned for 8.5% amount of the ex-showroom price of card and also termed as auto loan.
   - Home loans for construction or purchase of house.
   - Education Loan or Student Loan given to meet the tuition fee, maintenance cost, books and other equipments.

4. **Easy Banking :** The banking system has shown tremendous technological change by moving towards a system of easy banking. Banking is possible just at a fingertip these days. Now, there is no need to stand for hours waiting to check the account, transfer funds, make payment and many more things, which were too time consuming in physical banking. Now the following easy banking services are being provided by the banks :

(*a*) **Automated Teller Machine (ATM) :** ATM was first introduced in India by Hongkong and Shanghai Banking Corporation (HSBC) in the year 1987. Now, almost every commercial bank is offering this service to its customers. ICICI, UTI, HDFC and IDBI count for more 50% of the total ATMs in India. Public sector banks are also taking up the installation of ATMs seriously for Indian Market either on their own or in tie-up with other banks. Banks are also using a scheme called "Swadhan" Scheme under which they can use each other's ATM at a cost (usually Rs. 35 extra from customers). The main feature of "Swadhan Card" are as follows:

- The fiscal ceiling on "Swadhan Card" is Rs. 3000.
- No Exchange fee is charged to change an old ATM Card for a Swadhan Card.
- IBA gives Banks the discretion to decide a higher maximum amount on withdrawal.
- No overdraft facility is provided by "Swadhan Card" and the transactions conducted through the card appear on the bank statement given by the individual's bank.

(*b*) **Mobile Banking :** It is also called "Account that travels with a person. with, mobile banking a person can bank from anywhere, at anytime and in any condition or anyhow". The system is either through SMS or through WAP. The percentage of mobile banking has increased three times compared to debit or credit card. Using HTML & WAP technologies conducts the following operations:

- Bill Payments
- Fund Transfers
- Check Balances
- Any many more, which is also available in SMS Banking.

(*c*) **SMS Banking :** As business is in move and so are individuals, banks are providing services SMS. The following services are being provided by use of SMS technology:

- Balance Enquiry
- Last three transactions
- Cheque Payment Status
- Statement request
- DEMAT – Free Balance Holding
- DEMAT – Last Two Transactions
- Bill Payment

For getting this facility, the customer has to first get registered with the bank and fill the service brochure of the nearest branch. Registration is a one time process and once registered, the customer is able to purchase things from any of the registered merchant of the bank. The transaction will be validated online and immediately funds will be transferred from customer account to merchant account. Bank would send transaction confirmation as a message to both merchant and customer. An SMS report will be sent to both merchant and buyer everyday stating the total number of transactions made during previous day.

(*d*) **Net Banking :** It is conducting banking online through a computer and a net connection followed by immediate updating of the system automatically after every transaction. The following are the features of net banking:

(*a*) Banks offer only relevant information about their products and services to the masses.

(*b*) Few Banks provide interaction facility between the banks and its customers.

(*c*) Banks are coming up with arrangements of utility payments like telephone bills, electricity bills etc., which can be done through net banking.

Net Banking helps the customers in the following way:

(*a*) It removes traditional geographic barriers as it can reach out to customers of different countries.

(*b*) It has helped in saving customer's time and bank's cost.

But net banking has posed some risk challenges in terms of security of banking transactions, validity of electronic contact, customer's privacy etc. It led to loss of business to those banks who did not respond in time to this new technology. Services provided by net banking include:

- Check Balance
- See Statement
- Ask for a statement

- Ask for a cheque book
- Inquire about status, cheques
- Inquire about fixed deposit
- Check TDS details
- See DEMAT Account
- Update profile
- Pay bills
- Stop a cheque
- Ask for a demand draft
- Transfer funds between accounts
- Transfer funds to a third party
- Request for a new fixed deposit
- Shop on-line
- Pay bank credit card dues

5. **Banking Services for NRIs :** Banks in India provide services to Non Resident Indians. The following are the banking services provided to NRIs:

(*a*) **Non Resident (Ordinary) Account (NRO A/c) :** The funds credited to this account cannot be repatriated outside India in foreign exchange without prior permission of Reserve Bank of India. Interest earned is however eligible for repatriation outside India and no RBI permission is required for it.

(*b*) **Non Resident (External) A/c (NRE A/c) :** The funds standing in credit of this account, as well as interest earned thereon, are remittable outside India in free foreign exchange, without permission of RBI. The interest income is not subject to Indian Income Tax.

(*c*) **Foreign Currency Non Resident A/c (FCNR A/c) :** They can be opened in four foreign currencies:

- Pounds Sterling
- US Dollars
- Japanese Yen
- Euro

These accounts can be opened only as fixed deposits with a minimum maturity of one year and maximum of three years. The principal as well as interest earned on these accounts is remittable outside India, in some currency or, in other convertible currency as desired by the account holder.

METHODS OF LENDING

Like many other activities of the banks, method and quantum of short-term finance that can be granted to a corporate was mandated by the Reserve Bank of India till 1994. This control was exercised on the lines suggested by the recommendations of a study group headed by Shri Prakash Tandon.

The study group headed by Shri Prakash Tandon, the then Chairman of Punjab National Bank, was constituted by the RBI in July, 1974 with eminent personalities drawn from leading banks, financial institutions and a wide cross-section of the industry, with a view to study the entire gamut of Bank's finance for working capital and suggest ways for optimum utilisation of Bank credit. This was the first elaborate attempt by the central bank to organise the Bank credit.

The report of this group is widely known as *Tandon Committee Report*. Most banks in India even today continue to look at the needs of the corporates in the light of methodology recommended by the Group.

As per the recommendations of Tandon Committee,

- The corporates should be discouraged from accumulating too much of stocks of current assets and should move towards very lean inventories and receivable levels.
- The committee even suggested the maximum levels of Raw Material, Stock-in-process and Finished Goods which a corporate operating in an industry should be allowed to accumulate. These levels were termed as inventory and receivable norms.
- Depending on the size of credit required, the funding of these current assets (working capital needs) of the corporates could be met by one of the following methods:
  - **First method of lending:** Banks can work out the working capital gap, *i.e.,* total current assets less current liabilities other than bank borrowings (called Maximum Permissible Bank Finance or MPBF) and finance a maximum of 75 per cent of the gap; the balance to come out of long-term funds, *i.e.,* owned funds and term borrowings. This approach was considered suitable only for very small borrowers *i.e.,* where the requirements of credit were less than Rs.10 lakh.
  - **Second method of lending:** Under this method, it was thought that the borrower should provide for a minimum of 25% of total current assets out of long-term funds i.e., owned funds plus term borrowings. A certain level of credit for purchases and other current liabilities will be available to fund the build-up of current assets and the bank will provide the balance **Maximum Permissible Bank Finance (MPBF).** Consequently, total current liabilities inclusive of bank borrowings could not exceed 75% of current assets. RBI stipulated that the working capital needs of all borrowers enjoying fund based credit facilities of more than Rs. 10 lakh should be appraised (calculated) under this method.
  - **Third Method of Lending:** Under this method, the borrower's contribution from long-term funds will be to the extent of the entire CORE CURRENT ASSETS, which has been defined by the Study Group as representing the absolute minimum level of raw materials, process stock, finished goods and stores which are in the pipeline to ensure continuity of production and a minimum of 25% of the balance current assets should be financed out of the long-term funds plus term borrowings.

CONSORTIUM LENDING

Consortium Lending or syndicated loan facility is a lending facility, defined by a single loan agreement, in which several or many banks participate, *i.e.,* several banks or financial institutions associate to provide loan to a single person/group.There is usually one lead bank called the "Arranger" or "Agent" that takes a percentage of the loan and syndicates the rest to other banks. Unlike bilateral loan, which only involves one borrower and one lender consortium lending involves one borrower and a group of lenders.

To avoid that the borrower has to deal with all lending banks individually, one of the lender banks usually acts as an Agent for all consortium members and acts as the focal point between them and the borrower. Though there is a single loan agreement, each participant to a consortium loan maintains a separate claim on, and bears the credit risk for, the portion of the loan that it has provided. These loans therefore enable lenders to achieve greater diversification in their loan portfolios and maintain client relationships that can be beneficial in other ways.

REASONS FOR CONSORTIUM LENDING

The following are the reasons for consortium lending arrangements:

- Consortium lending is opted for large business loans. This is because if the bank has only one large business loan, and if that business happens to be one of the party that defaults, then the bank loses all its money. For this reason, it is in the best interest of all banks to split, their large loans with each other, so each bank gets a representative sample in their loan portfolios and the risk gets diversified. So, Consortium lending avoids large or surprising losses and instead usually provides small and more predictable losses.
- The borrowing requirements of businesses are sometimes beyond the funding and credit risk capacity of single lenders. As a result, some loans are arranged as consortium with the funds jointly provided by two or more lenders. So when a borrower wants to raise a relatively large amount of money quickly and conveniently consortium lending is opted for.
- When a single bank cannot meet all requirements of the borrower and the borrower does not want to deal with a large number of lenders separately so lending banks provide an arrangement in which they join hands and one of them, *i.e.,* the agent deals with him.

PARTICIPANTS IN CONSORTIUM LENDING

Arranger / Lead Manager

Arranger or Lead Manager includes the bank, *i.e.,* awarded the mandate by the prospective borrower, and-is responsible for placing the syndicated loan with other banks and ensuring that the syndication is fully subscribed.

Lead managers are responsible for structuring the loan facility, including negotiating the pricing and terms and conditions. Most of the banks in this lead group would be involved in funding the loan and, in larger deals, also responsible for marketing the loan to other banks.

Underwriting Bank

The underwriting bank commits to supply the funds to the borrower -if necessary from its own resources if the loan is not fully subscribed. Underwriting bank may be the arranging bank or another bank. Not all syndicated loans are fully underwritten.

Underwriting banks may bear the risk that the loan may not be fully subscribed.

Participating Bank

Participating bank participates in the syndication by lending a portion of the total amount required. It charges interest and participation fee. The risks borne by the bank is borrowers credit risk.

Facility Manager / Agent

Agent takes care of the administrative arrangements over the term of the loan (*e.g.,* disbursements, repayments, compliance) on behalf of the banks. Agent may be the arranging/underwriting bank. In case of larger syndications co-arranger and co-manager may be used.

BENEFITS OF CONSORTIUM LENDING

Benefits to the Borrower

- The borrower has to deal with a single bank.
- It is quicker and simpler than other ways of raising capital (*e.g.,* issue of bonds or equity).

Benefits to the Lead Banks

- It is a good lending arrangement in which fees can be earned without commitment of capital alone.
- It enhances of bank's reputation and relationship with the client.

Benefits to the Participating Banks

- It provides access to lending opportunities with low marketing costs.
- It provides opportunities to participate in future syndications.
- In case the borrower runs into difficulties, participating banks have equal treatment.
- Participant banks do not find themselves at a disadvantage *vis-à-vis* a dominant bank or one with high leverage over the client.

STAGES

1. Pre-mandate phase

In this phase the prospective borrower may liaise with a single bank or it may invite competitive bids from a number of banks.

The lead bank then:

- identifies the needs of the borrower.

- designs an appropriate loan structure.
- develops a persuasive credit proposal and obtains internal approval.

2. Placing the loan
   - The lead bank starts selling the loan in the marketplace.
   - For selling the loan the lead bank needs to prepare:
     (*i*) an information memorandum
     (*ii*) a term sheet
     (*iii*) legal documentation
   - Then it approaches selected banks and invites participation. Negotiations with the borrower may be needed if prospective participants raise concerns. The stage ends with closing of the syndication, including signing.
3. Post-closure phase

The agent now handles the day-to-day running of the loan facility.

PRICING

The following fees are involved in consortium lending arrangements:

- Fee for "front-end activities"-arrangement and underwriting fees.
- Interest (margin over base rate).
- Commitment fees for available but not drawn funds.

Apart from earning the spread on the portion of the loan that is drawn, consortium members also receive various fees depending on their role in the transaction as arranger, underwriter, agent or participant. Those involved in arranging the deal are paid a fee, often called a principium, for their role in putting the deal together. Any banks underwriting the transaction will earn a fee for guaranteeing the availability of funds, and the agent bank will earn an annual fee for administering the loan after origination. In some cases, participants may earn a participation fee for joining the syndicate, with the size of the fee usually dependent on the size of their commitment. Also, for that part of a facility that remains undrawn, the participants will typically receive an annual commitment or facility fee to compensate them for the cost of tying up regulatory capital. Even when the facility is drawn, some deals also incorporate a utilization fee, in which case the interest rate spread may be somewhat lower than otherwise.

In addition to interest rate spreads and fees, there are various non-pricing conditions, known as covenants, that are also attached to consortium loans. These are undertakings given by the borrower in a loan agreement that are designed to limit the lenders' risks. Typical covenants include limits on the amount of additional financing the borrower can obtain and restrictions on the use of any funds it might realize from asset sales.

DOCUMENTATION REQUIRED

Specialist lawyers are engaged to work closely with all the banks.The role of each party is clearly defined and some standard clauses are included.

Consortium loans have become an increasingly important source of finance for businesses over the past few years. Syndicated loans provide borrowers with a more set of choices of financing options. In effect, the syndication market completes a range between traditional private bilateral bank loans and publicly traded bond markets. This has resulted in a more competitive corporate finance market, which has permitted issuers to achieve more market-oriented and cost-effective financing.

CREDIT GAPS

Credit gaps occur when banks or financial institutions are unable to adequately meet the needs of particular groups of potential borrowers such as: *small firms*, *risky firms*, and *knowledge-based enterprises*. In general lenders ration credit in accordance with firm size, knowledge orientation, and risk

At times some private knowledge about the entrepreneur may not be shared with the lender. Consequently, lenders cannot differentiate between a 'high-quality' firm and a 'low-quality' firms which can result in adverse selection and credit rationing, *i.e.,* controlled distribution of credit which results in credit gaps. By practicing capital rationing banks may deny credit to particular classes of borrowers.

Credit gaps can be eliminated by reducing, information asymmetry which can be done in following ways:

- through a firm's ability to somehow signal its credit worthiness;
- by having developed a strong relationship with its lender; and,
- through due diligence and the lender's examination of the business plan and other lender requirements for documentation.

Bases for Credit Gaps

Collateral. Lenders may be more likely to approve loans to firms that are able to provide collateral and to those firms that have established long term relationships with lenders. The need for collateral may militate against technology based firms. But many technology-based firms are relatively young firms and may not yet have developed relationships with bankers. Moreover, intellectual assets of high technology firms are more difficult to value than those of low technology firms". This lack of information clarity may make it relatively difficult for knowledge-based firms to access debt.

Technology Orientation. It has been found that after allowing for traditional determinants of credit policy (sector, size of firm, age of firm, etc.), loan turndown rates and other dimensions of bank credit policy do not differ between technology based and non technology based firms. What appears to be a gap based on technology orientation is more related to technology-based firms being small and young.

Growth may be another dimension that forms a basis for a credit gap. High growth firms may be more informationally opaque and may face a greater degree of difficulty obtaining financing.

Gender may also be a dimension on which gaps may be present. As per Marleau (1995) women business owners face particular difficulty while obtaining credit.

Size of firm (or size of loan) may also be a dimension across which a financing gap may be present. It has been empirically found that small firms face particular challenges with terms of credit and access to bank loans. In addition, of course, the understanding that small firms face lack of access to credit is the basis for loan guarantee programs to small firms in many countries.

Risk. Finally risk may be a dimension across which a financing gap might exist. Moreover, it can be argued that the role of the banks is in fact to discriminate based on risk and insufficient risk information can lead to credit gap.

Therefore, it remains that credit gaps occur when firms are refused credit which may be based on certain characteristics and information assymetry. Thus, an empirical test for credit rationing must take into account firms' ability to meet terms of credit and then isolate the extent to which the credit decision is varied on the basis of the possible dimensions that may form a basis for disbursement of credit.

SHIFT TOWARDS UNIVERSAL BANKING

Universal banking is the combination of commercial banking with investment banking and insurance i.e. under universal banking the banks offered a wide range of services like accepting, deposits, issuing, under writing, investing and trading in securities.

So, universal banks are financial institutions, which offer entire range of financial services. They are thus multi-product organization with different businesses linked together in a complex network which draws on a set of various resources (financial, informational, human resources), which are managed in a way to achieve maximum utilization of invested capital. Advantages of Universal Banking:

1. **Cost Savings :** Banks already possess the necessary infrastructure and expertise for carrying all the functions under universal banking so this large or multi-functional operation helps in sharing of overheads and improving technology through joint production.
2. **Regulatory Monopoly :** It helps in preventing specific financial service suppliers from gaining monopoly positions in the market.
3. **Risk Diversification :** It helps the banks to diversify risk of loss, which is higher in case they restrict themselves to a particular activity. But diversifying in various activities helps in diversifying the risk of loss and puts banks in a better position.
4. **Higher Output and Better Products :** Shift towards universal banking has helped in increasing output of banks and providing better services and innovative products.

Issues in Universal Banking:

1. **Development of Capital :** Concentration of bank's efforts into one activity would help in developing by deploying entire capital to it but universal banking distributes the raised capital into several activities.
2. **Investment Advice Issue :** There may be conflicts in the bank's commercial and investment banking rules. There may be a conflict between investment bank's promotional role and disinterested commercial banks to give investment advice. So there may be a conflict of interest between the two to give investment advice.
3. **Bankruptcy Issues :** In case a bank has an outstanding loan from a firm whose bankruptcy risk has increased. In that case the bank being a universal bank will assist the firm to raise money through public issue of debt / equity for which its underwriting division may take up underwriting of the issue. In such cases bank transfers the bad debts risk from itself to outside investors' along with which it also earns and underwriting commission or fee.

4. **Third Party Loans :** To ensure that an underwriting goes well, a bank may move below market loans to third party investors on condition that this finance is used to purchase security underwritten by its security unit.

UNIVERSAL BANKING IN INDIA

Prior to liberalization commercial banks were meeting deposit and lending requirements while Developmental Financial Institutions, Refinancing Institutions were looking after sector specific needs, insurance was purely taken care by LIC. Underwriting and Merchant Banking activities were to some extent handled by brokers.

But after liberalization and deregulation of financial sector the distinction between commercial banking and investment banking has blurred, universal banking issue surfaced in 2000, when ICICI submitted its proposal to transform itself into a universal bank. After this RBI has asked financial institutions, interested in conversion to universal bank to submit three reports for consideration and further discussions. The permission to convert into universal base is given only if the prescribed norms are satisfied.

Universal Banking Approach (extracted from Mid-Term Review of Monetary and Credit policy of Reserve Bank of India for 1999-2000).

APPROACH TO UNIVERSAL BANKING

The Narasimham Committee II suggested that Development Financial Institutions (DFIS) should convert ultimately into either commercial banks or non-bank finance companies. The Khan Working Group held the view that DFIS should be allowed to become banks at the earliest. The RBI released a "Discussion Paper" (DP) in January, 1999 for wider public debate. The feedback on the discussion paper indicated that while the universal banking is desirable from the point of view of efficiency of resource use, there is need for caution in moving towards such a system by banks and DFIs. Major areas requiring attention are the status of financial sector reforms, the state of preparedness of the concerned institutions, the evolution of the regulatory regime and above all a viable transition path for institutions which are desirous of moving in the direction of universal banking. It is proposed to adopt the following broad approach for considering proposals in this area:

The principle of "Universal Banking" is a desirable goal and some progress has already been made by permitting banks to diversify into investments and long-term financing and the DFIs to lend for working capital, etc. However, banks have certain special characteristics and as such any dilution of RBI"s prudential and supervisory norms for conduct of banking business would be inadvisable. Further, any conglomerate, in which a bank is present, should be subject to a consolidated approach to supervision and regulation.

Though the DFIs would continue to have a special role in the Indian Financial System, until the debt market demonstrates substantial improvements in terms of liquidity and depth, any DFI, which wishes to do so, should have the option to transform into bank (which it can exercise), provided the prudential norms as applicable to banks are fully satisfied. To this end, a DFI would need to prepare a transition path in order to fully comply with the regulatory requirement of a bank. The DFI concerned may consult RBI for such transition arrangements. Reserve Bank will consider such requests on a case by case basis.

The regulatory framework of RBI in respect of DFIs would need to be strengthened if they are given greater access to short-term resources for meeting their financing requirements, which is necessary.

In due course, and in the light of evolution of the financial system, Narasimham Committee's recommendation that, ultimately there should be only banks and restructured NBFCs can be operationalized.

GLOBAL FACE OF INDIAN BANKING

Bright future of Indian Banking Industry can be ensured by meeting the emerging global needs. The primary reason behind this is increasing global competition. Foreign Banks either as branches or subsidiaries have grown. Foreign owned non-banking financial companies compete for deposit mobilization. Moreover cross border payments are becoming easy due to emergence of organizations such as Western Union, Money Changers licensed by RBI. With more companies becoming multinational, they expect banking services to be at par with international standards. Foreign Banks are also entering into transactions of non-public sector organizations.

For meeting the global standards and needs Indian Banks have been participating in the evolution of Basal Accord in line with the Basal Norms (Capital Adequacy Norms) of Bank for International Settlements (BIS). Consideration is being given to maintain financial stability, continued health and resistance of banking industry. There is an increased focus on improving operational efficiency, development of new policy as well as procedural actions.

Thrust is being put to remove issues leading to financial crisis and ensuring soundness and effectiveness of macroeconomic policy. For this norms related to banking supervision and restructuring of banking systems have been developed. A Financial Sector Assessment Program (FSAP) has been launched by IMF to identify financial system strengths and vulnerabilities and to reduce the potential for crisis in its member countries. In FSAP, a country's compliance with international standards is assessed on a priority basis and gets reflected in the Report on the Observance of Standards and Codes (ROSCs).

India has been very closely associated with IMF in developing these approaches and volunteered to be assessed under FSAP under the ROSC initiative. Indian Banks have also been closely following the developments in Bank for Informational Settlements and have adopted the Basal Standards.

Various issues, which must be resolved so as to reach the goal of achieving international standards include:

- Developments governing the real economy.

  Reduction of financial market risks like interest rate, foreign exchange settlement, legal, political, systematic etc.
- Policy environment including relationship between banks and large corporates, growth and competition with non-banks etc.

- Improvement of relationship between government and banking sector in terms of financing, contingent liabilities etc.
- Institutional arrangements for regulation and supervision.
- Arrangements with multilateral institutions to promote trade.
- Greater attention to be given to strengthen stronger banks in terms of resources and operational freedom.
- Finding/Measuring the gap between where we stand and how far we go.

All these need to be done as to achieve the objective of equaling global standards to comptete effectively and once the standards have been achieved, excel in those standards so as to make a respectable place in the fast growing global financial sector.

As per the speech of Governor Bimal Jalan on Banking and Finance in the New Millennium in January, 2001.

"The long-term vision for India's banking system to transform itself from being a domestic one to the global level may sound far-fetched at present. However, it is not beyond our capacity, provided we have the will and the determination. Taking the banking industry to the heights of international excellence will require a combination of new technologies, better processes of credit and risk appraisal, treasury management, product diversification, internal control and external regulations and, not the least, human resources. Fortunately, we have a comparative advantage in almost all these areas. Our professionals are at the forefront of technological change and financial developments all over the world. It is time to harness these resources for development of Indian Banking in the new century."

QUESTIONS

Fill in the blanks:

1. Banks provide plastic money through __________ and ___________.
2. Universal banking is the combination of commercial banking with ___________.
3. Private sector banks are run by _________ promoters.
4. __________, ________ and _________ are involved in easy banking.
5. Unlike __________loan, which only involves one borrower and one lender ________ lending involves one borrower and a group of lenders.
6. __________ may bear the risk that the loan may not be fully subscribed.
7. Credit gaps can be eliminated by reducing, _________________.

State whether true or false:

1. Scheduled foreign bank branches are not located in India.
2. Banking services in India are not offered to Non-Resident Indians.
3. Universal banking increases cost structure of structure of banks.

4. Consortium lending is less quick than other ways of raising capital (*e.g.,* issue of bonds)
5. Women business owners face particular difficulty while obtaining credit.

Answer in detail:

Q.1. Briefly classify the types of Banks in India.

Q.2. What are the various banking services offered in India?

Q.3. What is Universal Banking? Explain its concept with respect to Indian Banking System.

Q.4. What are the various opportunities and challenges before Indian banks in the context of globalization?

Q.5. What are the benefits of consortium lending over other methods? Who are the participants in consortium lending and what are their roles?

Q.6. What are the reasons of credit gaps? How can they be eliminated?

❑❑❑

16 COOPERATIVE BANKING IN INDIA

INTRODUCTION

The Cooperative banks have a history of almost 100 years. The Cooperative banks are an important constituent of the Indian Financial System, judging by the role assigned to them, the expectations they are supposed to fulfill, their number and the number of offices they operate. The cooperative movement originated in the West, but the importance that such banks have assumed in India is rarely paralleled anywhere else in the world. Their role in rural financing continues to be important even today, and their business in the urban areas also has increased phenomenally in recent years mainly due to the sharp increase in the number of primary cooperative banks.

While the cooperative banks in rural areas mainly finance agriculture based activities including farming, cattle, milk, hatchery, personal finance etc. along with some small scale industries and self-employment driven activities, the cooperative banks in urban areas mainly finance various categories of people for self-employment, industries, small scale units, home finance, consumer finance, personal finance, etc.

Some of the cooperative banks are quite forward looking and have developed sufficient core competencies to challenge state and private sector banks.

According to NAFCUB the total deposits and lending of Cooperative Banks is much more than Old Private Sector Banks and also the New Private Sector Banks. This exponential growth of Cooperative Banks is attributed mainly to their better local reach, personal interaction with customers, and their ability to catch the nerve of the local clientele.

Though registered under the Cooperative Societies Act of the Respective States (where formed originally) the banking related activities of the cooperative banks are also regulated by the Reserve Bank of India. They are governed by the Banking Regulations Act, 1949 and Banking Laws (Cooperative Societies) Act, 1965.

OVERVIEW

Cooperative movement is quite well established in India. The first legislation on co-operation was passed in 1904. In 1914, the Maclagen committee envisaged a three tier structure for cooperative banking *viz.* Primary Agricultural Credit Societies (PACs) at the grassroot level, Central Cooperative Banks at the district level and State Cooperative Banks at state level or Apex Level. The first urban cooperative bank in India was formed nearly 100 years back in Baroda.

Cooperative Institutions are engaged in all kinds of activities namely production, processing, marketing, distribution, servicing, and banking in India and have vast and powerful superstructure. Cooperative Banks are important cogs in this structure.

In the beginning of 20th century, availability of credit in India, more particularly in rural areas, was almost absent. Agricultural and related activities were starved of organized, institutional credit. The rural folk had to depend entirely on the moneylenders, who lent often at usurious rates of interest.

The cooperative banks arrived in India in the beginning of 20th Century as an official effort to create a new type of institution based on the principles of cooperative organization and management, suitable for problems peculiar to Indian conditions. These banks were conceived as substitutes for money lenders, to provide timely and adequate short-term and long-term institutional credit at reasonable rates of interest.

In the formative stage Cooperative Banks were Urban Cooperative Societies run on community basis and their lending activities were restricted to meeting the credit requirements of their members. The concept of Urban Cooperative Bank was first spelt out by Mehta Bhansali Committee in 1939 which defined on Urban Cooperative Bank. Provisions of Section 5 (CCV) of Banking Regulation Act, 1949 (as applicable to Cooperative Societies) defined an Urban Cooperative Bank as a Primary Cooperative Society was made applicable in 1966.

With gradual growth and also given fillip with the economic boom, urban banking sector received tremendous boost and started diversifying its credit portfolio. Besides giving traditional lending activity meeting the credit requirements of their customers they started catering to various sorts of customers *viz.,* self-employed, small businessmen/industries, house finance, consumer finance, personal finance etc.

CATEGORIES

There are two main categories of the cooperative banks:

(*a*) **Short-term lending oriented Cooperative Banks :** Within this category there are three sub categories of banks *viz.,* State Cooperative Banks, District Cooperative Banks and Primary Agricultural Cooperative Societies.

(*b*) **Long-term lending oriented Cooperative Banks :** Within the second category there are land development banks at three levels state, district and village.

The cooperative banking structure in India is divided into following main 5 categories –

1. Primary Urban Cooperative Banks
2. Primary Agricultural Credit Societies
3. District Central Cooperative Banks
4. State Cooperative Banks
5. Land Development Banks

Features of Cooperative Banks

- Cooperative Banks are organized and managed on the principal of co-operation, self-help, and mutual help.
- They function with the rule of "one member, one vote" function on "no profit, no loss" basis. Cooperative Banks, as a principle do not pursue the goal of profit maximization.
- Cooperative Banks perform all the main banking functions of deposit mobilization, supply of credit and provision of remittance facilities.
- Cooperative Banks provide limited banking products and are functionally specialists in agriculture related products. However, cooperative banks now provide housing loans also. UCBs provide working capital loans and term loans as well.
- The State Cooperative Banks (SCBs), Central Cooperative Banks (CCBs) and Urban Cooperative Banks (UCBs) can normally extend housing loans upto Rs 1 lakh to an individual. The scheduled UCBs, however, can lend upto Rs 3 lakh for housing purposes. The UCBs can provide advances against the shares and debentures also.
- Cooperative Bank do banking business mainly in the agriculture and rural sector. However, UCBs, SCBs and CCBs operate in semi urban, urban, and metropolitan areas also. The urban and non-agricultural business of these banks has grown over the years. The cooperative banks demonstrate a shift from rural to urban, while the commercial banks, from urban to rural.
- Cooperative Banks are perhaps the first government sponsored, government-supported, and government-subsidised financial agency in India.
- They get financial and other help from the Reserve Bank of India, NABARD, central government and state governments.
- They constitute the "most favoured" banking sector with risk of nationalization. For commercial banks, the Reserve Bank of India is lender of last resort, but for cooperative banks it is the lender of first resort which provides financial resources in the form of contribution to the initial capital (through state government), working capital, refinance.
- Cooperative Banks belong to the money market as well as to the capital market. Primary agricultural credit societies provide short-term and medium-term loans.
- Land Development Banks (LDBs) provide long-term loans. SCBs and CCBs also provide both short-term and long-term loans.

- Cooperative Banks are financial intermediaries only partially. The sources of their funds (resources) are (*a*) central and state government, (*b*) the Reserve Bank of India and NABARD, (*c*) other cooperative institutions, (*d*) ownership funds and, (*e*) deposits or debenture issues.
- Intra-sectoral flows of funds are much greater in cooperative banking than in commercial banking. Inter-bank deposits, borrowings, and credit from a significant part of assets and liabilities of cooperative banks. This means that intra-sectoral competition is absent and intra-sectoral integration is high for cooperative bank.
- Some cooperative banks are scheduled banks, while others are non-scheduled banks. For instance, SCBs and some UCBs are scheduled banks but other cooperative banks are non-scheduled banks. At present, 28 SCBs and 11 UCBs with Demand and Time Liabilities over Rs 50 crore each are included in the Second Schedule of the Reserve Bank of India Act. Cooperative Banks are subject to CRR and liquidity requirements as other scheduled and non-scheduled banks. However, their requirements are less than commercial banks.
- Since 1966 the lending and deposit rate of commercial banks have been directly regulated by the Reserve Bank of India.
- Although the Reserve Bank of India had power to regulate the rate cooperative bank but this have been exercised only after 1979 in respect of non-agricultural advances they were free to charge any rates at their discretion.
- Although the main aim of the cooperative bank is to provide cheaper credit to their members and not to maximize profits, they may access the money market to improve their income so as to remain viable.

RBI POLICIES

The Reserve Bank of India appointed a High Power Committee in May 1999 under the Chairmanship of Shri K.Madhava Rao, Ex-Chief Secretary, Government of Andhra Pradesh, to review the performance of Urban Cooperative Banks (UCBs) and to suggest necessary measures to strengthen this sector. With reference to the terms given to the committee, the Committee identified five broad objectives:

1. To preserve the cooperative character of UCBs
2. To protect the depositors' interest
3. To reduce the systemic risks to the financial system
4. To put in place strong regulatory norms at the entry level so as to sustain the operation efficiency of UCBs in a competitive environment and evolve measures to strengthen the existing UCB structure particularly in the context of ever increasing number of weak banks and
5. To align urban banking sector with the other segments of banking sector in the context of prudential norms *in toto* and removing the irritants of dual control regime.

RBI Policies can be put under the following:

- Branch Licensing
- Unit Banks
- Extension of Area of Operation
- Genesis and Architecture of UCBs
- Extension Counters
- Capital Adequacy Norms
- Classification of UCBs
- Investment of Funds
- Operations in Call/Notice Money Market
- Limits on discounting of UCBs Pay Orders
- Equity Finance
- Other investments
- Classification and Valuation of Investment
- No Abridged Names

COOPERATIVE BANKS RBI PERSPECTIVE

RBI has decided not to allow urban cooperative banks (UCBs) with less than Rs 50 crore net worth to spread their operations outside their state of jurisdiction. The main risk exposure of UCBs was not credit risk but interest rate risk. As interest rates paid by these banks, particularly on deposits, were not in synchronisation with the rest of the banking sector. The sheer number of weak UCBs, which is well over 200, is a cause for concern for the RBI.

Rehabilitation of these banks may involve strategies such as the registrars directing cooperative courts for speedy recovery process and execution of decrees, unviable branches being either relocated or closed down, exploring avenues for getting additional capital and merger with a well-managed bank.

RBI is in favour of ending dual control for UCBs. Therefore, demarcation of banking-related functions and those that warrant only state government's action were required.

As per RBI the issue of dual control could be resolved in three ways –

The **first** approach is by bringing the subject of co-operation under the concurrent list so as to enable the Union government to legislate in matters pertaining to cooperative banking. But such a move will involve constitutional amendments.

The **second** approach would be for the states to enact progressive legislations thereby making the registrars confine their functions only to registration and acceptance of be laws. This will lead to the dual command over UCBs ending automatically.

The **last** approach would be to demarcate the regulatory roles of state Governments and RBI in the state acts, as suggested by the Madhava Rao Committee. Mr. Capoor favours the third approach.

Government is considering incorporating amendments to the Banking Regulations Act to empower the Reserve Bank of India to change the management and chief executive officer (CEO) of urban cooperative banks (UCBs).

Meanwhile, the RBI had mooted a proposal to set-up a separate supervising and regulatory body for UCBs in its recent Credit Policy.

COOPERATIVE CREDIT STRUCTURE: COMMITTEE RECOMMENDATIONS

The committee on revitalization support to the cooperatives credit structure, headed by minister of state for finance Balasaheb Vikhe Patil recommended that financial support for each such credit institutions be split between the Centre and the respective State Governments in the proportion of 60:40. However, for the North-Eastern States and Jammu and Kashmir, it suggested that the Center's proportion be raised to 90 per cent.

Committee recommended that the revitalization assistance could be in the form of bonds issued by the Centre and State Governments. These bonds should be self-extinguishing in nature, and after 10 years, the bonds will be extinguished without any redemption of the principal amount.

The committee also said that a panel be constituted comprising of the Secretary (Finance), Secretary (Agriculture), Deputy Governor, RBI, Chairman, NABARD and representatives of State Governments for policy direction, review, and monitoring of the cooperative credit institutions. Similar committees may be constituted at the State-level, it added. The panel said that the decision on de-layering of the credit system should be left to the individual State.

For computation of assistance to the cooperative banks the committee suggested that accumulated losses and interest overdue for over three years should be the basis of calculation.

The committee also said that scheduling of district cooperative banks will allow them to borrow funds from Reserve Bank of India and National Bank for Agriculture and Rural Development (NABARD) which will reduce their dependence on state cooperative banks.

Committee hoped that recapitalization would help the cooperative banks transform themselves into scheduled commercial banks.

FUTURE OF COOPERATIVE BANKS

*Strengthening through Corporate Governance

1. To address this topic of tremendous relevane, focus and signficance in today's context. Needless to say, for the cooperative banks in India these are transitional times. Never before has the need for restoring customer confidence in the coperative sector beeen felt so much. Never before has the issue of good governance in the cooperative banks assumed such criticality. The literature on corporate governance in its wider connotation covers a range of issues such as protection of shareholders' rights; enhancing shareholders' value. Board issues including its composition and role, disclosure requirements, integrity of accounting practices, the control systems, in particular internal control systems. Corporate governance especially in the cooperative

sector has come into sharp focus because more and more cooperative banks in India, both in urban and rural areas, have experienced grave problems in recent times which has in a way threatened the profile and identity of the entire cooperative system. These problems include mis-management, financial impropriety, poor investment decisions and the growing distance between members and their cooperative society.

2. The purpose and objectives of cooperatives provide the framework for cooperative corporate governance. Cooperatives are organized groups of people which function as jointly managed and democratically controlled enterprises. They exist to serve their members and depositors and produce benefits for them. Cooperative corporate governance is therefore about ensuring cooperative relevance and performance by connecting members, management and the employees to the policy, strategy and decision-making processes. Infact, the very definition of corporate governance stems from its organic link with the entire gamut of activities having direct or indirect influence on the financial health of corporate entities. Cooperative banks as corporate entities possess certain unique characteristics. Although it may sound ironic, evolution of cooperatives in India as peoples' organizations rather than business enterprises adopting professional managerial systems has hindered growth of professionalism in cooperatives and proved to be a neglected area in their evolution.

3. Professionalism reflects the co-existence of high level of skills and standards in performing duties entrusted to an individual. The absence of a proper system of placement and skill up-gradation inputs constrain professional management in cooperative banks. Though there is a system of training in place in many cooperative banks, attempts are seldom made to match them with the current and future staff requirements. It is desirable that the training programmes encompass skill up-gradation and aptitude development in full measure. It is also necessary to keep the staff sufficiently motivated through periodic job rotation, job enrichment and recognition of performance. The cooperative banks should indeed work like professional organizations on sound managerial systems in tune with the needs of the time, taking care of future projections of requirements to retain and improve their market share and identity in the long run. It is in this context that professionalism and accountability of the banks' boards assume critical significance.

4. Regulators are external pressure points for good corporate governance. Mere compliance with regulatory requirements is not however an ideal situation in itself. In fact, mere compliance with regulatory pressures is a minimum requirement of good corporate governance and what are required are internal pressures, peer pressures and market pressures to reach higher than minimum standards prescribed by regulatory agencies. RBI's approach to regulation in recent times has some features that would enhance the need for and usefulness of good corporate governance in the cooperative sector. The transparency aspect has been emphasized by expanding the coverage of information and timeliness of such information and analytical content. Importantly, deregulation and operational freedom must go hand-in-hand with operational transparency. In fact, the RBI Governor's April, 2002 Monetary and Credit Policy announcements have made it clear that with the abolition of minimum lending rates for cooperative banks, it will be incumbent on these banks to make the interest rates charged by them transparent and known to all customers. Banks have therefore been asked to publish the minimum and maximum interest rates charged by them and display this information in every branch. Disclosure and

transparency are thus key pillars of a corporate governance framework because they provide all the stakeholders with the information necessary to judge whether their interests are being taken care of.

5. Another area which requires focused attention is greater transparency in the balance sheets of cooperative banks. The commercial banks in India are now required to disclose accounting ratios relating to operating profit, return on assets, business per employee, NPAs etc. as also maturity profile of loans, advances, investments, borrowings and deposits. RBI had advised Registrars of Cooperative Societies of the State Governments in 1996 that the balance sheet and profit and loss account should be prepared based on prudential norms introduced as a sequel to Financial Sector Reforms and that the statutory/departmental auditors of cooperative banks should look into the compliance with these norms. Auditors are therefore expected to be well versed with all aspects of the new guidelines issued by RBI and ensure that the profit and loss account and balance sheet of cooperative banks are prepared in a transparent manner and reflect the true state of affairs. Auditors should also ensure that other necessary statutory provisions and appropriations out of profits are made as required in terms of Cooperative Societies Act/Rules of the state concerned and the bye-laws of the respective institutions.
6. Appropriate internal control systems become even more critical in the context of the growing emphasis on diversification of business products as the prime need of all levels in cooperative credit institutions. It is indeed necessary for cooperative banks to devote adequate attention to maximizing their returns on every unit of resources through an effective funds management strategy and mechanism. One prime component of the investment portfolio of the cooperative banks, which has attracted a lot of attention, is their transaction in government securities.
7. The financial sector reforms in India have sought to achieve, among other things, improvement in the financial health and competitive capabilities by means of prescription of prudential norms. The cooperative banks have also thus been put under the prudential norms regime to bring about the desirable level of transparency in their balance sheets. While urban cooperative banks have been subjected to income recognition, asset classification, provisioning and other related norms in a phased manner beginning April, 1992, these prudential norms including asset classification and provisioning (excluding the capital adequacy ratio) were made applicable to the cooperative banks from the year 1996-97.
8. One important issue that has engaged much attention in the recent past is the duality of control over cooperative banks. In terms of the Cooperative Societies Act of respective States, the Registrar of Cooperative Societies was the sole regulator and supervisor of all the societies registered in his State including societies carrying on banking business. With the application of BR Act, 1949 to cooperative banks, this position has since changed. While RBI now regulates and supervises banking activities carried on by urban cooperative societies, supervision of State Cooperative Banks and District Central Cooperative Banks is carried out by NABARD. The core principles of supervision in relation to cooperative banks have thus to be formulated and implemented by RBI in respect of Urban Cooperative Banks and there is an emergent need to constantly beef up the supervisory system through proper on-site monitoring and adequate off-site surveillance.

We also need to analyze and pick up early warning signals, if any, in respect of any such irregularities in the investment portfolio of these banks from the periodic review reports on such transactions which are received from them. There is also an urgent need for clarity in defining the roles of various control institutions by streamlining processes, procedures, etc. for removing overlapping of controls over cooperative banks presently vested with State Government, RBI or NABARD, as the case It is in this context that the Governor's Monetary and Credit Policy announcement in April, 2001 had stressed the need for a separate regulatory agency for the cooperative banks. This issue is being debated in various quarters.

9. Credit institutions are linked to each other through a complex chain of inter-bank relationships which – as recent instances have showed – in any event of difficulty become mechanisms for spread of the contagion effect. Signs of financial mismanagement in an institution or a group of institutions regardless of the reasons are liable to set-off similar problems in other institutions and open serious risks in the financial system. Power and decision-making in cooperative banks are all too often concentrated at the top in too few hands. Cooperative performance has therefore been for a long time characterized by lack of participation and sense of involvement. Active members who feel that they are part of an organization that has goals in harmony with their own and clear roles for constructively engaged, competent governing bodies and management would be a powerful force to build cooperative identity and excellence. It is perhaps time that the State Governments refashioned management in cooperative banks by picking up threads of good corporate governance.

10. Success of economic decision depends after all on the human resources at the disposal of any organization. A change is needed today in the cooperative banks which is built on confidence in human capital – the most important of all resources – in commitment, creativity and innovation brought about by proactive management, membership and employees. The ability to capture knowledge and wisdom gives cooperative banks their competitive advantage. A pre-requisite is that participants from all parts of a cooperative organization know and understand its purpose, core values and visions.

11. In the years to come, the Indian financial system will grow not only in size but also in complexity as the forces of competition gain further momentum and financial markets acquire greater depth. The policy environment is expected to remain supportive of healthy growth and development with accent on more operational flexibility as well as greater prudential regulation and supervision. The real success of our financial sector reforms will however depend primarily on the organizational effectiveness of the banks, including cooperative banks, for which initiatives will have to come from the banks themselves. It is for the cooperative banks themselves to build on the synergy inherent in the cooperative structure and stand up for their unique qualities. With elements of good corporate governance, sound investment policy, appropriate internal control system, better credit risk management, focus on newly emerging business areas like micro finance, commitment to better customer service, adequate mechanization and proactive policies on house-keeping issues, cooperative banks will definitely be able to grapple with these challenges and convert them into opportunities.

QUESTIONS

Fill in the Blanks:

1. There are _________categories of cooperative banks.
2. Cooperative banks are registered under _______act of the respective state.

State whether true or false:

1. Cooperative banks finance rural areas for farming, cattle, milk and hatchery.
2. Cooperative banks are regulated by RBI.
3. Urban cooperative banks cannot provide advances against shares and debentures.

Answer in detail:

Q.1. What are Cooperative Banks? Discuss their categories and features.

Q.2. What is the future of Cooperative Banks in India? What strategies should they adopt to improve their performance?

❑❑❑

17 NON-BANKING FINANCIAL COMPANIES

DEFINITION

A Non-Banking Financial Company (NBFC) is a company registered under the Companies Act, 1956 and is engaged in the business of loans and advances, acquisition of shares/stocks/bonds/debentures/ securities issued by Government or local authorities or other securities of like marketable nature, leasing, hire-purchase, insurance business, chit business but does not include any institution whose principal business is that of agricultural activity, industrial activity, sale/purchase/construction of immovable property.

A non-banking institution which is a company and which has its principal business of receiving deposits under any scheme or arrangement or any other manner, or lending in any manner is also a non-banking financial company (Residuary non-banking company).

Difference between Banks and NBFCs

NBFCs are doing functions akin to that of banks, however there are a few differences:

- An NBFC cannot accept demand deposits;
- It is not a part of the payment and settlement system and as such cannot issue cheques to its customers; and
- Deposit insurance facility of DICGC is not available for NBFC depositors unlike in case of banks.

Registration of NBFCs

In terms of Section 45-IA of the RBI Act 1934, it is mandatory that every NBFC should be registered with RBI to commence or carry on any business of non-banking financial institution as defined in clause (*a*) of Section 45 I of the RBI Act, 1934.

However, to obviate dual regulation, certain categories of NBFCs which are regulated by other regulators are exempted from the requirement of registration with RBI *viz.,* Venture Capital Fund/

Merchant Banking companies/Stock broking companies registered with SEBI, Insurance Companies holding a valid Certificate of Registration issued by IRDA, Nidhi companies as notified under Section 620A of the Companies Act, 1956, Chit companies as defined in clause (b) of Section 2 of the Chit Funds Act, 1982 or Housing Finance Companies regulated by National Housing Bank.

The NBFCs that are registered with RBI are:

(*i*) Equipment Leasing Company;

(*ii*) Hire-Purchase Company;

(*iii*) Loan Company;

(*iv*) Investment Company;

The above type of companies may be further classified into those accepting deposits or those not accepting deposits.

(*v*) Residuary Non-Banking Company: Residuary Non-Banking Company is a class of NBFC which is a company and has as its principal business the receiving of deposits, under any scheme or arrangement or in any other manner and not being Investment, Leasing, Hire-Purchase, Loan Company. These companies are required to maintain investments as per directions of RBI, in addition to liquid assets. The functioning of these companies is different from those of NBFCs in terms of method of mobilisation of deposits and requirement of deployment of depositors' funds. However, prudential norms are applicable to these companies also.

NBFCS EXEMPTED FROM REGISTRATION

Housing Finance Companies, Merchant Banking Companies, Stock Exchanges, Companies engaged in the business of stock-broking/sub-broking, Venture Capital Fund Companies, Nidhi Companies, Insurance Companies and Chit Fund Companies are NBFCs but they have been exempted from the requirement of registration under Section 45-IA of the RBI Act 1934, subject to certain conditions.

Housing Finance Companies are regulated by National Housing Bank, Merchant Banker/Venture Capital Fund Company/Stock-Exchanges/Stock Brokers/Sub-Brokers are regulated by Securities and Exchange Board of India, Insurance Companies are regulated by Insurance Regulatory and Development Authority. Similarly, Chit Companies are regulated by the respective State Governments and Nidhi Companies are regulated by Ministry of Company Affairs, Government of India.

REQUIREMENTS FOR REGISTRATION WITH RBI

A company incorporated under the Companies Act, 1956 and desirous of commencing business of non-banking financial institution as defined under Section 45 I(a) of the RBI Act, 1934 should have

- A minimum net owned fund of Rs. 25 lakh (raised to Rs. 200 lakh w.e.f April 21, 1999).
- The company is required to submit its application for registration in the prescribed format along with necessary documents for Bank's consideration. The Bank issues Certificate of Registration after satisfying itself that the conditions as enumerated in Section 45-IA of the RBI Act, 1934 are satisfactory.

ACCEPTANCE OF PUBLIC DEPOSITS BY NBFCS

All NBFCs are not entitled to accept public deposits. Only those NBFCs holding a valid Certificate of Registration with authorisation to accept Public Deposits can accept/hold public deposits. The NBFCs accepting public deposits should have minimum stipulated Net Owned Fund and comply with the Directions issued by the Bank.

Moreover there is a ceiling on acceptance of Public Deposits. A NBFC maintaining required NOF/CRAR and complying with the prudential norms can accept public deposits as follows:

Category of NBFC	Ceiling on Public Deposits
EL/HP Companies maintaining CRAR of 15% without credit rating EL/HP Companies with CRAR of 12% and having minimum investment grade credit rating	1.5 times of NOF or Rs. 10 crore whichever is less 4 times of NOF
LC/IC with CRAR of 12% and having minimum investment grade credit rating.	1.5 times of NOF

Presently, the maximum rate of interest a NBFC can offer is 11%. The interest may be paid or compounded at rests not shorter than monthly rests.

The NBFCs are allowed to accept/renew public deposits for a minimum period of 12 months and maximum period of 60 months. They cannot accept deposits repayable on demand.

REGULATIONS ON ACCEPTANCE OF DEPOSITS BY NBFCS

Some of the important regulations relating to acceptance of deposits by NBFCs are as under:

- The NBFCs are allowed to accept/renew public deposits for a minimum period of 12 months and maximum period of 60 months. They cannot accept deposits repayable on demand.
- NBFCs cannot offer interest rates higher than the ceiling rate prescribed by RBI from time to time. The present ceiling is 11 per cent per annum. The interest may be paid or compounded at rests not shorter than monthly rests.
- NBFCs cannot offer gifts/incentives or any other additional benefit to the depositors.
- NBFCs (except certain equipment leasing/hire-purchase finance companies) should have minimum investment grade credit rating.
- The deposits with NBFCs are not insured.
- The repayment of deposits by NBFCs is not guaranteed by RBI.
- There are certain mandatory disclosures about the company in the Application Form issued by the company soliciting deposits.

ACCEPTANCE OF DEPOSITS FROM NRIS

Effective from April 24, 2004, NBFCs cannot accept deposits from NRI except deposits by debit to NRO account of NRI, provided such amount do not represent inward remittance or transfer from NRE/ FCNR (B) account. However, the existing NRI deposits can be renewed.

While making deposits with a NBFC, the following aspects should be borne in mind:

- Public deposits are unsecured.
- A proper deposit receipt which should, besides the name of the depositor/s state the date of deposit, the amount in words and figures, rate of interest payable and the date of maturity should be insisted. The receipt shall be duly signed by an officer authorised by the company in that behalf.
- The Reserve Bank of India does not accept any responsibility or guarantee about the present position as to the financial soundness of the company or for the correctness of any of the statements or representations made or opinions expressed by the company and for repayment of deposits/discharge of the liabilities by the company.
- An unrated NBFC, except certain equipment leasing/hire-purchase (EL/HP) companies, cannot accept public deposits.
- An exception is made in case of unrated EL/HP companies with CRAR of 15% which can accept public deposit up to 1.5 times of the NOF or Rs. 10 crore whichever is lower without having a credit rating.
- A NBFC may get itself rated by any of the four rating agencies namely, CRISIL, CARE, ICRA and FITCH Ratings India Pvt. Ltd.

The symbols of minimum investment grade rating of the Credit rating agencies are:

Name of rating agencies	Level of minimum investment grade credit rating (MIGR)
CRISIL	FA- (FA MINUS)
ICRA	MA- (MA MINUS)
CARE	CARE BBB (FD)
FITCH Ratings India Pvt. Ltd.	tA-(ind)(FD)

It may be added that A- is not equivalent to A, AA- is not equivalent to AA and AAA- is not equivalent to AAA.

If rating of a NBFC is downgraded to below minimum investment grade rating, it has to stop accepting public deposit, report the position within fifteen working days to the RBI and reduce within three years from the date of such downgrading of credit rating, the amount of excess public deposit to nil or to the appropriate extent permissible under paragraph 4(4) of Non-Banking Financial Companies Acceptance of Public Deposits (Reserve Bank) Directions, 1998; however such NBFC can renew the matured public deposits subject to repayment stipulations specified above and compliance with other conditions for acceptance of deposits.

PRUDENTIAL REGULATIONS APPLICABLE TO NBFCS

The Reserve Bank of India has issued detailed directions on prudential norms, *vide* Non-Banking Financial Companies Prudential Norms (Reserve Bank) Directions, 1998. The directions interalia, prescribe guidelines on income recognition, asset classification and provisioning requirements applicable to NBFCs, exposure norms, constitution of audit committee, disclosures in the balance sheet, requirement of capital adequacy, restrictions on investments in land and building and unquoted shares.

QUESTIONS

Fill in the blanks:

1. NBFCs cannot accept ________ deposits.
2. NBFCs must have a minimum net owned fund of ________.
3. NBFCs accept deposits for a minimum period of ________ months.
4. An unrated NBFC except ________ cannot accept public deposits.

State whether true or false:

1. Deposits with NBFCs are insured.
2. NBFC deposits are guaranteed by RBI.
3. NBFCs must get themselves rated.
4. Housing finance companies are exempt from registration with RBI.

Answer in detail:

Q.1. What is the difference between banks and NBFCs?

Q.2. How are NBFCs regulated in terms of acceptance of deposits?

❑❑❑

Section-III

Developmental Financial Institution

18 BRIEF PROFILE OF VARIOUS DEVELOPMENTAL FINANCIAL INSTITUTIONS IN INDIA

I. INDUSTRIAL CREDIT AND INVESTMENT CORPORATION OF INDIA LIMITED (ICICI)

ICICI Ltd. was established as a private sector company in 1955, offering a wide range of financial services. It set-up various subsidiaries in areas of commercial banking, investment, banking, non-banking finance, venture capital financing, investor service and state level infrastructure financing services. Its major objective was to provide medium-term and long-term project financing to Indian businesses. In 1999, ICICI became the first Indian company from non-Japan Asia to be listed on the New York Stock Exchange (NYSE).

In 2001, due to move towards Universal Banking and emerging competitive scenario in Indian banking industry the managements of ICICI and ICICI Bank framed the view that merger of ICICI with ICICI Bank would be an optimal strategic alternative for both the entities and would create an optimal legal structure for ICICI group's universal banking strategy. It would create value for ICICI's shareholders due to merged entity's access to low-cost deposits, greater opportunities for earning fee-based income, ability to participate in the payments system and provide transaction banking services. The merger was also considered to enhance the capital base, scale of operations, seamless access to ICICI bank's strong corporate relationships, entry into new business segments, higher market share in various business segments particularly in fee based services and access to the vast talent pool of ICICI and its subsidiaries.

So in October, 2001 Boards of directors of ICICI and ICICI Bank approved the merger of ICICI and ICICI Bank along with the two wholly owned subsidiaries, ICICI Personal Financial Services Limited and ICICI Capital Services Limited. After the merger, the ICICI groups financing and banking operations, both wholesale and retail, have been integrated in a single entity.

FUNCTIONS/SERVICES OFFERED BY ICICI

The services offered by ICICI include:

1. **Retail Banking :** It offers a wide range of investment and other banking services to the customers. These products include mortgages, automobile and two-wheelers loans, commercial loans, construction equipment loan, consumer durable loans, personal loans and credit cards.
2. **Wholesale/Corporate Banking :** It provides financial solutions tailored to customer's needs. It also provides working capital finance and focuses on transaction banking services like cash management, letters of credit and bank guarantees.
3. **Project Finance :** It involves financing new projects in manufacturing sector, oil, gas and petrochemical sectors. Along with this it also acts as arranger and facilitator in creating appropriate structure.
4. **International Business :** It has to establish its presence in international markets mainly in IT, investment banking and banking products.
5. **Corporate Center :** It involves investors' relationship management, risk management, legal, human resources management, corporate banking and communications.

Subsidiaries of ICICI Bank Ltd. : ICICI Bank has 12 subsidiaries out of which four are international and eight are domestic.

Domestic Subsidiaries –

1. **ICICI Securities Limited :** It takes up investment banking activities in both debt and equity market. It advises on corporate strategy, capital structure and capital raising. It also provides advisory services in case of mergers and acquisitions.
2. **ICICI Brokerage Services Limited :** It is engaged in business of broking and secondary market transactions.
3. **ICICI Venture Funds Management Co. Ltd. :** It specializes in making investments in new or expanding privately held business ventures. It also provides business skills and plays a full fledged role in Investee Company.
4. **ICICI Prudential Life Insurance Co. Ltd. :** It is a registered Life Insurance Company set-up after opening up of insurance sector in India. It provides Life Insurance Services similar to LIC.
5. **ICICI Lombard General Insurance Company Ltd. :** It undertakes general insurance business in India.
6. **ICICI International Management Company Ltd. :** It is the Asset Management Company of ICICI Securities Fund.
7. **ICICI Trusteeship Services Ltd. :** It acts as a trustee of mutual funds, off-shore funds, pension funds, venture capital funds etc.

International Subsidiaries

1. **ICICI Securities Holdings Inc. :** It was established as a wholly owned subsidiary of ICICI Securities Ltd. To provide investment banking services to US investors who wish to enter the Indian Financial Market and Indian Investors who wish to enter the US Market.

2. **ICICI Securities Inc. :** It was set-up to provide brokerage research and investment banking services to investors in USA, who wish to invest in Indian Securities Market.
3. **ICICI International Ltd. :** It is an Investment Fund Management Company incorporated in the Republic of Mauritius on January 18, 1996.

II. INDUSTRIAL FINANCE CORPORATION OF INDIA (IFCI)

The Industrial Finance Corporation of India was established on July 1, 1948 as the first Developmental Financial Institute in the country to cater to the long-term finance needs of the industrial sector.

It came out during the period when merchant banks and underwriting firms were almost non-existent and commercial banks were not equipped to provide industrial finance in any significant manner. IFCI provided access to low cost funds through central bank's Statutory Liquidity Ratio (SLR) which in turn enabled it to provide loan and advances to corporate borrowers at concessional rates.

Till 1993, IFCI continued to be a Developmental Financial Institution. After 1993 it was changed from a statutory corporation to a company under the Indian Companies Act 1956 and was named as IFCI Limited w.e.f. October 1999.

PRODUCTS AND SERVICES

IFCI has been functioning with the goal of providing medium and long-term financial assistance to manufacturing concerns and fulfill the overall goal of industrial and economic development in India. Services provided by IFCI include:

- **Project Finance**: IFCI provides credit and various other facilities to finance green field (new) projects as well as brown field (modernization, expansion, diversification of existing concerns) projects.
- **Financial Services:** They cover activities such as acquisition of assets, expansion, diversification and modernization programs. IFCI provides quick funds to suit the borrowers' requirement.
- **Non-Project Specific Assistance:** It is provided mainly in the form of corporate/short-term loans, working capital, bills discounting, etc. to meet expenditure not related to any specific project.
- **Corporate Advisory Services:** These were started by IFCI in 1986. This service was provided by IFCI to promote the activities of its Merchant Banking and Allied Business Department. It also plays a role in portfolio management services.
- **Ancillary Services :** Various ancillary services provided by IFCI include : -
  (*a*) **Advisory Services to Regulatory Agencies:** IFCI provides consultancy services to various regulatory agencies controlling sectors like electricity, telecom, oil & gas, education etc.
  (*b*) **Industry Research:** IFCI has a vast database and a professional research team which helps to resolve various micro as well as macro level issues of the corporate sector.
  (*c*) **Legal Advisory Services:** IFCI has a full fledged legal cell comprising of professionals

to handle various corporate disputes. It provides consultancy as well as investigation and report preparation services to the corporates.

(*d*) **Corporation Finance and Investment Banking :** This includes:—

- Deciding capital structure, preparation of prospectus, identification of potential investors and placement of instruments with Banks and FIs.
- Advice on strategic decisions like mergers and amalgamation, preparing amalgamation scheme and solving post-merger issues.
- PSU disinvestment services involving restructuring, pricing of equity, legal assistance & assistance in raising and listing of securities.

(*e*) **Catalyst in Channeling FDI into India:** IFCI also helps in promoting FDI into India in the following ways:

- Providing necessary office infrastructure for start-up operations.
- Facilitating clearance from government departments.
- Helping in important decisions regarding markets, materials, manpower available for enabling production of globally competitive products.
- Providing inputs for performing functions which can ensure long-term viability.
- Providing research and advisory services.

(*f*) **Infrastructure Advisory Services**: This includes services provided to the infrastructure sector and these include:—

- Credit locumentation
- Pre investment review
- Preparation of feasibility report
- Risk assessment and cost allocation
- Advising alternative financing options
- Financial analysis
- Project evaluation
- Credit syndication
- Arranging guarantee
- Raise of debt and equity
- Capital market advisory services

(*g*) **Project Advisory Services**: These include—

- Purchase, sale, transfer of assets, rights concerning technology usage
- Separation, liquidation and disposal of assets, liabilities;
- Preparation of all the information, structuring, negotiating terms and conditions and managing documentation transaction and transition process during mergers/joint venture.

(*h*) **Privatization Services** :

- Conducting SWOT qnalysis, assessment and valuation of assets.
- Suggesting alternatives to increase sale value.
- Bidding
- Preparation of information brochure and financial restructuring.

III. INDUSTRIAL DEVELOPMENT BANK OF INDIA (IDBI)

IDBI has been a leading development bank with the mission of promoting industrial growth by financing of medium and long-term projects in accordance with national plans and priorities. Over the years, IDBI has provided products and services to cover the entire spectrum of industrial activities, including manufacturing and services. IDBI Ltd. has been providing rupee as well as foreign currency loans or expansion, diversification as well as modernization purposes.

IDBI Ltd. has been providing customer's need oriented products like asset credit, equipment finance, corporate loan, working capital loan and bills discounting for acquisition of equipment and capital assets. It has also been meeting the capital expenditure and working capital requirements, offering credit for turnkey contracts and providing fee based services.

HISTORY AND GROWTH

IDBI was set-up July, 1964 under an Act of Parliament as a wholly-owned subsidiary of Reserve Bank of India. In February, 1976 ownership of IDBI was transferred to Government of India and it was designated as Principal Financial Institution for coordinating the working of institutions at national and state levels engaged in financing, promoting and developing industry. In March, 1982 International Finance Division of IDBI was transferred to Export-Import Bank of India, established as a wholly owned corporation of Government of India, under an Act of Parliament.

In April, 1990, Small Industries Development Bank of India (SIDBI) was established under SIDBI Act as a wholly-owned subsidiary to cater to specific needs of small-scale sector. In terms of an amendment to SIDBI Act in September 2000, IDBI divested 51% of its shareholding in SIDBI in favour of banks and other institutions in the first phase. IDBI has subsequently divested 79.13% of its stake in its erstwhile subsidiary to-date.

In January, 1992, IDBI accessed domestic retail debt market for the first time with innovative Deep Discount Bonds, registering path-breaking success. Afterwards in December, 1993, IDBI Capital Market Services Ltd. was set-up as a wholly-owned subsidiary of IDBI to offer a broad range of financial services, including Bond Trading, Equity Broking, Client Asset Management and Depository Services. IDBI Capital is currently a leading Primary Dealer in the country.

In September, 1994, IDBI Bank Ltd. was set-up in association with SIDBI as a private sector commercial bank subsidiary, a sequel to RBI's policy of opening up domestic banking sector to private participation as part of overall financial sector reforms.

In July, 1995, IDBI made Initial Public Offer of Equity and raised over Rs.2000 crore, thereby reducing Government stake to 72.14%. The Industrial Development Bank (Transfer of Undertaking and Repeal) Act, 2003 came into force from July 2, 2004.

The new entity "Industrial Development Bank of India" was incorporated on September 27, 2004 and Certificate of Commencement of Business was issued by the Registrar of Companies on September 28, 2004.

But, the Board of Directors of IDBI Ltd., at a meeting held on January 20, 2005, approved the Scheme of Amalgamation, envisaging merging of IDBI Bank Ltd. with IDBI Ltd. Pursuant to the scheme approved by the Boards of both the banks, IDBI Ltd. issued 100 equity shares for 142 equity shares held by shareholders in IDBI Bank Ltd.

Activities : IDBI has been involved in the following financing activities—

1. **Project Finance :** This scheme has the objective of providing long-term finance for expansion, diversification and modernization of existing projects in the form of rupee, foreign currency loan, underwriting direct subscription to equity capital and guarantees. To avail this scheme the following conditions must be satisfied:—
   - Long-term Debt to Equity Raito of 1.5:1.
   - 25% of project cost to be met through Promoters' Contribution.

   Fee charged by IDBI Ltd. For the above finances is:-
   - 1% of the loan amount as up front or processing fee.
   - Fixed or floating rate of interest on rupee loan as per borrower's creditworthiness, rating, tenure of loan etc.
   - Floating rate on Foreign Currency Loan – This rate is based on London Inter Bank Offer Rate (LIBOR) along with a fixed spread based on creditworthiness and rating of borrower as well as tenure of the loan.
   - Up to 2.5% of the amount to be paid as underwriting commission.

   Repayment of the loan may be done in monthly or quarterly installments. This is secured by personal guarantee of promoters or corporate guarantee or pledging of shares.
2. **Film Financing :** The objective of this finance is to assist in the production of feature films as defined under the Cinematograph (Certification) Rules, 1983. Documentaries, Short Films, Advertisements are not eligible for financing.

   The extent of financing provided is not less than 2 crore and should not exceed 50% of the estimated cost of the film.

   Criteria to be satisfied for availing this loan facility are:-
   - Debt Equity Ratio not to exceed 1:1.
   - Promoters' contribution should not be less than 30% of the estimated cost of the film.
   - The loan is sanctioned only to corporate entities, promoted by reputed producers, backed by satisfactory track record.

   Fees to be paid are:—
   - Interest at a prevailing interest rate band.
   - 1% of the loan amount to be paid as up front fee.

   Repayment must be made within a period of 2 years.
3. **Corporate Loan :** This loan is provided with the objective of financing normal capital expenditure, working capital margin, shortfall in working capital and general corporate purposes, including expenses on VRS (Voluntary Retirement Scheme) and business acquisition.

   Criteria to be satisfied to avail this loan are:—
   - Well performing corporates with minimum 5 years of operations and satisfactory track and credit record with lenders.

- Minimum BBB (Triple B) must be obtained by companies assisted by IDBI and 'A-' by companies not assisted by IDBI.
- Net worth of the company should not be less than 10 crore.
- Long-term Debt to equity ratio should be 1.25:1 and current ratio should be 1:1.

Fee charged for this financing includes:-

- Up front or processing fee depending on case to case basis.
- Fixed or floating rate of interest on rupee loan and foreign currency loan.

Repayment period of the loan is up to 5½ years from date of first disbursement of the loan.

4. **Direct Discounting of Bill :** This facility is provided to cover and promote sale of indigenous machinery and equipment.

The criteria to be satisfied to avail this loan facility are:-

- Long-term Debt to equity ratio should be 1.5:1.
- At least three years of track record of operations without default.

The interest charged depends on the rate prevailing at the time of discounting of bills. The repayment period varies from 2-7 years and repayment is assured by a bank guarantee or co-acceptance from a scheduled bank.

5. **Technology Upgradation Fund Scheme :** This scheme was introduced for the Textile and Jute industries and is intended to facilitate the induction of state-of-the-art or near state-of-the-art technology in Textile Industry.

   IDBI provides this facility to the non-Small Scale Industry (SSI) sector; on the condition that Debt Equity Ratio of borrower is 1.5:1 with minimum 20% contribution of project cost by promoter. Interest rate charged depends on the rates prevailing at the time of sanction/execution of loan documents.

6. **Refinance :** This facility is provided to fund medium scale industries. The institution eligible to get this loan include:-

   - All State Financial Corporations and State Industrial Development Corporations.
   - Banks in States of Bihar, Himachal Pradesh, J&K, Orissa and State in the North East.

The refinance facility is available only against loans or advances granted by above institutions SSIs are not eligible to avail this facility. The loan is provided in rupees and the cost of project for the same should not exceed Rs. 12 crore.

Conditions to be met by institutions to avail this facility include:-

- Debt Equity Ratio should not be more than 2:1.
- Promoter's Contribution should not be less than 25% of project cost.
- An up front fee of 1% will have to be paid on each disbursement.

Interest rate charged include rate announced from time to time by IDBI based on its Minimum Term Lending Rate. Repayment must be done between 3-10 years.

7. **Bill Rediscounting :** This facility is provided to cover and promote sale of indigenous machinery and equipment. Starting from a minimum amount of Rs. 10,000 the loan is provided up to 100% of the value of invoice. Fee charged depends on rate prevailing from time to time and repayment term varies from 2-5½ years, which can be extended to a maximum of 7 years on selective basis.
8. **FOREX Services/Treasury :** These are provided for corporate purposes with fund requirement of short-term nature.

   Well performing corporates with a minimum 5 years of record of operations and a satisfactory credit record with lenders are eligible to get this finance.

   The net worth of corporates must not be less than Rs. 25 crore and long-term debt to equity rates should be a minimum of 1.25:1.

   IDBI provides both Rupee and Foreign Currency Loan. The interest charged may be a fixed or floating rate varying on case to case basis.

   Repayment must be done within a maximum period of 18 months.

IV. NATIONAL BANK FOR AGRICULTURE AND RURAL DEVELOPMENT (NABARD)

NABARD was established on 12th July, 1982 with an initial capital of Rs.100 crore under National Bank for Agriculture and Rural Development Act 1981. Later its capital was enhanced to Rs.2000 crore by Government of India and RBI. NABARD is an apex institution handing all matters concerning policy, planning and operation in the field of credit for agriculture and other economic activities in rural areas of India.

As per the Preamble of the NABARD Act 1981, "NABARD is established as a development bank, for providing and regulating credit and other facilities for the promotion and development of agriculture, small scale industries, cottage and village industries, handicrafts and other rural crafts and other allied economic activities in rural areas with a view to promoting integrated rural development and securing prosperity of rural areas and for matters connected therewith or incidental thereto".

Role and Functions of NABARD —

- serves as an apex financing agency for the institutions providing investment and production credit for promoting the various developmental activities in rural area;
- takes measures towards institution building for improving absorptive capacity of the credit delivery system, including monitoring, formulation of rehabilitation schemes, restructuring of credit institutions, training of personnel, etc.;
- coordinates the rural financing activities of all institutions engaged in developmental work at the field level and maintains liaison with Government of India, State Governments, Reserve Bank of India (RBI) and other national level institutions concerned with policy formulations; and
- undertakes monitoring and evaluation of projects refinanced by it.

NABARD's refinance is available to State Cooperative Agriculture and Rural Development Banks (SCARDBs), State Cooperative Banks (SCBs), Regional Rural Banks (RRBs), Commercial Banks (CBs) and other financial institutions approved by RBI. While the ultimate beneficiaries of investment credit can be individuals, partnership concerns, companies, state-owned corporations or cooperative societies, production credit is generally given to individuals.

TYPES OF REFINANCE FACILITIES	
Agency	**Credit Facilities**
Commercial Banks	• Long-term credit for investment purposes. • Financing the working capital requirements of Weavers' Cooperative Societies (WCS) and State Handloom Development Corporations
Short-term Cooperative Structure (State Cooperative Banks, District Central Cooperative Banks, Primary Agriculture Credit Societies).	• Short-term (crop and other loans) • Medium-term (conversion) loans • Term loans for investment purposes • Financing WCS for production and marketing purposes • Financing State Handloom Development Corporations for working capital by State Cooperative Banks.
Long-term Co-operative Structure (State Co-operative Agriculture and Rural Development Banks, Primary Co-operative Agriculture and Rural Development Banks)	• Term loans for investment purposes.

V. SMALL INDUSTRIES DEVELOPMENT BANK OF INDIA (SIDBI)

SIDBI was established on April 2, 1990. It is a Principal Developmental Financial institution for promotion and development of Industries in the small scale sector and coordinating the functions of other institutions engaged in similar activities.

Provision of SIDBI Charter: The Charter establishing it, The Small Industries Development Bank of India 1989 Act envisaged SIDBI to be "the principal financial institution for the promotion, financing and development of industry in the small scale sector and to co-ordinate the functions of the institutions engaged in the promotion and financing or developing industry in the small scale sector and for matters connected therewith or incidental thereto".

SCHEMES

Direct Finance Schemes: SIDBI had been providing refinance to State Level Finance Corporations/ State Industrial Development Corporations / Banks etc., against their loans granted to small scale units.

Since the formation of SIDBI in April, 1990 a need was felt/representations were made that SIDBI being the principal financial institution for the small sector, should take up the financing of SSI projects directly on a selective basis.

So it was decided to introduce direct assistance schemes to supplement the other available channels of credit flow to the small industries sector. Since then, SIDBI has evolved itself into a supplier of a range of products and services to the Small and Medium Enterprises (SME) sector.

Bills Finance Schemes : This scheme involves provision of medium and short-term finance for the benefit of the small-scale sector. Bills Finance seeks to provide finance to manufacturers of indigenous machinery, capital equipment, components sub-assemblies set, based on compliance to the various eligibility criteria, norms etc. as applicable to the respective schemes.

To be eligible under the various bills schemes, one of the parties to the transactions to the scheme has to be an industrial unit in the small-scale sector within the meaning of Section 2(h) of the SIDBI Act 1989.

Refinance Schemes: Refinance scheme is introduced for catering to the need of funds of Primary Lending Institutes for financing small-scale industries. Under the scheme, SIDBI grants refinance against term loans granted by the eligible Prime Lending Institutes (PLI) to industrial concerns for setting-up industrial projects in the small scale sector as also for their expansion/modernization/ diversification.

Term loans granted by the PLIs for other specified eligible activities/purposes are also eligible for refinance.

Ceiling on re-financable term loan under the scheme is given below:

Banks

Types of PLI	**Revised Ceiling (Rs. Lakh)**
Scheduled Commercial Banks and State Cooperative Banks	300
Other Cooperative Banks / Urban Cooperative Banks	50
Regional Rural Banks	20

SFCs, SIDCs and TFIDCs >

Type of PLI	**Category (Amount in Rs. Lakh)**		
	A	**B**	**C**
SFC	500	500	500
SIDC	400	250	150
TFIDC	240	150	100

International Finance Schemes: The main objective of the various **International Finance** schemes is to enable small-scale industries to raise finance at internationally competitive rates to fulfill their export commitments.

The financial assistance is being offered in US Dollar and Euro currencies. Assistance in Rupees is also considered, independent of foreign currency limits.

SIDBI has a license to deal in foreign exchange as a **"restricted" Authorized Dealer** (*i.e.,* SIDBI confines its foreign exchange activities only to its own exposures and to exposures for its customers.

The Mumbai Head Office (MHO) of SIDBI operates as a Category 'A' branch that maintains foreign currency positions, nostro account with foreign correspondent banks and provides cover to other branches (Category 'B' branches) that carry out FOREX business.

Micro Finance: SIDBI identifies, nurtures and develops select potential (Micro Finance Institutions (MFIs) as long-term partners and provides credit support for their micro credit initiatives. The eligible partner institutions of SIDBI Foundation, therefore, comprise large and medium scale MFIs having minimum fund requirement of Rs.10 lakh per annum. In all, around 100-125 MFIs are planned to be developed as long-term partners over the next 4 years. Large and medium scale MFIs having considerable experience in managing micro credit programmes, high growth potential, good track record, professional expertise and committed to viability are provided financial assistance for on-lending. Under the present dispensation, annual need based assistance is provided to enable MFIs to expand their scale of operations and achieve self sufficiency at the earliest. Lending is based strictly on an intensive in-house appraisal supplemented with the capacity assessment rating by an independent professional agency. Relaxed security norms have also been adopted to reduce procedural bottlenecks as well as to facilitate easy disbursements.

Capacity Building: The long-term future of the micro-finances sector depends on MFIs in being able to achieve operational, financial and institutional sustainability. The constraints and challenges vary with the different types and development stage of MFIs. Most MFIs are currently operating below operational viability and use grant funds from donors for financing up-front costs of establishing new groups and covering initial losses incurred until the lending volume builds up to a break-even level. The MFIs are generally constrained in reaching a break-even and finally achieving sustainability primarily due to a narrow client and product base, high operational and administrative costs for delivering credit to the poor and their inability to mobilize requisite resources. Moreover lack of technical manpower, operational systems, infrastructure and MIS are prevalent. In view of above, to scale up micro-finance initiatives at a fast pace, a special effort is required for capacity building of the micro finance institutions.

In this background, it has been decided that need-based capacity building support in the form of grant be provided to the partner MFIs, in the initial years, to enable them to expand their operations, cover their managerial, administrative and operational costs and provide technical support besides helping them achieve self-sufficiency in due course. The grant support is being provided both as technical assistance as well as operational support. The technical assistance component is directed at helping the MFIs to strengthen their micro finance programmes through inputs such as human resource development, MIS development, effective financial and general management, training, efficient monitoring and control system etc, whereas operational support is provided to the MFIs to meet a part of their operational deficit arising due to expansion of their programme.

Liquidity Management: In view of the fact that liquidity is a major concern of many of the middle level MFIs and a small working capital support can go a long way in their better liquidity management and thus pave way for faster growth, SIDBI has introduced a special short-term loan scheme, Liquidity Management Support (LMS) for the long-term partners.

Equity Provision of equity capital to the NBFC-MFIs is perceived as an emerging requirement of the micro finance sector in India. SIDBI provides equity capital to eligible institutions not only to enable them to meet the capital adequacy requirements but also to help them leverage debt funds.

Direct Credit to Clients/Members of Select MFIs : SIDBI provides direct credit to select MFIs. However, these borrowers would be supported/supervised by the MFI. The scheme is targeted on larger MFIs which have strong credit and recovery mechanism, MIS and internal control. Under the arrangement, SIDBI would assess the MFIs ability to manage the projected micro credit portfolio and extend credit to the borrowers of MFI. There would be no restriction on the MFIs as regards their methodology for credit dispensation. The MFIs may pass the assistance directly to SHGs/individuals or route it through their partner NGOs and MFIs. They may also adopt any other channel so as to effectively reach financial assistance to poor clients.

Micro Enterprise Loans : In order to build and strengthen new set of intermediaries for Micro Enterprise Loans, the Bank has formulated new scheme for Micro Enterprise Loans. Institutions/MFIs with minimum fund requirement of Rs.25 lakh p.a.and having considerable experience in financial intermediation/facilitating or setting up of enterprises/providing escort services to SSI/tiny units/networking or active interface with SSIs etc. and having professional expertise and capability to handle on-lending transactions shall be eligible under the dispensation. The institutions would be selected based on their relevant experience, potential to expand, professional management, transparency in operations and well laid-out systems besides qualified/trained manpower. Lending to be based strictly on an intensive in-house appraisal supplemented with the credit rating by an independent professional agency. Relaxed security norms more or less on line with micro credit dispensation to be adopted to reduce procedural bottlenecks as well as to facilitate easy disbursements.

Promotional and Development Activities

As an apex financial institution for promotion, financing and development of industry in the small scale sector, SIDBI meets the varied developmental needs of the Indian SSI sector by its wide-ranging Promotional and Developmental (P&D) activities.

P&D initiatives of SIDBI aim at improving the inherent strength of small scale sector on one hand as also economic development of poor through promotion of micro-enterprises.

In pursuance of its multifaceted P&D activity, synergistic with its business activities aimed at development of small industries, SIDBI looks forward to a partnership with NGOs, associate financial institutions, corporate bodies, R&D laboratories, marketing agencies, etc. for national level programmes.

VI. EXIM BANK OF INDIA

Export-Import Bank of India was set-up in 1981 for the purpose of financing, facilitating and promoting foreign trade in India. EXIM is the principal financial institution in the country for coordinating working of institutions engaged in financing exports and imports.

Vision

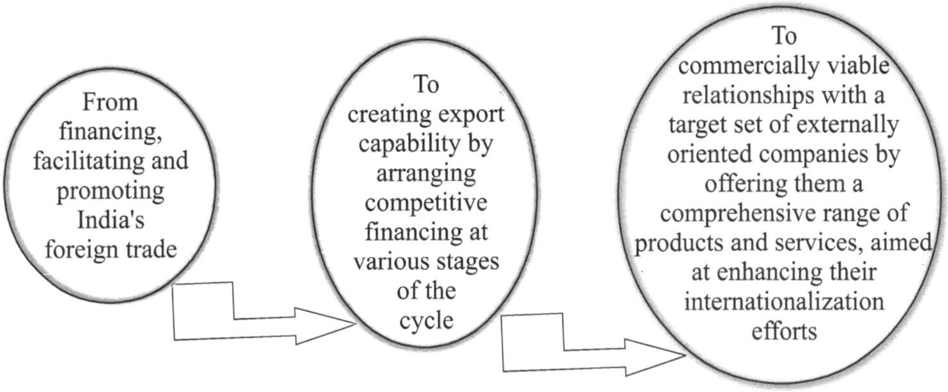

Operations–

- Bank provides exports of Indian machinery, manufactured goods, consultancy and technology services on deferred payment terms.
- Lines of credit/buyer's credits are extended to overseas entities, *i.e.,* governments, central banks, commercial banks, development finance institutions, regional development banks for financing export of goods and services from India.
- Project Finance
- Trade Finance

Export Capability Creation

- Export product development
- Export marketing finance
- Export oriented units
  (*i*) Project finance, (*ii*) Working capital, (*iii*) Production Equipment Finance
- European Community Investment Partners (ECIP)
- Asian Country Investment Partners (ACIP)
- Overseas investment finance
- Export facilitation programs
  (*i*) Software training institutes, (*ii*) Minor ports development

EXPORT SERVICES

In addition to finance, Bank provides a range of information and advisory services to Indian companies to supplement their efforts at globalization of Indian Business.

Supporting Groups

1. Planning and research
2. Corporate financing

3. Legal
4. Corporate affairs
5. Human resource management
6. Establishment

A Range of Programmes

- Financing Programmes — Export Credits / Export Capability Creation
- Export Services and Export Promotion Programmes
- Research and Analysis

DEVELOPMENT BANKS: FUTURE AHEAD

Financial liberalization is leading to the death of development banking in the country. On March 30, 2002, the Industrial Credit and Investment Corporation of India (ICICI) through a reverse merger was integrated with ICICI Bank. This was the result of a decision (announced on October 25, 2001) by ICICI to transform itself into a "universal bank" that would engage itself not only in traditional banking but investment banking and other financial activities. The new company was to become the first entity in India to serve as a financial supermarket and offer almost every financial product under one roof.

Since then similar moves have been underway to transform the other two principal development finance institutions in the country, the Industrial Finance Corporation of India (IFCI), established in 1948, and the Industrial Development Bank of India (IDBI), 1964. In early February, the then Finance Minister Jaswant Singh, announced the government's decision to merge the IFCI with a big public sector bank, like the Punjab National Bank. Following that decision, the IFCI board has approved the proposal, rendering itself defunct.

Reasons For Creation of Development Banks

- The principal motivation for the creation of such financial institutions was to make-up for the failure of private financial agents to provide certain kinds of credit to certain kinds of clients. Private institutions may fail to do so because of high default risks.
- Financial intermediaries seek to meet for credit from clients with their funds by adjusting not just interest rates, but also the terms on which credit is provided. The nature and quality of collateral for sending is adjusted according to the nature of the borrower and supply and demand conditions in the credit market.
- Industrial development banks also help deal with the fact that local industrialists may not have adequate capital to invest in capacity of the requisite scale in more capital-intensive industries characterized by significant economies of scale. They help promote such ventures through their lending and investment practices and often provide technical assistance to their clients.
- Some development banks are expected to focus on the small-scale industrial sector, providing them with long-tem finance and working capital at subsidized interest rates and longer grace periods, as well as offering training and technical assistance in areas like marketing.

- Fundamentally of course, development banking is required because social returns exceed private returns. This problem arises because private lenders are concerned only with the return they receive. On the other hand, the total return to a project includes the additional surplus (or profit) accruing to the entrepreneur. The projects that offer the best return to the private lender may not be those with the highest total expected return. As a result some good projects are necessitating measures such as development banking or directed credit.

THE ROLE OF DEVELOPMENT BANKS & IMPACT OF LIBERALIZATION

Developmental Financial Institutions have played a pivotal role in the development of Indian Industry and have fulfilled their initial objective, *i.e.,* to promote industrialization in the country over the last three to four decades.

The corporation, transformation into universal banks and subsequent privatization of the DFIs is bound to undermine this role of development banks.

It was the result of liberalization that the profitability of an institution like the IFCI was affected.

According to the Basu Expert Committee, which was appointed by IFCI's governing board to examine the causes of the large NPAs accumulated by the institution and suggest a restructuring policy, IFCI embarked upon a programme of rapid expansion of business. To scale up the volume of business it increasingly raised resources from the debt markets. This was at a time when interest rates were relatively high. In order to cover the high costs borrowings, the institution was forced to make investments in what were considered high yielding loan assets.

Unfortunately, this occurred at a time when financial liberalization had put an end to the traditional consortium mode of lending, in which all major financial institutions collaborated in lending to a single borrower as per a mutually agreed pattern of sharing.

Liberalization was introducing an element of competition among financial institutions. In the event, in search of high returns IFCI chose to take relatively large exposures in several greenfield projects (notably in the steel and oil sectors).

For a number of reasons these projects did not deliver on their promise. Many of these projects had expected to raise substantial equity from the capital market as well as from the internal resources of group companies.

Depressed conditions in the capital market was the first reason and recessionary conditions the second. Many of these groups were in the traditional commodity sectors such as iron and steel, textiles, synthetic fibers, cement, sugar, basic chemicals, synthetic resins, plastics, etc.

Besides the general recessionary environment, some of these sectors were particularly affected by the abolition of import controls and the gradual reduction of tariffs. Internal resource generation, therefore, fell short of expectations. As a result, with inadequate own-financing, in the pipeline many of these projects suffered from cost and time over-runs.

Unlike other financial institutions, IFCI had not diversified into other types of businesses. Project finance still accounted for 94 per cent of IFCI's business assets.

As a result, the impact of NPAs arising from the factors cited above was greater in the case of IFCI than in the case of other institutions.

In addition, there was sharp rise in IFCI's gross NPA level in 1998-99 (Rs.5,783.56 crores in the previous year) as a result of the implementation of the mandatory Reserve Bank of India guidelines for classifying non-performing assets.

As a result, certain loans particularly those relating to projects under implementation, which had been treated as performing assets in earlier years, had to be classified as non-performing.

The Basu Committee had noted that some of the factors referred to above such as impact of trade policy liberalization and tariff reduction, recessionary condition in the late 1990s, depressed conditions in the capital market, etc., affected other DFIs and banks as well.

However, the impact was particularly pronounced in the case of IFCI, as the concentration of risk relative to net worth was much higher.

Also, as already stated, other DFIs had started diversifying into non-project related lending and business. It was difficult to survive as development finance institutions in the new environment.

Thus the decline of development finance is clearly related to the process of economic liberalization. However, as a number of industry associations have noted in recent times, it hardly is true that in a time of growing competition for Indian firms from international business and a growing liberalization induced shift in the investment and lending practices of banks and NBFCs away from manufacturing, state support for domestic private investment is not relevant. But given the ethos of liberalization this does not seem to matter.

QUESTIONS

Fill in the Blanks:

1. ICICI has _______ subsidiaries.
2. IFCI provides finance for _______ and ___________ type of projects.
3. NABARD stands for ___________.
4. Micro finance institutions are funded by _____________.

State whether true or false:

1. IFCI caters to long-term finance needs of institutions.
2. IDBI provides film finance to cover the entire cost of film.
3. NABARD promotes development in rural areas.
4. EXIM Bank does not provide credit to overseas entities.
5. SIDBI helps small institutions to raise international finance.

Answer in detail:

Q.1. What are Development Banks? Discuss various development banks in brief in terms of their features and services offered.

Q.2. How has development banking led to economic development in India?

❑❑❑

19 INSURANCE INSTITUTIONS

I. LIFE INSURANCE CORPORATION OF INDIA (LIC)

Brief History of Insurance

- Though the concept of insurance is largely a development of the recent past, particularly after the industrial era – past few centuries – yet its beginnings date back almost 6000 years.
- Life Insurance in its modern form came to India from England in the year 1818.
- Oriental Life Insurance Company started by Europeans in Calcutta was the first life insurance company on Indian Soil.
- All the insurance companies established during that period were brought up with the purpose of looking after the needs of the European community and Indian natives were not being insured by these companies.
- However, later with the efforts of eminent people like Babu Muttylal Seal, the foreign life insurance companies started insuring Indian lives. But Indian lives were being treated as sub-standard lives and heavy extra premiums were being charged on them.
- Bombay Mutual Life Assurance Society heralded the birth of first Indian life insurance company in the year 1870, and covered Indian lives at normal rates. Starting as Indian enterprise with highly patriotic motives, insurance companies came into existence to carry the message of insurance and social security through insurance to various sectors of society.
- Bharat Insurance Company (1896) was also one of such companies inspired by nationalism. The Swadeshi movement of 1905-1907 gave rise to more insurance companies.
- The United India in Madras, National Indian and National Insurance in Calcutta and Cooperative Assurance at Lahore were established in 1906.
- In 1907, Hindustan Cooperative Insurance Company took its birth in one of the rooms of the Jorasanko, house of the great poet Rabindranath Tagore, in Calcutta.

- The Indian Mercantile, General Assurance and Swadeshi life [later Bombay life] were some of the companies established during the same period.
- Prior to1912 India had no legalization to regulate insurance business. In the year 1912, the Life Insurance Companies Act, and the Provident Fund Act were passed.
- The Life Insurance Companies Act, 1912 made it necessary that the premium rate tables and periodical valuations of companies should be certified by an actuary. But the Act discriminated between foreign and Indian companies on many accounts.
- The first two decades of the twentieth century saw lot of growth in insurance business. From 44 companies with total business-in-force as Rs.22.44 crore, it rose to 176 companies with total business-in-force as Rs.298 crore in 1938.
- During the mushrooming of insurance companies many financially unsound concerns were also floated which failed miserably.
- The Insurance Act 1938 was the first legislation governing not only life insurance but also non-life insurance to provide strict state control over insurance business.
- The demand for nationalization of life insurance industry was made repeatedly but it gathered momentum in 1944 when a bill to amend the Life Insurance Act, 1938 was introduced in the Legislative Assembly.
- It was much later on the 19th of January, 1956 that life insurance in India was nationalized. About 154 Indian insurance companies, 16 non-Indian companies and 75 provident funds were operating in India at the time of nationalization.
- Nationalization was accomplished in two stages; initially the management of the companies was taken over by means of an Ordinance, and later, the ownership too by means of a comprehensive bill.
- The Parliament of India passed the Life Insurance Corporation Act on the 19th of June, 1956, and the Life Insurance Corporation of India was created on 1st September, 1956, with the objective of spreading life insurance much more widely and in particular to the rural areas with a view to reach all insurable persons in the country, providing them adequate financial cover at a reasonable cost.
- LIC had 5 zonal offices, 33 divisional offices and 212 branch offices, apart from its corporate office in the year 1956.
- From about 200.00 crore of New Business in 1957 the corporation crossed 1000.00 crores only in the year 1969-70, and it took another 10 years for LIC to cross 2000.00 crore mark of new business.
- With re-organization happening in the early eighties, by 1985-86 LIC had already crossed 7000.00 crore Sum Assured on new policies.

Today LIC functions with 2048 fully computerized branch offices, 100 divisional offices, 7 zonal offices and the corporate office. LIC's Wide Area Network covers 100 divisional offices and connects all the branches through a Metro Area Network. LIC has tied up with some Banks and Service providers to offer on-line premium collection facility in selected cities. LIC's ECS and ATM premium payment facility is an addition to customer convenience. Apart from on-line Kiosks and IVRS, Info Centers have been commissioned at Mumbai, Ahmedabad, Bangalore, Chennai, Hyderabad, Kolkata, New Delhi, Pune and many other cities. With a vision of providing easy access to its policyholders, LIC has launched its SATELLITE SAMPARK offices. The satellite offices are smaller, leaner and closer to the customer. The digitalized records of the satellite offices will facilitate anywhere servicing and many other conveniences in the future.

LIC continues to be the dominant life insurer even in the liberalized scenario of Indian insurance and is moving fast on a new growth trajectory surpassing its own past records. LIC has issued over one crore policies in 2005, it has crossed the milestone of issuing 1,01,32,955 new policies by 15th Oct, 2005, posting a healthy growth rate of 16.67% over the corresponding period of the previous year.

From then to now, LIC has crossed many milestones and has set unprecedented performance records in various aspect of life insurance business. The same motives which inspired our forefathers to bring insurance into existence in this country inspire us at LIC to take this message of protection to light the lamps of security in as many homes as possible and to help the people in providing security to their families.

Some of the important milestones in the life insurance business in India are:—

- 1818: Oriental Life Insurance Company, the first life insurance company on Indian soil started functioning.
- 1870: Bombay Mutual Life Assurance Society, the first Indian life insurance company started its business.
- 1912: The Indian Life Assurance Companies Act enacted as the first statute to regulate the life insurance business.
- 1928: The Indian Insurance Companies Act enacted to enable the government to collect statistical information about both life and non-life insurance businesses.
- 1938: Earlier legislation consolidated and amended to by the Insurance Act with the objective of protecting the interests of the insuring public.
- 1956: 245 Indian and foreign insurers and provident societies were taken over by the central government and nationalized. LIC formed by an Act of Parliament, *viz.,* LIC Act, 1956, with a capital contribution of Rs. 5 crore from the Government of India.
- The General insurance business in India, on the other hand, can trace its roots to the Triton Insurance Company Ltd., the first general insurance company established in the year 1850 in Calcutta by the British.

Some of the important milestones in the general insurance business in India are:

- 1907: The Indian Mercantile Insurance Ltd. set-up, the first company to transact all classes of general insurance business.
- 1957: General Insurance Council, a wing of the Insurance Association of India, frames a code of conduct for ensuring fair conduct and sound business practices.

- 1968: The Insurance Act amended to regulate investments and set minimum solvency margins and the Tariff Advisory Committee set-up.
- 1972: The General Insurance Business (Nationalization) 1972, Act, nationalized the general insurance business in India with effect from 1st January, 1972.
- 107 insurers amalgamated and grouped into four companies *viz.,* the National Insurance Company Ltd., the New India Assurance Company Ltd., the Oriental Insurance Company Ltd. and the United India Insurance Company Ltd. GIC incorporated as a company.

Objectives of Life Insurance

- Spread life insurance widely and in particular to the rural areas and to the socially and economically backward classes with a view to reaching all insurable persons in the country and providing them adequate financial cover against death at a reasonable cost.
- Maximize mobilization of people's savings by making insurance-linked savings adequately attractive.
- Bear in mind, in the investment of funds, the primary obligation to its policyholders, whose money it holds in trust, without losing sight of the interest of the community as a whole; the funds to be deployed to the best advantage of the investors as well as the community as a whole keeping in view national priorities and obligations of attractive return.
- Conduct business with utmost economy and with the full realization that the moneys belong to the policyholders.
- Act as trustees of the insured public in their individual and collective capacities.
- Meet the various life insurance needs of the community that would arise in the changing social and economic environment.
- Involve all people working in the Corporation to the best of their capability in furthering the interest of the insured public by providing efficient service with courtesy.
- Promote amongst all agents and employees of the Corporation a sense of participation, pride and job satisfaction through discharge of their duties with dedication towards achievement of Corporate Objective.

Plans offered by LIC: LIC broadly offers the following plans:

1. Insurance Plans
2. Pension Plans
3. Group Schemes
4. Unit Plans and
5. Special Plans

II. UNIT TRUST OF INDIA (UTI)

UTI was established on January 14, 2003 as UTI Mutual Fund managed by UTI Asset Management Company Private Limited, appointed by the UTI Trustee Company Private Limited for managing the schemes of UTI Mutual Fund and the schemes transferred/migrated from UTI Mutual Fund.

UTI AMC is a registered portfolio manager under the SEBI (Portfolio Managers) Regulations 1993, on February 3, 2004, for undertaking portfolio management services and also acts as the manager and marketer to offshore funds through its 100% subsidiary, UTI International Limited, registered in Guernsey, Channel Islands.

UTI Mutual Fund has come into existence with effect from 1st February, 2003. UTI Asset Management Company presently manages a corpus of over Rs.20000 Crore.

UTI Mutual Fund has a track record of managing a variety of schemes catering to the needs of every class of citizens. It has a nationwide network consisting 56 UTI Financial Centers (UFCs) and representative offices in Dubai and London. With a view to reach to common investors at district level, 11 satellite offices have also been opened in select towns and districts. It has well-qualified, professional fund management team, who have been highly empowered to manage funds with greater efficiency and accountability in the sole interest of unit holders. The fund managers are also ably supported with a strong in-house equity research department. To ensure better management of funds, a risk management department is also in operation.

It has reset and upgraded transparency standards for the mutual funds industry. All the branches, UFCs and registrar offices are connected on a robust IT network to ensure cost-effective quick and efficient service. All these have evolved UTI Mutual Fund to position as a dynamic, responsive, restructured, efficient, and transparent and SEBI compliant entity.

Sponsors

Three leading public sector banks – Bank of Baroda (BOB), Punjab National Bank (PNB) and State Bank of India (SBI) and Life Insurance Corporation of India (LIC), the largest public financial investment institution and life insurer in India have entered into an agreement with the Sponsors of the UTI Mutual Fund.

Schemes Floated by UTI Include :

1. Liquid Funds
2. Income Funds
3. Index Funds
4. Balanced Funds
5. Equity Funds and Asset Allocation Funds

US. 64. FUNCTIONING AND DOWNFALL OF THE SCHEME

Unit Scheme, 1964 (US-64) of UTI came as a bombshell to the millions of its small investors. After the share market scandal induced by Harshad Mehta, Hiten Desai and their likes in the very first year of liberalization, perhaps no other economic news has caused so many ripples in the country and invited so many comments from journals, newspapers and TV channels. Let us begin with how the US-64 used to function in the past and what benefits it used to provide to its small investors.

THE SCHEME'S FUNCTIONISING

As the very name of the scheme suggests, the US-64 functioned in terms of units which small investors used to purchase from UTI and sell back to the latter whenever they needed hard cash.

In every calendar year, the transactions used to start in July after UTI declared the sale and repurchase prices of its units. Sales price meant the rate an investor paid to purchase units from UTI and repurchase price was the rate at which he could sell his units back to UTI.

These prices used to appreciate month by month, they were duly notified through newspaper ads, and the transactions used to be closed at May end next year. The month of June was reserved for book-keeping and calculation exercises within UTI, after which it used to declare a rate of dividend for its investors.

To illustrate it concretely, let us take the example of July 1994-June 1995 period — the year just before US-64 suffered its first major jolt at the hands of a leading corporate house of the country. In July 1994, as in previous years, UTI offered to the investors US-64 units at a premium — at Rs. 15.30 per unit against the book value of Rs. 10 per unit. As in previous years, again, the sale price of the units went on appreciating and had, for example, reached Rs. 18.30 per unit in October 1994, only after three months. At the end of its transaction years, that is, towards the end of June 1995, the UTI announced a dividend of 26 per cent. Thus, every unit of a book value of Rs. 10 earned a profit of Rs. 2.60, which meant that if a person had bought a unit at the actual price of Rs. 15.30 in July 1994, he earned an interest of around 17 per cent after a year. The highest bank interest rate at that time was 13.5 per cent per annum.

After the end of June every year, the investor had two options before him: He could either get a cheque for the dividend accrued to him in the previous 12 months or he could reinvest the same, that is, get it converted into units and thus increase the number of units in his hand. In the latter case, the amount of dividend due to him automatically increased year after year, till chose to withdraw money by selling his units back to UTI.

BENEFITS TO INVESTORS

Compared to other instruments of investment, US-64 offered several benefits to investors.

First, as is evident from the above example small investors found investing in US-64 units far more lucrative in terms of interest amount than putting their money in a bank.

Secondly, compared to some other instruments like Kisan Vikas or National Saving Certificates, US-64 offered its investors the benefit of a very high degree of liquidity. While one's money was locked in the above instruments for (five to six years), a US-64 unit holder could sell his units back to UTI any time in the year, at the previously declared repurchase price. In any month, the repurchase price used to be only 15 to 25 paise less than the sale price, and did not mean any loss to the investor. After surrendering his units to UTI, the investor got a cheque for his money in a week or so.

Thirdly, US-64 was considered to be totally free from the risks of volatility that are associated with speculative investments. For about three decades since its inception, that is, as long as the US-64 money was not invested in stock market shares, the investor's money was perfectly safe from the ups and downs (mostly downs) of the stock market. The investor had full faith in US-64 units and thought that his money was safe in the custody of the "government of India".

Fourthly, contrary to the monthly deposit schemes run by the post office, some banks and even private organizations like the Peerless or Sahara, US 64 investors faced no risk of forfeiting any part of their principal or dividend or both, in case of default in payment for a couple of months. This was particularly to the liking of those who had no regular or fixed income.

Fifthly, under the US-64, an investor was required to purchase a minimum of only 100 units; that meant an investment of only Rs. 1500 or so. Thus, even those with modest incomes and savings could become members of the scheme.

Lastly, US-64 investor had two options before him, of getting a cheque for the dividend earned by him or of reinvesting the same into more units, the conversion from one option to the other was not difficult in the least and could be effected through simple correspondence. This offered another attraction for the investors.

It was these factors that made US-64 investments highly attractive for the investor. The scheme, on the whole, was a haven for small investors, particularly those working in the private or unorganized sector, who did not have any security of post-retirement or post-retrenchment benefits. Factory workers, peasants of all hues, artisans, middle class employees, pensioners, hawkers, small shopkeepers and vendors, head-load workers and even rickshaw pullers – all used to confide in US-64 units, taking this form of investment as their best security in bad days. This is what explains the tremendous success of the scheme and the very high number of investors it attracted — more than 20 million. This also explains how the US-64 alone accounted for about 23 per cent of the Rs. 60,000 crore plus corpus of the UTI that runs a number of other schemes. In fact, no scheme of UTI achieved such tremendous success as US-64 did, making UTI the biggest mutual fund of the country and one of the biggest in the world.

POINTS OF DOWNFALL

But then, it was the new economic policy of 1991 that hindered the so far smooth functioning of US-64 and of UTI as a whole.

If US-64 was hitherto a debt-oriented instrument, its fund managers now chose to make it equity-oriented.

Deviating from its earlier path of investing in the fixed income securities, these fund managers now turned into stock market players with a huge corpus of others' money in their hands. Capitalizing on the stock market boom of 1992 was their ostensible plea.

In this atmosphere of liberalization, US-64 suffered its first major jolt in 1995 when UTI invested US-64 money in Reliance group's shares and the group offered it fake share certificates.

However, when the media got scent of this bungling and some adverse comments came, the Reliance group offered to take back the fake share certificates and issue new ones in their stead.

But US-64 heavily lost in this process which involved a re-valuation of the shares, the UTI held. At that time, the involvement of UTI fund managers and its then chairman in the building was widely suspected.

By that time, the Reliance group had also earned notoriety for some of its arbitrary actions. Those who had once purchased Reliance Petro shares were, for instance, later made shareholders in other companies of the group, without their consent. Nor did the Reliance Petro issue carry any clause informing the subscribers that such a conversion could be effected.

However, the UTI persisted in its new found love for stock market investments. Even though another major mutual fund, namely the SBI Mutual Fund had already gone under because of the stock market volatility, never to regain its earlier importance, the US-64 fund managers chose not to learn any lessons from it.

This was indeed the point from where the downfall of US-64 started and the scheme never recovered its earlier coveted status.

Because of the volatility of the stock market, and after the dreamy phase of the 1992 boom was over, the net asset value (NAV) of the US-64 units constantly went downhill, finally turning negative in 1998.

GRAVEST MISENDEAVOUR

It was in this situation that UTI dropped a bombshell on its investors by announcing a freeze on all US-64 transactions for the next six months.

This was something of the gravest nature as it badly shook the investors' confidence in UTI and, more particularly in US-64 – virtually beyond redemption. The investor confidence in US-64 was not shaken even when the SBI Mutual Fund went under. The investor did not desert US-64 even when the Canara Bank started a unit scheme of its own and offered its units at par value – Rs 10 units for Rs 10 only. But the same cannot be said after the latest misendeavour committed by the UTI fund mangers.

The nefarious link of these fund managers with the corporate houses is clear from the fact of that they had inside information about the impending downfall of US-64. It was widely reported these houses withdrew their money, about Rs. 4,000 crore, from the US-64 before downfall. It was only the small investors who were kept in the dark and eventually left in the lurch. The units these corporate houses held were mainly those purchased before 1995, before the UTI launched another similar scheme (US-95) specifically for corporates.

Newspaper reports also go to show how the UTI invested heavily in the patently loss-making companies including Pritish Nandy Communications, Business India, Pioneer and Himachal Futuristic.

Finally, UTI announced a repurchase price of Rs. 10 per unit in a bid to console the investors and offset the criticism. The least they had paid for these units in July, 2000 was Rs 13.40 per unit, not to talk of those who had purchased units mid-year. This means that these small investors lost at least Rs 3.40. Thus a person holding, say, 1,000 units stood to lose Rs. 3,400 on this count.

QUESTIONS

Fill in the Blanks:

1. Life insurance started in ____________.
2. LIC promotes _________ savings.
3. ____,________,_____and________ are sponsors of UTI.
4. US-64 suffered the first major jolt in year __________.

State whether true or false:

1. GIC is a subsidiary of LIC.
2. US-64 was considered to be less risky than NSC, KVP, etc by investors.
3. The downfall of US-64 started with stock market investments.
4. UTI does not offer insurance linked products.

Answer in detail:

Q.1. Discuss the impact of globalization on insurance sector?

Q.2. How has UTI been able to recover after the setback received in the US-64 scandal?

Q.3. What was US-64? Discuss the reasons for its downfall.

Q.4. Discuss how UTI has regained investor confidence after the crash of US-64.

❑❑❑

PART–III
FINANCIAL SERVICES

20

VENTURE CAPITAL

DEFINITION

The term venture capital refers to the financing of start-up and early businesses as well as businesses in "turnaround" situations. In other words, it can be called as money provided by investors to new firms or small business with long-term growth potential. So it is a very important source of funding for start-up firms who do not have access to capital markes.

Venture capital being involved in new firms has a high risk for investors but a potential of providing a return of ten times more in less than five years. The investor making such investment is called a Venture Capitalist. They manage the investment in return of investment, venture capitalists receive not only a major equity stock in the firm but also demand seats on the board of directors. Their involvement extends to several functions like recruitment of personnel, strategic advice, introduction to potential customers, strategic financiers, investment bankers and various other contacts.

HISTORY OF VENTURE CAPITAL

The origin of venture capital traces back to World War II. Prior to World War II, the source of risk capital for entrepreneurs all over the world was either the government, government sponsored institutions meant to invest in such venture, or informal investors that had some prior linkage to the entrepreneur.

After the Second World War, a set of intermediaries, the venture capitalists emerged whose only activity was investing in firms that they considered were capable of rapid growth and capital appreciation.

In 1946, American Research and Development Corporation was formed by General Georges Doroit who is called "The Father of Venture Capital". The organization produced Digital Equipment and was highly successful in its venture.

Followed by this J H.Whitney and Co.was formed in 1946 and produced Minute Maid Juice, which was also used to give nourishment to troops in the field.

In 1957, (SBIC) was established to leverage private capital borrowing from feudal government at below market interest rates. Nearly 600 SBICs came into operation within a span of few years. Also a number of venture capital firms formed private partnerships outside the SBICs format.

In 1960, IPO market boomed giving an opportunity to venture capital firms to demonstrate their ability of creating companies and producing huge investment returns.

A setback to venture capital industry came in 1970s, when the public markets went into a slump. Due to poor market performance and legislation the venture capital market hit a bottom in 1975.

But from 1978 due to improved legislative measures recovery started. A number of high profile IPOs by venture-backed companies came up namely Federal Express in 1978, Apple Computer and Genetech Inc. in1981 which again lit the hope and interest in venture capital among wealthy families and institutional investors. The greatest growth period recorded by the industry was in 1980 when the number of venture capital industry touched a high investment of $ 4bn. During this period the venture capitalists' primary source shifted from wealthy individuals to institutions, pension funds, endowment funds etc. The internal rates of return from projects increased from 15% to 25%.

So during its period of growth, venture capital industry has witnessed several stages of growth from early or seed funds, mature-stage funds and bridge funds.

GROWTH AND DEVELOPMENT OF VENTURE CAPITAL IN INDIA

Due to highly bureaucratized economy, conservative social and business world and a risk averse financial system; India provided little institutional space for the development of venture capital. The first formal venture capital organization in India was set-up in the public sector. Later the role of Developmental Finance in India was an extension of the developmental financial institutions like IDBI, ICICI, SIDBI and SFCs.

The origin of venture capital in India can be traced to the setting-up of Technology Development Fund (TDF) in year 1987-88 to provide financial assistance for innovative and high risk technological programs through Industrial Development Bank of India.

The industry growth rate in India can be divided into 2 phases. First phase started in 1991 soon after liberalization. Attempts were made to raise funds from public for funding new ventures. But it was then realized that the concept of venture capital funding needs to be institutionalized and regulated. So in 1996, new guidelines were given by SEBI on venture capital funds which marked the beginning of second phase of growth in which bureaucratic hassles were removed and foreign funds were allowed to enter into India. As a result of increase in competition, access to global and professional business practices increased.

Indian Venture Capital Association was set-up in 1992 and has become the nodal center for all venture fund activity in the country.

TYPES OF VENTURE FUNDS IN INDIA

Genesis

Financial Institutions Led by ICICI Ventures, RCTC, ILFS,etc.

- Private venture funds like Indus, etc.
- Regional funds like Warburg Pincus, JF Electra (mostly operating out of Hong Kong).
- Regional funds dedicated to India like Draper, Walden, etc.

- Offshore funds like Barings, TCW, HSBC, etc.
- Corporate ventures like Intel.

Investment Philosophy

Early stage funding is avoided by most funds. Funding growth or mezzanine funding till pre IPO is the segment where most players operate.

Size of Investment

The size of investment is generally less than US$1mn, US$1-5mn, US$5-10mn, and greater than US$10mn.

How does the Vc industry work?

Venture capital firms typically source the majority of their funding from lare invesment institutions such as fund of funds, financial institutions, endowments, pension funds and banks. These institutions typically invest in a venture capital fund for a period of up to ten years.

To compensate for the long term commitment and lack of both security and liquidity, investment institutions expect to receive very high returns on their investment. Therefore, venture capitalists invest in either compaines with high growth potential where they are able to exit through either an IPO or a merger/acquisition. Although the venture capitalist may receive some return through dividends, their primary return on investment comes from capital gains when they eventually sell their shars in the company, typically between three to five years after the investment.

Venture capitalists are therefore in the business of promoting growth in the companies they invest in and managing the associated risk to protect and enhance their investors' capital.

What do VC's look for?

Venture capitalists are higher risk investors and in accepting these risks, they desire a higher return on their investment.

The venture capitalist manages the risk/reward ratio by only investing in businesses which fit their investment criteria and after having completed extensive due diligence.

Venture capitalists have differeing operating approaches. These differences may relate to location of the business, the size of the investment, the stage of the company, industry specialization, structure of the investment and involvement of the venture capitalists in the companies activities.

The rejection of a business proposal by a venture may not be a reflection of the quality of the business, but rather a matter of the business not fitting with the venture capitalist's particular investment criteria. Often entrepreneurs may want to ask the venture capitalist for other firms that might be interested in the investment opportunity. Venture capital is not suitable for all business. As a venture capitalist typically seeks.

Superior Business

Venture capitalists look for compaines with products or services targeted at large, fast growing or untapped markets with a defensible strategic position such as intellectual property or patents.

Quality and Depth of Management

Venture capitalists must be confident that the firm has the quality and depth in the management team to achieve its aspirations. Venture capitalists seldom seek managerial control, rather they want to add value to the investment where they have particular skills including fund raising, mergers and acquisitions, international marketing, product development and networks.

Appropriate Investment Structure

As well as the requirement of being an attractive business opportunity, the venture capitalist will also seek to structure a deal to produce the anticipated financial returns to investors. This includes making an investment at a reasonable price per share (valuation).

Exit Opportunity

Lastly, venture capitalists look for the clear exit opportunity for their investment such as public listing or a third party acquisition of the investee company.

Once a short list of appropriate venture capitalists has been selected, the entrepreneur can proceed to identify which investors match their funding requirements. At this point, the entrepreneur should contact the venture capital firm and identify an investment manager as an initial contact point. The venture capital firm will ask prospective investee companies for information concerning the product or service, the market analysis, how the company operates, the investment required and how it is to be used, financial projections, and importantly questions about the management team.

In reality, all of the above questions should be answered in the Business Plan. Assuming the venture capitalist expresses interest in the investment opportunity, a good business plan is a pre-requisite.

INVESTMENT PROCESS

The investment process begins with the venture capitalist conducting an initial review of the proposal to determine if it fits with the firm's investment criteria. If so, a meeting will be arranged with the entrepreneur/management team to discuss the business plan.

Preliminary Screening

The initial meeting provides an opportunity for the venture capitalist to meet with the entrepreneur and key members of the management team to review the business plan and conduct initial due diligence on the project. It is an important time for the management team to demonstrate their understanding of their business and ability to achieve the strategies outlined in the plan. The venture capitalist will look carefully at the team's functional skills and backgrounds.

Negotiating Investment

This involves an agreement between the venture capitalist and management of the terms of the term sheet, often called memorandum of understanding (MoU). The venture capitalist will then proceed to study the viability of the market to estimate its potential. Often they use market forecasts which have been independently prepared by industry experts who specialize in estimating the size and growth rates of markets and market segments.

The venture capitalist also studies the industry carefully to obtain information about competitors, entry barriers, potential to exploit substantial niches, product life cycles, and distribution channels. The due diligence may continue with reports from other consultants.

Approvals and Investment Completed

The process involves due diligence and disclosure of all relevant business information. Final terms can then be negotiated and an investment proposal is typically submitted to the venture capital fund's board of directors. If approved, legal documents are prepared.

Problems with Venture Capitalists in India

1. **Licensing:** Till early 90s license regime prevailed to fund a cement plant *e.g.,* venture capital was not needed but what was needed was the ability to get a license and then get the project funded by Banks & Discount & Finance Houses. Conventional sources were available for raising funds.
2. **Lack of Scalability:** Most products of Indian markets lack scalability in, needed to make value addition and move towards the higher end of value chain.
3. **Mindset of People:** People were averse to invest in risky avenues and most venture capitalists wanted to provide secured debt capital to business with profit track record.
4. **Regulatory Environment:** There has been a lack of clarity between investors due to multiplicity of regulations. Domestic funds follow SEBI guidelines. There is difference in taxation policy of funds in India and abroad.
5. **Valuation Mismatches:** Promoters do not agree to a valuation and have risky high valuation expectation. So it becomes difficult for deals to reach financial closure and the numbers of quality deal available to venture funds get reduced.

Regulatory Issues Involved in Venture Capital Finance

Venture Capital Funds in India are subject to various guidelines. These are:

1. Indian Trust Act, 1882 or the Company Act, 1956, depending on whether the fund has been set-up as a trust or company.
2. While setting up abroad the funds have to take permission from FIPB, while in India clearance from RBI is needed.
3. CBDT also regulates the taxation aspect of the venture funds in India.
4. SEBI has given a set of guidelines to regulate venture capital funds in India.

In addition to this government of India and various other agencies regulate the venture capital financing.

The Venture Capital Process

The process of venture capital involves the following stages:-

- Creating/exploring investment opportunities.
- Analyzing the investment proposal
- Investment valuation
- Pricing and structuring the deal
- Value addition and monitoring
- Exit

EXPLORING INVESTMENT OPPORTUNITIES

In the venture capital investor creates a pipeline of 'deals' or investment opportunities that he would consider investing in. This is achieved primarily through looking into an appropriate network. The most popular network obviously is the network of venture capital funds/investors. It is also common for venture capitalist to develop working relationships with R&D institutions, academia, etc., which could potentially lead to business opportunities. The composition of the network would depend on the investment focus of the venture capital funds/company. Thus venture capital funds focusing on early stage technology based deals would develop a network of R&D centers working in those areas. The network is crucial to the success of the venture capital investor. It is almost imperative for the venture capital investor to receive a large number of investment proposals from which he can finally select a few good investment candidates.

The venture capital investor focuses on opportunities with a high degree of innovation. The technique of generating a deal can vary from country to country. In India, different venture capital funds/companies have their own methods varying from promotional seminars with R&D institutions and industry associations to direct advertising campaigns targeted at various segments.

ANALYZING THE INVESTMENT PROPOSAL

It includes carrying out reference checks on the proposal related aspects such as management team, product, technology and market. It focuses on the qualitative aspects of an investment opportunity.

Venture Capital Fund/Companies set-up an 'investment screen'. The screen is a set of qualitative (sometimes quantitative criteria such as revenue are also used) criteria that help venture capital funds/ companies to quickly decide on whether an investment opportunity warrants further diligence. Screens can be sometimes elaborate and rigorous and sometimes specific and brief. The nature of screen criteria is also a function of investment focus of the firm at that point. Venture capital investors rely extensively on reference checks with 'leading lights' in the specific areas of concern being addressed in the due diligence.

A venture capitalist tries to maximize the upside potential of any project. He tries to structure his investment in such a manner that he can get the benefit of the upside potential, *i.e.,* he would like to exit at a time when he can get maximum return on his investment in the project. Hence, his due diligence appraisal has to keep this fact in mind.

INVESTMENT VALUATION

The investment valuation process is an exercise aimed at arriving at 'an acceptable price' for the deal. Typically in countries where free pricing regimes exist, the valuation process goes through the following steps:

- Evaluate future revenue and profitability
- Forecast likely future value of the firm based on experienced market capitalization or expected acquisition proceeds depending upon the anticipated exit from the investment.
- Target an ownership position in the investee firm so as to achieve desired appreciation on the proposed investment. The appreciation desired should yield a hurdle rate of return on a Discounted Cash Flow basis.

STRUCTURING A DEAL

Structuring refers to putting together the financial aspects of the deal and negotiating with the entrepreneurs to accept a venture capital's proposal and finally closing the deal. To do a good job in structuring, one needs to be knowledgeable in areas of accounting, cash flow, finance, legal and taxation. Also the structure should take into consideration the various commercial issues (*i.e.,* what the entrepreneur wants and what the venture capital would require to protect the investment). Documentation refers to the legal aspects of the paperwork in putting the deal together.

The instruments to be used in structuring deals are many and varied. The objective in selecting the instrument would be to maximize (or optimize) venture capital's returns/protection and yet satisfy the entrepreneur's requirements. The instruments could be as follows:

Instrument	Issues
Loan	clean *vs* secured
	Interest bearing *vs* non interest bearing
	convertible *vs* one with features (warrants)
	1st Charge, 2nd Charge,
	loan *vs* loan stock
	Maturity
Preference shares	redeemable (conditions under Company Act)
	Participating

Instrument	Issues
	par value
	nominal shares
Warrants	exercise price, expiry period
Common shares	new or vendor shares
	par value
	partially-paid shares
Options	exercise price, expiry period, call, put

In India, straight equity and convertibles are popular and commonly used. Nowadays, warrants are issued as a tool to bring down pricing.

MONITORING AND FOLLOW-UP

The role of the venture capitalist does not stop after the investment is made in the project. The skills of the venture capitalist are most required once the investment is made. The venture capitalist gives ongoing advice to the promoters and monitors the project continuously.

It is to be understood that the providers of venture capital are not just financiers or subscribers to the equity of the project they fund. They function as a dual capacity, as a financial partner and strategic advisor. Venture capitalists monitor and evaluate projects regularly. They keep a hand on the pulse of the project. They are actively involved in the management of the of the investee unit and provide expert business counsel, to ensure its survival and growth. Deviations or causes of worry may alert them to potential problems and they can suggest remedial actions or measures to avoid these problems. As professional in this unique method of financing, they may have innovative solutions to maximize the chances of success of the project. After all, the ultimate aim of the venture capitalist is the same as that of the promoters – the long-term profitability and viability of the investee company.

Exit

One of the most crucial issues is the exit from the investment. After all, the return to the venture capitalist can be realized only at the time of exit. Exit from investment varies from the investment to investment and from venture capital to venture capital. There are several exit routes, buy-buck by the promoters, sale to another venture capitalist or sale at the time of Initial Public Offering, to name a few. In all cases specialists will work out the method of exit and decide on what is most profitable and suitable to both the venture capitalist and the investee unit and the promoters of the project.

Conclusion

At present many investments of venture capitalists in India remain on paper as they do not have any means of exit. Appropriate changes have to be made to the existing systems in order that venture capitalists find it easier to realize their investments after holding on to them for a certain period of time. This factor is even more critical in small and mid-sized companies, which are unable to get listed on any stock exchange, as they do not meet the minimum requirements for such listings. Stock exchanges could consider how they can assist in this matter for listing of companies, keeping in mind the requirement of the venture capital industry.

QUESTIONS

Fill in the Blanks:

1. Venture capital originated in ________.
2. Venture capital has a potential of providing return of __________ in less than 5 years.
3. Most favoured by venture capitalist are _______ companies.
4. Venture capial firms usually invest in ________and_______scale industries.

State whether true or false:

1. The basic objective of investment through venture capital route is capital appreciation.
2. CBDT regulates the taxation aspect of the venture funds in India.
3. Venture capital is also avaible for trading concerns.

Answer in detail:

Q.1. What is venture capital and discuss the steps in venture capital process?

Q.2. Site evidence of successful venture capital projects in India.

Q.3. Discuss the role and activities of SEBI in Indian Securities Market.

❑❑❑

21

CREDIT RATING

INTRODUCTION

Credit Rating is a simple and easy to understand symbolic indicator of the opinion of a credit rating agency about the risk involved in a borrowing programme of an issuer with reference to the capability of the issuer to repay the debt as per terms of the issue. This is neither a general purpose evaluation of the company nor a recommendation to buy, hold or sell a debt instrument.

Credit rating is an opinion expressed by an independent professional organization, after making a detailed study of all relevant factors. Such an opinion will be of great assistance to investors in making investment decisions. It also helps the issuers of debt instruments to price their issues correctly and to reach out to new investors. Regulators like Reserve Bank of India (RBI) and Securities and Exchange Board of India (SEBI) often use credit rating to determine eligibility criteria for some instruments. For example, the RBI has stipulated a minimum credit rating by an approved agency for issue of Commerce Paper. In general, credit rating is expected to improve quality consciousness in the market and establish over a period of time, a more meaningful relationship between the quality of debt and the yield from it. Credit Rating is also a valuable input in establishing business relationships of various types.

ROLE OF CREDIT RATING AGENCIES IN THE EVALUATION OF ISSUERS OF SECURITIES

General Procedures for Evaluating Issuers

The larger credit rating agencies engaged in traditional, fundamental credit analysis generally approach the rating process with similar procedures and organizational structures. Organizationally, the larger rating agencies divide the rating universe into separate categories by industry (*e.g.*, energy or banking) and type of instrument (*e.g.,* corporate debt, government securities, structured finance). At the core of the rating process is the rating committee. Rating committees are generally formed *ad hoc* to initiate, withdraw, or change a rating. They typically are composed of a lead credit analyst, managing directors or other area supervisors, and junior analytical staff. Rating decisions are made-upon a simple majority vote of the committee and are, at their most basic level, an opinion regarding the likelihood the issuer will repay its financial obligation. Rating agencies generally designate ratings of long-term debt through some variation of an alphabetical combination of lower and upper case letters.

In the Indian context, the rating is done at the instance of the issuer, which pays rating fees for this service. If it is unsatisfied with the rating assigned to its proposed instrument, it is at liberty not to disclose the rating given to it. There are 4 rating agencies in India. These are as follows:

CRISIL — The oldest rating agency was originally promoted by ICICI. Standard & Poor, the global leader in ratings, has recently taken a small 10% stake in CRISIL.

ICRA — Promoted by IFCI. Moody's, the other global rating major, has recently taken a small 11% stake in ICRA.

CARE — Promoted by IDBI.

Duff and Phelps — Co-promoted by Duff and Phelps, the world's 4th largest rating agency.

CRISIL is believed to have about 42% market share followed by ICRA with about 36%, CARE with 18% and Duff and Phelps with 4%.

Grading System in India

Each of the rating agencies has different codes for expressing rating for different instruments; however, the number of grades and subgrades is similar *e.g.,* for long-term debentures/bonds and fixed deposits, CRISIL has 4 main grades and a host of subgrades. In decreasing order of quality, these are AAA, AA+, AA, AA-, A+, A, A-, BBB-, BBB, BBB+, BB+, BB, BB-, B+, B, B-, C and D. ICRA, CARE and Duff and Phelps have similar grading systems.

Rating Committee Process

Rating committees typically convene at the behest of a lead analyst or sector supervisor to, among other things: (*a*) rate a new issuer or instrument; (*b*) assess a major transaction or event that might impact a current rating; or (*c*) consider putting a rating on review for change.

Ratings are based on a variety of public and nonpublic information. Public information reviewed in the ratings process typically includes filings with the Commission, news reports, industry reports, bond and stock price trends, data from central banks etc. Nonpublic information can include credit agreements, acquisition agreements, private placement memoranda, and business projections and forecasts. Nonpublic information is often provided pursuant to a confidentiality agreement between the rating agency and the issuer, or is provided premised upon the rating agency's policy to keep such information confidential. Questionnaires and detailed document and information request letters also are used to gather information from issuers. Rating agencies generally do not, however, conduct audits or due diligence reviews of issuer-provided information.

Rating Decisions and Publication

Rating agencies generally advise issuers in advance of an imminent rating action and allow the issuers to appeal the decision. However, the right of appeal is limited both in time and to the submission of new and important information. The time between a committee decision and publication varies from a few hours to a few days, in order to minimize the inappropriate and premature disclosure of information to the marketplace. Issuers may be allowed to review and edit press releases to ensure factual accuracy and prevent the disclosure of confidential information. Rating agencies do not, however, allow issuers to delete the primary basis of a rating action if the disclosure of confidential information is not at issue. Rating agencies generally survey ratings over time by reviewing corporate filings, monitoring industry trends, and maintaining a dialogue with corporate management.

CREDIT RATING PROCESS

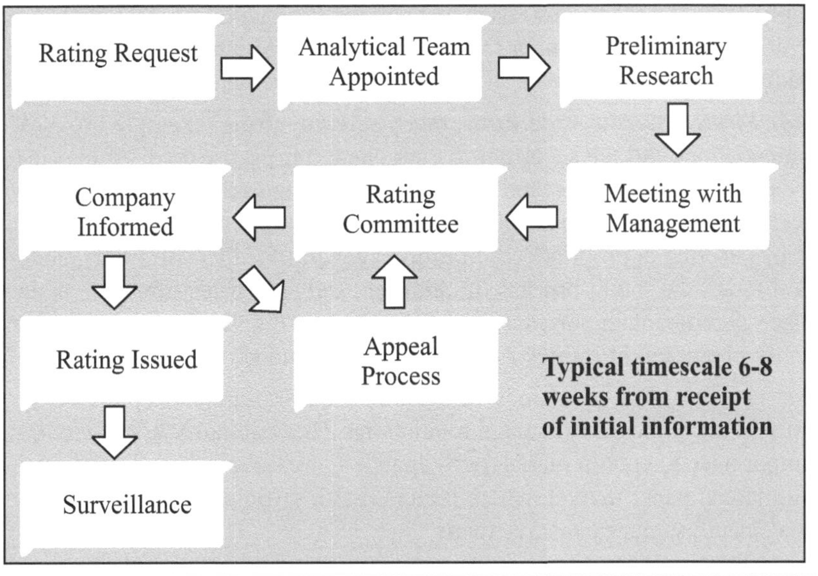

IMPORTANCE OF THE ROLE OF CREDIT RATING AGENCIES

Credit ratings can play a significant role in the investment decisions of investors, and the value investors place on such ratings is evident from, among other things, the impact ratings have on an issuer's ability to access capital. Set forth below is a brief description of how various market participants use credit ratings, and the importance of rating agencies to their market activities.

1. *Investors*: For the investors, credit rating is an information regarding the relative ranking of the default loss probability for a given fixed income investment in comparison with other rated instruments. The rating provides the investors with an independent and professional judgement of the credit quality of the instrument which the individual investor would not otherwise be able to evaluate. Rating provides low cost supplement to the in-house appraisal system of organised institutional investors. The rating replaces name recognition by objective opinion. Ratings can be used by the investor to optimise his risk return preference as ratings seek to establish a link between risk and return. Large institutional and other investors also make use of these ratings to make investment decisions. Other benefits to the investors come from the industry reports, company reports, investor information and protection seminars and other on-line assistance provided by the rating agencies.

2. *Issuers*: Issuers seek credit ratings for a number of reasons, such as to improve the marketability or pricing of their financial obligations, or to satisfy investors, lenders, or counterparties who want to enhance management responsibility.
3. *Buy-Side Firms*: Buy-side firms, such as mutual funds, pension funds, and insurance companies, are among the largest owners of debt securities, preferred stock. Most of the large buy-side firms active in the fixed income markets are substantial users of information from credit rating agencies. Buy-side firms use credit ratings as one of several important inputs to their own internal credit assessments and investment analyses. Buy-side firms also may use credit ratings to comply with internal by-law restrictions or investment policies that require certain minimum credit ratings for investments, or to identify acceptable counterparties. Finally, buy-side firms use credit ratings to ensure compliance with various regulatory requirements.
4. *Sell-Side Firms*. Like buy-side firms, many sell-side firms (example brokerdealers that make recommendations and sell securities to their clients) firms use credit ratings in a fashion similar to buy-side firms. One difference between buy-side and sell-side firms, however, is that many broker-dealers also maintain rating advisory groups. These groups generally assist underwriting clients in selecting appropriate credit rating agencies for their offerings, and help guide those clients through the rating process. In addition, sell-side firms often act as dealers in markets that place significant importance on credit ratings. Finally, large broker-dealers themselves frequently obtain credit ratings as issuers of long- and short-term debt.
5. *Regulatory Use of Ratings:* Credit ratings are used for regulatory purposes around the world, primarily in the context of financial regulations. The regulatory use of credit ratings increases their importance to certain market participants. For example, ratings play an important role in the commercial paper market, where issuers find it difficult to sell paper that does not qualify for investment by money market funds
6. *Use of Ratings in Private Contracts*: The extensive use of credit ratings in private contracts also has enhanced the importance of credit ratings to the marketplace. For example, the widespread use of "ratings triggers" in financial contracts recently has received considerable attention as a result of certain high-profile bankruptcies, such as

Enron and Pacific Gas and Electric Company ("PG&E"). In cases such as these, contractual ratings triggers can seriously escalate liquidity problems at firms faced with a deteriorating financial outlook.

Credit Rating

- Assists in portfolio monitoring by investors.
- Serves as a benchmark for risk premium. Lower the rating, higher will be the risk premium required by an investor.
- Serves as an information and reference point.
- Is a simple global measure of credit risk.
- Acts as an independent benchmark of creditworthiness.
- Is widely accepted by investors/counterparties as a convenient and objective tool for differentiating credit quality.
- Higher the Credit quality transparency more will be the efficiency in capital market.

LIMITATIONS OF CREDIT RATING - RATING DOWNGRADES

Rating agencies all across the world have often been accused of not being able to predict future problems.

- In part, the problem lies in the rating process itself, which relies heavily on past numerical data and standard ratios with relatively lower usage of judgement and understanding of the underlying business or the country economics.
- Data does not always capture all aspects of the situation especially in the complex financial world of today.
- Indian rating agencies have lost some amount of credibility in the last two years due to their inability to predict defaults in many companies, which they had rated quite highly. Sometimes, some of the agencies had an investment grade rating in place when the company in question had already defaulted to some of the fixed deposit holders.
- Rating agencies resorted to mass downgrading of 50-100 companies as a reaction to public criticism, which further eroded their credibility. The major reasons for these downgrades are as follows:
    1. Corporate earnings fell very sharply due to persistent recessionary conditions prevailing in the economy. Many of the corporates are in commodity sectors where fluctuations in selling prices of products can be very sharp - leading to complete erosion of profitability. This problem was compounded by the Asian crisis, which led to increased competition from cheap imports in many product categories.
    2. Rating agencies substantially overestimated financial flexibility of corporates especially from traditional corporate houses. Much of the financial flexibility was implicit on raising money from new issues from the capital market, which has been impossible in the last 3 years.
    3. In the case of finance companies, widespread defaults like CRB and tightening of regulations made it virtually impossible for them to raise money in any form. These finance companies had been in the habit of investing in longer-term, illiquid assets by borrowing shorter-term fixed deposits. When the flow of credit stopped, they faced liquidity problems. These were further compounded by defaults by some of the companies to which they had on lent money.

By and large, the rating is a very good estimate of the actual creditworthiness of the company; however, it is not able to predict extreme situations such as the ones described above, which are unlikely to have been predicted by most investors in any case. Investors should realize that a credit rating is not sacrosanct and that one has to do one's own due diligence and investigation before investing in any instrument and they should use the rating as a reference and a base point for their own effort.

QUESTIONS

Fill in the Blanks:

1. Rating committee formed for credit rating is constituted on an ________ basis.
2. Four rating agencies in India are _______, _________, ________ and ________.
3. Rating is based on two types of information _________ and __________.
4. Major use of credit rating by investors is in __________.
5. Credit rating committee comprises of ________ and _________.
6. CRISIL is currently promoted by ________.

State whether true or false:

1. Credit rating is an opinion expressed by independent professional organizations.
2. Rating agencies conduct audit of issuer provided information.
3. Rating agencies do not allow issuers to prevent the disclosure of confidential information.
4. Financial regulators use ratings to qualify investments.

Answer in detail:

Q.1. Discuss the importance of credit rating for various users.

Q.2. What is the process of credit rating? What types of grading systems are used by various rating agencies in India?

Q.3. What have been the reasons for loss of credibility of Indian rating agencies?

❑❑❑

22 MERCHANT BANKING

INTRODUCTION

A "Merchant Banker" could be defined as "An organisation that acts as an intermediary between the issuers and the ultimate purchasers of securities in the primary security market"

Merchant Banker has been defined under the Securities and Exchange Board of India (Merchant Bankers) Rules, 1992 as "any person who is engaged in the business of issue management either by making arrangements regarding selling, buying or subscribing to securities as manager, consultant, advisor or rendering corporate advisory service in relation to such issue management".

ORIGIN OF MERCHANT BANKING IN INDIA

Merchant Banking, as a commercial activity, took shape in India through the management of Public Issues of Capital and Loan Syndication. It was originated in 1969 with the setting up of the Merchant Banking Division by ANZ Grindlays Bank. The main service offered at that time to the corporate enterprises by the merchant banks included the management of public issues and some aspects of financial consultancy. The early and mid-seventies witnessed a boom in the growth of merchant banking organisations in the country with various commercial banks, financial institutions, broker's firms entering into the field of merchant banking.

Reform measures were initiated in the capital market from 1992, starting with the conferring of statutory powers on the Securities and Exchange Board of India (SEBI) and the repeal of Capital Issues Control Act and the abolition of the office of the Controller of Capital Issues. These have brought about significant improvement in the functional and regulatory efficiency of the market, enabling the Merchant Bankers shoulder greater legal and moral responsibility towards the investing public. Commercial banks and foreign development finance institutions have organized them through formation divisions, nationalized banks have formed subsidiaries companies and share brokers and consultancies constituted themselves into public limited companies or registered themselves as private limited companies. Some merchant banking outfits have entered into collaboration having merchant bankers abroad with several branches.

NATURE OF MERCHANT BANKING

The services of merchant bank cover project counseling, pre-investment activities, feasibility studies, project reports, design of capital structure, issue management, underwriting, loan syndication, mobilization of funds, foreign currency finance, mergers, amalgamation, takeover, venture capital and public deposits. Merchant banking is a skill based activity and involves serving financial needs of every client. Merchant bankers can turn to any of the activities depending upon resources, such as capital, foreign tie-ups for overseas activities and skills.

MERCHANT BANKING FUNCTIONS

The depth and sophistication in merchant banking business are improving since the avenues for raising funds are widening and demands for funds is increasing. Various services offered by merchant banks include:

PRE-ISSUE MANAGEMENT

Introduction

The public issue of securities is the core of merchant banking function. At one time merchant banking was constructed as the sole function. Merchant bankers were identified as issue houses. It was perceived that they provide other financial services. When companies seek to raise resources for implementation of a new project or finance expansion or modernization or diversification of an existing unit or fund long-term working capital requirement, they retain the services of a merchant banker.

The issue function may be both broadly divided into pre-issue management and post-issue management. In both stages legal requirements have to be complied with and since several agencies are involved, activities connected with issue have to be coordinated. For convenience of treatment pre-issue management is divided into: 1.) issue through prospectus, offer for sale and private placement, 2.) marketing and underwriting and 3.) pricing of issues; and post-issue management dealing with stock exchange and collection of subscriptions, allotment and dispatch of shares/refund orders through registrar to the issue.

TYPES OF ISSUES

Public Issue: Public issues of securities, debentures or shares are made in the primary market. The funds mobilized through primary market constitute investment. An offer to public is made through issue of prospectus or subscribed directly. Different media newspapers televisions periodicals are used for publicity. The intermediaries who organize these activities are merchant bankers. In past, stock brokers used to organize public issue. Initial issues are issues of shares for the first time either after incorporation or conversion from private limited to public limited company. The initial as well as further issues may be offered for cash subscription or for consideration other than cash such as change of ownership either of physical assets or technical know-how.

Exchange Issue: An exchange issue is one in which shares of one company are exchanged for another as in case of takeover and mergers. It does not add to funds of the company making the exchange although the merger may result in synergy.

Bonus Issues: Like the Exchange Issues the bonus issue also does not result in raising new funds. Bonus shares are distributed to determine proportion to existing shareholders.

Right issues: Right issue is the issue of new shares in which existing shareholders are given pre-emptive rights to subscribe to new issue. They are issued at a premium, which is freely determined by the company making the issue.

Contents of Prospectus—

A prospectus specifies the following:

- objective of the company
- memorandum of association
- number and classes of shares
- number of redeemable preference shares
- qualification of directors and their remuneration
- particulars about managing directors and directors
- minimum subscription for shares
- the time and opening of subscription lists
- amount payable for application and allotment of each shares
- shares issue for consideration other than cash
- name of the underwriter
- underwriting commission
- preliminary expenses and issues expenses
- particulars of the auditors
- interest of directors and promoters
- voting and dividend rights
- time of business
- capitalization of profits and surplus from reevaluation of assets

ROLE OF MERCHANT BANKER IN PRE-ISSUE MANAGEMENT

Merchant bankers have to coordinate the activities of different government and public bodies, professionals and private agencies relating to issues to bring out a public issue. Also the requirements under the companies act and stock exchange and the guidelines of SEBI have to be met.

Prospectus

Merchant bankers have to ensure that the information required by companies act is furnished in the prospectus. They arrange for drafting of prospectus and vetting thereof by reputed solicitors. The merchant bank is expected to exercise due diligence ensuring compliance by company in regard to prospectus and after the prospectus is ready it has to be sent to SEBI that for vetting. It is only after clearance by SEBI it is filed with the registrar office.

Appointment of Brokers to Issue

Members of recognized stock exchange are appointed as brokers to issue. They can canvass subscription by mailing the literature to clients and undertaking wide publicity. The appointment of brokers is similar to appointment of underwriters. A profile of the project is sent to brokers to the issue. Appointment is made on the preference of the management of the company (issuers) they ensure wide geographical distribution, reputation of the brokers inspire confidence among the investors and track record in the securing subscriptions to issue early.

Appointment of Principal Brokers

Principal brokers assist merchant bankers to devise strategy for success of the public issue, keep liaison between merchant banker and stock exchange and canvass support for the issue among the stockbrokers. Sometimes they centralize mailing of prospectus, applications forms and others publicity materials at the instance of the merchant banker.

Appointment of Banker's Issues

Bankers to the issue accept application with the subscriptions tender at their designated branches and forward them to the register. Bankers to the issue also undertake publicity to the issue by distributing publicity materials, application forms and prospectus. There are eligible for brokerage on shares allotted against application bearing their stamps.

Registrar to Issue or Issue House

An outside agency is employed when merchant banker cannot attend issue house work. Merchant bankers have a panel of issue house and help the issuing company in finalizing the terms and conditions of appointment.

Marketing

Grooming the Issue : The merchant bankers should arrange a meeting with company representatives and advertising agents to finalize arrangements relating to

- Date of opening and closing issue
- Registration of the prospectus
- Launching publicity campaign
- Fixing the date of board meeting to approve and sign prospectus and pass the necessary resolution.

Publicity Campaign : Publicity campaign covers the preparation of all publicity materials and brochures, prospectus, announcement, advertisements in the press, radio, TV, conferences, and hoardings. Success of an issue depends on the size of the publicity materials. Merchant bankers play a key role by helping them in the choice of media, size, and publications in which advertment should appear. Publicity is a function of size of issue, image of issuer and company location. Effective marketing include arrangements of conferences at potential centers to explain nature and strength of the project to various cross section of investors and their counsellors.

Free Pricing of Issues

Pricing of issues is done by companies themselves in consultation with merchant bankers. If a premium is too low the issue gets over subscribed and fails. The merchant bankers apart from taking into account earning per share, book value and average market price for two or three years have to take into account future prospects of the company and assess whether the market can absorb the premium on issue.

POST ISSUE MANAGEMENT

Introduction

Post-management consist of collection of application forms form bankers and the statement of amounts are received, screening applications and deciding allotment procedure in consultation with stock exchange. Post- management concludes with the mailing of allotment letters/share certificates and refund orders.

Registrars to the Issue

Registrars to the issue management play a major role in post issue-management. They work in collaboration with bankers to issue. The registrar to issue get the application forms together, sorts them, and arranges in then order .Merchant banks assist the company by coordinating this activity till final allotment is made and allotment letters and refund orders are posted. Registrars reconcile the total applications collected by the bankers to the issue on behalf of the company with the amount collected, cash/checks/stock invested. They should verify the applications received from the public and multiple applications and applications with technical defects or which do not conform to the conditions stipulated on the application form are removed and rejected. They submit a proposed basis of allotment with the details of applications received. After the basis of allotment is approved by the stock exchange and allotted by the board, the auditor has to certify allotment .registrars have to ensure that the applications are processed and allotment, share certificates /refund orders are sent within 70 days of the close of issue.

Loan Syndication

These financial intermediaries arrange loans for their clients, by analysing their cash flow pattern so that the terms of borrowing meet the clients cash requirements. They also offer assistance in loan documentation procedures.

Mergers and Acquisitions

Merchant banks often represent firms in mergers, acquisitions, and divestitures. Example projects include the acquisition of a specific firm, the sale of a company or a subsidiary of the company, and assistance in and executing a merger or joint venture. In each case, the merchant bank should provide a thorough analysis of the entity bought or sold, as well as a valuation range and recommended structure.

General Advisory Services

Advisory services include assignments such as strategic planning, business valuations, assisting in financial restructurings, and providing an opinion as to the fairness of a proposed transaction.

Restructuring Strategies

Merchant bankers assist the management of the client company to successfully restructure various activities, which include mergers and acquisitions, divestitures, management buyouts, joint venture among others. To help companies achieve the objectives of these restructuring strategies, the merchant banker participates in different activities at various stages which include understanding the objectives behind the strategy (objectives could be either to obtain financial, marketing, or production benefits), and help in searching for the right partner in the strategic decision and financial valuation of the proposal.

What to look for in a Merchant Bank?

Merchant banking is a service business, and the client should expect a premium service from the merchant banking firm. Some criteria to evaluate a merchant bank include:

Services Offered

For all functions except sales and trading, the services should go well beyond simply making introductions, or "brokering" a transaction. For example, most projects will include detailed industry and financial analysis, preparation of relevant documentation such as an offering memorandum or presentation to the Board of Directors, assistance with due diligence, negotiating the terms of the transaction, coordinating legal, accounting, and other advisors, and generally assisting in all phases of the project to ensure successful completion.

Experience

It is extremely important to make sure that experienced, senior members of the merchant banking firm will be active in the project on a day-to-day basis. Depending on the type of transaction, it may be preferable to work with a merchant bank that has some background in the specific industry segment. The merchant bank should have a wide network of relevant contacts, such as potential investors or companies that could be approached for acquisition.

Record of Success

Although no reputable merchant bank will guarantee success, the firm must have a demonstrated record of closing transactions.

Ability to Work Quickly

Often, merchant banking projects have very specific deadlines, for example when bidding on a company that is for sale. The merchant bank must be willing and able to put the right people on the project and work diligently to meet critical deadlines.

Fee Structure

Generally, a merchant bank will charge an initial retainer fee, which may be one-time or monthly, with the majority of the fee contingent upon successful completion of the transaction. It is important to utilize a fee structure that aligns the merchant bank's incentive with organizational benifit.

Ongoing Support

Having worked on a transaction for a company, the merchant bank will be intimately familiar with the company business. After the transaction, a good merchant bank should become a trusted business advisor that can be called upon informally for advice and support on an ongoing basis.

Because merchant banks are intermediaries, and generally not providers of capital, some executives elect to execute transactions without a merchant bank in order to avoid the fees. However, an experienced, quality merchant bank adds significant value to a transaction and can pay for its fee many times over.

The merchant banker has vested interest in making sure the transaction closes, that the project is completed in an efficient time frame, and with terms that provide maximum value to the client. At the same time, the client is able to focus on running the business, rather than on the day-to-day details of the transaction, knowing that the transaction is being handled by individuals with experience in executing similar projects.

DIFFERENCE BETWEEN MERCHANT BANKERS AND INVESTMENT BANKERS

Merchant banks and investment banks, in their purest forms, are different kinds of financial institutions that perform different services. In practice, the fine lines that separate the functions of merchant banks and investment banks tend to blur. Traditional merchant banks often expand into the field of securities underwriting, while many investment banks participate in trade financing activities. In theory, investment banks and merchant banks perform different functions.

- Traditionally, investment banks only participated in underwriting and selling securities in large blocks. Investment banks facilitate mergers and acquisitions through share sales and provide research and financial consulation to companies. Traditionally, investment banks did not deal with the general public. Traditional merchant banks primarily perform international financing activities such as foreign corporate investing, foreign real estate investment, trade finance and international transaction facilitation. Some of the activities that a pure merchant bank is involved in may include issuing letters of credit, transferring funds internationally, trade consulting and co-investment in projects involving trade of one form or another.

- The current offering of investment banks and merchant banks varies by the institutions offering the services, but there are a few characteristics most companies that offer in both investment and merchant banking share. As a general rule, investment banks focus on initial public offerings (IPOs) and large public and private share offerings. Merchant banks tend to operate on small-scale companies and offer creative equity financing, bridge financing, mezzanine financing and a number of corporate credit products. While investment banks tend to focus on larger companies, merchant banks offer their services to companies that are too big for venture capital firms to serve properly, but are still too small to make a compelling public share offering on a large exchange. In order to bridge the gap between venture capital and a public offering, larger merchant banks tend to privately place equity with other financial institutions, often taking on large portions of ownership in companies that are believed to have strong growth potential.
- Merchant banks still offer trade financing products to their clients. Investment banks rarely offer trade financing because most investment banking clients have already outgrown the need for trade financing and the various credit products linked to it.

Without holding a certificate of registration granted by the Securities and Exchange Board of India, no person can act as a merchant banker. Only a corporate body other than a non-banking financial company shall be eligible to get registration as a merchant banker.

Registration with SEBI as Merchant Banker

Categories of Registration

The categories for which registration may be granted are given below:

Category I : To carry on the activity of issue management and to act as adviser, consultant, manager, underwriter, portfolio manager.

Category II : To act as adviser, consultant, co-manager, underwriter, portfolio manager.

Category III : To act as underwriter, adviser or consultant to an issue

Category IV : To act only as adviser or consultant to an issue.

Capital Requirement

The capital requirement depends upon the category. The minimum net worth requirement for acting as merchant banker is given below:

- Category I : Rs. 5 crore
- Category II : Rs. 50 lakh
- Category III : Rs. 20 lakh
- Category IV : Nil

Procedure for Getting Registration

An application should be submitted to SEBI in Form A of the SEBI (Merchant Bankers) Regulations, 1992. SEBI shall consider the application and on being satisfied issue a certificate of registration in Form B of the SEBI (Merchant Bankers) Regulations, 1992

Registration fee Payable to Sebi

Rs. 5 lakh which should be paid within 15 days of date of receipt of intimation regarding grant of certificate.

Validity Period of Certificate of Registration

The validity period of certificate of registration is three years from the date of issue. For renewal of registration three months before the expiry period, an application should be submitted to SEBI in Form A of the SEBI (Merchant Bankers) Regulations, 1992. SEBI shall consider the application and on being satisfied renew certificate of registration for a further period of 3 years. A renewal fee of Rs. 2.5 lakh should be paid within 15 days of date of receipt of intimation regarding renewal of certificate. The person whose registration is not current shall not carry on the activity as merchant banker from the date of expiry of validity period.

Conclusion

The merchant banker plays a vital role in channelising the financial surplus of the society into productive investment avenues. Hence before selecting a merchant banker, one must decide what the services for which he is being approached are. Selecting the right intermediary who has the necessary skills to meet the requirements of the client will ensure success for a firm.

QUESTIONS

Fill in the Blanks:

1. Merchant banking originated in the year ________ with the setting up of merchant banking division by _________.
2. Core function of merchant banking is _________.
3. Merchant bankers arrange ________ and ________ of prospectus
4. Merchant bankers provide general advisory services to the clients such as ______, ________ and _________.
5. Registration fee payable by merchant bankers to SEBI is __________.

State whether true or false:

1. Merchant bankers are not involved in in marketing and publicity of an issue.
2. An outside agency is employed as issue house when merchant banker cannot attend issue house work
3. Merchant bankers do not assist in mergers and acquisitions.

4. Merchant bankers usually carge an initial retainer fee and rest of the fee on successful completion of transaction.
5. Merchant banker should have wide network of contacts.
6. Merchant bankers serve the companies that are too big for venture capitalists to serve.

Answer in detail:

Q.1. What is the need of merchant bankers for a company? What are the criteria for judging a merchant banker?

Q.2. What is the difference between an investment banker and a merchant banker?

❑❑❑

23

MUTUAL FUNDS

DEFINITION OF A MUTUAL FUND

A Mutual Fund is a trust that pools the savings of a number of investors who share a common financial goal and are called shareholders or unitholders of the fund. The money, thus, collected is then invested in capital market instruments such as shares, debentures and other securities. The income earned through these investments and the capital appreciation realized is shared by its unitholders in proportion to the number of units owned by them.

A mutual fund provides income to the investors in three ways:

(1) In the form of dividends on stocks and interest on bonds. In this case the fund pays out nearly all of the income it receives over the year to fund owners in the form of a distribution.

(2) In the form of capital gain the fund sells securities that have increased in price, most funds also pass on these gains to investors in a distribution.

(3) If fund holdings increase in price but are not sold by the fund manager, the fund's shares increase in price and these can be sold by the investor for a profit.

Funds will also usually give the investor a choice either to receive cash distributions or to reinvest the earnings and get more shares

Thus, a Mutual Fund is the most suitable investment for the common man as it offers an opportunity to invest in a diversified, professionally managed basket of securities at a relatively low cost. The working of a mutual fund can be described by Fig. 22.1.

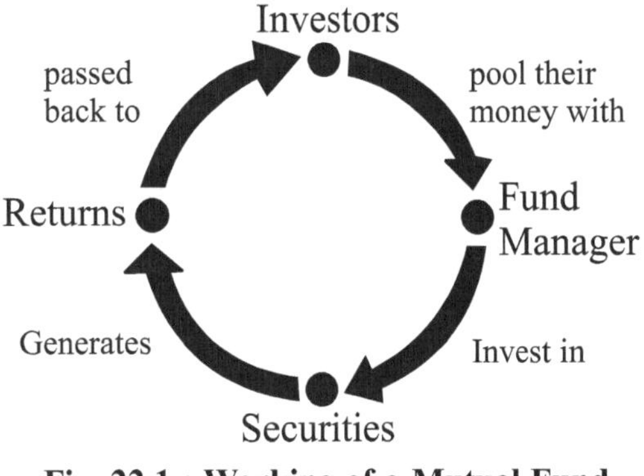

Fig. 22.1 : Working of a Mutual Fund

EVOLUTION AND GROWTH OF MUTUAL FUNDS IN INDIA

The mutual fund industry in India started in 1963 with the formation of Unit Trust of India, at the initiative of the Government of India and Reserve Bank. The evolutionary history of mutual funds in India can be broadly divided into four distinct phases.

First Phase – 1964-87

The beginning of mutual fund industry in India was marked by the establishment of Unit Trust of India (UTI) in 1963, by an Act of Parliament. It was set-up by the Reserve Bank of India and functioned under the Regulatory and Administrative Control of the Reserve Bank of India. In 1978, UTI was de-linked from RBI and the Industrial Development Bank of India (IDBI) took over the regulatory and administrative. UTI launched the first Unit scheme in 1964 called US-64.

At the end of 1988, UTI had Rs.6,700 crore of assets under management.

Second Phase – 1987-1993 (Entry of Public Sector Funds)

In 1987, non- UTI, public sector mutual funds set-up by public sector banks and Life Insurance Corporation of India (LIC) and General Insurance Corporation of India (GIC), entered the Indian market. SBI Mutual Fund was the first non-UTI mutual fund established in June, 1987, followed by Canbank Mutual Fund (Dec 87), Punjab National Bank Mutual Fund (Aug 89), Indian Bank Mutual Fund (Nov 89), Bank of India (Jun 90), Bank of Baroda Mutual Fund (Oct 92). LIC established its mutual fund in June 1989 while GIC had set-up its mutual fund in December 1990.

At the end of 1993, the mutual fund industry had assets under management of Rs.47,004 crore.

Third Phase – 1993-2003 (Entry of Private Sector Funds)

A new era started in the Indian mutual fund industry in 1993,when private sector funds entered the market giving the Indian investors a wider choice of funds for investment. Also, 1993 was the year in which the first Mutual Fund Regulations came into being, under which all mutual funds, except UTI were to be registered and governed. The erstwhile Kothari Pioneer (now merged with Franklin Templeton) was the first private sector mutual fund registered in July 1993.

The 1993 SEBI (Mutual Fund) Regulations, were substituted by a more comprehensive and revised Mutual Fund Regulations in 1996. The industry now functions under the SEBI (Mutual Fund) Regulations 1996.

The number of mutual fund houses went on increasing, with many foreign mutual funds setting-up funds in India and also the industry has witnessed several mergers and acquisitions.

At the end of January, 2003, there were 33 mutual funds with total assets of Rs. 1,21,805 crore. The Unit Trust of India with Rs.44,541 crore of assets under management was way ahead of other mutual funds.

Fourth Phase – since February 2003

In February 2003, following the repeal of the Unit Trust of India Act 1963, UTI was bifurcated into two separate entities. One became the Specified Undertaking of the Unit Trust of India with assets under management of Rs.29,835 crores as at the end of January 2003, representing broadly, the assets of US

64 scheme, assured return and certain other schemes. The Specified Undertaking of Unit Trust of India, functions under an administrator and under the rules framed by Government of India and does not come under the purview of the Mutual Fund Regulations.

The second is the UTI Mutual Fund Ltd, sponsored by SBI, PNB, BOB and LIC. It is registered with SEBI and functions under the Mutual Fund Regulations. With the bifurcation of the erstwhile UTI which had in March 2000, more than Rs.76,000 crore of assets under management and with the setting up of a UTI Mutual Fund, conforming to the SEBI Mutual Fund Regulations, and with recent mergers taking place among different private sector funds, the mutual fund industry has entered its current phase of consolidation and growth.

At the end of September 2004, there were 29 funds, which manage assets of Rs.1,53,108 crore under 421 schemes.

The Fig. 22.2 describes the growth in assets of mutual fund industry since inception till 2006:

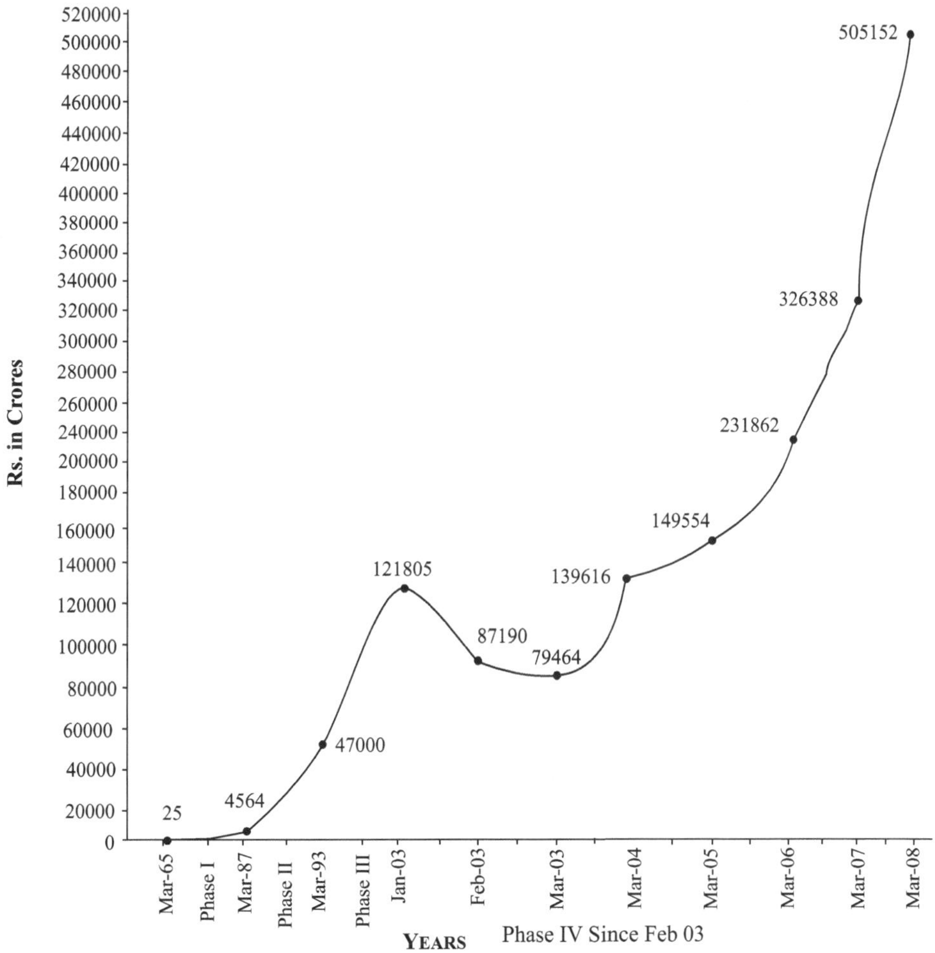

Fig. 22.2 : Growth in assets of mutual fund industry

ORGANISATION OF A MUTUAL FUND

Sponsor: The sponsor of a mutual fund performs the same functions as the promoter of a company and may be a bank, an FI or a financial services company. The sponsor is responsible for setting up and establishing a mutual fund and settling the mutual fund trust. In order to be able to perform all these functions the sponsor has to obtain a license from SEBI for which it has to satisfy certain conditions related to capital, profits, track records, default free dealings etc. For example the sponsors of ICICI Prudential mutual fund are Prudential Plc. and ICICI Bank.

Mutual Fund Trust: The mutual fund is set-up as a trust under Indian Trusts Act, 1881, and is registered with SEBI. This trust enters into contract in the name of its trustees who may be individuals or a corporate. The investors of the fund are beneficiaries of this trust. For examples ICICI Prudential mutual fund has been set-up as a trust named Prudential ICICI Mutual Fund Trust. This trust holds the units of holders in the fund and enters into agreement with SEBI and ensures compliance. The trustees appoint and monitor the asset management company which in turn are responsible for fund's financial regularity, secure necessary compliance and hold the properties of various schemes in the interest of investors.

Asset Management Company: The Asset Management Company, appointed by the trustees, performs the function of investment banker for a fund. It designs the mutual fund schemes, floats them and manages them as per SEBI guidelines. In return for these services the AMC receives an annual investment management and advisory fee linked to the size of the scheme. This fee should not exceed 1.25 per cent if collections are below Rs 100 crore and 1 per cent if collections are above Rs 100 crore. AMC exercises due diligence on investments and submits quarterly reports to the trustees. A fund's AMC can neither act for any other fund nor undertake any business other than asset management. Its net worth should not fall below Rs 10 crore SEBI can pull up an AMC if it deviates from its prescribed role. For example, the AMC of ICICI Prudential Fund is Prudential ICICI Asset Management Company.

Custodian: Often an independent organisation, it takes custody of securities and other assets of a mutual fund. Among public sector mutual funds, the sponsor or trustee generally also acts as the custodian. A custodian's responsibilities include receipt and delivery of securities, collecting income, distributing dividends, safekeeping of units and segregating assets and settlements between schemes. Their charges range between 0.15-0.2 per cent of the net value of the holding. Custodians can service more than one fund. SEBI's regulations specify each constituent's role clearly. How well they act in concert determines the quality of the investor's experience with the mutual fund. For example, the custodian of ICICI Prudential Fund is HDFC Bank limited.

Registrar and Transfer Agents: Registrar and transfer agent handles communications with investors, performs data entry services, maintains investor data and dispatches account statements reflecting the holding and transactions of the investors. For example, the RTA of ICICI Prudential Mutual Fund is ICICI Infotech Services Limited.

Along with this there are distributors who sell the schemes to the investors for which they are paid an incentive in the form of commission.

The structure of a Mutual Fund may be shown as:

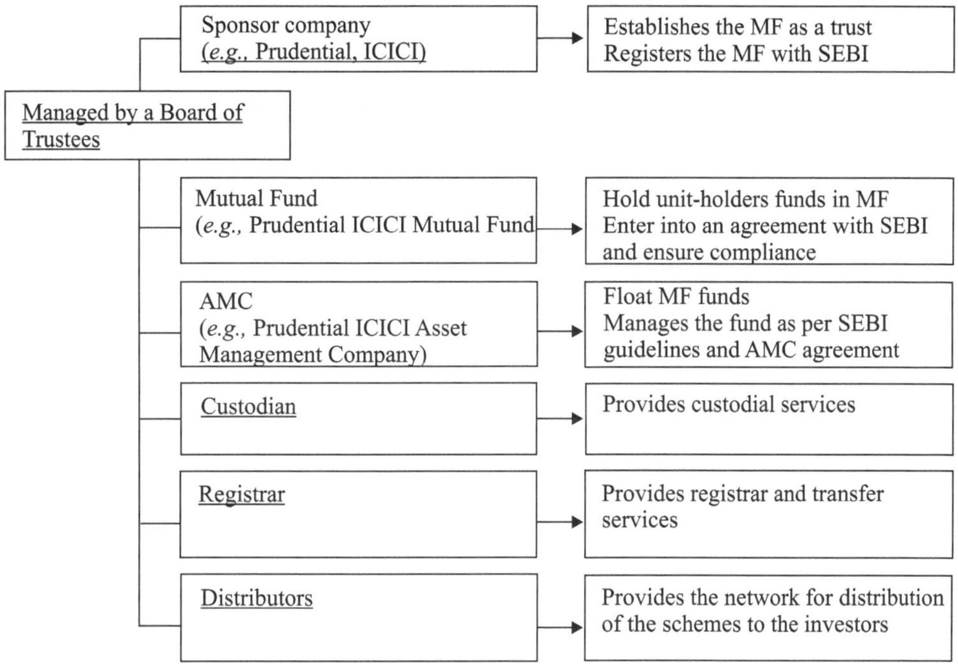

TYPES OF MUTUAL FUNDS

By Structure:

Ooen Ended Scheme: An open ended mutual fund scheme has the following features:

- It accepts funds from investors by offering its units or shares on a continuing basis.
- It permits investors to withdraw from the fund any time on a continuing basis under a repurchase agreement.
- The scheme has no maturity period.
- These schemes are not ordinarily listed on stock market.
- For example, Principal Global Opportunities Fund, Sundaram Select Midcap, UTI contra fund, UTI infrastructure fund etc.

Closed Ended Scheme: A closed ended mutual fund scheme has the following features:

- It does not accept funds from investors by offering its units or shares on a continuing basis.
- It does not permit investors to withdraw from the fund any time.
- The scheme has a fixed maturity period which is usually 5 to 15 years.
- These schemes are ordinarily listed on stock market.
- For example, HDFC Long-term Equity Fund, Morgan Stanley Growth Fund, Franklin India Smaller Companies Fund, UTI Master Value Unit Plan.

In case of closed ended scheme the value of units generally falls and they sell at discount over their net asset value leading to capital loss to investor while open ended schemes generally sell close to their net asset value. However capital appreciation in case of these units may invite tax liability for the investors and sometimes their value may also fall below NAV due to fall in the market. In case of closed ended scheme the portfolio does not face a continuous shuffle as no investor can withdraw funds before maturity leading to stability in liquidity while an open ended scheme may lead to liquidity problems and continuous revamp of portfolio by the fund managers.

Exchange Traded Funds: An exchange traded fund is a combination of open and closed ended fund. For example SPIC of ICICI Pudential

The open ended part of the fund is sold to limited participants called authorized participants who can get or redeem units in kind. In case they want to get new units they have to give the basket of stocks underlying the fund and when they wish to redeem the units they are paid the underlying stocks.

Investors can buy or sell ETF units listed on stock exchange in cash.

This hybrid nature of ETF helps authorized participants to make arbritrage. In case the market value of ETF units increases above NAV then APs sell ETF units and buy underlying basket of stocks from the exchange, deliver these to the ETF and redeem their units thus making an arbitrage profit. On the other hand if the market value of ETF units falls below NAV then these APs buy ETF units from the market, sell them to ETF and get underlying basket of stocks in return, sell these in the market to make arbitrage profit.

ETF units generally sell near to their face value and their open ended part involves dealing in kind rather than cash so the fund does not face liquidity problems.

The Fig. 22.3 shows the working of ETF as explained above:

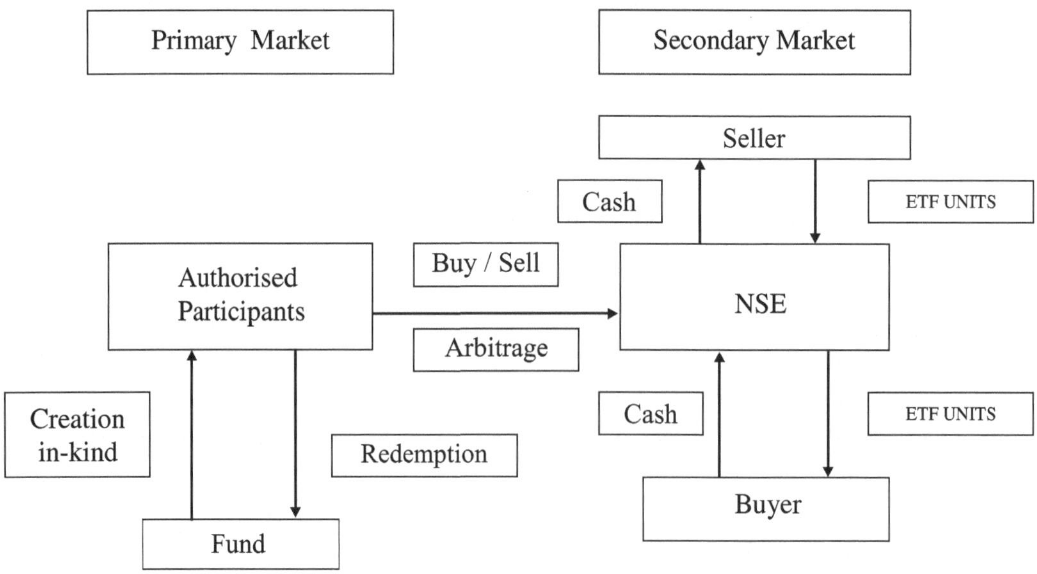

(Adapted from Investment Analysis and Portfolio management by Prasanna Chandra)

Fig. 22.3 : The working of ETF

BY INVESTMENT ORIENTATION

Each mutual fund has a predetermined investment objective according to which it selects the assets in which it will invest regions of investments and investment strategies. According to the investment orientation, there are four types varieties of mutual funds:

Equity Funds: Funds that invest in equity shares or equity linked instruments are called equity funds.The investment objective of this class of funds is generally long-term capital growth with some income. There are, however, many different types of equity funds because there are many different types of equities. These funds are considered to be risky as the underlying assets are equities which have variable return. These funds may give the investor the option of dividend or growth which may give current income or lead to capital appreciation that increases the value of shares. For example, Allianz Equity Fund, Birla MNC Fund, DSP Merill Lynch Equity Plan.

Bond Funds or Income Funds or Debt Funds: When referring to mutual funds, the terms "fixed-income," "bond," and "income" are synonymous. These terms denote funds that invest primarily in government and corporate debt. While fund holdings may appreciate in value, the primary objective of these funds is to provide a steady cashflow to investors. As such, these funds attract conservative investors and retirees. Bond funds are likely to pay higher returns than certificates of deposit and money market investments, but bond funds aren't without risk. Because there are many different types of bonds, bond funds can vary dramatically depending on where they invest. For example, a fund specializing in high-yield junk bonds is much more risky than a fund that invests in government securities. Furthermore, nearly all bond funds are subject to interest rate risk, which means that if rates go up the value of the fund goes down. For example, LIC Bond Fund, Prudential ICICI Multiplier.

Money Market Mutual Funds: These funds invest in money market instruments such as treasury bills, government securities, and certificate of deposit etc., these funds are totally risk free but don't offer great returns; however there is no chance of losing the principal. For example, UTI's G-Sec Invest Fund, KIC MF Liquid Fund.

Balanced Fund: The objective of these funds is to provide a balanced mixture of safety, income and capital appreciation. The strategy of balanced funds is to invest in a combination of fixed income and equities. A typical balanced fund might have a weighting of 60% equity and 40% fixed income. The weighting might also be restricted to a specified maximum for each asset class. A similar type of fund is known as an asset allocation fund. Objectives are similar to those of a balanced fund, but these kinds of funds typically do not have to hold a specified percentage of any asset class. The portfolio manager is therefore given freedom to switch the ratio of asset classes as the economy moves through the business cycle. For example, Franklin India Balanced Fund, HDFC Balanced Fund etc.

OTHER SCHEMES

Global/International Funds: International mutual funds are those funds that invest in non-domestic securities market throughout the world. Investing in international markets provides greater portfolio diversification and lets investor capitalize on some of the world's best opportunities. If investments are chosen carefully, international mutual fund may be profitable when some markets are rising and others are declining. However, fund managers need to keep close watch on foreign currencies and world markets as profitable investments in a rising market can lose money if the foreign currency rises against the dollar. For example UTI MNC Fund, Kotak MNC Fund etc.

Sector Funds: Sector Funds are targeted at specific sectors of the economy such as financial, technology, health, etc. Sector funds are extremely volatile. There is a greater possibility of big gains, as well as big losses in such a fund. For eg. Magnum IT Fund (technology sector), JM auto sector fund (automobiles sector), Reliance Pharma Fund (pharmaceutical sector) etc.

Tax Saving Schemes: These schemes are Equity Linked Saving Schemes open to individuals and HUF. These scheme provide tax relief upto Rs. 1 lakh under Section 80C to investors. For example, Prudential ICICI Tax, SBI Magnum Tax Gain 1993 fund, Tata Tax Saving Fund.

Index Funds: This type of mutual fund replicates the performance of a broad market index such as the S&P CNX Nifty,Sensex etc. An investor in an index fund figures that most managers can't beat the market. An index fund merely replicates the market return and benefits investors in the form of low fees. For example, Benchmark Bank BEES, Prudential ICICI Index Fund Nifty Plan etc.

Fund of Funds: Fund of fund schemes invest in other mutual fund schemes instead of investing in debt or equity.

Funds of Funds uses a particular strategy to hold a portfolio of several other investment funds instead of directly investing in various kinds of bonds, shares and different kind of other securities. The Fund of Funds is often termed in other words as multi-manager investment. One can find a great variety in Fund of Funds and all of these types have one thing in common and that is they are all investing in various types of collective investment scheme.

Fund of Funds has various advantages and disadvantages in its parts. Some of the advantages and disadvantages are:

Advantages of Fund of Funds

1. **Simplicity of the Fund of Funds:** A person to achieve good results while can invest in one Fund of Funds rather than investing in several different funds. This helps the person to concentrate on only one thing and also helps the investor to take care of limited number of papers.

2. **Cheap for the New Investors:** An investor may find it very difficult to diversify initially as he has minimum number of accounts. For this problem the Fund of Funds become very popular for the new investors as this would help them to diversify among thousands of funds through this .

3. A mutual fund generally diversifies through a great number of stocks but a Fund of Funds goes through many different funds which provides the Fund of Funds double diversification.

4. An investor can also have the institutional advantages as he can make investments in various funds which are in other ways off-limit for the retail investors. The investor also gets the advantages of load funds and for that one does not have to pay the load.

Disadvantages of Fund of Funds

1. **Expense Ratios:** Nearly all Fund of Funds carry an expense ratio that are on the higher side. These higher ratios can bring down the amount of returns one was scheduled to get.

2. The investors have to pay some extra charges for keeping the Fund of Funds in force and this can also curtail the amount of income one expected to get.

Gold funds: A gold Exchange Traded Fund (ETF) is a financial instrument like a mutual fund whose value depends on the price of gold. In most cases, the price of one unit of a gold ETF approximately reflects the price of 1 gram of gold. As the price of gold rises, the price of the ETF is also expected to rise by the same amount. Similarly, a fall in the price of gold will also be reflected by a drop in the price of the ETF. A mutual fund will sell units. Each unit will cost a particular amount, called the Net Asset Value.

In an equity fund, the NAV depends on the current market prices of the shares of the companies the fund has invested in, the amount of cash the fund is holding and the number of units the fund has.

As the prices of the shares of the invested companies rise, so will the NAV.

Abroad, the practice with gold traded funds is that one unit represents one-tenth of an ounce of physical gold.

1 ounce	28.35 grams
1 troy ounce	31.1035 grams

So if there are investors in the fund who hold 10,000 units, that means the fund must have physical gold worth 100 ounces. As the price of gold rises and falls, the value of the unit will move accordingly. Just like a mutual fund, the value per unit will be the total value of gold held divided by the number of units, minus the expenses of the fund.

However, unlike a mutual fund, the units of a gold ETF have to be purchased or sold on the stock market. To do so, one needs to have a demat account and a brokerage account with an online brokerage like ICICIdirect, or it may be purchased a local stock broker. Most gold ETFs are traded on the National Stock Exchange (NSE), so one will need a broker who is a member of the NSE. There are five gold ETFs in the market today, namely Gold BeEs, Kotak Gold, Quantum Gold, Reliance Gold, and UTI Gold ETF.A gold exchange traded fund means they are funds focused only on one asset: gold. They do not derive their value from the share prices of various companies. Instead, they do so from gold.

The underlying asset is not equity, but gold.

There are three ways of owning gold.

1. Buying the shares of mining companies.
2. Buying physical gold (gold bars or coins).
3. Investing in a gold traded fund.

Unfortunately, the first option is not really available. Mining companies do not go public (list their shares on a stock exchange) do it is not possible to buy their shares. From the other two, there are a number of factors to look at:

***(i)* Convenience**

The only area where a gold traded fund will score over owning actual gold is in convenience and actual storage. One does not have to worry about safety and keeping it in a bank locker.

***(ii)* Cost**

It may be cheaper to buy a few units of the fund if one cannot afford a gold bar.

***(iii)* Fees**

When buying a gold bar, the actual cost of the gold and a 1% sales tax is paid. This is higher than the fees applicable while buying a gold mutual fund: entry fee, exit fee, transaction tax.

REAL ESTATE MUTUAL FUNDS (REMFS)

An REMF is a scheme much like any other closed-end MF scheme (that invests in shares and bonds) except for the fact that the new entity will invest in real estate. There are two conditions of investment set by SEBI.

First, it is mandatory for an REMF to invest at least 35 per cent of its corpus in completed real estate assets (read flats, row houses, bungalows, shops). These could be either residential or commercial properties, but must be finished and ready-to-use and not under construction.

The REMF will get title deeds and will be the owners of these premises - it's like an investor is buying a second home or a small office.

The REMF will then rent out these properties and earn rental income that it will pass on to the unit holder. When an REMF's tenure ends, it will sell these properties and generate capital appreciation and eventually pass on these earnings to investor. With money as low as Rs 5,000, one can now own a part of this flat through REMF.

Let us assume an REMF collects Rs 500 crore (Rs 5 billion) and invests Rs 200 crore (Rs 2 billion) out of it (40 per cent of the collections) in 40 flats costing Rs 5 crore (Rs 50 million) each. If one has invested Rs 10,000 in this fund, then the share out of the appreciation and rental income of these flats would be 0.0002 per cent.

The second investment condition of SEBI mandates that at least 75 per cent of the corpus should be invested in real estate or related securities. These can be debentures of real estate companies and mortgage-backed securities and equity shares of real estate companies listed on the stock exchange.

Under this, REMF can also invest in 'under-development' properties. But it can neither buy barren land, nor can it undertake construction activities. It will partner with a real estate developer and then take a stake in a special purpose vehicle that the developer will have set up for constructing a particular project. This REMF will take a stake in that project and not in the developer company or its other projects across the country.

REMF will buy unlisted shares in that SPV, not more than 15 per cent of its own corpus. Once the project is completed, the gains arising out of it are of an investor to the extent of hid/her REMF's stake in the SPV. An REMF will be closed-end (this means limited tenure and no ongoing sales of units) and units will be listed on the stock exchanges. Also the investor will be able to trade units on the exchanges very much like shares.

Risks in REMFs: Although REMFs open up a new asset class to investors that was otherwise restrictive, they come with a set of risks.

REMFs are free to invest the 25 per cent of the corpus that is left after investing in real estate or related securities in any security, related or unrelated to real estate. This can be either directly in the equity markets and debt instruments, or kept as cash. Sebi has allowed REMFs to take a call on this. But, how an REMF opts to invest this portion can have a bearing on its risk profile.

Flexible asset allocation: That is not the only flexibility that Sebi has allowed for REMFs. Beyond the mandated 35 per cent in finished real estate projects and within 75 per cent of the scheme's corpus, they have about four different types of securities to choose from.

Here's where one REMF can significantly look and behave differently from another. An REMF may choose to hold 35 per cent in completed real estate assets and deploy 40 per cent in equity shares of real estate companies and then invest the balance 25 per cent in another set of equity shares.

Asset allocation will be riskier in cases like above as against those that have a healthy dose of mortgage-backed securities and debentures of real estate companies and money market securities that earn a fixed interest income.

INVESTMENT PLANS OF MUTUAL FUNDS

Growth Plan : The Growth Plan is designed for investors interested in capital appreciation on their investment and not in regular income. Accordingly, the Scheme will not declare dividends under the Growth Plan. The income earned on the Growth Plan's corpus will remain invested in the Growth Plan.

The Growth Plan has two options :

- **Growth Option :** Under this option, there will be no distribution of income and the returns to the investor is only by way of capital gains/ appreciation, if any, through redemption at applicable NAV of the units held by them.
- **Bonus Option :** Under this plan Bonus in the form of additional units will be allotted.

Dividend Plan : The Dividend Plan has been designed for investors who require regular income in the form of dividends. Under the Dividend Plan, the Scheme will endeavour to make regular dividend payments to the unit holders. Dividend will be distributed from the available distributable surplus.

***Dividend Plan has two options* :**

- **Dividend Payout Option :** Under this option the Dividend declared under the Dividend Plan will be paid to the unit holders within 30 days from the declaration of the dividend.
- **Dividend Reinvestment Option :** The Dividend Plan has a Reinvestment Option whereby the dividend distributed under the plan will be automatically reinvested at the ex-dividend NAV on the transaction day following the date of declaration of dividend and additional units will be allotted accordingly.

Systematic Investment Plan (SIP) : When an investor chooses to invest via an SIP, he makes investments (usually) in smaller denominations (as small as Rs. 100) at pre-specified regular time intervals as opposed to making a single lump sum investment. The underlying intention is to benefit from the volatility in equity markets by lowering the average purchase cost. The concept underlying SIP is of Rupee Cost Averaging.

Rupee Cost Averaging is an effective market-timer mechanism that eliminates the need to time the markets. It involves investing a fixed, pre-decided amount of money on a regular basis over a long period of time. Since the amount invested per month is constant, one buys more units when the price is low and fewer units when the price is high.

As a result the average unit cost will always be less than the average sale price per unit, irrespective of the market rising, falling or fluctuating.

Lets take an example of Mr.X wherein he started investing Rs. 2,000 every month in a Systematic Investment Plan

Period	Amount invested in SIP	NAV per unit	Number of units
5th May, 2009	2,000	11.01	181.6530427
5th June, 2009	2,000	12.05	165.9751037
5th July, 2009	2,000	13.13	152.3229246
5th Aug., 2009	2,000	13.67	146.3057791
5th Sept., 2009	2,000	15.81	126.5022138
5th Oct., 2009	2,000	16.78	119.1895113
5th Nov., 2009	2,000	18.28	109.4091904
5th Dec., 2009	2,000	18.71	106.8947087
5th Jan., 2010	2,000	21.48	93.10986965
5th Feb., 2010	2,000	21.49	93.06654258
5th March, 2010	2,000	21.98	90.99181074
Total Amount Invested	22,000		

Actual Average NAV = (11.34 + 11.01 + 12.05 + 13.13 + 13.67 + 15.81 + 16.78 + 18.28 + 18.71 + 21.48 + 21.49 + 21.77) / 12 = **Rs.16.76.**

NAV for Mr.X = (2,000 * 12) / (352.73 + 363.31 + 331.95 + 304.65 + 292.61 + 253.00 + 238.38 + 218.82 + 213.79 + 186.22 + 186.13 + 183.74) = **Rs.15.87**

So, whatever may be the direction of the market Mr. X has to pay less by going for SIP than if he purchased in lump sum

Moreover, suppose the monthly SIP is for Rs 1,000 and the fund's net asset value (NAV) is Rs 50; this will lead to 20 units being credited to the investor. However, in the next month on account of the volatile markets, the fund's NAV falls to Rs 40. This will lower the average purchase cost; as a result, the investor will have 25 units credited to his account. This is how an SIP can help investors benefit from volatility in equity markets.

Other Advantages of SIP

Disciplined investing: One of the major reasons for investors not achieving their financial goals is lack of disciplined investing. For example, often monies that are kept aside for investments end up getting used for other purposes. As a result, the investor is even further divorced from his goals. An SIP ensures that the investor stays the course by investing in a disciplined manner.

SIP takes care of the problem of lack of money with the investor by lowering the minimum investment amount. For example, the minimum investment amount for a lump sum investment in a diversified equity fund could typically be Rs 5,000; conversely for an SIP, it can be as low as Rs 500. As a result, investing via the SIP route is gives less burden of financial commitment to investor

Timing the market is a popular pastime with several investors. Investors generally have the habit of getting invested when markets have bottomed out. Moreover timing markets to perfection and doing so consistently is beyond most investors. SIPs make market timing irrelevant.

How to Choose a Mutual Fund?

The following points should be kept in mind while choosing a mutual fund:

Investment objective of the fund and its assets allocation pattern, *i.e.,* in what proportion does the scheme plans to invest its money.

If the fund is an old fund then the past record of the fund and the fund management abilities should be analyzed. Relative performance and rating by independent agencies can give a clearer picture.

The extent of diversification is important in judging the risk underlying a fund.SEBI prohibits equity schemes from holding more than 10% in a stock at the time of investment. But later on this limit is not applicable. So overshooting of the limit can give warning signal and higher risk exposure of the fund.

Apart from stock diversification the fund should also have a diversified investor base as major holding by a single investor can destroy the NAV of the fund if the investor sells off/redeems his units.

Expense ratio of the fund which expresses costs of the fund as a percentage of its corpus should be lower. For equity funds the maximum ratio has been capped at 2.25% and for debt it is 2.5%

Load structure of the fund (entry and exit load) should be reasonable. Most of the funds charge this between 0.5-2.5 %.Schemes charging more than this can be avoided.

How to Track a Mutual Fund?

The performance of a mutual fund can be tracked by:

Reading the half yearly and annual reports.

Reading the fact sheets and newsletters which give details about schemes' performance statistics as well as views of fund managers, investors etc.

Tracking the NAV of fund from newspapers, websites etc.

Comparing the fund with its benchmark.

WHEN TO SELL A MUTUAL FUND

1. Financing a need

A very obvious reason to sell would be when one needs money which may be to buy a car or a house; or need to pay your child's fees; or may be you want to take a vacation abroad. However, proper choice is essential in deciding which fund(s) to sell. An investor can either sell those funds, whose performance has not been encouraging; or those where the tax impact is minimal; or those where the amounts are not very significant; etc.

2. Poor performance

For performance one should look at long-term returns — 1-year, 3-year & 5-year — and compare it with both the benchmark index and other funds in the peer group. In the short term there could be a genuine reason for under-performance. If the performance of the fund continues to be consistently below par over long periods of time, then it may be worthwhile considering switching over a better performing fund. If possible, one should also try and assess the reasons for poor performance.

3. Rebalancing the portfolio

An investor has certain asset allocations across various investment options such as debt, equity, real-estate, gold, etc. A change in financial position may require an investor to rebalance his portfolio. Suppose a person is presently having a well-paid job and is unmarried with no liabilities. He can, therefore, take much higher exposure in equity MFs. But with marriage and kids responsibilities may increase, which would require him to reduce you equity risk to more manageable levels. Hence he would need to sell equity and re-invest in debt to restore the original balance.

4. Change in taxation policy

A change in the tax policy could become a reason to sell and reinvest somewhere else. Suppose our risk profile is such that we can take around 50:50 equity to debt exposure. Thus, we had invested in the balanced funds. But, in the recent budget, the tax laws have been changed wherein a fund would classify as an equity fund only if the equity component is more than 65%.Therefore, the balanced funds would have to increase the equity component to 65% so that they can continue to enjoy the lower tax applicable to equity funds. But with 65% equity it becomes riskier. Hence, it could be time to exit.

5. Change in Fund-Style or Objective

Suppose, an investor has exposure in mid-cap funds and in order to diversify his portfolio he chooses a large-cap fund. However, after some time he observes that the fund is taking exposure in mid-cap sector too. This increases investor's overall exposure to mid-cap. Thus, it may be time to sell and move to a truly large-cap fund.

Similarly if the investor chooses a fund for its' passive style of investing; but later the fund manager starts following an aggressive style with frequent churning. If this style does not suit investor's risk profile then it would be better to quit the fund.

6. Change in the Fund Manager

When investing, one of the criteria is to evaluate the expertise, knowledge, experience and past performance of the fund manager. However, while the fund manager is a key player in managing our money, one should not forget the contribution of the research team, the investment committee, the top management and AMC's investment philosophy. Therefore, a change the fund manager need not necessarily mean exiting the fund. But it may be worthwhile keeping the fund under a close watch. If there is a perceptible decline in the performance, one could consider selling.

7. Change in the Fund's Size

Sometimes the size of the fund starts affecting the returns. For example, certain mid-caps funds took a voluntary step to stop accepting fresh money into the fund, when the size became too large to manage. The moment a fund becomes too large to manage or say too small to capture new investment opportunities, it may be time sell the units of the fund

There could, of course, be other reasons to sell, more specific to one's circumstances. The basic idea is to define, beforehand, certain rules for oneself for selling one's investments. This would reduce the day-to-day dilemma and ad-hoc decision-making, thereby make investing more scientific and unemotional.

8. When you have achieved your investment objective

A mutual fund investment is made with the intent of achieving a specific investment objective. Some of these investment objectives include, among others, planning for child's education, planning for retirement, saving for a house/car. If an investor does not achieve his investment goal, it is better to the mutual fund.

9. When a mutual fund revises its mandate

Mutual funds have an investment mandate. The mandate sets the 'guidelines' for fund managers about how they should manage their funds. Since the mandate is formally stated, investors know about this beforehand and invest in the fund if they believe that it will enable them to achieve their investment goals. Mutual funds are known to revise their mandates if they believe that the existing mandate does not serve the mutual fund's interests anymore. For instance, in the recent past a leading private sector fund house converted its index fund into an actively managed fund. From investor's perspective, he will have to evaluate whether the mutual fund with a revised mandate merits a place in your portfolio. If it does not, then its time to redeem it.

10. When the star fund manager quits

A category of investors track the fund managers more than they track the fund house and its schemes. These investors invest in a mutual fund relying mainly on the star fund manager's investment prowess and skills. If the fund manager quits the fund house, then there is a case for investor to redeem his investments because it is unlikely that the rest of the fund management team will be able to replicate the performance in the star fund manager's absence.

Advantages of Mutual Funds:

- **Professional Management :** The primary advantage of funds (at least theoretically) is the professional management of investor's money. Investors purchase funds because they do not have the time or the expertise to manage their own portfolios. A mutual fund is a relatively inexpensive way for a small investor to get a full-time manager to make and monitor investments.
- **Diversification :** By owning shares in a mutual fund instead of owning individual stocks or bonds, investment risk is spread out. The idea behind diversification is to invest in a large number of assets so that a loss in any particular investment is minimized by gains in others. In other words, the more stocks and bonds an investor owns, the less is the risk of loss. Large mutual funds typically own hundreds of different stocks in many different industries. It would not be possible for an investor to build this kind of a portfolio with a small amount of money.
- **Economies of Scale :** Because a mutual fund buys and sells large amounts of securities at a time, its transaction costs are lower than what an individual would pay for securities transactions.
- **Liquidity :** Just like an individual stock, an open-ended mutual fund allows conversion of shares into cash at any time.
- **Simplicity :** Buying a mutual fund is easy most of the funds allow investors to invest in mutual fund units on monthly basis under plan called Systematic Investment Plan(SIP) where a regular amount is invested at regular intervals to facilitate investment by the investor.

Disadvantages of Mutual Funds:

- **Professional Management :** Many investors debate whether or not the so-called professionals are any better at picking stocks. Management is by no means infallible, and even if the fund loses money, the manager still takes his/her cut. So although managed professionally, managers investing in loss making securities for their personal interests can not be ruled out as had happened in case of US-64.
- **Costs :** Mutual funds do not simply invest investor's money without earning any profit. They have charges in form of annual fees along with the cost of entering and exit from the fund, called load (discussed later).
- **Dilution :** It's possible to have too much diversification. Because funds have small holdings in so many different companies, high returns from a few investments often do not make much difference on the overall return. Dilution is also the result of a successful fund getting too big. When money pours into funds that have had strong success, the manager often has trouble finding a good investment for all the new money.
- **Taxes :** When making decisions about investor's money, fund managers do not consider investor's personal tax situation. For example, when a fund manager sells a security, a capital-gains tax is triggered, which affects how profitable the individual is from the sale. It might have been more advantageous for the individual to defer the capital gains liability.

COSTS INVOLVED IN MUTUAL FUND INVESTMENT

Mutual fund investment does not simply involve putting in the principal amount but some fees is also charged by the fund companies for making such investment on investor's behalf. Fees can be broken down into two categories:

1. Yearly fees to keep the investor invested in the fund.
2. Transaction fees paid when an investor buys or sells shares in a fund; also called loads.
   Yearly fees
   - The yearly fees involves the investment management and advisory fees charged by the AMC and other expenses such as postage, marketing expenses, brokerage, audit fees, costs of proving account statements, dividend redemption cost etc.
   - The ceiling for investment management and advisory fee by AMC is:
     - In case of funds with net assets up to Rs. 100 crore: 1.25% of net assets.
     - In case of funds with net assets above Rs. 100 crore: 1% of net assets.
     - In case of no load funds an additional fee not above 1% of the weekly average net assets outstanding each year can be charged by the AMC.

The total yearly fee is subject to following limits:

- Up to 100 crore of the average weekly net assets: 2.50%
- On next 300 crore of the average weekly net assets: 2.25%
- On next 300 crore of the average weekly net assets: 2%
- On balance net assets: 1.75%.

Loads

Loads are just fees that a fund uses to compensate brokers or other salespeople for selling the mutual fund. Various types of loads are:

- Front-end loads or entry loads: These are the fees paid at the time of purchasing the fund. If one invests in a mutual fund with a 1.5% front-end load, and the net asset value per unit is Rs.15 then the investor will end up paying 15.225 per unit due to the load charged. The maximum load for a scheme may be 2% and many schemes may be without any load.
- Exit load – This load is levied when the investor redeems the mutual fund units and may range between 0 to 3%. Another charge which may be levied is contingent deferred sales charge or back end load. This may be levied if the investor exits out of the scheme before a stipulated time frame say a year or so and may be between 0.5-1%. The exit and contingent deferred sales load may not be applicable if the scheme carries an entry load.

Along with these a fund may also have some invisible charges such as transaction costs incurred on investing in securities which may be deducted from the return and may range between 0.5-2% of the fund's assets.

All these charges may reduce the returns from the fund. A no-load fund sells its shares without a commission or sales charge. Some in the mutual fund industry may say that the load is the fee that pays for the service of a broker choosing the correct fund for an investor. According to this argument, investor returns will be higher because the professional advice will lead to better stock selection and fund performance. However there is little to no evidence that shows a correlation between load funds and superior performance. In fact, when the fees charged is taken into account, the average load fund performs worse than a no-load fund.

SEBI GUIDELINES ON: CONSTITUTION AND MANAGEMENT OF ASSET MANAGEMENT COMPANY

1. **Application by an asset management company**

   (*i*) The application for the approval of the asset management company shall be made in Form D.

   (*ii*) The provisions of Regulations 5, 6 and 8 shall, so far as may be, apply to the application made under sub-regulation (1) as they apply to the application for registration of a mutual fund.

2. **Appointment of an asset management company**

   (*i*) The sponsor or, if so authorised by the trust deed, the trustee shall, appoint an asset management company, which has been approved by the Board under sub-regulation (2) of Regulation 21.

   (*ii*) The appointment of an asset management company can be terminated by majority of the trustees or by seventy five per cent of the unit-holders of the scheme.

   (*iii*) Any change in the appointment of the asset management company shall be subject to prior approval of the Board and the unitholders.

3. **Eligibility criteria for appointment of asset management company**

(*i*) For grant of approval of the asset management company the applicant has to fulfil the following: -

(*a*) In case the asset management company is an existing asset management company it has a sound track record, general reputation and fairness in transactions; Explanation: For the purpose of this clause sound track record shall mean the networth and the profitability of the asset management company. 16*[(aa) The asset management company is a fit and proper person.]

(*a*) The directors of the asset management company are persons having adequate professional experience in finance and financial services related field and not found guilty of moral turpitude or convicted of any economic offence or violation of any securities laws;

(*b*) The key personal of the asset management company17*[have not been found guilty of moral turpitude or convicted of economic offence or violation of securities laws] 18*[or worked] for any asset management company or mutual fund or any intermediary19*[during the period when its] registration has been suspended or cancelled at any time by the Board;

(*c*) The board of directors of such asset management company has at least fifty per cent directors, who are not associate of, or associated in any manner with, the sponsor or any of its subsidiaries or the trustees;

(*d*) The Chairman of the asset management company is not a trustee of any mutual fund;

(*e*) The asset management company has a networth of not less than rupees ten crores: Provided that an asset management company already granted approval under the provisions of Securities and Exchange Board of India (Mutual Funds) Regulations, 1993 shall within a period of twelve months from the date of notification of these regulations increase its networth to rupees ten crores. 20*[Provided that the period specified in the first proviso may be extended in appropriate cases by the Board upto three years for reasons to be recorded in writing. Provided further that no new schemes shall be allowed to be launched or managed by such asset management company till the net worth has been raised to Rupees ten crores]. 21*[Explanation: For the purposes of this clause, "net worth" means the aggregate of the paid up capital and free reserves of the asset management company after deducting therefrom miscellaneous expenditure to the extent not written off or adjusted or deferred revenue expenditure, intangible assets and accumulated losses].

(*ii*) The Board may, after considering an application with reference to the matters specified in sub-regulation (1), grant approval to the asset management company.

4. **Terms and conditions to be complied with**

The approval granted under sub-regulation (2) of Regulation 21 shall be subject to the following conditions, namely:

(*a*) Any director of the asset management company shall not hold the office of the director in another asset management company unless such person is an independent director referred to in clause (d) of sub-regulation (1) of Regulation 21 and approval of the board of asset management company of which such person is a director, has been obtained;

(*b*) The asset management company shall forthwith inform the Board of any material change in the information or particulars previously furnished, which have a bearing on the approval granted by it;

(*c*) No appointment of a director of an asset management company shall be made without prior approval of the trustees;

(*d*) The asset management company undertakes to comply with these regulations;

(*e*) No change in the controlling interest of the asset management company shall be made unless, -

(*i*) Prior approval of the trustees and the Board is obtained;

(*ii*) A written communication about the proposed change is sent to each unitholder and an advertisement is given in one English daily newspaper having nationwide circulation and in a newspaper published in the language of the region where the Head Office of the mutual fund is situated; and

(*iii*) The unitholders are given an option to exit on the prevailing Net Asset Value without any exit load] 23*[Provided that in case of an open ended scheme, the consent of the unitholders shall not be necessary if;

- The change in control takes place after one year from the date of allotment of units
- The unitholders are informed about the proposed change in the controlling interest of asset management company by sending individual communication and an advertisement is given in one English daily newspaper having nationwide circulation and in a newspaper published in the language of the region where the head office of the mutual fund is situated.
- The unitholders are given an option to exit at the prevailing Net Asset Value without any exit load."

(*f*) The asset management company shall furnish such information and documents to the trustees as and when required by the trustees.

5. **Procedure where approval is not granted :** Where an application made under regulation 19 for grant of approval does not satisfy the eligibility criteria laid down in Regulation 21, the Board may reject the application.

6. **Restrictions on business activities of the asset management company:** The asset management company shall

Not act as a trustee of any mutual fund;

(*a*) Not undertake any other business activities except activities in the nature of 24*[portfolio management services] management and advisory services to offshore funds, pension funds, provident funds, venture capital funds, management of insurance funds, financial consultancy and exchange of research on commercial basis if any of such activities are not in conflict with the activities of the mutual fund; Provided that the asset management company may itself or through its subsidiaries undertake such activities if it satisfies the Board that the key personnel of the asset management company, the systems, back office, bank and securities accounts are segregated activity wise and there exist systems to prohibit access to inside information of various activities. Provided further that asset management company shall meet capital adequacy requirements, if any, separately for each such activity and obtain separate approval, if necessary under the relevant regulations.]

(*b*) The asset management company shall not invest in any of its schemes unless full disclosure of its intention to invest has been made in the offer documents 25*[in case of schemes launched after the notification of these regulations.] Provided that an asset management company shall not be entitled to charge any fees on its investment in that scheme.

7. Asset Management Company and its obligations

The asset management company shall take all reasonable steps and exercise due diligence to ensure that the investment of funds pertaining to any scheme is not contrary to the provisions of these regulations and the trust deed.

(*a*) The asset management company shall exercise due diligence and care in all its investment decisions as would be exercised by other persons engaged in the same business.

(*b*) The asset management company shall be responsible for the acts of commissions or omissions by its employees or the persons whose services have been procured by the asset management company.

(*c*) The asset management company shall submit to the trustees quarterly reports of each year on its activities and the compliance with these regulations.

(*d*) The trustees at the request of the asset management company may terminate the assignment of the asset management company at any time: Provided that such termination shall become effective only after the trustees have accepted the termination of assignment and communicated their decision in writing to the asset management company.

(*e*) Notwithstanding anything contained in any contract or agreement or termination, the asset management company or its directors or other officers shall not be absolved of liability to the mutual fund for their acts of commission or omissions, while holding such position or office. 26*[(6A) The Chief Executive Officer (whatever his designation may be) of the asset management company shall ensure that the mutual fund complies with all the provisions of the regulations and the guidelines or circulars issued in relation thereto from time to time and that the investments made by the fund managers are in the interest of the unit holders and shall also be responsible for the overall risk management function of the mutual fund. Explanation: For the purpose of this sub-regulation, the words 'these regulations' shall mean and include the Securities and Exchange Board of India (Mutual Funds) Regulations, 1996 as amended from time to time. (6B) The fund manager (whatever the designation may be) shall ensure that the funds of the schemes are invested to achieve the objectives of the scheme and in the interest of the unit holders.]

(*f*) 27*{(7) (*a*) An asset management company shall not through any broker associated with the sponsor, purchase or sell securities, which is average of 5% or more of the aggregate purchases and sale of securities made by the mutual fund in all its schemes. Provided that for the purpose of this sub-regulation, aggregate purchase and sale of securities shall exclude sale and distribution of units issued by the mutual fund. Provided further that the aforesaid limit of 5% shall apply for a block of any three months. (*b*) An asset management company shall not purchase or sell securities through any broker [other than a broker referred to in clause (a) of sub-regulation (7)] which is average of 5% or more of the aggregate purchases and sale of securities made by the mutual fund in all its schemes, unless the asset management company has recorded in writing the justification for exceeding the limit of 5% and reports of all such investments are sent to the trustees on a quarterly basis. Provided that the aforesaid limit shall apply for a block of three months.}

(*g*) An asset management company shall not utilise the services of the sponsor or any of its associates, employees or their relatives, for the purpose of any securities transaction and distribution and sale of securities Provided that an asset management company may utilise such services if disclosure to that effect is made to the unit holders and the brokerage or commission paid is also disclosed in the half yearly annual accounts of the mutual fund. 28*[Provided further that the mutual funds shall disclose at the time of declaring half-yearly and yearly results;

- Any underwriting obligations undertaken by the schemes of the mutual funds with respect to issue of securities associate companies,
  (*a*) Devolvement, if any,
  (*b*) Subscription by the schemes in the issues lead managed by associate companies
  (*c*) Subscription to any issue of equity or debt on private placement basis where the sponsor or its associate companies have acted as arranger or manager].

(*h*) The asset management company shall file with the trustees the details of transactions in securities by the key personnel of the asset management company in their own name or on behalf of the asset management company and shall also report to the Board, as and when required by the Board.

(*i*) In case the asset management company enters into any securities transactions with any of its associates a report to that effect shall be sent to the trustees 29*[***] 30*[at its next meeting].

(*j*) In case any company has invested more than 5 per cent of the net asset value of a scheme, the investment made by that scheme or by any other scheme of the same mutual fund in that company or its subsidiaries shall be brought to the notice of the trustees by the asset management company and be disclosed in the half yearly and annual accounts of the respective schemes with justification for such investment 31*[provided the latter investment has been made within one year of the date of the former investment calculated on either side.]

(*k*) The asset management company shall file with the trustees and the Board:

- Detailed bio-data of all its directors along with their interest in other companies within fifteen days of their appointment; and \
  (*a*) Any change in the interests of directors every six months.
  (*b*) A quarterly report to the trustees giving details and adequate justification about the purchase and sale of the securities of the group companies of the sponsor or the asset management company as the case may be, by the mutual fund during the said quarter.]

(*l*) Each director of the Asset Management Company shall file the details of his transactions of dealing in securities with the trustees on a quarterly basis in accordance with the guidelines issued by the Board.]

(*m*) The asset management company shall not appoint any person as key personnel who has been found guilty of any economic offence or involved in violation of securities laws.

(*n*) The asset management company shall appoint registrars and share transfer agents who are registered with the Board. Provided if the work relating to the transfer of units is processed in-house, the charges at competitive market rates may be debited to the scheme and for rates higher than the competitive market rates, prior approval of the trustees shall be obtained and reasons for charging higher rates shall be disclosed in the annual accounts.

(*o*) The asset management company shall abide by the Code of Conduct as specified in the Fifth Schedule.

INVESTMENT OBJECTIVES AND VALUATION POLICIES

I. The moneys collected under any scheme of a mutual fund shall be invested only in transferable securities in the money market or in the capital market or in privately placed debentures or securitised debts. Provided that moneys collected under any money market scheme of a mutual fund shall be invested only in money market instruments in accordance with directions issued by the Reserve Bank of India; Provided further that in case of securitised debts such fund may invest in asset backed securities 47*[and] mortgaged backed securities.

II. Investment, borrowing, restriction, etc.

1. Any investments to be made under Regulation 43 shall be invested subject to the investment restriction specified in the Seventh Schedule. 48*[(1A) The mutual fund having an aggregate of securities which are worth Rs.10 crore or more, as on the latest balance sheet date, shall subject to such instructions as may be issued from time to time by the Board settle their transactions entered on or after January 15, 1998 only through dematerialised securities.]
2. The mutual fund shall not borrow except to meet temporary liquidity needs of the mutual funds for the purpose of repurchase, redemption of units or payment of interest or dividend to the unit holders. Provided that the mutual fund shall not borrow more than 20% of the net asset of the scheme and the duration of such a borrowing shall not exceed a period of six months.
3. The mutual fund shall not advance any loans for any purpose.
4. 49*[(4) The mutual fund may lend securities in accordance with the Stock Lending Scheme of the Board.

Option Trading, etc.

The funds of a scheme shall not in any manner be used in option trading or in short selling or carry forward transactions. 50*[Provided that mutual funds shall enter into derivatives transactions in a recognised stock exchange for the purpose of hedging and portfolio balancing, in accordance with the guidelines issued by the Board].

Underwriting of Securities

Mutual funds may enter into underwriting agreement after obtaining a certificate of registration in terms of the Securities and Exchange Board of India (Underwriters) Rules and Securities and Exchange Board of India (Underwriters) Regulations, 1993 authorising it to carry on activities as underwriters.

Explanation:

5. For the purpose of these regulations, the underwriting obligation will be deemed as if investments are made in such securities.
6. The capital adequacy norms for the purpose of underwriting shall be the net asset of the scheme. Provided that the underwriting obligation of a mutual fund shall not at any time exceed the total net asset value of the scheme.

III. Method of Valuation of Investments

Every mutual fund shall compute and carry out valuation of its investments in its portfolio and publish the same in accordance with the valuation norms specified in Eighth Schedule.

IV. Computation of Net Asset Value

1. Every mutual fund shall compute the Net Asset Value of each scheme by dividing the net assets of the scheme by the number of units outstanding on the valuation date.
2. The Net Asset Value of the scheme shall be calculated and published at least in two daily newspapers at intervals of not exceeding one week: Provided that the Net Asset Value of any scheme for special target segment or any monthly income scheme which are not mandatorily required to be listed in any stock exchange under Regulation 32, may publish the Net Asset Value at monthly or quarterly intervals as may be permitted by the Board.

V. Pricing of Units

1. The price at which the units may be subscribed or sold and the price at which such units may at any time be repurchased by the mutual fund shall be made available to the investors.
2. The mutual fund, in case of open ended scheme, shall at least once a week publish in a daily newspaper of all India circulation, the sale and repurchase price of units.
3. While determining the prices of the units, the mutual fund shall ensure that the repurchase price is not lower than 93% of the Net Asset Value and the sale price is not higher than 107% of the Net Asset Value. Provided that the repurchase price of the units of a close ended scheme shall not be lower than 95% of the Net Asset Value:
4. The price of units shall be determined with reference to the last determined Net Asset Value as mentioned in sub-regulation (3) unless,

   (*a*) The scheme announces the Net Asset Value on a daily basis; and

   (*b*) The sale price is determined with or without a fixed premium added to the future net asset value which is declared in advance

QUESTIONS

Fill in the Blanks:

1. The company which sets up a mutual fund is called __________.
2. Small investors can enter into big companies through _________.
3. _________ actually manages a mutual fund.
4. Each scheme of a mutual fund must be registered with a __________.

State whether true or false:

1. Mutual fund schemes involve both open and close ended schemes.
2. Units of mutual fund schemes can be publicly traded.
3. Mutual funds are free from risks.
4. The repurchase price of a mutual fund unit is always sinked to its net asset value.

Answer in detail:

Q.1. Discuss the dynamics of a mutual fund.

❑❑❑

24 AMERICAN AND GLOBAL DEPOSITORY RECEIPTS

ADR DEFINED

An American Depository Receipt (ADR) is a physical certificate evidencing ownership in one or several ADSs. The terms ADR and ADS are often used interchangeably.

An American Depository Share (ADS) is a US dollar denominated form of equity ownership in a non-US company. It represents the foreign shares of the company held on deposit by a custodian bank in the company's home country and carries the corporate and economic rights of the foreign shares, subject to the terms specified on the ADR certificate.

CONCEPT OF ADRS

ADRs provide US investors with a convenient way to invest in non-US securities without having to worry about the complex details of cross-border transactions; they offer the same economic benefits enjoyed by the domestic shareholders of the non-US company. ADRs are issued by a US bank, such as JP Morgan, that functions as a depositary on behalf of the non US company. Each ADR is backed by a specific number or fraction of shares in the non-US company. The relationship between the number of ADRs and the number of foreign shares is typically referred to as the ADR ratio.

ADRs can be listed on any of the US exchanges, such as the New York Stock Exchange (NYSE) and the American Stock Exchange (AMEX), and may be quoted for trading on the National Association of Securities Dealers Automated Quotation System (NASDAQ), the NASD's over-the-counter market, or the pink sheets. They can also be privately placed and traded. The concept of ADR has been extended to other geographical markets, resulting in structures known as global depositary receipts (GDRs), international depositary receipts (IDRs), and European depositary receipts (EDRs), which are generally traded or listed in one or more international markets.

Although ADRs are US dollar denominated securities and pay dividends in US dollars, they do not eliminate the currency risk associated with an investment in a non-US company.

TYPES OF ADRS

Sponsored and Unsponsored ADR Programs

These ADRs are created and offered to the investors with a company's active participation hence the name sponsored ADRs.

Issuers seeking the benefits of ADRs generally pursue what are called sponsored ADR programs. They initiate the process and, working with a depositary bank, actively manage the program going forward.

The issuer benefits by making a strategic foray into the US market, controlling its image and reputation in the capital markets. In general, only sponsored ADRs can be listed on the major stock exchanges or quoted under the NASDAQ system. While most new ADR programs are sponsored, many unsponsored programs (in which the ADRs are created and offered to investors without a company's active participation) still exist.

LEVEL I ADR

The most basic form of sponsored ADR program is a Level I ADR. Level I ADR is used when the issuer is not initially seeking to raise capital in the US markets or does not wish to, or can't, list its ADRs on an exchange or on NASDAQ Level I ADR program offers an easy and relatively inexpensive way for an issuer to gauge interest in its securities and begin building a presence in the US securities markets.

Trading

Level I ADRs are traded in the over-the-counter (OTC) market, with bid and ask prices published daily and distributed by the National Daily Quotation Bureau in the pink sheets. Prices may also be posted on the OTC Bulletin Board (OTCBB). Due to the SEC's recent permanent approval of the OTCBB system, however-effective April 1, 1998-all non-US equity securities, inculding ADRs, must be registered with the SEC pursuant to Secion 12 of the 1934 Securities Exchanges Act to remain eligible for quotation in the OTCBB system.

Regulations and Disclosure

Level I ADR programs currently require minimal Securities Exchange Commission (SEC) registration: The issuer seeks exemption from the SEC's traditional reporting requirements. Under this exemption, the company agrees to send to the SEC summaries or copies of any public reporting documents required in its home market (including documents for regulatory agencies, stock exchanges, or direct shareholder communications). The depositary, working with the issure, also files the Form F-6 registration statement with the SEC in order to establish the program.

LEVEL II ADR

In a Level II ADR program, the ADRs are listed on the US securities exchange or quoted on NASDAQ, thereby offering higher visibility in the US market, more active trading, and greater liquidity.

Trading

Level II ADRs can be listed and traded on one of the US securities exchanges (including NYSE, AMEX, and others). Alternatively, they can be quoted on NASDAQ.

Regulations and Disclosure

Level II ADR programs must comply with the full registration and reporting requirements of the SEC's Exchange Act, which entails the following:

- Form F-6 registration statement, to register the ADRs to be issued
- Form 20-F registration statement, which contains detailed financial disclosure about the issuer, including financial statements and a reconciliation of those statements to US GAAP, to register the listing of the ADRs
- Annual reports and any interim financial statements submitted on a regular, timely basis to the SEC

LEVEL III ADR

In the most high-profile form of sponsored ADR program, Level III, an issuer floats a public offering of ADRs in the United States and lists the ADRs on one of the US exchanges or NASDAQ. The benefits of a Level III program are substantial: It allows the issuer to raise capital and leads to much greater visibility in the US market.

Trading

Level III ADRs can be listed and traded on one of the U.S. securities exchanges (including NYSE and AMEX) or on NASDAQ.

Regulations and Disclosure

Level III ADR programs must comply with various SEC rules, including the full registration and reporting requirements of the SEC's Exchange Act. This entails the following:

- Form F-6 registration statement, to register the ADRs.
- Form 20-F registration statement, an annual filing that contains detailed financial disclosure from the issuer, including financial statements and a full reconciliation of those statements to US GAAP
- Form F-1, to register the equity securities underlying the ADRs that are offered publicly in the US for the first time, including a prospectus to inform potential investors about the company and the risks inherent in its businesses, the offering price for the securities, and the plan for distributing the shares
- Annual reports and any interim financial statements submitted on a regular, timely basis to the SEC and to all registered public shareholders.

OTHER KINDS OF ADRS

Rule 144A ADRs

Many companies seek to raise capital in the US markets privately by issuing restricted securities under Rule 144A, which do not require SEC review. Rule 144A facilitates the trading of privately placed securities by sophisticated institutional investors (also known as Qualified Institutional Buyers, or QIBs; they must own or manage at least $100 million in securities).

Global Depositary Recepits (GDRs)

GDRs allow issuers of raise capital in two or more markets simultaneously, thus broadening their shareholder base. They can be settled outside the US (using a link connecting the two major European clearance and settlement facilities, Euroclear and Cedel, with the major US clearance and settlement facility, the Depository Trust Company, or DTC) and can be traded in the Rule 144A private market. Under SEC Regulation S, securities offered or sold to investors outside the US are not subject to SEC registration requirements.

Mechanics of Issuance and Cancellation of ADRs

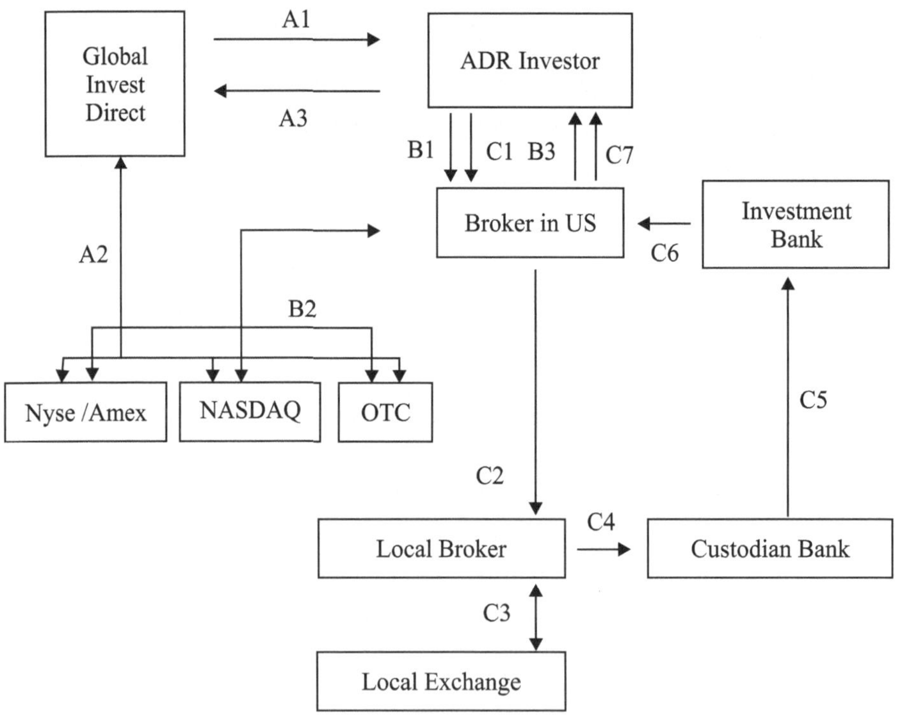

A broker-dealer can purchase existing ADRs in the United States or purchase underlying shares in an issuer's home market and have new ADRs created, or issued, by the depositary bank. While the pool of available ADRs is constantly changing, the broker-dealer decides whether to purchase existing ADRs or have new ones issued, depending on such factors as availability, pricing, and market conditions in the United States and the issuer's home market. To create new ADRs, underlying shares are deposited with a custodian bank in the issuer's home market. The depositary then issues ADRs representing those shares. The process for canceling ADRs is similar to the issuance process, but the steps are reversed. The above chart and description provide a more detailed explanation, including the parties and steps involved.

THE ADR PURCHASE AND ISSUANCE PROCESS: THREE SCENARIOS

Purchase

Global Invest Direct

A1 Investor enrolls and places order through Investment Bank's investment program such as Global Invest Direct Program.

A2 Investment Bank purchases ADRs in the applicable market.

A3 This is followed by Settlement of the ADRs and credit to the account of the investor.

Existing ADRs

B1 Investor places order with broker in the United States

B2 Broker in the United States purchases ADRs in the applicable market.

B3 Settlement and delivery of the ADRs (in book-entry or certificate form).

New ADRs

C1 Investor places order with broker in the United States.

C2 Broker in the United States places order with local broker (outside US) for equivalent shares.

C3 Local broker purchases shares in local market.

C4 Local shares are deposited with Investment bank's custodian.

C5 Investment bank receives confirmation of share deposit.

C6 Investment bank issues new ADRs and delivers them to broker in the US.

C7 Settlement and delivery of the ADRs (in book-entry or certificate form).

Issuance

To request the issuance of new ADRs, a broker needs to own or purchase share in the local market

The shares are then deposited with the designated local custodian.

The custodian informs investment bank that the shares have been deposited in its account.

Investment bank issues ADRs and delivers them through the Depositary Trust Company to the broker.

Cancellation of ADR

To cancel ADRs, a broker needs to deposit the ADRs with investment bank and submit a cancellation request.

Investment bank instructs the custodian to release the shares.

The custodian delivers the shares as instructed.

Pricing of ADR

As per the norms laid down by the finance ministry, companies going in for domestic offering of shares and a simultaneous or follow-on offering in the ADR/GDR would be exempt from the pricing guidelines for overseas offerings , provided the ADR/GDRs are priced at or above the domestic offer price.

To avail oneself of the exemption, the follow-on overseas offering has to be within 30 days of the domestic issue.

The Finance Ministry has said that companies going for such simultaneous or immediate follow-on offering will have to take SEBI's approval and that the capital market regulator would specify the percentage to be offered in the domestic and ADR/GDR markets.

In its guidelines for GDRs/FCCBs issued in August, the Government had stipulated that the overseas offering should be made at a price not less than the higher of the following two averages : (*i*) The average of the weekly high and low of the closing prices of the related shares quoted on the stock exchange during the six months preceding the relevant date; (*ii*) The average of the weekly high and low of the closing prices of the related shares quoted on a stock exchange during the two weeks preceding the relevant date.

The 'relevant date' would be the date 30 days prior to the date on which the meeting of the general body of shareholders is held, in terms of Section 81 (IA) of the Companies Act, 1956, for considering the proposed issue.

The pricing guidelines were part of a major revision of the guidelines on ADRs/GDRs/FCCBs whereby the Finance Ministry has made it mandatory for unlisted companies that have raised funds from such overseas offerings to list on the domestic stock exchanges within a stipulated time frame.

It had said that such listing would have to be done within three years of the issuance of GDRs/FCCBs or on making profit in any financial year starting from 2005-06, whichever is earlier.

It had been stipulated that unlisted companies that have not yet accessed the GDR/FCCB route for raising funds overseas would require a prior or simultaneous listing in the domestic market along with the overseas offering. Listed companies not eligible to raise funds from the domestic market had been barred from raising funds abroad.

Advantages Of ADRs

For issuers, there are several reasons for launching and managing an ADR program:

- An ADR program can stimulate investor interest, enhance a company's visibility, broaden its shareholder base, and increase liquidity.

- By enabling a company to tap US equity markets, the ADR offers a new avenue for raising capital, often at highly competitive costs. For companies with a desire to build a stronger presence in the United States, an ADR program can help finance US initiatives or facilitate US acquisitions.
- ADRs can provide enhanced communications with shareholders in the United States.
- ADRs provide an easy way for US employees of non-US companies to invest in their companies' employee stock purchase plans.
- Features such as dividend reinvestment and direct purchase programs can help ensure a continual stream of investment into an issuer's program.
- ADR ratios can be adjusted to help ensure that an issuer's ADRs trade in a comparable range with those of its peers in the US market.

The core benefit for investors - individuals and institutions alike - is that ADRs make it easy to purchase and hold a non-US issuer's securities. Furthermore:

- ADRs trade easily and conveniently in US dollars and settle through US clearinghouses.
- Publicly traded ADRs are registered with the US Securities and Exchange Commission (SEC).
- For companies that typically pay dividends, ADRs mean those dividends are paid promptly and in US dollars.
- Many institutional investors are restricted from investing in securities that do not trade on a US exchange, so listed ADRs represent a way to add international exposure to a portfolio.

GDRS and EDRS

Two other forms of Depository Receipts are: European Depositary Receipts (EDRs) and Global Depositary Receipts (GDRs). They are similar to ADRs except that they are primarily aimed at non-US resident investors and are intended to trade mainly in markets outside the US.

EDRs are used by corporations (of whatever country) to enable their shares to be indirectly purchased by individuals in Europe but not in the US market or other markets. EDRs in Europe trade through various Euromarket clearing systems such as Euroclear and Cedel and many are listed on the major European stock exchanges.

By way of contrast, GDRs will trade in two or more markets such as Europe and Asia.

Normally, EDRs and GDRs are priced in US dollars thereby enabling non-resident investors to indirectly trade in the issuing company's stock without the risk of holding investments denominated in a possibly weak local currency.

EDRs and GDRs provide several other benefits to global investors including the following:

A share ownership interest in overseas companies may be easily purchased by non-resident investors even though the non-resident companies involved do not have their actual shares listed on the stock exchanges of the non-resident's jurisdiction.

EDRs and GDRs have low commission costs compared with shares bought directly in the overseas markets. EDRs and GDRs also provide the following benefits to issuer companies such as the following:

- They serve to increase the liquidity of the shares of the issuer company globally;
- They provide a means of accessing international capital markets;

EDRs and GDRs may be purchased through most major brokerage firms and international financial institutions.

QUESTIONS

Fill in the Blanks:

1. ADRs carry the _______ and _________ rights of foreign shares.
2. The relationship between ADRs and number of foreign shares is referred to as ______.
3. There are two types of ADRs _________and ___________.
4. Depository Receipts issued in Europe are called _________ and those issued in other countries are called ______.
5. than USA are called _______.
6. The most high profile ADR program is _______.

State whether true or false:

1. ADRs cannot be placed privately.
2. ADRs do not bear currency risk.
3. Level I ADRs are not listed on an exchange.
4. ADRs/GDRs priced at or above the domestic offer price are exempt from pricing guidelines.
5. ADR ratio is non adjustable.

Answer in detail:

Q.1. Explain the mechanism of issue of ADR.

Q.2. What are the various types of ADRs and what are the benefits of issue of ADRs?

Q.3. What is the difference between ADRs, GDRs & EDRs. What are the benefits of GDRs and EDRs over ADRs?

❑❑❑

25 DEBT SECURITIZATION

DEFINITION OF SECURITIZATION

Securitization, or Debt securitization of debt, or asset securitization, is a process by which selected receivables, which are usually not liquid on their own, are converted into marketable securities through restructuring of cash flows generated by them. Securitization, in fact involves credit enhancement and repackaging of assets in the form of collateralized securities or loans. It is a form of credit arbitrage transaction that allows risk management by separating a specific pool of assets from the balance sheet of the originator of securitization. Moreover, unlike the case of conventional debt financing, where the interest and principal obligations of a borrowing entity are serviced out of its own general cash flows, servicing of debt with asset backed securities (Asset Backed Securities) created through securitization is from the cash flows originating from its underlying assets.

HISTORY OF SECURITIZATION

In the middle of the 1900's banks who acted as principal lenders funded loans primarily by deposits and sometimes through debt. But after World War II, banks and depository institutions simply could not meet the rising demand for credit. So, Banks, as well as other financial intermediaries who found a great opportunity in lending market, ways of increasing the sources of mortgage funding. To attract investors, investment bankers eventually developed an investment vehicle that segregated mortgage pools, segmented the credit risk, and structured the cash flows from the underlying loans.

In February, 1970, the U.S. Department of Housing and Urban Development did a transaction using a mortgage-backed security. In this year the Government National Mortgage Association (GNMA) sold securities backed by a portfolio of mortgage loans.

By 1985, securitization techniques that had been developed in the mortgage market were applied for the first time to a class of non-mortgage assets — automobile loans.

An early auto loan deal was a $60 million securitization originated by Marine Midland Bank and securitized in 1985 by the Certificate for Automobile Receivables Trust.

The first significant bank credit card sale came to market in 1986 with a private placement of $50 million of outstanding bank card loans. This transaction demonstrated to investors that, if the yields were high enough, loan pools could support asset sales with higher expected losses and administrative costs than was true within the mortgage market. After the success of this initial transaction, investors grew to accept credit card receivables as collateral, and banks developed structures to normalize the cash flows.

The market has evolved a lot and at the end of 2004, the larger sectors of this market were credit card-backed securities (21 per cent), home-equity backed securities (25 per cent), automobile-backed securities (13 per cent), and collateralized debt obligations (15 per cent). Among the other market segments are student loan-backed securities (6 per cent), equipment leases (4 per cent), manufactured housing (2 per cent), small business loans (such as loans to convenience stores and gas stations), and aircraft leases.

SECURITIZABLE ASSETS

All assets generating stable and certain cash flows can be taken up for securitization. Most of the securitized paper issued has underlying periodic cash flows which are secured through contracts that lay down cash flow volumes, yield and timing which will be coming through the underlying assets. Securitization of auto loans, credit card receivables, computer leases, unsecured consumer loans, residential and commercial mortgages, franchise/royalty payments, and other receivables relating to telecom, trade, toll road and future export are being done in practice. Generally securitization involves creation of asset portfolios which have homogeneity with regard to credit, maturity and interest rate risk.

REASONS FOR SECURITIZATION

Securitization effort involves considerable investments in time and resources. Hence, as compared to other financing alternatives available to borrowers it can even be more expensive, at least in the initial stages. However, it has been established that a continuing securitization program rather than a single deal often tends to reduce the costs, as over a period of time economies of scale develop. Keeping this in mind, many securitization programs are run with a long-term strategic perspective. However, the main motives behind securitization are:

Financing source

Securitization is separate from the originator's own obligations. So a well structured Asset Backed Securities stands on its own credit rating and thus generates genuine incremental funding. This is so as the originator's existing creditors may invest in the Asset Based Securitization in addition to providing lines of credit to the originator.

Moreover, there may also be other investors in the Asset Backed Securities who do not have a lending relationship with the originator. It is also possible to achieve a superior credit rating for the Asset

Backed Securities than the originator's own rating through appropriate structuring and credit enhancement. This involves focusing on high grades, which otherwise may not be possible for an originator. Also, at times when the originator is not permitted to issue capital market instruments on his own Asset Backed Securities could help overcome financial constraints.

Improvement in Balance Sheet Statistics

The benefit of underlying a cash sale, *i.e.,* freeing up the capital of the originator would apply in the case of all securitization transactions. As a result of this, the balance sheet gets compressed and becomes more robust. Its financial ratios also get improved. Alternately, reduction in leverage after securitized sale can be obtained by adding on new assets to the balance sheet. Securitization can also generate matched funding for balance sheet assets. Further, it may also enable the disposal of non-core assets through suitable structuring.

Transfer of Risk

Securitization transfers most of the credit risk in the portfolio to the Asset Backed Securities investors and helps to quantify the residual credit risk that the originator is exposed to. This helps, the originator to take larger exposure to individual obligors as well as provide a higher degree of comfort to his creditors.

Securitization also transfers the originator's market risks, *i.e.,* liquidity, interest rate and prepayment risks, to Asset Backed Securities investors and reduces risk capital requirement. This can lead to more competitive pricing of the underlying asset products.

Improvement in Efficiency in Operating processes

Securitization involves portfolio analysis and information collection which often leads to serious re-examination and consequent reengineering of operating processes within the originator organization.

Further, handling of various functional components, such as origination, funding, risk management and administration, through specialists often achieved through outsourcing, promotes efficiency across operating processes.

Improvement in Operating Leverage

The originator of securitization usually assumes the function of the servicer, the issuing and paying agent, and sometimes that of the credit enhancer. As a result of all these functions fees is collected by the originator on account of these the difference between yield generated by the assets and the cost of funds which is called excess servicing, is also normally taken by the originator. These income streams can increase the operating leverage of the originator generating income from a larger asset base than what may be otherwise possible for a given capital structure.

Reduces Funding Costs

Through Securitization, a company rated BB but with AAA worthy cash flow would be able to borrow at possibly AAA rates. This is the number one reason to securitize a cash flow and can have tremendous impacts on borrowing costs.

Reduces Asset-liability Mismatch

Depending on the portfolio structure chosen, securitization can offer perfect matched funding of liabilities with assets by eliminating funding exposure in terms of both duration and pricing basis.

Lower Capital Requirements

Some firms, due to legal, regulatory, or other reasons, have a limit or range upto which leverage is allowed . By securitizing some of their assets, which qualifies as a sale for accounting purposes, these firms will be able to lessen the equity on their balance sheets while maintaining the "earning power" of the asset.

Locking in Profits

For a given block of business, the total profits have not yet emerged and thus remain uncertain. Once the block has been securitized, the level of profits get locked in for that company.

Admissibility

Future cashflows may not get full credit in a company's accounts (life insurance companies, for example, may not always get full credit for future surpluses in their regulatory balance sheet), and a securitization effectively turns an admissible future surplus flow into an admissible immediate cash asset.

Liquidity

Future cashflows may simply be balance sheet items which currently are not available for spending, whereas once the book has been securitized, the cash would be available for immediate spending or investment.

BENEFITS OF SECURITIZATION TO INVESTORS

Decreased risk due to diversification

The pack assets representing the obligations of a number of entities is usually more flexible to event risks than the obligations of a single borrower. This means the risk that the credit rating of the security will deteriorate due to circumstances usually beyond the obligor's control is much higher in the case of single borrower. The diversification that the securitization pool represents makes the Asset Backed Securities largely immune to event risks.

Higher yields for constant risk

Asset Backed Securities usually offer higher yields over securities of comparable credit and maturities. The yield spread typically represents the premium paid to compensate for prepayment risk, amortizing cash flows and the uniqueness of the instrument. In some cases, Asset Backed Securities also provide an opportunity to invest into a pool of otherwise illiquid and inaccessible assets.

Structured issuances

Through appropriate structuring, Asset Backed Securities can be structured to meet investor standards on credit quality, yield and maturity. Working with a pool of receivables gives the originator the needed flexibility to be able to offer investors a variety of options around which issuances could be made.

Increased Secondary Market Liquidity

Institutional investors place a considerable weight age to instrument liquidity while devising their investment portfolios. Asset Backed Securities does fit the requirement in this regard. While the ideal scenario would be to have an active secondary market trading in Asset Backed Securities, institutional investors are often willing to settle for credible liquidity backstops provided by well-rated institutions.

PARTIES IN A SECURITIZATION TRANSACTION

Securitization programs usually involve several participants, each carrying out a specialist function, such as, creating and analyzing the asset pool, administration, credit rating, accounting, legal negotiation, etc. These include:

- The Originator – also interchangeably referred to as the Seller – is the entity whose receivable portfolio forms the basis for Asset Backed Securities issuance,
- Special Purpose Vehicle (SPV), which as the issuer of the Asset Backed Securities ensures adequate distancing of the instrument from the originator,
- The Servicer, who bears all administrative responsibilities relating to the securitization transaction,
- The Trustee or the Investor Representative, who act in a fiduciary capacity safeguarding the interests of investors in the Asset Backed Securities ,
- The Credit Rating Agency, which provides an objective estimate of the credit risk in the securitization transaction by assigning a well-defined credit rating,
- The Regulators, whose principal concerns relate to capital adequacy, liquidity, and credit quality of the Asset Backed Securities, and balance sheet treatment of the transaction,
- Service providers such as Credit Enhancers and Liquidity Providers, and,
- Specialist functionaries such as legal and tax counsels, accounting firms, pool auditors.

However, the most important than all the aforementioned are the investors in the securitised paper. Investors are the ultimate judges of any securitization effort. Originators should therefore interact actively with the investor community to get to know investor preferences and concerns for effective structuring and distribution of Asset Backed Securities. Such knowledge would also make the origination process more efficient.

Further, investors have their constraints in the form of legal restrictions, complexity of credit analysis, house name limits, long response time for in-house approvals, etc., all of which can block a deal, and more so in the case of Asset Backed Securities , which, on account of their uniqueness and complexity, present a host of issues which are not normally encountered, say in a straightforward bond investment.

SECURITIZATION PROCESS

Essential features of a securitization transaction comprise the following:

1. Creation of asset pool and its sale

The originator/seller (of assets) creates a pool of assets and executes a legal true sale of the same to a special purpose vehicle (SPV). An SPV in such cases is either a trust or a company, as may be appropriate under applicable law, setup to carry out a restricted set of activities, management of which would usually rest with an independent board of directors.

2. Issuance of the securitized paper

This activity is usually performed by the SPV. Design of the instrument however would be based on the nature of interest that investors would have on the asset pool. In the case of pass-through securities issuances, the investors will have a direct ownership interest in the underlying assets, while pay-through securities are debt issued by the SPV secured by the assets and their cash flows.

3. Credit Risk

In case of securitization the accretions on the asset-backed security, *i.e.,* interest, amortization and redemption payments, are entirely dependent on the performance of the pooled assets, and will have nothing to do with the credit of the originator. By the same argument, such cash flows would also be not influenced by events affecting the condition of the originator, including insolvency.

4. Pool Selection

The process of selecting assets to build a securitization pool would take into careful consideration, loan characteristics that are important from a cash flow, legal, and credit points of view, such as type of asset, minimum and maximum loan size, vintage, rate, maturity and concentration limits geographic, single-borrower, etc.). 'Cherry-picking' to include only the highest quality assets in the pool should be consciously avoided. Ideal selection should be a random choice among assets conforming only to cash flow or legal criteria. Often, substitution of eligible assets in the place of original assets that mature/ prepay in order to maintain the level of asset cover would also be required.

5. Administration

Formal delineation of duties and responsibilities relating to administration of securitised assets, including payment servicing and managing relationship with the final obligors must be spelt out clearly through a contractual agreement with the entity who would perform those functions.

In addition, the following features are often included as part of a securitization transaction:

- Credit enhancement to support timely payments of interest and principal and to handle delinquencies,
- Independent credit rating of the securitised paper from a well-known credit rating agency, and,
- Providing liquidity support to investors, such as appointment of market makers.

DOCUMENTATION

Documentation is of great significance in securitization. Although the specific procedure may vary from one jurisdiction to another, there is a laid down body of documentation that is normally applicable in most cases.

On the first priority the legal opinions must provide clearance on all fundamental, such as the legality of the transaction, the bankruptcy remoteness of the issuer from the originator, the issuer's authority to enter into such transactions, the legal true sale of receivables to the issuer, the creation of security over the receivable pool, etc.

Other documentation relate to receivables, security, administration and operational aspects. Receivable documentation should first establish the existence and nature of underlying obligations, such as payment schedules, the conditions under which the obligors may either default or disclaim payments, and terms of sale of such receivables. It must also confirm that the receivables have been originated in compliance with the applicable statutes. When receivables are sold, documentation specifying the items sold, the mechanics of sale and the representations and warranties made by the seller on their characteristics would be drawn up. Further, the claims of investors in Asset Backed Securities over such flows need to be established clearly through the security documentation. Service documentation specifying the duties and responsibilities of the servicer or servicing agent would also be a key one. Related documentation in addition to the above would typically comprise those relating to credit enhancement, liquidity and market-making, listing agreements with stock exchanges, as well as transaction prospectus or information memoranda, as may be appropriate.

STRUCTURING CONSIDERATIONS

These considerations determine certain specifications related to Asset Backed Securitization such as, the issuer, the relevant tax and accounting treatment, and other key factors. Every Asset Backed Securities issuance may have to be developed differently in order to take the best advantage of the various factors.

First, the structuring decisions would concern the manner in which the pool of assets will be sold/transferred.

This would be followed by the design of the Asset Backed Securities instrument, as either a pass through or a pay through security. Pass-throughs represent direct ownership interests in the underlying assets, which are typically held in trust for the investors, so that payments on the assets are passed through to the investors directly from the assets (after payment of all fees and expenses, including excess servicing).

Pay through, on the other hand, are general obligations or preferred stock of the issuer (SPV), substantially all the assets of which consist of a pool of receivables and the related credit enhancement or other structural support.

Payments on these assets are said to be paid rather than passed through to the investors. As the assets are owned by this entity rather than the investors, who as a matter of law receive payments on a separate security backed by the general credit of the entity rather than an interest in the assets.

Tax and accounting treatments constitute other important dimensions of structuring. Typical tax issues that need to be addressed relate to transfer charges (stamp duty), capital gains taxation as applicable to the originator on sale of assets, taxation of the issuer, and withholding tax or taxes deducted at source as applicable to the issuer and the investors.

Accounting treatment of securitization could fall into one of the following three categories, *viz.,* full derecognition, partial derecognition where only transferred assets receive derecognition, and full on-balance sheet recognition. Specialist opinion must be obtained on both tax and accounting aspects. These would be environment specific Credit enhancement of the Asset Backed Securities would also be an important structuring consideration, as it strives to strike a balance between the investor and the issuer needs on the credit quality of the instrument.

Typical forms of credit enhancement include: Spread Account or Reserve Account, Overcollateralisation, Letters of credit, Insurance company guarantees, Senior/Subordinated structure, etc. Other structuring issues that need to be addressed relate to extraction of excess servicing, identification of payment and loss priorities, etc.

SECURITIZATION IN INDIA

Since 1996, an estimated Rs.700 crore of asset-backed securities have been issued in the Indian market. This includes issuances of some high quality securitised paper structured largely in accordance with international standards. Majority of the Asset Backed Securities issued in India have been backed by auto loan receivables. Due to boom in real estate property developer receivables has also been issued. But securitization involving credit cards, mortgages, and future receivables are yet to come, as the existing legal framework is not supportive in this regard. Much of the securitization effort in the country till now has been done by commercial banks, in collaboration with credit rating agencies. However, of late, some investors have emerged from the mutual funds and insurance sectors, although their level of interest at present seems limited.

BENEFITS OF SECURITIZATION IN INDIA

In the Indian context, the benefits that securitization can bring about can be quite significant. In any economy, an opportunity that permits effective use of available capital is of importance. In addition, the ability to diversify one's funding base by reaching out to new investor markets, without increasing the financial leverage, which may otherwise have regulatory implications in some cases, is also of definite value. Obtaining matched funding leading to effective balance sheet management is particularly significant from commercial banks' perspective. Reallocation of risks in a planned and transparent manner helps in managing them better. In securitization originators also stand to benefit on account of possible gains that would come in the form of improvements in their credit and operating processes.

As the Indian banking system has a long history it is possible to create substantial amount of Asset Backed Commercial paper in accordance with the rating required about the credit quality This would ensure continuous supply of assets that can be tailored to meet the credit appetites of investors.

Institutional investors may not only benefit from such customized issuances, but also may have access to invest into otherwise illiquid assets at superior yields without compromising on their credit standards.

In the medium to longer term, the securitization process could upgrade the level of sophistication of banking and finance in the country. This, in combination with an appropriate regulatory framework, can make securitization an important catalyst in mobilizing domestic savings as well as attracting foreign capital, which can be of immense value, particularly in the context of capital requirements to develop the country's infrastructure sector.

Securitization has developed a lot but areas such as project finance, telecom, toll road and other similar receivables which are left could well become reality for securitization in the medium term future.

FUTURE STRATEGIES

It is important to draw inspiration from various factors that have led to the development of global Asset Backed Securities markets as successes and evaluate if some of those factors, apply in the Indian context. Major factors that have spurred the development of Asset Backed Securities markets in the world include:

- Competitive pressures released due to deregulation, forcing sharp declines in bank lending margins,
- Successive financial sector crises (some of which may actually be attributable to credit quality dilution on account of fierce competition) leading to sectoral level credit deterioration,
- Universal adoption of capital adequacy standards, with efficiency of capital usage increasingly becoming the basis of evaluating banks and financial institutions,
- Increasing functional specialization leading to large scale outsourcing,
- Giant strides in information technology,
- Global trend towards making all debt issuances in tradable form, and, most importantly,
- The patronage (including credit support) of national governments by enacting supportive legislation, setting up specialized agencies to provide credit enhancement, etc.

On evaluation of the above factors it could be found that much of these factors do apply to the Indian financial system, more so at present in an era of economic liberalization, than before.

- Deregulation, shrinking margins, capital adequacy are all present over here, and the benefits of progress in information technology are as much available to India as they are to other countries. In the presence of all these, it may be said that an enabling legal framework and institutional support from the government and its agencies could form the necessary foundations from which an active Asset Backed Securities market could emerge in this country.
- Recognizing that ultimately it is the investor who determines success in this regard, it is worthwhile to examine first as to what regulatory changes are needed from an investor perspective. All over the world, large fixed income investors, such as insurance companies and

pension/provident funds, are the natural choices for distributing Asset Backed Securities . However, in the current scenario in India, the list of instruments permitted for investment by such entities does not include Asset Backed Securities. In fact, a legal definition for Asset Backed Securities does not even exist at present. Hence, it would be ideal to firstly define Asset Backed Securities as a security under the Securities Contracts Regulation Act.

- As the next logical step, appropriately rated Asset Backed Securities may be ranked on par with debentures through a suitable umbrella definition of fixed income securities. This would simplify operational aspects relating to Asset Backed Securities, such as listing on the exchange, as its treatment would then be similar to that of a debenture. The Asset Backed Securities instrument may then become available for investment by insurance companies and registered FIIs.
- Rated Asset Backed Securities may also be permitted for investments by provident funds, pension funds, et al.
- In the case of institutions that come under mandated sectoral asset allocations, Asset Backed Securities backed by receivables from such sectors may be permitted as acceptable equivalents.
- For the longer term viability of securitization, it is vital to broaden the investor base to include sophisticated fixed income investors. Opening up insurance and pension fund sectors would have to be done in this regard.
- The next set of legislative changes concern stamp duty on transfers and the taxation of the issuer. The law should be able to distinguish between revolving and non-revolving asset-backed structures and charge a uniform level of stamp duty. In other words, in the case of revolving asset securitization such as credit cards, replacement assets should not be subject to stamp duty and in such cases, the law should provide a methodology for defining proportionate interest.
- Further, it is also important to rationalise stamp duties at least for the purpose of securitization across the various states.
- The issuer (Special Purpose Vehicle) shall be given a tax status similar to trusts under U.S. law. *i.e.,* the special purpose entity used in pass-throughs, the income of which is not taxed at the entity level, but at the level of the beneficiaries of the entity; the beneficiaries in this case being the investors who hold the Asset Backed Securities issued by the entity. This may be achieved by according securitization SPVs, a tax treatment similar to that of mutual funds. At the initial stages, adequately capitalised banks may be allowed to set up such vehicles.
- Further, setting up of a banking matters tribunal on the lines of consumer courts could also be of help in early enforcement of security interests and this would facilitate the development of Asset Backed Securities market.
- Other than the legal and regulatory changes required, securitization efforts should also cater to some specific preferences of investors. As the Asset Backed Securities market is only at its beginnings at present, it is perhaps necessary for investors to ask for a high level of credit

enhancement that is easily visible and understood, While the economics of catering to such an investor preference will have to be evaluated, it may perhaps be the way to start the Asset Backed Securities market, possibly with some assistance from the government. Yields on such paper may be kept tight initially and once the investor awareness and the level of comfort with the instrument increases, such credit enhancements may be made selective or phased out.

- Indian institutional investors also have a preference for liquidity in the Asset Backed Securities instrument. The facility also needs to be formalized through appropriate documentation. Support from a Government agency or an institution of repute would be of considerable value in this regard.
- In addition to such preferences, institutional investors such as mutual funds also require reliable valuation benchmarks on Asset Backed Securities in order to evaluate their portfolio performance. Until the Asset Backed Securities market reaches a certain critical volume and level of activity, it would be difficult to receive market maker quotations. The liquidity facility required may therefore act as a surrogate valuation benchmark in the interim.

It has been established that in the case of several developed financial markets, asset securitization is an important building block in creating an efficient and broad-based financial system. The concept is highly relevant to emerging economies, given their capital constraints. An enabling policy framework and affirmative actions in this regard from the government can immensely facilitate the development of the asset-backed securities market in India.

Long term advantages of securitization are that, if used strategically, it will enable originators to grow as well as create a sustainable competitive advantage. The growth will come from the funding flexibility it can provide, as balance sheet will pose lesser constraints and the demand for regulatory capital will be proportionately lower.

From a developmental perspective, Asset Backed Securities are essential to develop the domestic debt capital markets in the country in order to mobilize long term savings. While pension funds, insurance companies, etc may function as agents to create such resource mobilization, it is important to bring forward a range of high quality financial assets into which they can invest. In suitable destinations which are in the interest of the nation.

QUESTIONS

Fill in the blanks:

1. Securitization is a form of ____________ arbitrage transaction.
2. Securitization reduces risk due to ____________.
3. ____________ is an issuer of Asset Backed Securities.
4. Asset Backed Securities can be structured to meet investor requirements of _______, ________ and ________.
5. Around ________ crores of Asset Backed Securities have been issued in India since 1996.
6. Accounting treatement of Asset Backed Securities falls into three categories namely _________, __________ and __________.

State whether true or false:

1. All assets whether generating stable and certain cash flows or not can be taken up for securitization.
2. Majority of the Asset Backed Securities issued in India have been backed by auto loan receivables.
3. Institutional investors place a considerable weight age to instrument liquidity while devising their investment portfolios. Asset Backed Securities does not fit the requirement in this regard.
4. In the medium to longer term, the securitization process could upgrade the level of sophistication of banking and finance in the country.

Answer in detail:

Q.1. Define securitization. Explain various participants in securitization process.

Q.2. What is the advantage of securitization? What type of assets should be securitized?

Q.3. What should be the future strategies towards development of securitization in India? Explain the milestones achieved in the area of securitization in India *vis-à-vis* other nations of the world.

❑❑❑

26 DISINVESTMENT

Disinvestment may be defined as the sale of equity and bond capital invested by the government in PSUs. It also involves the sale of government's debt capital in PSUs through securitization.

Disinvestment is generally done to bring in private management to improve the company's performance and to add to the Government's revenue.

GLOBAL PERSPECTIVE

Taking in context the global perspective, the root of disinvestment can perhaps be traced back to 1970s. It was observed in many countries that the performance of the public enterprises was far below the expectations and often worse than that of the private sector. The public sector seemed to perform well only when protected through Government created monopolies, entry reservations, high tariffs and quotas etc. The problems got further accelerated due to pre-emption of massive resources by the under performing public sector which left little money for more urgent social needs and public welfare. These problems were brought in sharp focus after the second oil shock of 1979, when it became clear that the experiments with Government ownership of commercial activities were not succeeding.

In the 1980s, around the globe, it was considered that the proportion of the GNP due to Government economic activity should be reduced to the extent possible. This coincided with the belief that even for natural monopolies, effective regulatory substitutes for competition could be devised that would protect the consumers from the abuse of the monopoly or dominance power of these companies.

It has been argued that Government must not venture into those areas where the private sector can undertake the job efficiently. Lot of emphasis was laid on market driven economies, rather than state administered economies. The collapse of socialist economy of the Soviet block convinced the policy planners, around the world, that role of the state should be that of a regulator and a facilitator rather than of the producer. The resources deployed by the Government for undertaking commercial activities should be unlocked and deployed in social activities.

During the 1980s, USSR started the economic reforms under Perestroika, which swept the economies of Eastern Europe. China also introduced far reaching economic reforms and it was recognized that public sector did not optimise efficiency and productivity of capital. It was realized that the large number of public enterprises working under mixed economies were plagued by over-centralization in decision-making and excessive bureaucratisation.

A new trend of global integration began to emerge and countries all over the world, whether developed or developing, capitalist or socialist, started undergoing vast economic changes, witnessed by the decline in the role of the State in commercial activities and increasing privatisation of state owned enterprises. In 1980s, privatisation had started in real sense in several parts of the world. This was facilitated by the gradual integration of the world economies, which ensured that capital and goods flowed more freely to countries suffering from lack of resources. Foreign capital became freely available to finance large infrastructure projects, for want of which the domestic private parties were unable to come forward, and State support was necessary.

Acceptance of the WTO regime by most of the countries has since led to gradual abolition of quantitative restrictions, reduction in duties and removal of restrictions on inter country trade. As a result, the relevance of the State in providing resources for various commercial activities and protecting the interests of consumers has considerably reduced.

It became increasingly evident that to maximize choice before the consumers, all bureaucratic controls over business activities should be removed. Business and private entrepreneurship are to be encouraged to face competition for optimal utilization of capital and resources – leading to greater consumer choice and enhanced efficiency of production and services.

EVOLUTION OF PUBLIC SECTOR IN INDIA

Before independence, there was almost no 'Public Sector' in the Indian economy. The only instances worthy of mention were the Railways, the Posts and Telegraphs, the Port Trust, the Ordnance and the Aircraft factories and few Government managed undertakings like the Government salt factories, quinine factories etc.

After independence and with the advent of planning, India opted for the dominance of the public sector, firmly believing that political independence without economic self-reliance was not good for the country. The passage of Industrial Policy Resolution of 1956 and adoption of the socialist pattern of society led to a deliberate enlargement of our public sector. It was believed that a dominant public sector would reduce the inequality of income and wealth, and advance the general prosperity of the nation. The planners also seemed to believe that by placing the management and workers in public enterprises in a position of responsibility and trust, they would develop a sense of the public good and their actions and aspirations would naturally reflect what was best for the country.

Main objectives for setting up the Public Sector Enterprises

The main objectives for setting up the Public Sector Enterprises as stated in the Industrial Policy Resolution of 1956 were:

- To help in the rapid economic growth and industrialisation of the country and create the necessary infrastructure for economic development;
- To earn return on investment and thus generate resources for development;
- To promote redistribution of income and wealth;

- To create employment opportunities;
- To promote balanced regional development;
- To assist in the development of small-scale and ancillary industries; and
- To promote import substitutions, save and earn foreign exchange for the economy.

In tune with the widespread belief at that time, the 2nd Five Year Plan stated very clearly that 'the adoption of socialist pattern of society as the national objective, as well as the need for planned and rapid development, require that all industries of basic and strategic importance, or in the nature of public utility services, should be in the public sector. Other industries, which are essential and require investment on a scale, which only the state, in the present circumstances, could provide, have also to be in the public sector. The state has, therefore, to assume direct responsibility for the future development of industries over a wider area.

The Second Plan further emphasized that ' the public sector has to expand rapidly. It has not only to initiate developments which the private sector is either unwilling or unable to undertake, it has to play the dominant role in shaping the entire pattern of investment in the economy, whether it makes the investments directly or whether these are made by the private sector. The private sector has to play its part within the framework of the comprehensive plan accepted by the community.'

GENESIS AND RATIONALE FOR DISINVESTMENT IN INDIA

For almost four decades, India was pursuing a path of development in which public sector was expected to be the engine of growth. However, the public sector had overgrown itself and their shortcomings started getting reflected in the shape of low capacity utilization and low efficiency due to over manning and poor work ethics,. They also suffered from over capitalisation due to substantial time and cost overruns, inability to innovate, take quick and timely decisions, large interference in decision making process etc.

The Government started to deregulate the areas of its operation and subsequently, the disinvestment in Public Sector Enterprises was announced. The process of deregulation was aimed at enlarging competition and allowing new firms to enter the markets. The market was thus opened up to domestic entrepreneurs / industrialists and norms for entry of foreign capital were liberalised.

Because of the current revenue expenditure on items such as interest payments, wages and salaries of Government employees and subsidies, the Government is left with hardly any surplus for capital expenditure on social and physical infrastructure.

The Government likes to spend on basic education, primary health and family welfare, large amount of resources are blocked in several non-strategic sectors such as hotels, trading companies, consultancy companies, textile companies, chemical and pharmaceuticals companies, consumer goods companies etc.

Not only this - the continued existence of the PSUs is forcing the Government to commit further resources for the sustenance of many non-viable PSUs. The Government continues to expose the taxpayers' money to risk, which it can readily avoid. To top it all, there is a huge amount of debt overhang, which needs to be serviced and reduced before money is available to invest in infrastructure. All this makes disinvestment of the Government stake in the PSUs absolutely imperative.

Primary objectives for disinvesting the Public Sector Enterprises

The primary objectives for privatising the PSEs are, therefore, as follows:

- Releasing large amount of public resources locked up in non-strategic PSEs, for redeployment in areas that are much higher on the social priority, such as, basic health, family welfare, primary education and social and essential infrastructure;
- Reducing further outflow of scarce public resources for sustaining the unviable non-strategic PSEs;
- Reducing the public debt that may assume unmanageable proportions;
- Transferring the commercial risk, to which the taxpayers' money is locked up, the money that is deployed in the PSEs is really the public money and is exposed to an entirely avoidable and needless risk, in most cases;
- Releasing other tangible and intangible resources, such as, large manpower currently locked up in managing the PSEs, and their time and energy, for redeployment in high priority social sectors that are short of such resources.

Other benefits expected from disinvestment:

The other benefits expected to be derived from privatisation are:

- Disinvestment would expose the PSUs to market discipline, thereby forcing them to become more efficient and survive or cease on their own financial and economic strength. They would be able to respond to the market forces much faster and cater to their business needs in a more professional manner. It would also facilitate in freeing such companies from Government control and introduce corporate governance among them.
- Disinvestment should result in wider distribution of wealth through offering of shares of privatised companies to small investors and employees.
- Disinvestment would have a beneficial effect on the capital market as it would increase the floating stock; give the market more depth and liquidity, give investors easier exit options, help in establishing more accurate benchmarks for valuation and pricing, and facilitate raising of funds by the privatised companies for their projects or expansion, in future.
- Opening up the public sector to appropriate private investment would increase economic activity and have an overall beneficial effect on the economy, employment and tax revenues in the medium to long term.
- In many areas, *e.g.,* the telecom and civil aviation sector, the end of public sector monopoly and privatisation has brought to consumers greater satisfaction by way of more choices, as well as cheaper and better quality of products and services.
- With the quantitative restrictions removed and tariff levels revised owing to opening of world markets/WTO agreements, domestic industry has to compete with cheaper imported goods. In the bargain, the common man now has access to a whole range of cheap and quality goods. This would require Indian industries to become more competitive and such restructuring would be easier in a privatised environment.

DISINVESTMENT POLICY

The policy of the Government on disinvestment has evolved over a period and it can be briefly stated in the form of following policy statements made in chronological order:

- In 1991-92, the Government, decided to divest up to 20% of the Government equity in selected PSEs in favour of public sector institutional investors. The objective of the policy was stated to be to broad-base equity, improve management, enhance availability of resources for these PSEs and yield resources for government.
- In 1993, the Rangarajan Committee recommendations emphasised the need for substantial disinvestment. It stated that the percentage of equity to be divested could be up to 49% for industries explicitly reserved for the public sector. It recommended that in exceptional cases, such as the enterprises, which had a dominant market share or where separate identity had to be maintained for strategic reasons, the target public ownership level could be kept at 26%, that is, disinvestment could take place to the extent of 74%. In all other cases, it recommended 100% divestment of Government stake. However, the Government did not take any decision on the recommendations of the Rangarajan Committee.
- In 1996, the policy formulated by the United Front Government focussed on the following:
  1. To carefully examine the public sector non-core strategic areas;
  2. To set up a Disinvestment Commission for advising on the disinvestment related matters;
  3. To take and implement decisions to disinvest in a transparent manner; thereby ensuring Job security, opportunities for retraining and redeployment to be assured.
- From 1997- 1999 Disinvestment Commission made recommendations on 58 PSEs. The recommendations indicated a shift from public offerings to strategic / trade sales, with transfer of management.
- From 1998-99, the new Government decided to bring down Government shareholding in the PSUs to 26% in the generality of cases, (thus facilitating ownership changes, as was recommended by the Disinvestment Commission). It however, stated that the Government would retain majority holdings in PSEs involving strategic considerations and that the interests of the workers would be protected in all cases.
- From 1999-2000, the policy for 1999 - 2000, as enunciated by the Government, was to strengthen strategic PSUs, privatise non-strategic PSUs through gradual disinvestment or strategic sale and devise viable rehabilitation strategies for weak units. One highlight of the policy was that the expression 'privatisation' was used for the first time.
- The Government classified the Public Sector Enterprises into strategic and non-strategic areas for the purpose of disinvestment. Arms and ammunitions and the allied items of defence equipment, defence air-crafts and warships; Atomic energy and Railway transport were considered strategic whereas; all other Public Sector Enterprises were to be considered non-strategic. For the non-strategic Public Sector Enterprises, it was decided that the reduction of Government stake less than 51% or to 26%, would be taken on the following considerations:

1. Whether the industrial sector requires the presence of the public sector as a countervailing force to prevent concentration of power in private hands, and
2. Whether the industrial sector requires a proper regulatory mechanism to protect the consumer interests before Public Sector Enterprises are privatised.

- In the year 2000 - 01, for the first time the Government made the statement that it was prepared to reduce its stake in the non-strategic PSEs even below 26% if necessary, that there would be increasing emphasis on strategic sales and that the entire proceeds from disinvestment / privatisation would be deployed in social sectors, restructuring of PSEs and retirement of public debt.
- The Government's approach to PSUs had a three-fold objective: revival of potentially viable enterprises; closing down of those PSUs that cannot be revived; and bringing down Government equity in non-strategic PSUs to 26 per cent or lower. The Government decided to disinvest a substantial part of its equity in enterprises such as Indian Airlines, Air India, ITDC, IPCL, VSNL, CMC, BALCO, Hindustan Zinc, and Maruti Udyog.
- In 2001 – 2002, government decided for

  Restructuring assistance to PSUs

  Safety net to workers

  Reduction of debt burden

Government decided to continue to ensure that disinvestment does not result in alienation of national assets, which, through the process of disinvestment, remain where they are. It also kept in mind that disinvestment does not result in private monopolies.

In order to provide complete visibility to the Government's continued commitment of utilisation of disinvestment proceeds for social and infrastructure sectors, the Government set up a Disinvestment Proceeds Fund to be used for financing fresh employment opportunities and investment, and for retirement of public debt.

MAJOR ISSUES IN DISINVESTMENT

Profitability

The return on investments in PSEs, at least for the last two decades, has been quite poor, and the PSEs have not been able to generate resources for development. As a whole, PSUs never earned post tax profits that exceeded 5% of total sales or 6% of capital employed. Also, the PSEs' highest return on Capital Employed is at least 3% points below the interest paid by the Government on its borrowings. Thus, adjusted for the effective interest rate, they had actually been giving negative return on capital. Besides, huge relief had to be given to the loss making PSEs, to help them survive.

Cost Control

On comparing cost structure PSEs and the private sector companies it was revealed how the cost structure in PSEs was increasing as compared to private sector, which was able to contain costs on all parameters. The manufacturing industry was able to take measures to cut costs, while the public sector could not take such measures, perhaps owing to the nature and compulsions of its ownership. With the advent of WTO, and in a falling tariff protection regime, the private sector had been taking measures to cut costs. Public Sector Enterprises have not been successful in this regard. PSEs' performance with regard to manpower costs has also been disappointing.

Recurring Budgetary Support to PSEs

Despite huge investment in the public sector, the Government is required to provide more funds every year that go into maintaining of the unviable / weak PSEs and the extent of drain that the PSEs continue to cause on the exchequer.

Industrial Sickness in PSUs

To save the PSUs from sickness, the government had been sanctioning restructuring packages from time to time. The revival packages include a combination of some or all of the following:

1. Conversion of cash losses to interest free loans or equity
2. Moratorium on payment of all loans
3. Interest holiday on outstanding government loans
4. Write off of outstanding non-plan loans
5. Write off interest on government loans
6. Conversion of loans into equity, etc.
7. Conversion of outstanding cash credit into working capital term loan
8. Concession on existing power tariff (by State Government)
9. Release of fresh loans
10. Conversion of loans into equity, etc.

Despite huge investments shown above the Government had not even been able to achieve turnaround in any of the sick companies

As regards the objective of balanced regional development, despite five decades of attempted industrialisation through the PSEs, there are still many pockets, especially in the eastern and northeastern parts of the country, which woefully lack in industrial growth and infrastructure. Commendable growth has, no doubt, taken place as far as the small scale and ancillary industries are concerned. However, most of these have not been able to keep pace with the times and the changing scenario and suffer from lack of economies of scale, obsolete technologies and many other ills.

The objectives of import substitution, saving and earning foreign exchange through the PSEs too, have met with only limited success.

It has been widely observed that the PSEs have no commercial motivation. Their financial eeds have often to be subordinated to other macro-economic considerations and they often face shortage of funds. They generally survive on monopolistic profits. Apart from all this, the increasing integration of the Indian financial, capital and foreign exchange markets with global markets, starting with the economic reforms of July, 1991 and the recent WTO Agreements, have exposed the public sector to market forces, as a result of which it now finds itself unable to stand on its own feet without State support.

EMPLOYEE ISSUES

Barring the organized private sector, employment levels were stagnant in the 1990's. Of the 1.6 million jobs added in the organized sector 1 million, or two thirds, were added in the private sector during the period 1991 to 2000. This indicates that the private sector has become the major source for incremental employment in the organized sector of the economy over the last decade.

The following must be kept in mind at the time of disinvestment:

- PSEs functioning in competitive markets, or in markets easily made competitive, are prime candidates for privatisation. Their sale is simple compared with that of public monopolies, and they require little or no regulation.
- An appropriate regulatory framework must be in place before monopolies are privatised. Failure to regulate properly can hurt consumers and reduce public support for privatisation.
- Countries can benefit from privatising management through management contracts, leases, contracting out, or concessions.
- The primary objective of privatisation should be to increase efficiency, not to maximize revenue
- Experience shows that labour does not, and need not, lose in privatisation, if governments pay attention to easing the social cost of unemployment through adequate severance pay, unemployment benefits, retraining and job search assistance.

METHODS OF DISINVESTMENT

I. Strategic Sale

Features

- It involves Pricing through Optimisation / maximisation by getting competitive bids. Investors targeted in this are ones with strategic fit - techno-commercial credentials
- Transaction costs involved are low. Time involved is 6-10 months. It is covered under Companies Act, SEBI Take-over code, Stock Exchange, RBI regulations, FIPB clearance (for foreign investors).
- This method is suitable for
    - Non-strategic Companies
    - Companies where Government is willing to give significant management control

Companies disinvested through this method include MFIL, BALCO, CMC, HTL, VSNL, IBP, HZL, PPL, IPCL etc.

Methodology

The transaction is structured in terms of:

- Extent of stake to be divested along with the extent of management rights is decided.
- Decisions on pre-qualification criteria, bid evaluation criteria and bidding process are made

- Information Memorandum are prepared and circulated of to pre-qualified buyers. Due diligence is kept while preparation of transaction documents
- Valuation of Assets/shares is done
- Bids are received and evaluated.
- Sale Agreement is signed.

Advantages of strategic sale method include:

- Strategic sale maximises price because of transfer of management rights
- It brings technical / marketing / financial / managerial expertise of the buyer to the company
- It increases the value of residual Govt. shareholding
- It involves low cost and less regulation

Disadvantages of the strategical sale method include:

- It is highly time consuming
- Issues relating to management, land and labour etc. are considerable and need to be resolved

II. Capital Market Method

This method includes the following:

(*a*) Offer for Sale to Public at Fixed Price

Features

- Here price is decided before the transaction; offer is made at a discount to market to ensure success and immediate capital appreciation for investors.
- Target investor set for sale offer include a mix of retail and wholesale, with some reservation for small investors .
- Transaction costs involved are in the range of 2-5% depending on issue size .
- Time involved for the sale offer to complete is 3 - 4 months .
- The method is regulated through SEBI guidelines and needs to follow all the Stock Exchange requirements .
- The method is suitable for
    - Companies for which small investor interest is expected to be substantial .
    - Profit making companies with good future prospects.
    - Companies not in need of significant technical, managerial and marketing inputs .

For eg. offer of 1 million shares of VSNL @ Rs.750 per share.

Methodology of Offer for sale method

- At the first step an issue of Equity Shares held by GoI to the public at large at a pre-determined price. This is done:
    1. Through an Offer Document
    2. By sweeteners such as warrants

- This helps in automatically obtaining the Issue amount. Issue may or may not be underwritten by the Syndicate Members

Advantages

- This method ensures broad-based shareholding.
- It sets valuation benchmarks for further fund raising.
- It is relatively quick and transparent method.

Disadvantages

- It is dependent on capital market conditions
- In order to ensure good response offer has to be made at a discount to market/ intrinsic price to ensure good response
- The entire process is expensive and costs approx. 2 – 5 %
- It requires various regulatory compliances from SEBI and Stock Exchanges.

(*b*) Offer for Sale to Public through Book Building

Features

- In this method price is discovered through a bidding process
- Target investor set includes essentially wholesale but small investors also
- Transaction costs are high, in the range of 2 - 5% depending on issue size
- Time involved in offer is approximately 3-4 months
- It is also regulated through SEBI guidelines and Stock Exchange requirements
- The method is Suitable for:
  - Companies for which institutional interest is expected to be substantial
  - Profit making companies with good intrinsic value and future prospects
  - Companies not in need of significant technical, managerial, marketing inputs

Methodology

- Equity Shares are issued to the public at large
- In this method the number of securities to be issued is pre-determined and disclosed
- Price discovery is done through bidding by interested investors. Issue amount is thus automatically obtained through No. of securities multiplied by price.

Advantages

- It optimises price and ensures broad based shareholding
- It also sets valuation benchmarks for further fund raising / offer for sale for IPOs
- It is relatively quick and transparent method

Disadvantages

- The cost involved is 2 - 5% of the issue amount.

(*c*) Secondary Market Operation

- The offer is made at market prices
- Target investor set includes wholesale or at times retail investors also
- Transaction costs are low, in terms of brokerage
- It involves spot transactions and takes less time.
- It is regulation: Stock Exchange requirements.
- It is suitable for:
  - Companies which have a sizeable floating stock with good intrinsic value and good future prospects
  - Companies which are not in need of significant technical, managerial, marketing inputs etc.

Methodology

- Sale is done through market operations in which secondary market sale of Equity shares is done through brokers at trading market prices.
- Sale is done to interested buyers which may be both - institutional and retail

Advantages

- It involves low costs as only brokerage is to be paid.

Disadvantages

- It is unsuitable for Companies with low floating stock.
- Price is dependent on day to day market conditions.
- Amount of proceeds is uncertain and there is possibility of price rigging.
- It is highly dependent on the day-to-day demand for the shares.
- The method may not be considered transparent.

(*d*) International Offering [Global Depository Receipts (GDR) / American Depository Receipts (ADR)]

Features

- Valuation is done by International Qualified Institutional Buyers (QIBs) (through book building) and related to domestic market prices.
- Target investor set includes Essentially foreign institutional investors.
- Transaction costs are high, in the range of 2-5% depending on issue size.
- Time involved is 3-5 months.
- It is regulated by disclosure requirements by Securities Exchange Commission (SEC) and accounting in accordance with US Generally Accepted Accounting Practices (GAAP) (for ADRs), NASDAQ / NYSE/ LSE listing requirements.

- It is suitable for:
  - Companies which have stocks listed in the international markets or companies with actively traded stock in domestic markets
  - Companies with good intrinsic value, good future prospects and of international repute

Companies disinvested by this method include VSNL, MTNL, GAIL

Methodology

- An offer to international investors is made through issue of Depository Receipts, which represent underlying shares and are called ADRs in the USA market and GDRs in markets other than the USA.
- The accounts for issue of ADRs are recasted as per US GAAP and are consolidated for issue of GDRs
- The issue is usually fully underwritten.Red herring prospectus is prepared and price discovery is done through bidding and allocations made at cut-off price which is called Dutch Auction or at bid price called French Auction.

Advantages

- It provides access to deeper international markets and capital, sometimes at better price by creating price competition between the overseas and home market
- The issue has enhanced visibility

Disadvantages

- It is a time consuming process.
- It requires following stringent regulatory requirements, accounting norms and disclosures and regular reporting to SEC in case of ADRs.
- It has a high cost about 4-5% for ADRs and about 3% for GDRs.

(*e*) Private Placement of Equity

- In this method valuation is done by merchant banker and feedback is obtained from institutional investors or price is discovered through book building.
- Target investor set includes institutional including multilateral agencies, private equity funds.
- Transaction costs are low.
- Time involved is 1-2 months.
- It is regulated by Foreign investment guidelines in case of overseas investors, SEBI guidelines in case of domestic listed companies.
- It is suitable for:
  - Unlisted companies
  - Listed companies with low floating stock and low volumes
  - Companies with good intrinsic value and good future prospects

Such disinvestments made include CONCOR, GAIL (Domestic issue with FIIs participation)

Methodology of sale

- Placement of equity to a set of institutional investors is done at a negotiated price arrived at through valuation or price discovery through book building.
- The issues of management rights and exit option are resolved and an information memorandum is circulated among institutional investors.

Advantages

- It is less time consuming and involves no regulatory compliance requirements, except in case of foreign investment.
- It involves low transaction cost.

Disadvantages

- It does not ensure widespread shareholding and therefore may not be considered transparent.

(*f*) Auction

- Here pricing is done through bidding. In case of Dutch Auction, allotments are made at single price. In case of French Auction, allotments are made at bid price.
- Target investor set are institutional investors.
- Transaction costs involved are low.
- Time involved is 1-2 months.
- Regulation includes SEBI Take-over code.
- It is suitable for
  - Companies with good intrinsic value
  - Unlisted companies
  - Listed companies with low floating stock

Initially disinvestments made in Central PSUs was done by this method.

Methodology

- Auction is done through the Dutch / French Auction to a set of institutional investors is done at a price discovered through the bidding process and for a pre-determined number of Equity Shares.
- Allocations are made at a cut-off price to all investors above the cut-off price in case of Dutch Auction and at the bid price in case of French Auction.
- Marketing is done through Analysts' meet and one-on-one discussions.

Advantages

- It optimises receipts to the Government of India (amount higher in case of French Auction).
- It is a transparent mechanism; is less time consuming with no regulatory compliance requirements.
- It involves low transaction cost.

Disadvantages

- It does not ensure broad based shareholding.

Warehousing

- Pricing is done at market determined price, after building in returns to the warehouser. Profit on sale and net of selling expenses by warehouser are shared in pre-determined ratio
- Target investor set includes institutional investors.
- Transaction costs involved are fixed return to warehouser less cost of funds for Government of India.
- Time for completion of deal is within a month.
- It is regulated by RBI restrictions on bank investments.
- It is Suitable for:
  - Listed companies with adequate liquidity.
  - Companies with potential for growth in market prices.

Disadvantages

- In this deal shares are offered at a discount to the market price and have to be sold at a later date in the market, within a specified time frame.

Conversion of Equity Into Another Instrument

- Pricing is done at book value / market price.
- Transaction costs are low.
- Time involved is up to 3 months.
- It is regulated by Companies Act.
- It is suitable for:
  - Cash rich companies with no immediate capital expenditure plans.
  - Low geared companies with good intrinsic value which is not reflected in accretion to shareholder value and market price.

NALCO was disinvested through this strategy.

Methodology

- Equity is converted into an attractive and suitable capital market instrument such as, simple bonds, deep discount bonds, fully / partially convertible bonds, bonds with warrants attached, preference shares with / without warrants.
- An information memorandum (IM) is prepared and circulated among institutional investors and the instrument is placed.

Advantages

- It results in improvement in the capital structure of the Company combined with funds inflow to seller.

- It also reduces capital and thus improves EPS, Book Value & RoE of the Company.
- It has low cost of transaction and is relatively quick method.
- There is no reduction in cash surplus with the Company by disinvesting through this method.

Disadvantages

- More regulatory compliance is required for listed companies.

Trade Sale

- Trade Sale means sale of a business or a division or a non-core activity. In addition to price, the auction takes into account factors such as capital investment to which the bidder is willing to commit and guarantees the bidder makes to employees and customers.
- Though the total amount offered is an important factor in the auction, there is also a trade-off for the seller between.
    1. obtaining the maximum amount of sale proceeds and
    2. ensuring that charges to the customers remain at affordable prices.
- For this reason, the seller generally develops a number of selection criteria *e.g.,*
    1. Indicative bids
    2. Strengths and capabilities of prospective operators
    3. Financial strength and credentials of bidders
- Any special conditions/assumptions attached to the bids such as spelling out in advance the extent to which rate increase will be permitted over a transition period.

A Trade Sale is generally regarded as a quicker option to execute. Public offerings make more sense when the company to be sold has a reasonable strong skill base and capital markets are liquid. In UK, Trade sales have generally been used with smaller industries or enterprises.

Asset Sale and Winding up

This is normally resorted to in companies that are either sick or facing closure. The Asset Sale is normally done either by open auction or by tender method. Sick companies under SICA are wound up on the findings of BIFR and orders of the concerned High Court and handed over to the official liquidator for realisation of dues through liquidation.

Management/Employees Buyout (M/EBO)

For smaller companies, particularly those that are highly dependent on their personnel, management/ employee buyouts may be suitable privatisation techniques. Although most buyouts are led by management, active participation by the workforce is a pre-requisite for success. The workforces are to be necessarily taken along, contributing some of their own money towards the enterprise. London's Bus service was reorganized into companies, which were purchased by their managers and employees. Other than National Freight Corporation of UK, which is often cited as the classic case of 100% employee buyout, there are not well-known examples of such cases in large companies with huge manpower. Perhaps such option is suitable in highly profit–making, low asset based companies with small and highly motivated manpower.

Sale Through Demerger/Spinning Off

Sections 391-394 of the Companies Act, 1956 govern demerger. The basic concept of demerger requires transfer of an undertaking from an existing company ("Transferor Company") to another existing company (Transferee Company"). The demerged companies have their shareholding as that of the Transferor Company. For a government Company, the scheme of demerger has to be approved by Department of Company Affairs. To minimize time, new transferee companies can be incorporated as shell companies in which the properties of Transferor Company can be transferred as per the order of Department of Company Affarirs. These new companies continue as Government Companies under Section 617 of the Companies Act and are formed for the limited purpose of facilitating the demerger. On transfer of shares to successful bidders, they cease to be Government Companies. Successful sale of a few hotels of ITDC and HCI (a subsidiary of Indian Airlines) has taken place through this method.

Disinvestment from April, 1991 till November 30, 2002; Realisation and Methodologies Adopted

S. no.	Particulars	Sale of shares – 1991-92 to 1999-2000	Strategic sale 1999-2000 till date	Total
1	No. of Companies	39 *	36 *^^	68 *
2	Equity sold (Rs. in crore)	2347.5	894	3241.5
3	As % of total equity of central Govt. and holding cos. (as on march 2000)	3 %	1.13 %	
4	Total Receipts (Rs. in crore)	19573	11344 ^	30917 ^
5	Realisation as multiple of equity sold	7 **	12	

* Seven companies are common in both modes

** Of profit making companies in monopoly days

^ Includes expected accruals from deals finalised

^^ From 25 loss making & 11 profit making

QUESTIONS

Fill in the blanks:

1. Disinvestment exposes the PSUs to __________ thereby forcing them to become more efficient.
2. In 1991-92 the Government, decided to divest up to ________of the Government equity in selected PSEs in favour of public sector institutional investors.
3. The Government classified the Public Sector Enterprises into ________ and __________ areas for the purpose of disinvestment.
4. The Government set up a _________to be used for financing fresh employment opportunities and investment, and for retirement of public debt.
5. Companies that are either sick or facing closure follow _________.
6. Transfer of an undertaking from one company to another company is called __________.

State whether true or false:

1. Disinvestment is done to only to add to the Government's revenue.
2. Strategic sale involves high cost and regulation.
3. Capital Market Offer has to be made at a discount to market/ intrinsic price to ensure good response.
4. For smaller companies, particularly those that are highly dependent on their personnel, management/employee buyouts may be suitable privatisation techniques.
5. Opening up the public sector to appropriate private investment would decrease economic activity.

Answer the following in detail:

Q.1. Why was disinvestment needed in India? What were the major concerns for disinvestment and what agenda did government formulate for disinvesting its strategic PSUs?

Q.2. What are the various methods of disinvestment? Which one is considered to be the most favored method?

Q.3. Has disinvestment been successful in India? If yes, how?

❑❑❑

27 INSURANCE

Insurance may be defined as a technique of risk management primarily used to hedge against the risk of a probable loss. It is defined as the transfer of the risk of a potential loss, from one entity to another, in exchange for a premium. The company that sells insurance is called **Insurer.** The Insurer decides about the amount of premium to be charged for certain amount of insurance coverage and that is called Insurance rate.

PRINCIPLES OF INSURANCE

Insurance involves the following basic principles:

A Large Number of Homogeneous Insurable Units: Insurance provides a vast majority of policies individuals belonging to very large classes. The existence of a large number of homogeneous exposure units allows insurers to benefit from the law of large numbers, which states that as the number of exposure units increases, the actual results are increasingly likely to become close to expected results. In case of absence of large classes insurance may cover select units. For example, Large commercial property policies may insure exceptional properties for which there are no 'homogeneous' exposure units.

Definite Loss: The event that gives rise to the loss that is subject to insurance should, take place at a known time, in a known place, and from a known cause. For example, death of an insured on a life insurance policy. Other types of losses such as occupational disease,may involve prolonged exposure to injurious conditions where no specific time, place or cause is identifiable and are therefore not identifiable.

Accidental Loss: The event that leads to a claim should be accidental, or at least outside the control of the beneficiary of the insurance.Events that contain speculative elements, such as ordinary business risks, are generally not considered insurable.

Large Loss: The size of the loss must be meaningful from the perspective of the insured. Insurance premiums need to cover both the expected cost of losses, plus the cost of issuing and administering the policy, adjusting losses, and supplying the capital needed to reasonably assure that the insurer will be able to pay claims. For small losses the above costs may be several times the size of the expected cost of losses therefore there is little point in paying such costs unless the protection offered has real value to a buyer.

Affordable Premium: If the likelihood of an insured event is so high, or the cost of the event so large, that the resulting premium is large relative to the amount of protection offered, it is not likely that anyone will buy insurance, even if on offer.

Calculable Loss: The probability of loss, and the attendant cost should be estimable. Probability of loss is generally an empirical exercise and there should be a reasonably definite and objective evaluation of the amount of the loss recoverable as a result of the claim.

Limited Risk of Catastrophically Large Losses: If any event can cause losses to numerous policyholders of the same insurer, the ability of that insurer to issue policies becomes constrained, not due to claims made by given policyholder but the sum of all claims made by policyholders so exposed. Typically, insurers prefer to limit their exposure to a loss from a single event to some small portion of their capital base, on the order of 5%. Where the loss can be aggregated, or an individual policy could produce exceptionally large claims, the capital constraint will restrict an insurers appetite for additional policyholders. For example, earthquake insurance, where the ability of an underwriter to issue a new policy depends on the number and size of the policies that it has already underwritten. Wind insurance in hurricane zones, particularly along coast lines, is another example of this phenomenon. In extreme cases, the aggregation can effect the entire industry, since the combined capital of insurers and reinsurers can be small compared to the needs of potential policyholders in areas exposed to aggregation risk. In commercial fire insurance it is possible to find single properties whose total exposed value is well in excess of any individual insurer's capital constraint. Such properties are generally shared among several insurers, or are insured by a single insurer who syndicates the risk into the reinsurance market.

INSURANCE *VS* GAMBLING

Both gambling and insurance transfer risk and reward. But they are different in many respects:

- Gambling transactions offer the possibility of either a loss or a gain. Gambling creates losers and winners. Insurance transactions do not present the possibility of gain. Insurance offers financial support sufficient to replace loss, not to create pure gain.
- Gamblers can continue spending, buying more risk than they can afford to pay for. Insurance buyers can only spend up to the limit of what carriers will accept to insure; their loss is limited to the amount of the premium.
- Gamblers create a risk that may have no link whatsoever to their personal and family situation. Insurance buyers must have an insurable interest in the insurance transaction. Insurance transactions are, usually economic or familia.
- Gamblers, by creating new risk transfer without regard to existing risk, are risk seekers. Insurance buyers are risk avoiders, creating risk transfer in terms of their need to reduce exposure to large losses.
- Insurance involves avoiding, mitigating and transferring of risk, which creates greater predictability for individuals and organizations. Insurance enables risk to be handled intelligently to achieve stability and growth.

HISTORY OF INSURANCE

In early periods methods of transferring or distributing risk were practiced by Chinese and Babylonian traders as long ago as the 3rd and 2nd millennia BC, respectively.

Chinese merchants travelling acreoss rivers would redistribute their wares across many vessels to limit the loss due to any single vessel being lost.

The Babylonians developed a system practiced by early Mediterranean sailing merchants. If a merchant received a loan to fund his shipment, he would pay the lender an additional sum in exchange for the lender's guarantee to cancel the loan should the shipment be stolen.

The insurance tradition was performed each year in beginning of the Iranian New Year.

A thousand years later, the inhabitants of Rhodes invented the concept of the 'general average'. Merchants whose goods were being shipped together would pay a proportionally divided premium which would be used to reimburse any merchant whose goods were damaged during storm or sinkage.

The Greeks and Romans introduced the origins of health and life insurance c. 600 AD when they organized guilds called "benevolent societies" which cared for the families and paid funeral expenses of members upon death.

Toward the end of the seventeenth century, London's growing importance as a center for trade increased demand for marine insurance. ;

Insurance as we know it today can be traced to the Great Fire of London, which in 1666 devoured 13,200 houses and led to the establishment of England's first fire insurance company, "The Fire Office," to insure brick and frame homes.

TYPES OF INSURANCE

Automobile insurance covers both legal liability claims against the driver and loss of or damage to the insured's vehicle itself.

Aviation insurance insures against hull, spares, deductible, hull war and liability risks.

Boiler insurance (also known as boiler and machinery insurance or equipment breakdown insurance) insures against accidental physical damage to equipment or machinery.

Builder's risk insurance insures against the risk of physical loss or damage to property during construction.

Business insurance provides (*a*) the various kinds of *professional liability insurance*, also called *professional indemnity insurance*, and (*b*) the businessowners policy (BOP), which bundles into one policy many of the kinds of coverage that a businessowner needs, in a way analogous to how homeowners insurance bundles the coverages that a homeowner needs.

Casualty insurance insures against accidents, not necessarily tied to any specific property.

Credit insurance repays some or all of a loan back when certain things happen to the borrower such as unemployment, disability, or death. Mortgage insurance is a form of credit insurance, although the name *credit insurance* more often is used to refer to policies that cover other kinds of debt.

Crime insurance insures the policyholder against losses arising from the criminal acts of third parties. For example, a company can obtain crime insurance to cover losses arising from theft or embezzlement.

Crop insurance Farmers use crop insurance to reduce or manage various risks associated with growing crops. Such risks include crop loss or damage caused by weather, hail, drought, frost damage, insects, or disease, for instance.

Disability insurance policies provide financial support in the event the policyholder is unable to work because of disabling illness or injury. It provides monthly support to help pay such obligations as mortgages and credit cards.

Expatriate insurance provides individuals and organizations operating outside of their home country with protection for automobiles, property, health, liability and business pursuits.

Financial loss insurance protects individuals and companies against various financial risks. For example, a business might purchase cover to protect it from loss of sales if a fire in a factory prevented it from carrying out its business for a time. Insurance might also cover the failure of a creditor to pay money it owes to the insured.

Health insurance policies cover the cost of private medical treatments

Liability insurance is a very broad superset that covers legal claims against the insured.

Environmental liability insurance protects the insured from bodily injury, property damage and cleanup costs as a result of the dispersal, release or escape of pollutants.

Professional liability insurance, also called *professional indemnity insurance*, protects professional practitioners such as architects, lawyers, doctors, and accountants against potential negligence claims made by their patients/clients.

Life insurance provides a monetary benefit to a decedent's family or other designated beneficiary, and may specifically provide for burial, funeral and other final expenses.

Life insurance policies often allow the option of having the proceeds paid to the beneficiary either in a lump sum cash payment or an annuity.

Locked funds insurance is a little-known hybrid insurance policy jointly issued by governments and banks. It is used to protect public funds from tamper by unauthorised parties. In special cases, a government may authorise its use in protecting semi-private funds which are liable to tamper. The terms of this type of insurance are usually very strict. Therefore it is used only in extreme cases where maximum security of funds is required.

Marine insurance and marine cargo insurance cover the loss or damage of ships at sea or on inland waterways, and of the cargo that may be on them. Mortgage insurance insures the lender against default by the borrower.

Property insurance provides protection against risks to property, such as fire, theft or weather damage. This includes specialized forms of insurance such as fire insurance, flood insurance, earthquake insurance, home insurance, inland marine insurance or boiler insurance.

Travel insurance is an insurance cover taken by those who travel abroad, which covers certain losses such as medical expenses, lost of personal belongings, travel delay, personal liabilities, etc.

TYPES OF INSURANCE COMPANIES

Insurance companies may be classified as :

Life insurance companies, which sell life insurance, annuities and pensions products.

Non-life or *general* insurance companies, which sell other types of insurance.

Reinsurance companies are insurance companies that sell policies to other insurance companies, allowing them to reduce their risks and protect themselves from very large losses.

Captive insurance companies may be defined as limited-purpose insurance companies established with the specific objective of financing risks emanating from their parent group or groups.The types of risk that a captive can underwrite for their parents include property damage, public and products liability, professional indemnity, employee benefits, employers liability, motor and medical aid expenses. The captive's exposure to such risks may be limited by the use of reinsurance.

INSURANCE IN INDIA

Insurance in India and has history dating back till 1818. But still Life and general insurance in India is still a nascent sector with huge potential for various global players with the life insurance premiums accounting to 2.5% of the country's GDP while general insurance premiums to 0.65% of India's GDP. The Insurance sector in India has gone through a number of phases and changes, particularly in the recent years when the Govt. of India in 1999 opened up the insurance sector by allowing private companies to solicit insurance and also allowing FDI up to 26%. Ever since, the Indian insurance sector is considered as a booming market with every other global insurance company wanting to have a significant share.

History of Insurance in India

Insurance in India has its history dating back till 1818, when Oriental Life Insurance Company started was started by Europeans in Kolkata to cater to the needs of European community. Pre-independent era in India saw discrimination among the life of foreigners and Indians with higher premiums being charged for the latter. It was only in the year 1870, Bombay Mutual Life Assurance Society, the first Indian insurance company covered Indian lives at normal rates.

At the dawn of the twentieth century, insurance companies started mushrooming up. In the year 1912, the Life Insurance Companies Act, and the Provident Fund Act were passed to regulate the insurance business. The Life Insurance Companies Act, 1912 made it necessary that the premium rate tables and periodical valuations of companies should be certified by an actuary. However, the disparage still existed as discrimination between Indian and foreign companies.

The insurance sector went through a full circle of phases from being unregulated to completely regulated and then currently being partly deregulated. It is governed by a number of acts, with the first one being the Insurance Act, 1938.

The Insurance Act, 1938

The Insurance Act, 1938 was the first legislation governing all forms of insurance to provide strict state control over insurance business.

Life Insurance Corporation Act, 1956

On 19 January, 1956, that life insurance in India was completely nationalized, through the Life Insurance Corporation Act, 1956. There were 245 insurance companies of both Indian and foreign origin in 1956. Nationalization was accomplished by the govt. acquisition of the management of the companies. The Life Insurance Corporation of India was created on 1st September, 1956, as a result and has grown to be the largest insurance company in India as of 2006.

General Insurance Business (Nationalisation) Act, 1972

The General Insurance Business (Nationalisation) Act, 1972 was enacted to nationalise the 100 odd general insurance companies and subsequently merging them into four companies. All the companies were amalgamated into National Insurance, New India Assurance, Oriental Insurance, United India Insurance which were headquartered in each of the four metropolitan cities.

Insurance Regulatory and Development Authority (IRDA) Act, 1999

Till 1999, there were not any private insurance companies in Indian insurance sector. The Govt. of India, then introduced the Insurance Regulatory and Development Authority Act in 1999, thereby de-regulating the insurance sector and allowing private companies into the insurance.

Liberalization

The opening up of Insurance sector was a part of the ongoing liberalization in the financial sector of India. The domain of State-run insurance companies was thrown open to private enterprise on December 7, 1999, with the introduction of the Insurance Regulatory and Development Authority (IRDA) Bill. The opening up of the sector gave way to the world known names in the industry to enter the Indian market through tie-ups with the eminent business houses. What was once a quiet business is becoming one of the hottest businesses today.

Post Liberalization

The changing face of financial sector and the entry of several companies in the field of Life Insurance segment are one of the key results of these liberalization efforts. Insurance business by way of generating premium income adds significantly to the GDP. Despite the fact that the market is vast in India for the Insurance business, the coverage is far less compared with the international standards. Estimates show that a meager 35-40 million, out of a population of 950 million, have come so far under the umbrella of the insurance industry. The potential market is so huge that it can grow by 15 to 17 per cent per annum. With the entry of private players, the Indian Insurance Market may finally be able to make deeper penetration in to newer segments and expand the market size manifold. The quality of service will also improve and there will be wide The Life insurance market in India is likely to be risky in the initial stages, but this will improve in the next three to five years Therefore, it may be advantageous to be a second-round entrant. In the Life insurance market the need risk assessment systems and data that are the key to success in the Life insurance market are significantly underdeveloped in India even today.

LIFE INSURANCE

The Indian insurance industry is segmented into two distinct markets: the life insurance market and the non-life, or general, insurance market. The history of life insurance in India can be traced from 1818.

Some of the important milestones in the life insurance business in India are:

- 1818: Oriental Life Insurance Company, the first life insurance company on Indian soil started functioning.
- 1870: Bombay Mutual Life Assurance Society, the first Indian life insurance company started its business.
- 1912: The Indian Life Assurance Companies Act enacted as the first statute to regulate the life insurance business.
- 1928: The Indian Insurance Companies Act enacted to enable the government to collect statistical information about both life and non-life insurance businesses.
- 1938: Earlier legislation consolidated and amended to by the Insurance Act with the objective of protecting the interests of the insuring public.
- 1956: 245 Indian and foreign insurers and provident societies are taken over by the central government and nationalized. LIC formed by an Act of Parliament, *viz.,* LIC Act, 1956, with a capital contribution of Rs. 5 crore from the Government of India.

KEY FEATURES OF LIFE INSURANCE INDUSTRY

Death Benefit: The primary feature of a life insurance policy is the death benefit it provides. Permanent policies provide a death benefit that is guaranteed for the life of the insured, provided the premiums have been paid and the policy has not been surrendered.

Cash Value: The cash value of a permanent life insurance policy is accumulated throughout the life of the policy. It equals the amount a policy owner would receive, after any applicable surrender charges, if the policy were surrendered before the insured's death.

Dividends: Many life insurance companies issue life insurance policies that entitle the policy owner to share in the company's divisible surplus.

Policy Loans: Some life insurance policies allow a policy owner to apply for a loan against the value of their policy. Either a fixed or variable rate of interest is charged. This feature allows the policy owner an easily accessible loan in times of need or opportunity.

BENEFITS OF LIFE INSURANCE

Risk cover: Life Insurance contracts allow an individual to have a risk cover against any unfortunate event of the future.

Tax Deduction: Under Section 80C of the Income Tax Act of 1961 one can get tax deduction on premiums up to one lakh rupees. Life Insurance policies thus decrease the total taxable income of an individual.

Loans: An individual can easily access loans from different financial institutions by pledging his insurance policies.

Retirement Planning: What had provided protection against the financial consequences of premature death may now be used to help them enjoy their retirement years. Moreover the cash value can be used as an additional income in the old age.

Educational Needs: Similar to retirement planning the cash values that flow from ones life insurance schemes can be utilized for educational needs of the insurer or his children.

ROLE OF LIFE INSURANCE IN THE GROWTH OF THE ECONOMY

The Life Insurance Industry has an enviable track record among public sector units. It has a Consistent profit and dividend paying record accompanied by a steady growth in its financial resources. Through investments in the Government sector and socially- oriented sectors the Industry has contributed immensely to the nation's development. The industry is recognized as one of the largest financial Institutions in the country. The ventures initiated by the industry in the areas of Mutual Fund, Housing Finance has done exceedingly well in recent years. To protect the country's foreign exchange reserves, the reinsurance arrangement are so organized that maximum retention is made possible within the country while at the same time protecting interests of the policy holders.

MAJOR MARKET PLAYERS

Presently there are 15 Life insurance companies in the country. There is only one public sector company LIC and the rest 14 are private sectors. Although LIC has been dominating the Life Insurance business since past few years the private players have now started to take the momentum.

Birla Sun Life Insurance Company : Birla Sun Life Insurance Company is a 74:26 joint venture between Birla group and Sun Life Financial. It is a private sector company. The company was registered on 31/1/2001.

HDFC – Standard : HDFC standard is a 74:26 joint venture between HDFC and Standard Life. It is a private sector company. The company was registered on 23/10/2000. The market share for the first eight months of FY 2005-06 is 2.96%.

ICICI Prudential Life Insurance : ICICI Prudential Life is a 74:26 joint venture between ICICI and Prudential. It is a private sector company. The company was registered on 24/11/2000. The market share for the first eight months of FY 2005-06 is 7.11%.

Life Insurance Corporation of India (LIC) : Life Insurance Corporation of India is a 100% government held Public Sector Company. Being the first to be established LIC is the forerunner in the Life Insurance sector. The market share for the first eight months of FY 2005-06 is 73.91%.

OM Kotak Mahindra old Mutual : OM Kotak Mahindra is a 74:26 joint venture between Kotak Mahindra bank and Old Mutual. It is a private sector company. The company was registered on 10/1/2001. The market share for the first eight months of FY 2005-06 is 0.71%.

Royal Sundaram : Royal Sundaram marks the coming together of Sundaram Finance, one of India's most respected and trusted finance companies, and Royal and Sun Alliance, one of the largest insurance groups in the world.

Max New York Life : Max New York Life is a 74:26 joint venture between J & Bank, Pallonji & Co and MetLife. It is a private sector company. The company was registered on 6/8/2001.

The market share for the first eight months of FY 2005-06 is 1.32%.

AMP SANMAR : Amp Sanmar was purchased by Reliance group in 3Q2005. It was registered as a private sector insurance company on 3/1/2002.The market share for the first eight months of FY 2005-06 is 0.54%.

Aviva Life Insurance India : Aviva Life insurance is a 74:26 joint venture between Aviva and Dabur. It is a private sector company. The company was registered on 14/5/2002. The market share for the first eight months of FY 2005-06 is 1.12%.

ING Vysya Life insurance : ING Vysya Life Insurance is joint venture between Exide (50%), Gujarat Cements (14.87%), Enam (9.13%) and ING (26 %). It is a private sector company. The company was registered on 2/8/2001. The market share for the first eight months of FY 2005-06 is 0.63%.

Met Life India : Met Life India is a 74:26 joint venture between 74:26 JV between J & K Bank, Pallonji & Co and MetLife. It is a private sector company. The company was registered on 6/8/2001. The market share for the first eight months of FY 2005-06 is 0.40%.

Allianz Bajaj Life Insurance Co : Allianz Bajaj Life Insurance Company is a 74: 26 Joint venture between Bajaj Auto limited and Allianz AIG. The company was registered on 3/8/2001. The market share for the first eight months of FY 2005-06 is 6.12%.

SBI Life Insurance Company Ltd : SBI Life Insurance Company is a 74: 26 Joint venture between SBI and Cardiff S.A. The company was registered on 31/3/2001.It is a private sector company. The market share for the first eight months of FY 2005-06 is 1.52%.

The TATA AIG Group : TATA AIG group is a 74:26 JV between Tata Group and AIG. It belongs to the private sector. The company was registered on 12/2/2001. The market share for the first eight months of FY 2005-06 is 1.78%.

Sahara India Life Insurance Company Ltd : First Wholly Indian Owned Private Life Insurance Company. The Company commenced operations from 30th October, 2004.

Shriram life insurance company Ltd : Shriram Life is a recent entrant into the life insurance sector It is a 74:26 joint venture between the Shriram group through its Shriram Financial Holdings and Sanlam Life Insurance Limited, South Africa. The company expects to start operations soon.

PRODUCTS

Life insurance provides financial protection to help families or business to manage after the key person does not remain.

Whole life policies : These policies cover the insured for entire life. The insured does not receive money while he is alive; the nominee receives the sum assured plus bonus upon death of the insured.

Endowment policies : These policies cover the insured for a specific period. The insured receives money on survival of the term and is not covered thereafter.

Money back policies : The nominee receives money immediately on death of the insured. On survival the insured receives money at regular intervals during the term. These policies cost more than endowment with profit policies.

Children's policies : The nominee receives a guaranteed amount of money at a pre-determined time and not immediately on death of the insured. On survival the insured receives money at the same pre-determined time. These policies are best suited for planning children's future education and marriage costs.

Annuities/Pension schemes : These schemes are policies that provide benefits to the insured only upon retirement. If the insured dies during the term of the policy, his nominee would receive the benefits either as a lump sum or as a pension every month.

NON-LIFE INSURANCE/GENERAL INSURANCE

General Insurance is a form of insurance mainly concerned with protecting the policyholder from loss or damage caused by specific risks. Examples include Property/Casualty Insurance, Health/ Disability Insurance Business/ Commercial Insurance.

General insurance business in the country was nationalised with effect from 1st January, 1973 by the General Insurance Business (Nationalisation) Act, 1972. More than 100 non-life insurance companies including branches of foreign companies operating within the country were amalgamated and grouped into four companies, *viz.,* the National Insurance Company Ltd., the New India Assurance Company Ltd., the Oriental Insurance Company Ltd., and the United India Insurance Company Ltd. with head offices at Calcutta, Bombay, New Delhi and Madras, respectively.

General Insurance Corporation (GIC) which was the holding company of the four public sector general insurance companies has since been delinked from the later and has been approved as the "Indian Reinsurer" since 3rd November, 2000. The share capital of GIC and that of the four companies are held by the Government of India. All the five entities are Government companies registered under the Companies Act.

The general insurance business has grown in spread and volume after nationalisation. The four companies have 2699 branch offices, 1360 divisional offices and 92 regional offices spread all over the country. GIC and its subsidiaries have representation either directly through branches or agencies in 16 countries and through associate/ locally incorporated subsidiary companies in 14 other countries.A wholly- owned subsidiary company of GIC, *i.e.,* Indian International Pte. Ltd. is operating in Singapore and there is a joint venture company, *viz.,* Kenindia Assurance Ltd. in Kenya. A new wholly owned subsidiary called New India International Ltd., UK has also been registered. Besides this a number of companies in private sector have also been set up in association with foreign companies.

Various Non-Life Insurance Policies

Property/Casualty Insurance

Provides protection for properties like home, car and house-hold possessions. It may also protect from liability as a result of their use.

Health and Disability Insurance

Pays for costs related to health

(*i*) Room rent

(*ii*) Surgeon/Physician's fees

(*iii*) Diagonstics tests

Business and Commercial Insurance

This caters to the need of business insurance requirements, provides wide coverage to property at work for example offers protection against loss/damage to the building and its contents. It also covers liabilities of employees, buyers and users.

Non-life Insurance companies in Public Sector

The following are the non-life insurance companies in public sector in India:

National Insurance Company Limited

New India Assurance Company Limited

Oriental Insurance Company Limited

United India Insurance Company Limited

Non-life Insurance companies in Private Sector

The following are the non-life insurance companies in private sector in India:

Bajaj Allianz General Insurance Co. Ltd.

ICICI Lombard General Insurance Co. Ltd.

IFFCO-Tokio General Insurance Co. Ltd.

Reliance General Insurance Co. Ltd.

Royal Sundaram Alliance Insurance Co. Ltd.

TATA AIG General Insurance Co. Ltd.

Cholamandalam General Insurance Co. Ltd.

Export Credit Guarantee Corporation

HDFC Chubb General Insurance Co. Ltd.

QUESTIONS

Fill in the blanks:

1. Insurance companies may be classified into ______, ______, ______and _____.
2. The domain of State-run insurance companies was thrown open to private enterprise on_______.
3. _________ policies often allow the option of having the proceeds paid to the beneficiary either in a lump sum cash payment or an annuity.
4. Insurance in India has its history dating back till ___________, when ________ started was started by Europeans in Kolkata to cater to the needs of European community.
5. General insurance business in the country was nationalized with effect from _________ by the _________ Act, 1972.

State whether true or false:

1. The event that gives rise to the loss that is subject to insurance should, take place at a known time, in a known place, and from a known cause
2. Both insurance and gambling are similar
3. Some Life insurance policies allow a policy owner to apply for a loan against the value of their policy.

Answer in detail

Q.1. What is the need for insurance for an individual? What are the various types of insurance? State their features.

Q.2. What are the principals of insurance? How did life insurance develop in India?

Q.3. How is life insurance different from non-life? Who are the major market players in both the sectors?

❑❑❑

28

INTERNET BANKING : AN INNOVATION IN BANKING SERVICES

The Internet has emerged as a cost-effective and time saving tool for conducting business transactions in an online global marketplace. Million of customers interact over myriad of products. It has become a door way to vast storehouse of business information accessible alike to individuals and enterprises. With the rising cost of traditional transactions, competition among companies is increasing to provide better services at lower cost to customers. E-commerce has opened the gateway for such transactions by being easier, faster and cheaper. Internet seems to be creating the possibility of a permanent worldwide bazaar in which no prices are ever fixed for long, and information is instantly available. Internet provides a perfect medium for aggregating buyers and sellers from all over the world. There are several signs that e-commerce is on the verge of taking off in India.

The corporate sector witnessed catalytic changes during the nineties. Globalization, deregulation M&A's and the new economy are the driving forces of business. However, many of these forces materialized into new initiatives that became difficult to be handled with traditional business practices. Information Technology has become the predominant element in many business deployments. IT has introduced capabilities that enabled new business paradigms. The power of the Internet transformed everything; e-commerce has redefined markets, industries and the way they do business. Those companies who choose to compete in capturing new market segments or even maintain there current customer base, will be require to face dramatic changes in management philosophies and business practices.

E-Business is all about using the Internet, digital communication and IT applications to enable the buying and selling process. E-Business involves the continuous optimization of an organization's value proposition and value chain position through the adoption of digital technology and the use of the Internet as the primary communications medium. This transformed business is E-Business. It outperforms tradition businesses by adapting more rapidly to market changes, responding faster to customer need, operating at the lowest possible cost, and managing the creation and termination of market relationships as needed. E-business enterprise must implement and integrate E-commerce systems, as well as CRM, knowledge asset management, SCM and logistics applications. The concept of E-business has reached banking services also.

E-business is poised to remove the barriers of time, space and distance making communication and collaboration available to all. This will result in an unprecedented shift in power from the producer of goods and services to the consumer who buys them.

TRADITIONAL BANKING

Banking in India has undergone a sea change. It has transformed from mobilizing savings and providing short-term finance to being an instrument of socioeconomic transformation.

Immediately after independence when India embarked upon planned economic development, the country had an inadequately developed financial structure, which was incapable of responding to the needs of a growing and diversifying economy. The branch network was concentrated in cities and towns. Rural areas, where 80 per cent of the population resided were barely touched by these branches. In these circumstances, the banking system was able to neither effectively mobilize savings of the community nor provide credit to the vast majority of the population.

The government initiated a series of measures commencing with the passage of Banking Companies Act, nationalization of the Imperial Bank of India, social control of banking and subsequent nationalization of major banks, etc. The concerted efforts of the government and the Reserve Bank of India bore fruit over the years.

During the same period the CRR and the SLR requirements were used as effective instruments of not only monetary policy but also as mechanism for mobilizing cheaper resources for financing the governments budget deficit. The socioeconomic obligations thrust on the Banks coupled with socio-political pressures on credit dispensation affected adversely the profitability of Banks and contaminated the assets portfolio of Banks and resulted in accumulation of non performing assets. These negative factors, however, did not minimize the creditable achievements of the Banking system of our country.

The world is changing at a rapid pace. Transformation can be witnessed in various fields such as politics, economy, science etc. at the same time, with the advancement of the information age, the world is becoming increasingly intertwined; resulting in elimination of a sense of remoteness which existed in past.

Perhaps the key driving force underlying these developments is the momentum of innovation in a broad range of information processing technology including telecommunications and computer technology. Information processing technology is an essential element of banking. The basis of banking or its source of income is not simple intermediation between deposits and loans to earn a margin. it is rather the financial intermediary's information processing ability in a broad sense including their ability to screen potential borrowers and their skill to help organize business projects supported by loans.

Competition both within the banking sector and between banks and non-banks for many areas of business has become more and more intense. Banks are becoming much more of a multifaceted provider of financial services with an increasing tendency to become either financial super markets or niche players.

Margins on traditional business have been eaten away and banks have been forced to look to new markets and new products to sustain profitability. As the banks are searching for new profit sources, they are becoming more conscious of the need to control risk.. the problem, therefore, is to disentangle the two from the data provided and determine where legitimate and prudent hedging ends and speculation begins.

Traditional banking can be done either physically or through computerized system. Anyone who wishes to deposit/withdraw money or makes any other banking transaction has to personally visit the bank. A lot of time can be wasted if one has to stand in long queues waiting for their turn to come. Moreover one cannot bank after 2 p.m in public sector banks and 4 p.m in private sector banks. Banks also remain closed on holidays as well as on Sundays.

Banks also have to invest a lot in infrastructure, staff, etc. the speed and service remains low. Banks having computerized system also involve a lot of time to clear transactions. So basically to cater to the needs of business class, executive class and to some extent common man, traditional banking remains inefficient.

In this scenario what do we do to survive? The solution lies in trying to understand the development and its driving forces and training and shifting human resources according. There is also a need to recognize business in a way we believe we can successfully operate and cope with change. The catchword is reengineering; the idea is not just cost cutting and rationalization but creating new interfaces with customers to generate added value.

Accepting the challenge for excellence and assuring that quality prevails throughout the product line are simply not enough in their own. Because the market is not willing to pay just any price since production economies play a decisive role. To realize these economies you need a rigorous cost management program that tunes your processes to optimum level of efficiency. Just in Time production is a fashionable term in the industry right now, but we still have difficulties trying to imagine something similar in service sector.

Nevertheless, it is astonishing how close the Banks can come to the industrial model with intelligent out-sourcing and managing their internal staff units so that they too focus their operations on clients and profits. Naturally all this requires top IT systems which often means very large front end cost in the form of investment. Besides retail Banking, custody business is a good example; think of the recent swapping of the entire custody business between some major International Banks.

INTERNET BANKING

There was a time when man was wanderer or nomad and he used to wander from place to place in search of various necessities of life. But now things have changed completely. With Information Technolgy becoming supreme Internet has completely changed the way we live. Internet has brought every thing right at our doorstep just at the click of a mouse. Gone are the days when we used to go to the banks standing in long queues depositing or crediting money. Now we can perform every bank transaction a calm and coordinated way through Internet Banking.

Internet Banking is the new game in town these days. Internet has touched almost all aspects of lives. The emergence of e-commerce has revolutionized the way we live, shop, entertain and interact.

Therefore, it should not come as a surprise if it tries to influence the way we save and the we invest.

Today, when the customer is King and the service providers are rushing to pay obeisance to the King, financial service providers cannot be left behind. In their quest to differentiate their services and gain competitive advantage over their competitors, the financial service providers are trying to provide their services to the customers in the comfort of their homes. The Internet has emerged as a convenient channel for these service providers.

Internet Banking is the latest in this series of technological wonders in the recent past involving use of Internet for delivery of Banking products and services. Even the Morgan Stanley Dean Witter Internet Research emphasized that web is more important for retail financial services than for many other industries.

Internet Banking is changing the Banking industry and is having the major effects on Banking relationships. Banking is now no longer confined to the branches where one has to approach the branch in person, to withdraw cash or deposit a cheque or request a statement of accounts. In true Internet Banking, any inquiry or transaction is processed online without any reference to branch (anywhere banking) at any time. Providing Internet Banking is increasingly becoming a "need to have" than a "nice to have" service. The Internet Banking, thus, is now is more of a norm rather than an exception in many developed countries due to the fact that it is the cheapest way of providing Banking services.

Fundamental shifts are taking place in the Banking scene with the dividing lines between banks, non-banking financial institutions, credit card issuers and even software providers getting blurred. M&A among Banks largely driven by the market are bringing synergy. But the biggest driving force in banking is going to be the use of Internet and underlying technologies such as EDI, electronic fund transfer, smart cards, interactive multimedia satellite and wireless communication. Internet that is considered to be the most transforming innovation in human history is catching on fast.

EVOLUTION OF INTERNET BANKING

In its evolutionary history, a start had been made in Internet Banking as early as 1920s. But this technology or this form of banking did not get a widespread acceptance till the 1960s. This is true for both Electronic Funds Transfers (EFT) and for credit cards. It required almost a complete before this form of Banking found popularity with a sizable group of consumers and bankers who are comfortable with technology as a part of their day to day lives. Weich (1993) explains the reason for this. He says, " In the early days, the effectiveness of Electronic Banking systems was inhibited by three main factors:

- Communication Technology was in its infancy and inadequate for local or global coverage- banks and customers could not communicate internationally within their own organizations or with each other.
- Most Companies and Banks had incompatible systems- sometimes even different branches of the same bank had different systems.
- Computer Manufacturers were unable to agree on the development of technology standards, which would permit data exchange directly between computer systems.

After the 1960s, Internet Banking and its use recorded a quantum jump. To explain this, Kalakota and Whinston (1996) say that, "recently several innovations helped to simplify consumer payments.

These can be broadly classified into:

1. *Innovations affecting consumers*: credit and debit cards and automated teller machines (ATMs), stored value cards and electronic banking.
2. *Innovations enabling electronic commerce*: digital cash, electronic cheques, smart cards(also called electronic wallets) and encrypted credit cards and EDI and Internal Technologies.
3. *Innovations effecting companies*: such as inter bank transfer through automated clearing houses that allow companies to pay dividends to their shareholders directly, or utility companies to debit their customers' accounts electronically through standing instructions.

Anthony Rohiwink (1991) explains how this form of banking is becoming a competitive advantage. According to him, "technological advances have made home,office and telephone banking more effective and efficient as a means of selling and delivering products, and these channels are gradually gaining more acceptance among customers. At the same time, the rapidly rising costs of operating a physical branch network, particularly in terms of staff and premises, are making this traditional channel less attractive. Such developments are changing the relative competitive advantage of various distribution channels. They can thus pose a major threat to established competitors with extensive branch networks while creating specific opportunities for new entrants to improve their competitive position with respect to this key success factor.

NEED FOR INTERNET BANKING

In the post liberalization era, technology is enabling banks to provide the convenience of anytime anywhere banking to increasingly demanding customers. Banks are now re-engineering the way in which their services can be reached to their customers by bringing in flexibility in their distribution channels. The earlier brick and mortar branch is no longer sufficient, technology is now taking banks to the homes or offices, 24 hours a day, 365 days a year through ATMs, telephones and PCs. The financial supply chain is undergoing a fundamental strategic change.

For a long time, customers could do their banking only by coming to a bank branch, whether it was an individual customer wishing to encash or deposit a cheque or a corporate customer wanting to open a letter of credit. The brick and mortar building of the bank branch defined the periphery of service delivery of banking products. Funds could be transferred only through mail transfers by issuing demand drafts that needed to be physically transported from its place of issuance to its place of payment. Realization, of such payments used to take times, often a couple of months.

The concept of banking through web sites started gaining popularity in Europe and US in the beginning of 1980s. by then, this concept of home banking was restricted to small segments of wealthy and tech savvy customers. But today the following the convergence of PC and television, nearly 40 percent of the banking transactions are expected to be done on the Internet involving around six million customers by 2002. The potential benefits of the Internet supported by empirical evidences provide the compelling reasons why banks should go for Internet Banking.

Internet Banking is becoming a strategic necessity for banks. Even as the brick and mortar models collapse into smaller kiosks or retail outlets, the Internet has destroyed all geographical advantages enjoyed by them. This is calling for newer, less expensive and more customer friendly technologies. And Internet is being seen as the ultimate answer to survival in the New World order.

INTERNET BANKING IN INDIA

India got the Internet connectivity in 1989 and a recent assessment places the total number of Internet users at more than 1.1 million, if only, cities and towns with population exceeding 10 lakh are considered. A majority of them could be potential customers for Internet Banking.

The new Private Sector Banks and the Foreign Banks are handicapped by the lack of a strong branch network in comparison with Public Sector Banks. In the absence of such networks, the market place has seen the emergence of a lot of innovative services by these players to increase their market share and reduce their cost of service delivery through direct distribution strategies of 'Non-Branch Delivery'. All these Banks are using 'Home Banking' as key 'pull' factor to wean customers away from the well-entrenched Public Sector Banks.

In India, new Private Sector Banks like ICICI Bank, HDFC Bank, Global Trust Bank, and Axis Bank, have taken the lead in Internet Banking. Among the Foreign Banks, Citibank, has noticeable presence, while others like HSBC, Deutsche Bank and ABN Amro Bank, have become big players in Internet Banking. Even almost all the state run banks have realized the advantages of such services.

DRIVERS OF INTERNET BANKING

Advantages previously held by large financial institutions have shrunk considerably. The Internet has leveled the playing field and afforded open access to customers in the global marketplace. Internet Banking is a cost effective delivery channel for financial institutions. Customers are embracing the many benefits of Internet Banking. Access to ones accounts at anytime and from any location via the World Wide Web is a convenience unknown a short time ago. Thus, a Banks Internet presence transforms from 'brochureware' status to 'Internet Banking' status once the Bank goes through a technology integration effort to enable the customer to access information about his or her specific account relationship. The six primary drivers of Internet Banking includes, in order of primacy are:

- Improve customer access.
- Facilitate the offering of more services.
- Increase customer loyalty.
- Attract new customers.
- Provide services offered by competitors.
- Reduce customer attrition.

INDIAN BANKS ON WEB

The Banking Industry in India is facing unprecedented competition from non-traditional banking institutions, which now offer banking and financial services over the Internet. The deregulation of the Banking Industry coupled with the emergence of new technologies, are enabling new competitors to enter the financial services market quickly and efficiently.

Indian Banks are going for the retail banking in a big way. However, much is still to be achieved. A study conducted by students of IIML show this interesting facts:

- Throughout the country, Internet Banking is in the nascent stage of development (only 50 Banks are offering varied kinds of Internet Banking services).
- In general, these Internet sites offer only the most basic services. 55 per cent are so called 'entry level' sites, offering a little more than company information and basic marketing materials. Only 8 per cent offer 'advanced transactions' such as online funds transfer, transactions and cash management services.
- Foreign and Private Banks are much advanced in terms of sites and their level of development.

COST ADVANTAGE

Branch Networks, once powerful competitive tools for gathering cheap deposits, are becoming costly white elephants. Internet Banking costs, in an operational sense are a fraction of Banking through other channels. In addition, this facility will allow for reduction in peaking of volumes and thus reduce the need to capitalize for these.

And statistics reveal it all. Rough estimates assuming teller at Re.1 per transaction put ATM transaction costs at 45P, phone banking at 35P, debit cards at 20P and Internet Banking at measly 10P.

The infrastructure costs of providing such services are quite high. A Bank not only has to automate its front end systems which the customer interfaces with but also the back end systems so that the Bank is able to provide 'robust functionality'. The heavy costs are in the development of the back end systems.

The main infrastructural costs are for security software, Internet Banking software and security hardware, which is very high. These are one time costs. The recurring cost is about 15per cent. Add to this, communications and other costs and it can run upto Rs.7-8 crore.

CUSTOMER SERVICE

Despite restructuring, reforms and branch automation, the standard of customer service in Banks is far below the expectations. Added to this is the inconvenience of driving to the Bank, finding a parking slot and spending time in transacting business which Net completely avoids to the customer. Besides, the financial statements can be viewed, printed or downloaded in any format for ease of analysis. Thus, Internet as a service delivery channel shifts the control of transactions from the bank staff to the customer. Net Bank customers find better information through websites than from the unwilling, less knowledgeable and non-cooperative banking staff.

INTERNET BANKING SERVICES AVAILABLE

1. Downloading Account Opening Form.
2. Opening an Account.
3. Making Balance Inquiries.

4. Requesting ChequeBooks.
5. Making a Fixed Deposit.
6. Stopping payment of a cheque.
7. Request for issuance of Demand Draft.
8. Establishing Letter of Credit.
9. Submitting Stock Statements.
10. Arranging forward contracts.
11. Making inquiries about TDS.
12. Bill payments.
13. Rechargins of Pre-Paid costs.
14. Payment of Income tax and many more to name.

STEPS IN NETTING THE TRANSACTIONS

1. The consumer either an individual or a corporate goes to the world wide web and logs on to a website.
2. The website server verifies user ID and Password. If a person is a first time user he has to fill in a registration form.
3. The server processes request via firewalls.
4. If password and ID match, the Webster allows transaction. It asks for a credit card or asks for a telephone number where it can reach you for offline transaction verification.
5. If a website allows online credit checking information about the credit card is passed on to the Bank, and the issuing Bank (for credit cards) verifies account status, credit limits and its own security measures. If everything is OK, transaction is approved and done.

How do Banks Secure Online?

The various security options which Banks use in order to secure the transactions of the customers are:

1. Encryption
2. Branch Connection Encryption
3. Fire Walls
4. Digital Certificates
5. Automatic Sign Off
6. Random Prop Ups
7. Disaster Recovery Sites

Typically, Internet based Banking involves four key security aspects-

Authentication: At the minimum, Banks use a Personal Identification Number (PIN) and a unique customer ID number whereby users can access their accounts or send payment instructions. Users are required to enter the PIN each time they connect to the Bank, in order to prove that the connection request is coming from an authorized user. Digital certificate technology provided by Verisign is also used in many companies.

Privacy: In order to assure that only the right person accesses data, state-of-the-art 1024 bit RSA, SSL and RCS technologies along with triple DES encryption are used while communicating. This encryption system from RSA data security incorporation scrambles data packets sent from your computer to your server, which prevents people from snooping on a network connection and viewing your information while in transit. Financial software programs such as Quicken come loaded with password features.

Integrity: Message integrity is provided by SSL and RCS security technology so that the message received has not been altered after it left the sender.

Transaction Confirmation/Monitoring: Almost all Banks and software vendors provide a 'special feature' that displays a list of instructions to be sent to the Bank before going online and provide a record of all completed transactions.

CONDITIONS FOR GROWTH OF INTERNET BANKING

For Internet Banking, to pick up in a big way, the following issues must be properly addressed:

1. The infrastructure costs of providing such services are quite high. A bank has not only to automate its front-end systems, which the customer interfaces with but also the back-end systems. This entails heavy cost.
2. The Reserve Bank of India, does not still allow inter-bank funds transfer through the Net, since cyber law I still to take effect.
3. The verification of digital certificates is another major constraint. A certificate authority needs to be set up to verify the digital signatures, which however, is being done.
4. The major issue in Internet Banking continues to be the security aspect, especially in the case of corporate, as bulk transactions are done in a day. Net is now, more like an unlocked diary and is vulnerable for being hacked. There are security risks that affect the web servers, the local area networks that host web sites and even the browser. These security gaps need to be plugged for building customer confidence in Internet Banking. The various security options like encryption (a process through which a password, accounting information, transactions and other information get transmitted is scrambled so that no one can figure out the key), branch connection encryption, firewalls, digital certificates, automatic sign off, random prop ups and disaster recovery sites are under trial of the banks to ensure the safety of money in the cyber world.

The number of Internet users, on which Net Banking depends, will increase once the government implements its policy by setting up Kiosks and offering Internet access through cable TV. For the moment owing to low PC and Internet penetration and non-existence of adequate cyber laws in the country, Internet Banking has many miles to cover.

Potential Online Banking Advantages

- Less amount of time is consumed in the transaction.
- In general one will find lower fees and higher interest rates for deposits due to the reduced cost of operating online and not needing numerous physical bank branches.
- One will have easy access to account information and transactions, due to the fact that any Internet enabled computer can become your 'bank terminal'.
- One will generally have up to the minute current bank account information due to the automation of most systems.
- In many cases, online banks offer free bill pay, which can be a big saving in both money and time.
- You can transfer funds electronically between accounts.
- Since online banks are marketing for new customers, there may be special offers available.

Potential Online Banking Disadvantages

- A very heavy infrastructure has to be developed in order to maintain an Internet Banking web site.
- Security from frauds is another issue of concern.

EMERGING CHALLENGES

One of the challenges before a bank, which is trying to be e-enabled is that the data is scattered across the countries. Integration of this data is necessary if the banks have to succeed on the net. The second challenge is related to the move towards expanding the basket of financial products being offered by financial service providers. In developed countries, financial service providers are using the Internet as a media for expanding into new products. However, in India archaic regulations do not allow companies to have a close relationship with the bank owned by them or to offer products, which are offered by another category of service providers. As a result, companies like ICICI are forced to keep their banking arms separate from the main company. They are also prevented from offering products,which fall under the purview of banks. This is a serious impediment for innovation in the financial service sector. Moreover, it prevents Indian financial service providers from exploiting the power of the web.

Given these challenges, only a bank (or financial service provider) which moves fast and tries to capture the first mover advantage can think of succeeding in this sector. Another key success factor will be the value, which the online operations of the banks will be offering to the consumers. This is what will differentiate between similar offerings from many providers of financial products and services. Starting now, will give the organization an advantage in terms of the networking it will be able to achieve. This will help it in meeting the first challenge. Banks (or financial service providers) should be ready to launch their operations within days of liberalization of the sector. This will allow them to reach a critical mass and establish themselves in the e-world.

Growth of Internet Banking will be postered by :

- Demand side pressure due to increasing access to low cost electronic services.
- Emergence of open standards for banking functionality.
- Growing customer awareness and need of transparency.
- Global players in the fray.
- Close integration of the bank services with web based e-commerce or even disintermediation of services through direct electronic payments (e-cash).
- More convenient international transactions due to the fact that the Internet along with general deregulation trends, eliminate geographic boundaries.
- Move from one stop shopping to 'Banking Portfolio' *i.e.* unbundled product purchases.

Certainly some existing brick and mortar banks will go out of business. But that's because they fail to respond to the challenge of the Internet. The Internet and its underlying technologies will change and transform not just banking, but all aspects of finance and commerce. It represents much more than a new distribution opportunity. It will enable nimble players to leverage their brick and mortar presence to improve customer satisfaction and gain share. It will force lethargic players who are struck with legacy cost basis, out of business since they are unable to bring to play in the new context.

❑❑❑

29

LEASING

CONCEPT OF LEASING

Leasing involves a contractual relationship in which the owner (lessor) of an asset or property grants to a firm or a person (lessee) the use of the asset's services for a specified period of time, usually for an agreed sum of rent. Leasing, therefore, enables a firm to avail the services of a plant of equipment without making the investment or incurring debt obligation. The firms can use the asset by paying a series of periodic amount called 'lease payments' of 'lease rentals' to the owner of the asset at the predetermined rates and generally in advance. The payments may be made monthly, quarterly or annually. Often there is no initial deposit or fee.

Lease contracts have two parties, namely, lessor and lease. A lessor may be a leasing company, a manufacturer, a subsidiary or an associate of a large business organisation including the trading firms looking for avenues to invest surplus to avail of the tax benefits or a banker or a finance house conducting the leasing business at times, through a subsidiary. A lessee may be a company, a cooperative society, a partnership firm, an individual, government or its agencies.

Conceptually, leasing may be distinguished from hire-purchase and instalment purchase. Under hire purchase, the buyer acquires the ownership of goods only after he has paid to total price in an agreed number of installments. Technically speaking, the hire purchase transaction becomes the full-fledged purchase only after the full price is paid and remains only a hire arrangement, if there is default in the payment of the full price. The buyer takes possession of the articles concerned on the payment of the initial sum but does not become their owner until the last instalment has been paid.

Under their instalment purchase, the ownership in assets passes to the buyer as soon as first instalment is paid. If the buyer fails to pay the installments in accordance with the agreement, the seller can sue the buyer for balance but cannot recover the goods.

In case of a lease transaction, however, the lessee (user) acquires only the usage or custody of the property and is not the owner therefor; ownership vests with the lessor.

Thus, the essential distinction between hire purchase, installant purchase and leasing is that the property in assets gets transferred automatically to the user if the first instalment, in case of instalment purchase and all instalments, in case of hire purchase are paid, it is not necessary that the ownership of the assets is transferred. In case of leasing, even if all instalments (lease rentals) are paid, it is not necessary that the ownership of the assets in transferred. In lease agreements the lessor and the lessee must specify explicitly regarding the transfer of the ownership. In the absence of such explicit specification, the ownership of assets will rest with the lessor only.

In general, leases can be classified into two types: (*a*) Finance Lease, and (*b*) Operating Lease.

(*a*) Finance Lease

A finance lease is known by various names, such as, 'Full Payout Lease', 'Capital Lease', "Long Term Lease' and 'Net Lease'. It is defined as a lease that transfers the risks and rewards incidental to ownership of an asset to lessee. Title may or may not, eventually, be transferred. Under this form of leasing, the lessee selects the equipment, settles the price and other terms of sale and requests the leasing company to buy it. The lessee, then, takes the equipment from the leasing company on lease. He uses the equipment, maintains and insures it and avails of the after sale service directly through an arrangement with the manufacturer/original seller. The lessee also bears the risk of obsolescence. He has to pay the rentals for the entire lease period even through the equipment may become obsolete during the period of lease.

The rental paid by the lessee is expected to take care of the capital cost of the equipment, the lessor's expenses, interest on money and lessor's margin of profit. Normally, the lessor and the lessee enter into a noncancellable lease agreement for a fixed period of time called the primary period depending upon the useful economic life of the equipment. Lessor recovers almost the total investment in the leased asset during the primary period itself. Upon the expiry of the primary period, either the equipment is returned to the lessor or the contract is renewed perpetually at a nominal rental 'pepper corn rentals' for whatever period of time he desires. This is known as secondary period and it is, sometimes, an indefinite period.

Thus, if at its inception a lease meets one or more of the following four criteria, the lease is classified as finance lease:

(*i*) Ownership is transferred at the end of the lease period;

(*ii*) Lease contains bargain purchase option;

(*iii*) Lease is for major part of asset's useful life. The lease term is equal to 75 per cent or more of the estimated economic life of the leased property;

(*iv*) The present value of minimum lease payments exceeds or at least is substantially equal (90 per cent) to the fair market value of the leased assets.

Under a finance lease, the rate of lease rental is generally fixed on the basis of the amount of lease, the period of lease, periodicity of rental payment, the rate of depreciation and other tax benefits available. The periodicity of lease rentals can be monthly, quarterly, half-yearly or annually. Usually, an advance of three to four months' rental is taken by the leasing company and is adjusted at the end of the lease period. The leasing company also charges nominal charges/management fees to cover legal and other costs. It can also insist on collaterals or banker's guarantee in individual cases.

(*b*) Operating Lease

When benefits and risks associated with the ownership of the leased assets are not transferred to the lessee, it is treated as operating lease.

Operating lease, sometimes called service lease, provides for both financing and maintenance. Ordinarily, these leases require the lessor to maintain and service the leased equipment. The cost of the maintenance is built into the lease payments. Operating leases are, frequently, not fully amortised during the period of lease agreement. The payment required under the lease contract are not sufficient to recover the full cost of the equipment. However, the lease contract is written for a period, considerably less than the expected economic life of the leased equipment and the lessor expects to recover all costs either in subsequent reviewal payments through leases to other lessees or by sale of the leased equipment.

Under operating lease, a cancellable clause is contained which gives the lessee the right to cancel the lease and return the equipment before the expiry of the basic lease agreement. This is an important consideration to the lessee, for it means that the equipment can be returned if it is rendered obsolete by technological developments or is no longer needed because of a decline in the lessee's business.

In addition to these two major forms of leases, recent years have experienced emergence of certain other type of leases. Among these, some important ones are : (*i*) Leverage Leasing, (*ii*) Sale and Leaseback Leasing, (*iii*) International Leasing, and (*iv*) In-House Leasing.

(*i*) *Leverage Leasing*

The leverage lease arrangement are made when very large and capital-intensive assets are to be acquired such as nuclear power plants, telecommunication units, etc. These agreements are generally made when a single lessor cannot provide the entire purchase price of the asset. In a non-leveraged lease, the lessor provides 100 per cent of the fiancee from his own funds. However, in leverage leases, the lessor provides any percentage (generally 20 per cent to 40 per cent) of the necessary capital and yet becomes the owner of the equipment. The remainder of the capital is borrowed by the lessor.

In a leverage lease agreement, three parties are involved, the lessor who provides a part of assert price as the equity contribution to the purchase, the lender or loan participant who contribution to the purchase, the leader or loan participant who contributes rest of the asset price and the lessee. This is in contrast with other type of lease agreements where only two parties, namely, lessor and lessee are involved.

(*ii*) *Sale and Leaseback Leasing*

Under the sale and leaseback arrangement, a firm sells an asset to another firm, generally a leasing company, which is turn leases it back to the former. The asset is sold at market price and seller firm receives the sale price in cash. Through this transaction, the manufacturing firm unlocks its investment in the existing asset by its sale, realises liquidity but continues in the existing asset by its sale, realises liquidity but continues to enjoy the use of the asset. The lessee firm, however, contracts to pay lease rentals which are fixed with reference to the selling price. The sale and leaseback arrangement can be operating lease or a finance lease depending upon the agreement.

Sale and Leaseback financing is used widely in the retail field in the western countries, where there are many large firms with no ownership interest in the buildings and fixtures in selling their merchandise. All maintenance expenses, property taxes, insurance etc. have to be born by lessee.

(iii) International Leasing

The term 'International Leasing' covers three separate types of activities : (*a*) Cross Border Leasing, (*b*) Overseas Subsidiaries, and (*c*) Import Leasing.

***(a) Cross Border Leasing* :** Leasing across national frontiers is Cross Border leasing. Cross Border leasing exists where the lessee and lessor are domiciled in different countries. It includes export leasing.

***(b) Overseas Subsidiaries* :** When a financial institution sets up leasing subsidiaries overseas, each conducting purely domestic business involving lessees in the same country they are called overseas subsidiaries. In this field, Barclays and Lloyds Bank International are the leaders. They have set up their leasing subsidiaries in Belgium, the Netherlands, Switzerland, Canada, USA, Hongkong, Australia etc.

***(c) Import Leasing* :** Import leasing is an arrangement by which a leasing company, a manufacturing company or the government enters into an agreement with a foreign company to acquire sophisticated equipments on lease basis. In fact, this activity requires a lot of government support and suitable changes in the import regulations.

(iv) In-House Leasing

When an industrial house promotes a leasing company for the benefit of companies in the same group, that company is known as 'In-House Company'. These companies are normally floated to take advantage to tax benefits and creating an additional source of finance through public issues by them. The in-house leasing companies enable through public issues by them. The in-house leasing companies enable the industrial house to claim otherwise. If the industrial house floats a leasing company, it can charge depreciation on the leased assets in the books of the leasing company the lease rentals in the books of lessee company of the group as tax deductible charges. As such from the point of view of the industrial house as a whole the lease rentals as well as depreciation on the leased assets are claimed as tax deductible charges reducing the amount of taxable income.

QUESTIONS

Q.1. What is Lease ? How is it different from hire purchase and instalment sale ?

Q.2. What do you understand by the finance lease ? How is it different to operating lease ?

Q.3. Differentiate between leverage lease and sale and lease back.

❑❑❑

BIBLIOGRAPHY

Avadhani,V.A., *Studies in Indian Financial System*, Jaico, Bombay,1978.

Bajpai J.N., *Indian Securities Markets— New Benchmarks*; SEBI-FICCI Convention on Capital Markets, Mumbai, August 6, 2003.

Bhatt, V.V., *On Financial Innovations and Credit Market Evolution*, Economic and Political Weekly, November 8, 1985.

Bhatia, B., *New Issue Markets of India*, Vora Bombay, 1976.

Bhatt. R.S., *Unit Trust of India and Mutual Funds: A Study*, UTI Institute of Capital Markets, Bombay, 1996.

Bhattacharya, S., *Venture Capital Financing Economic and Political Weekly,* November 25, 1989.

Bhole, L.M., *Financial Institutions & Markets: Structure, Growth & Innovations*, 3rd Edition, Tata McGraw Hill, New Delhi.

Chandra Prasanna, *Financial Management,* 5th edition, Tata McGraw Hill, New Delhi.

Chandra Prasanna, *Security Analysis & Portfolio Management,* 2nd edition, Tata McGraw Hill, New Delhi, 2005.

Claessens, S, *"The Emergence of Equity Investments in Developing Countries: Overview"*, The World Bank Economic Review, January 1995.

Dossani Rafiq & Kenney Martin, *Creating an Environment: Developing Venture Capital in India*; BRIE Working Paper 143, June 6, 2002

Disinvestment Manual; government of India ; February 2003.

Edminister R.O., *Financial Institutions, Markets & Management*, McGraw-Hill, New York 1992.

Fama E.F., *Foundations of Finance*, Basil Blackwell, Oxford, 1997.

Financial Sector Reforms: An Alternative Agenda, Denoument, August-September 1995.

Gupta, U.L., *Working of Stock Exchanges in India*, Thompson Press, New Delhi, 1972.

History of Reserve Bank of India, 1935-1951, Bombay 1970.

Indian Institute of Bankers, *Commercial Banking*, Volumes I & II, Vora, Bombay, 1978.

Industrial Credit & Investment Corporation of India, *Annual Report.*

Industrial Development Bank of India, *Annual Report.*

"Issues in Strengthening Commercial Paper Market in India": Address by Shyamala Gopinath, January 1, 1992.

Levi M.D., *International Finance*, Third Edition, McGraw-Hill, New York, 1996.

Life Insurance Corporation, Annual Report and Accounts.

Life Insurance Corporation, *Saga of Security: Story of Indian Life Insurance*, 1870-1890, Bombay, 1970.

Malhotra R.N., *India's Monetary Policy & Role of Banking System in Economic Development*, RBI Bulletin, December 1985.

Muranjan S.K., *Modern Banking in India*, Kamla Publishing House, 1992.

Mutual Funds, AMFI Publications.

NABARD Annual Report.

Norms Regarding Capital Adequacy, Asset Classification, Income Recognition & Provisioning: Committee on Banking Sector Reforms Narsimham Committee II RBI Report, October 31,2001.

NCFM: Debt Market.

Rangarajan, C., *Financial Sector Reforms: The Indian Experience*, RBI Bulletin, 1997.

Reddy, Y.V., *Development of Money Market in India*, Fifth J.V. Somayajulu memorial lecture, February 1, 1989.

Reddy, Y.V., *Indian Banking in International Perspective* A.D. Shroff Memorial Trust Publications 2002.

Report on Trend & Progress of Banking in India.

SEBI Annual Report, Various Issues.

Shapiro, A.C., *Multinational Financial Management*, Fourth Edition, Prentice Hall of India, New Delhi, 1995.

"The Indian Capital Market at Crossroads", Vikalpa, April-June, 1995.

Verma, J.C., *A Manual of Merchant Banking,* Bharat Law House, New Delhi, 1989.

❑❑❑

INDEX

A

Accidental Loss 327
Adhoc Treasury Bills 56
American Depositary Receipt (ADR) 291
Annuities/Pension Schemes 336
Asset Backed Commercial Paper 40
ASSET BACKED SECURITIES 299
Asset Classification and NPAs 153
Asset Management Company 268
Authorized Clerks 99
Automobile Insurance 329
Aviation Insurance 329

B

Balanced Fund 271
Bankers to the Issue 78
BENPOS 90
Boiler Insurance 329
Bombay Stock Exchange (BSE) 135
Bond Funds or Income Funds or Debt Funds 271
Book Building 72
Bought-Out-Deals 83
Broad Market Index 94
BSE Sensex-Bombay Stock Exchange Sensitive Index 96
Builder's Risk Insurance 329
Business and Commercial Insurance 337
Business Insurance 329

C

Call Market 27
Call Rates 29
Capital Adequacy 164
Capital Market 5
Capital Market Method 317
Carry Forward/Badla 100
Casualty Insurance 329
CD Redemption Account 46
CDSL 87
Certificates of Deposits (CDs) 43
Cherry-picking 302
Children's Policies 336
Circuit Filters 137
Closed Ended Scheme 269
CNX NIFTY Junior 140
Commercial Banks 4
Commercial Paper 35
Commission Brokers 98
Consortium Lending 185
Contract Note 99
Cooperative Banks 4, 195
Credit Cards 179
Credit Gaps 188
Credit insurance 329
Credit Rating 279
Credit Rating Agency (CRA) 37
Crime Insurance 330

Crop 330
Cross Border Leasing 354
Custodian 268

D

Dated Securities 49
Debit Card 179
Debt Market 11
Debt Securitization 297
Definite Loss 327
Delivery vs. Payment 66
DEMAT Account 88
Dematerialization 87
Depositories 90
Depository 90
Depository Participant (DP) 87
Depository System 88
Derivatives 16
Development Banks 219
Developmental Banks 4
Disability Insurance 330
Discretionary Order 99
Discriminatory Price Auction 51
Disinvestment may 311
Dot Ex International Limited 139
Dow Jones Indexes 96
Dutch Auction 51

E

Endowment Policies 336
Environmental Liability Insurance 330
Equal Weighted Index 95
Equity Funds 271
Euro Issue Market 5
European Depositary Receipts (EDRs) 289
Exchange Issue 257
Exchange Traded Funds 270
Expatriate Insurance 330
Export-Import Bank of India 215

F

Finance Lease 352
Financial Loss Insurance 330
Financial Markets 3
Financial System 1
Flat yield Curve 61
FOREX Market 5
French Auction 51

G

General Insurance 332
Gilt Edged Securities 49
Global Depositary Recepits (GDRs) 292
Global/International Funds 271

H

Health and Disability Insurance 337
Health Insurance 330
Hire Purchase Companies 4
Housing Companies 4

I

ICICI Ltd. 211
IDBI 215
Immediate or Cancel Order 99
Import Leasing 354
Income Recognition and Provisions Norms 170
Index Funds 272
India Index Services & Products Ltd. (IISL) 139
In-House Leasing 353
Insider Trading 100
Insurance 306
International Leasing 353
International Offering 319
Inverted Yield Curve 62
Investment Banks 261
Investment Companies 4
Investment Institutions 5

Investor Education and Protection Fund (IEPF) 129
Issuing & Paying Agent (IPA) 38

J

Jobbers or Tarawanwiwallas 98

L

Large Loss 327
Lease Financing 4
Leasing 351
Level I ADR 290
Level II ADR 290
Level III 291
Leverage Leasing 353
Liability Insurance 329
LIC 227
Life Insurance 329
Limit Order 99
Liquidity Preference Theory 62
Loads 281
Locked Funds Insurance 330
Lock-in Requirements 80

M

Management/Employees Buyout (M/EBO) 323
Marine Insurance and Marine Cargo 330
Mark to Market Margin 147
Market Expectations (Pure Expectations) Hypothesis 62
Market Order 99
Market Segmentation Theory 63
Merchant Banker 73,255
Money Back Policies 338
Money Market 5
Money Market Mutual Funds 271
Mutual Fund 265
Mutual Fund Trust 268

N

NABARD 218
NASDAQ (National Association of Stock Dealers Automated Quotations) 96
National Securities Clearing Corporation Ltd. (NSCCL) 138
National Securities Depository Limited (NSDL) 139
New Issue Market 5
Non-Banking Finance Companies 4
Non-Banking Financial Company (NBFC) 205
Normal Yield Curve 61
Notice Money 22
NSDL 87
NSE IT Lld 139
NSE's S & P CNX Nifty 96
NYSE Composite Index 96

O

Objectives of RBI 157
Offer for Sale to Public 317
Offer for Sale to Public Through Book Building 318
On Line Real Time (OLRT) Surveillance System 137
On-tap Treasury Bills 58
Ooen Ended Scheme 269
Operating Lease 352
OTCEI 139
Overseas Subsidiaries 354

P

Plastic Money 179
Post-Issue Obligation 82
Preferred habitat theory 63
Pre-Issue Obligation 81
Price Weighted Method 95
Primary Market 72
Private Placement 5, 83
Professional liability insurance 329
Property 304
Property/Casualty Insurance 336

Prospectus 79
Public Issue 71

R

RBIs Subsidiary General Ledger (SGL) Account 49
Ready Forward Transaction 65
Reference Rate 40
Registrar & Share Transfer Agents 78
Registrar and Transfer Agents 268
REPO 66
Reserve Bank of India (RBI) 154
Rights Issue 83
Role of SEBI in Collective Investment Schemes 154
Rolling Settlement 99

S

S & P CNX 500 141
S & P CNX NIFTY 141
S & Ps Indices 97
Sale and Leaseback Leasing 353
Sale Through Demerger/Spinning off 324
Scheduled Commercial Banks 174
SEBI & Derivatives Trading 154
SEBI & Mutual Funds 153
SEBI & Primary Market 152
SEBI & Secondary Market 153
SEBI and Foreign Institutional Investors 154
SEBI and Secondary Market 155
SEBI and Takeover Norms 154
Secondary Market 93
Sector Funds 266
Securities Exchange Board of India (SEBI) 151
SGL Account 49
SIDBI 215
Special Purpose Vehicle (SPV) 301
Specialized Financial Institutions 4
Specialized Index 94
Sponsor 268
Sponsored ADR Programs 290
State Level Institutions 5
Stock Brokers & Sub-Brokers 79
Stock Indexes 94
Stop Loss Order 99
Strategic Sale 313
Sub-Brokers 98

T

Tax Saving Schemes 272
The Chakravorty Committee 28
The Economic Times Index of Ordinary Share Prices 96
The Financial Express Equity Index 96
The Narsimhan Committee-II 28
Trade Sale 323
Travel Insurance 330
Treasury Bills 55

U

Underwriters 78
Uniform Price Auction 51
Unit Scheme 1964 (US-64) 231
Universal Banking 189
Unsponsored Programs 292
UTI 230

V

Vagrul Committee 28
Value at Risk Margin 147
Value Weighted Index/Market Capitalization Weighted Index 95
Venture Capital 239

W

Warehousing 322
Whole life policies 336

Y

Yield Curve 60